THE ARMY OF THE ROMAN REPUBLIC

To my wife Judith for all of her help and encouragement.

THE ARMY OF THE ROMAN REPUBLIC

From the Regal Period to the Army of Julius Caesar

Michael M Sage

Pen & Sword
MILITARY

First published in Great Britain in 2018 by
PEN & SWORD MILITARY
an imprint of
Pen & Sword Books Ltd
47 Church Street
Barnsley
South Yorkshire
S70 2AS

ISBN 978-1-78346-379-4

Printed and bound in England By
TJ International Ltd, Padstow, Cornwall

Pen & Sword Books Ltd incorporates the Imprints of Pen & Sword Aviation, Pen & Sword Family History, Pen & Sword Maritime, Pen & Sword Military, Pen & Sword Discovery, Pen & Sword Politics, Pen & Sword Atlas, Pen & Sword Archaeology, Wharncliffe Local History, Wharncliffe True Crime, Wharncliffe Transport, Pen & Sword Select, Pen & Sword Military Classics, Leo Cooper, The Praetorian Press, Claymore Press, Remember When, Seaforth Publishing and Frontline Publishing.

For a complete list of Pen & Sword titles please contact
PEN & SWORD BOOKS LIMITED
47 Church Street, Barnsley, South Yorkshire, S70 2AS, England
E-mail: enquiries@pen-and-sword.co.uk
Website: www.pen-and-sword.co.uk

CONTENTS

Introduction ix

1. The Sources 1

2. The Army of the Kings 9

3. A Time of Troubles 29

4. Recovery and Expansion 59

5. A New Model Army I 93

6. A New Model Army II 125

7. The Army on Campaign I 145

8. The Army on Campaign II 183

9. A Newer Model Army 219

10. The Late Republican Army 247

Notes 277

Select Bibliography 311

Index 321

Roman Italy at the End of the First Century

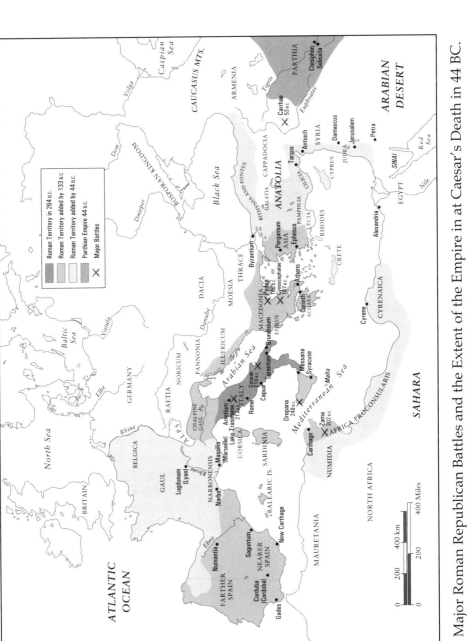

Major Roman Republican Battles and the Extent of the Empire in at Caesar's Death in 44 BC.

INTRODUCTION

By the end of the first century BC Rome had grown from a city-state on the Tiber to the greatest empire the Western world had ever seen. The empire had a population of 50,000,000 to 60,000,000 and an area of approximately 1,610,000km square. Originally centred on the Mediterranean, the empire had expanded to include large areas of northwestern and central Europe, the Near East and the North African coast. No other ancient city-state even remotely approached the extent of Rome's military success.

However, this growth was the result of more than a succession of military victories. Political acumen and the ability to respond to changing circumstances were also crucial. But the most important factor in the growth of Rome's hegemony was its ability to develop a military system that was tactically innovative and able to successfully adapt to the varied fighting styles of the enemies the Romans encountered.[1] In addition, Rome perfected a system of alliances and annexations that allowed her to sustain tremendous losses, beyond what any other Mediterranean state could bear, and still emerge victorious.[2]

Ancient Mediterranean states and peoples existed in an anarchic political system. They faced the constant need to wage war both to survive and to gain the security and wealth that domination over weaker groups could provide.[3] For instance, between the Persian Wars in 490 and 480–79 and 338, Athens was at war in two out of every three years (although in part this was a consequence of Athens being an imperial state). With the development of larger, more powerful states in the wake of the disintegration of Alexander's conquests in the eastern Mediterranean, the scale and intensity of warfare increased dramatically. From Alexander's death until their destruction by Rome, the Hellenistic successor monarchies with their much greater resources waged war on a far larger scale and over a much larger area than had been the case earlier. Kingship was closely tied to war both ideologically and practically. First and above all else, kings had to be victorious in warfare. They wore military dress and in battle kings often fought in the front rank to demonstrate their courage and their fitness to rule. War also provided the kings with the wealth necessary to maintain their armies and enrich their friends, both of which were fundamental for the maintenance of their power.[4]

Even in a world where war was the norm Rome seems to have been more aggressive and expansionist than most.[5] Augustus, the first Roman emperor and adopted son of Julius Caesar, died in August of AD 14.

In addition to his will he left behind three documents. The first consisted of instructions for his funeral, the second a survey of the empire's resources and the third was an account of his own achievements the *Res Gestae*. It was inscribed on two bronze pillars set up in front of his tomb.

The *Res Gestae* is a document designed to present a picture of Augustus as the justified avenger of his assassinated father and as the defender of the Republic against internal and external threats. Military victory and the extension of the limits of Roman dominion feature prominently. The emperor added more territory to the empire than anyone else had. Peace is also a theme. He had ended the disastrous civil wars that had almost destroyed the Roman state and pacified Rome's enemies.

Augustus presents himself as a bringer of peace. He claims that, when he was the leading citizen of Rome the temple of Janus Quirinus was closed three times, having been closed only twice before his time[6]. The small, square temple was located in the forum at the busiest inter-section in the city, just southwest of the Capitoline Hill. The Janus Temple was intimately connected with war so it is no surprise that the opening and the closing of gates signalled the presence or absence of conflict. The closing of the temple gates symbolized the fact that peace had been established throughout the Roman world. The first closing supposedly took place during the reign of Rome's legendary second king Numa Pompilius. The second occurred after the First Punic War, probably in 235, but the gates were reopened almost immediately. The dates of the three closings under Augustus are uncertain. The first was in 29 after the defeat of Antony, announcing the end of the civil wars. The second marked what was thought to be the end of war in Spain. The date and reason for the third are unclear.[7]

Augustus stresses that this peace is not simply the cessation of hostili-ties but a peace created by Roman victories. Later in the document he enu-merates the details of his military successes against foreign peoples. The Roman idea of peace is closely linked to military victory. It signals pacifi-cation as well as the end of hostilities. There is no clearer demonstration of this view than Caesar's report in his account of his war in Gaul of the reply of Quintus Cicero to the Gauls who were besieging his camp in the winter of 52. Quintus, the brother of Marcus and one of Caesar's legates, in answer to a request for a parlay by the Gauls replied:

> *It is not the custom of the Roman people to accept terms from an enemy still under arms. But if they would disarm he would support the sending of envoys to Caesar. He was hopeful given Caesar's sense of fairness that they would obtain what they sought.*[8]

The same theme of peace through victory appears frequently in Roman writers.

But for Roman authors, peace brought its own dangers. The most striking formulation occurs in late second century war against the Numidian king Jugurtha, by the mid-first century writer Sallust.[9] Sallust sees peace as a threat to Roman moral fibre. The absence of an external threat leads to a loss of self-control that leads to moral degeneration. The author claims that destruction of Carthage in 146 removed Rome's greatest external threat which then led to the growth of parties and factions which tore the state apart. He holds that fear of the enemy preserved good morals and that its absence led to the growth of luxury and arrogance. Sallust sums up his attitude in a crucial sentence:

> *Thus the peace for which they had longed in time of adversity, after they had gained it, proved to be crueller and bitterer than adversity itself.*[10]

Although in origin the idea has a long Greek pedigree, it seems to have been widely adopted by the Romans. References to this idea can be found in Roman literature as late as the fourth century AD.[11]

In addition to an ideology that valued conquest and encouraged foreign wars as central to maintaining peace and virtue within Roman society, there were practical benefits as well both for the elite and for the rest of the community.

Although the individual status of members of the Roman elite was in part based on wealth and family connections, it was closely tied to office-holding during the Republican period. Perhaps, as a reaction to the regal period that preceded it, methods of limiting the power of individual office-holders were instituted from the beginning of the Republic. The two principles employed were a limitation of the length of time that any individual could hold office, which was normally a year, and the use of collegiality so that each colleague could serve as a check on the other.

Office-holding was crucial to the status and political power of the elite and this held true not only for individuals but also families. The number and functions of these offices developed over time. Additional offices were added, often in conjunction with new duties. They formed a hierarchy of status and power.

Their connection to the military is clear. By the third century aristocrats had to serve in the army for ten years before they were eligible to stand for office, although by the first century this requirement had been relaxed. They normally fulfilled that obligation either by service in the cavalry or as one of the twenty-four military tribunes elected for the newly levied legions each year.[12] With his ten-year requirement fulfilled, the young aristocrat could now enter upon a hierarchy of offices that narrowed as he climbed the ladder. The highest prize of all, except for the censorship, was the consulate.[13] Even though the two consuls of each year had some power over most areas of political life, their most important function was military command. It was the one area where consuls could operate untrammelled by any limitations to their power.

In the intense competition for office and status, warfare was the single most important factor in gaining popular support for election to office. It was probably the major justification for the elite's position in the state.

The importance of military glory was so great that Roman commanders attacked peaceful peoples so that they could provoke a conflict and enjoy the prestige that victory that war brought. So in 151 L. Licinius Lucullus, the governor of Nearer Spain, attacked the tribe of the Vaccei in an effort to provoke a war despite his predecessor as governor concluding a treaty with the tribes in the area. The sources make clear that war against the tribe had not been sanctioned.[14]

Perhaps the most striking example of the importance of military glory came in 105 at Arausio (modern Orange) in southern France. The two Roman commanders, one senior to the other, refused to cooperate with one another because of their personal quest for military glory; that and their personal difficulties with each other, resulted in the worst Roman defeat since the battle of Cannae against Hannibal in 216. Between 60,000 and 80,000 troops were killed. Given the limited time a consul had in office he had a strong incentive to fight. The results of victory were worth it. It aided the prospect of a possible re-election to the consulship or election to the censorship as well as the ability to influence policy. These rewards were well worth the risks.[15]

A commander's success in warfare also brought an immediate tangible benefit: wealth. Given the low productivity of ancient economic activity, the quickest route to wealth was to seize it from others. A prime example is Julius Caesar's tenure as governor of Further Spain from 61–60. When he left for his province his finances were in terrible shape and his creditors barely allowed him out of Rome. On his return his finances had been repaired by the booty captured during tenure in Spain.[16] His governorship in Gaul was even more lucrative; in 55 Caesar was so wealthy that he could afford to raise and pay two new legions.[17]

Without wealth neither an aristocratic lifestyle nor a political career were possible. The booty that flowed from victory was at the disposal of a general. He could and did distribute it among his friends and officers, his soldiers, and in any other way he chose to do so. Often the choice was the construction of some amenity for the city or a monument to his victories. Perhaps most importantly if the commander had been awarded a triumph he could display it to the whole of the city.[18]

It was not only generals who benefitted. Private contractors profited from state contracts for army supplies and transportation. This included the large scale contractors who first appear in the course of the Second Punic War[19] and the small-scale merchants[20] who followed armies. Economic motives also operated among the men serving in the legions.

Cash distributions or donatives to the troops had by the third century become an expected benefit of military service. The recorded size of the donatives increased in the course of the second and first centuries. The absence of a donative or giving too little could cause problems with the troops. Pompey after his successful campaign in the civil war of the 80s was given permission by Sulla to celebrate a triumph that was dubious to begin with. His soldiers almost wrecked it since they were dissatisfied with the amount of cash that they had received.[21] Although in theory, the Romans had developed a rigid system of collecting booty, especially after a difficult siege where there had been a heavy loss of life the commander might allow soldiers to seize booty for themselves. In addition, in the confusion that often followed engagements soldiers must have sequestered booty for themselves. Livy mentions the number of volunteers who came forward for the war against Perseus in 171 because earlier service in the East against Philip V and Antiochus III had made soldiers rich.[22] The levies for Spain in the second century produced the opposite result with a lack of volunteers and occasional riots. Granted that the wars in the Iberian Peninsula were more difficult, it was also the case that they produced little profit for the legionaries serving there. As long as the Romans campaigned in Italy soldiers had the possibility of being given a land grant from the territory confiscated from the defeated enemy.

Despite the enormous burden of warfare, opposition to war in the assemblies was infrequent. Such opposition is recorded only twice, in 264 and 200. Both times resistance was the product of special circumstances and soon collapsed. This was notwithstanding the enormous burden that military service imposed on the men between the ages of 17 and 46 who had sufficient property to qualify for service in the legions. It has been estimated that to staff the legions generally enlisted in the second century each year, between 18 per cent and 24 per cent of those eligible were called up for service.[23]

The state also benefitted from successful warfare. The profits from wars in the east enabled the state to abolish the war tax in 167. Booty was not the only advantage that warfare brought. During the wars of expansion in Italy large amounts of land were confiscated from the defeated and turned into public land. After overseas wars Rome was often able to impose enormous indemnities on the losers. It has been pointed out that the vast amount of construction at Rome in the second century must have been financed by the profits from Rome's eastern wars.[24]

The army created by these factors remained a citizen militia almost to the end of the Republic in the first century. Most of those eligible for service assembled when they were called and served for a campaigning season that usually extended from late April or May to October. As Roman interests expanded, the campaigning season lengthened, especially for troops serving overseas. This type of service created problems, even though most of those serving were young men between the ages of 17 and 30 with fewer demands upon them at home.[25] Despite the problems that military service created, it was this citizen army that made Rome the master of the Mediterranean and extended her empire far beyond its shores.

The army changed over time, although some tactical formations endured over the centuries. By the beginning of the first century AD and the reign of Augustus, the citizen army had disappeared, replaced by a professional army stationed along the empire's frontiers.

CHAPTER ONE

THE SOURCES

Any attempt to trace the history and development of the Roman army during the regal period and the Republic faces serious difficulties, particularly with the literary sources that are fundamental to any reconstruction of the Greek army organization, tactics, and strategy.

The major sources for the history of early Rome and its army are Livy and Dionysius from Halicarnassus in southwestern Asia Minor. The texts of both suffer from a number of gaps. Of the 142 books of Livy, 1 to 10 and 20 to 45 are extant. The founding of the city, the period of the monarchy, the early Republic and the conquest of Italy to 293 are contained in books 1 to 10. Books 21 to 45 narrate the Second Punic War and the expansion of Rome into the Greek world until the middle of the second century.[1] The rest is lost, although we do have material that gives us at least some idea of what Livy wrote in the lost books. These include the *Periochae,* which is a summary of Livy's work of uneven quality, but does contain material from the lost books. In addition, there is a short summary of books 37 to 40 and 48 to 55 known as the *Epitome.* Dionysius' history consisted of twenty books. 1 to 11 have survived. They cover much the same ground as Livy and end in 444.[2] The quality of his information in 1 to 11 varies with the sources he used. There are also quotations from the last ten books in the works of later authors, which on occasion supply valuable information. However, there are clear differences between Livy and Dionysius that indicate that, at times, they used different sources.

Both wrote towards the end of the first century under Augustus and at about the same time. They were far removed in time from the events they narrated. And this has had an effect on their presentation of the army. Their picture of the earliest army is basically that of the army of the second century and so whatever their value for other aspects of the beginnings of Roman history, their portrait of the Roman army before 200 is an uncertain value and must be approached with caution.[3] A further problem is that for the most part they were uninterested in the technical aspects of warfare, as was the case with ancient history writing in general. There are occasional exceptions to this indifference, but they mostly concern modifications to weapons such as changes in the javelin (*pilum*) attributed to Marius and Caesar, and seem to be more the product of interest in well-known historical figures than in military weaponry.

Besides Dionysius, the work of another Greek author who covered Rome's early history survives in part: Diodorus Siculus writing in the late first century. He wrote a 'universal history' in forty books.[4] Its focus is Sicily and the western Mediterranean, especially Rome. It covered world history from the beginning until about 60. Books 1 to 5 and 11 to 20 have survived. Books 17 to 20 cover events from Alexander the Great's successors to about 300. There are also citations of the lost books in later authors that are of use. The work is of variable quality as Diodorus was not an original author, but copied earlier historians, many of whose works are now lost. The quality of his information varies with the worth of his source.

History writing in Rome first makes its appearance during the Second Punic War (218–201) with the work of Fabius Pictor. It is indicative of the Greek origin of Roman history writing that he wrote in Greek rather than Latin. He seems to have arranged his work year by year starting with the origin of the city down to his own time. It is no longer extant but was quoted and clearly used by later writers including Livy and Dionysius. The first history in Latin was written by Cato the Elder and did not appear until the 170s. Cato was followed by a series of writers who related the history of the city year by year and are collectively known as the 'annalists'. Their works were of differing quality. Little of these histories survive beyond quotations in later writers, especially Livy, and it is clear that some of them fabricated many of the events they describe. Almost all of them were senators and tended to enhance the role of the senate in their histories.[5]

The sources available to these historians were fairly numerous. Among them were narrative histories by non-Romans. There was a Greek tradition stretching back to the end of the fifth century including a mention of Rome's sack by the Gauls in 390 in Aristotle. Of particular importance was the history of Timaeus from Sicily (356–260). His *Histories,* in thirty-eight books, formed a crucial basis for later narratives from the early period.[6] It primarily focused on the history of Sicily but touched upon events in Italy, Libya, and elsewhere in the west Mediterranean. Timaeus began his history in mythological times and took it down to either the end of the Pyrrhic War in 275 or the beginning of the First Punic War in 264. His interest in Rome is noticeable and seems to stem from the greater interest in Rome in the Greek world as a result of her victory in the war against Pyrrhus (280–275). He accepted the story that Rome was a Greek city and synchronized its founding with that of Carthage. Timaeus is important because of his influence on Fabius and others; his work has not survived, but quotations from it in other writers can be used to partially reconstruct it. There are also other Greek historians who dealt with Rome, whose accounts are also not extant.

Out of these diverse sources the ancient Roman historians forged what was for the most part an internally consistent version of Rome's early military history. There are variations and contradictions in this account, but the broad outlines of this narrative appear to have been fixed fairly early and have remained essentially unchanged in later writers. That still leaves open the question of its trustworthiness. It is now generally accepted that the main lines of this tradition are valid, but not its details which must be evaluated on their own merits, on the basis of their agreement with other types of evidence, and also on the grounds of their inherent plausibility. This is vital for the history of Rome's armed forces as military developments and achievements seem to have been particularly subject to later elaboration and falsification.

The most important source for the Roman army of the mid-Republican period is the sixth book of Polybius' *Histories*, which chronicles the rise of Rome to a world power and the gradual intertwining of events in the eastern and western Mediterranean.[7] The work covered the period from the start of the First Punic War (264) down to 146. Originally in forty books only the first five books have survived intact. The rest have to be pieced together from quotations in other writers. Among them is Livy who depended heavily on Polybius for his account of the Second Punic War and for political events in mid-second century Rome.

Polybius, who lived from 200–118, came from Megalopolis (modern Megalopoli) in Achaea in the central Peloponnese. His father was a leading politician in the Achaean League and Polybius himself had both political and military experience.

After the Roman defeat of the Macedonian king Perseus in 167 in the Third Macedonian War (171–168), Polybius along with a thousand other Achaeans was deported to Rome as a hostage. At Rome, Polybius became close friends with Scipio Aemilianus, the son of the conqueror of the last Macedonian king Perseus and the adopted grandson of Scipio Africanus, the conqueror of Hannibal. Their close relationship gave Polybius access to some of Rome's most powerful and aristocratic families. In 151 he travelled with Scipio and was present with him during the siege and destruction of Carthage in 146. Polybius is a valuable witness not only because of his military experience (he had already written a work on tactics), but also because of his careful evaluation of the events he covered in his work. His history is far superior to any other source for the army of the mid-Republic.

Also significant is the work of Appian. He was born in Alexandria between AD 90 and 95 and died in Rome in AD 160. He wrote a vast work, which he entitled *Roman History*, that covered material from the reigns of the Roman kings until the early second century AD. It focused on Roman wars and was organized by the peoples and kings with whom Rome fought, as well as being arranged chronologically. There is also an important section on the Roman civil wars of the last century BC. Extensive fragments of the history have survived. Sometimes they offer invaluable information. For instance, the five books on the civil war period provide the only full and detailed source on this period that is available. In general, the work is useful but must be used with caution and compared with other available sources when possible.[8]

The first century produced in Julius Caesar's (100–44) *Gallic War* and *Civil War*, the only contemporary account of a Roman war written by the commander himself.[9] The *Gallic War* consists of seven books written by Caesar covering 58–52, with an eighth book added by Aulus Hirtius, who had been a lieutenant of Caesar's in Gaul. His book took events down to 50 on the eve of the outbreak of the civil war.[10] It seems likely that each year's campaign was written up after the campaigning season ended, and there is no reason to doubt the truth of the events in the *Gallic War*. Caesar's lieutenants, his political friends and enemies must have been well informed on the course of the war and could have easily exposed wholesale fabrication. Rather, the work's purpose is to depict Caesar in the best possible light as an ideal commander. This had a political purpose, which was to convince the Roman public that Caesar's accomplishments in Gaul merited his election to further office.

Caesar's *Civil War* continued the narrative down to 48. Three books survive, the third of which breaks off mid narrative, but there is no reason to think that further work was written and lost. Unlike the *Gallic War*, the purpose and time of composition are uncertain, but again the narrative presents Caesar as an incredibly effective commander who was ready to pardon his enemies if they ceased to be a threat. The work as a whole is sketchier and less accurate than the *Gallic War*. It was continued by later writers; Hirtius seems to have added an account of the civil war in Egypt, while the narratives of the wars in Africa and Spain – which are of lower quality – are by unknown writers.

Caesar's accounts were not formal history but rather written in a form that the Roman called a commentary. Historical works were composed within a moralistic framework and with conscious literary art. The commentary was bare of rhetorical decoration and not directed to the reader's moral improvement. It developed from memoranda, official dispatches and administrative reports which commanders and governors sent back to the senate to report on their activities. It could serve as a source for the writing of a formal history. A clear example is provided by the request by Cicero to his friend Lucceius to write a history of his consulship. Cicero promises to supply his commentary on his consulship so that Lucceius can use it as a basis for his history.[11] By the generation before Caesar, publication of such factual accounts of their achievements by the elite had developed into a means of self-promotion and justification and as a way to enhance the influence and standing of their families.

Besides narrative histories, the lives of Plutarch are a valuable resource. Plutarch lived from AD 45 to sometime after AD 120 in a small town in central Greece. During his life he travelled to Rome and was given an honorary office by the Roman government. His literary output was enormous. He wrote on philosophy, religion and many other topics. From the historical point of view, his most important work is the *Parallel Lives*. It is a series of forty-six biographies that pair together important Greeks and Romans; their main purpose is the moral improvement of Plutarch's readers, but they contain valuable historical information. In some cases, these lives are the most detailed sources we have.

Further, we have an account of the war against the Numidian prince Jugurtha (111–105), written by Sallust. During the civil war he had joined Caesar and fought for him in Africa. As a reward Caesar made him governor of one of the African provinces. However, he was charged with extortion and Caesar had to intervene to have the charges dropped. After Caesar's assassination he dropped out of politics and devoted the rest of his life to writing history. He wrote a number of works but the *War against Jugurtha* is of special importance in a discussion of the late Republican Roman army.[12]

The main historical tradition embodied in Livy and Dionysius presents a static picture, based on the army of the second century. Polybius' history forms a major exception to the general lack of interest shown in the technical side of warfare. His detailed discussion of the organization and equipment of the contemporary Roman army in Book VI, and his comparison of the manipular formation to the Macedonian phalanx in Book XVIII, as well as in his accounts of the major battles and scattered comments throughout the rest of his work, offer detailed information on Roman army organization, weapons and tactics.

Other literary sources are also useful. Plays which began to be shown on the stage in Rome from the middle of the third century provide valuable evidence. These plays, such as Plautus' *Amphitruo* (produced around 189), although based on Greek originals, contain important information on the ideological views of war as well as occasional details of army life and individual solders in action. The *Amphitruo* provides the earliest account we have of a Roman army in battle. Occasional references in poems provide further information, much of it earlier than the extant prose histories. Gnaeus Naevius, who died towards the end of the third century, composed an epic poem on the First Punic War containing the earliest account of a Roman war, and had first-hand experience of the war since he had fought in it. The first extended treatment of Roman warfare was Quintus Ennius' (239–169) monumental poem the *Annales,* basically a history of Rome from the founding of the city to 189 in verse. It was written late in life and became almost a Roman national poem. The poem has occasional references to military equipment which are useful in reconstructing the army of the late third and early second centuries.

The surviving quotations from antiquarian writers provide the basis for much of our understanding of early military organization and tactics. They were a product of the last two centuries of the Republic. The greatest antiquarian of them all was Marcus Terentius Varro, who flourished towards the end of the first century.[13] Antiquarians were interested in the origins and development of institutions and especially in the history and development of language. They supply much of the evidence for early weapons and army structure. Unfortunately, none of their works survive, but quotations are found in later writers. It is likely that antiquarian sources lie behind the digressions on the sixth century Servian army in Livy, Cicero and Dionysius of Halicarnassus. The fragmentary nature of most of the material and its narrow focus prevents it from offering a coherent account. At most it can serve as a starting point for the construction of one.

The sources from which historians and antiquarian writers ultimately drew their material are hard to evaluate. There is a tradition mentioned by Cato the Elder in his history that in earlier times banqueters were accustomed to sing the praises of famous men. There has been much debate as to whether this ever happened or whether this is a fabricated tradition. But there are parallels in the Greek world and it certainly is a possibility. It is difficult not to suspect that although the events mentioned were genuine, the presentation of them was not. The same can be said for the records elite families kept of their kinsmen's past achievement. They most probably did keep them, but given Roman elite culture, there is every reason to suspect the contained a great deal of bias and fiction designed to exaggerate the achievement of their ancestors.

One early source that was probably much less subject to distortion was the *Annales Maximi*.[14] These were annual records written on whitened boards, posted up and kept by the *pontifex maximus,* the chief Roman priest. From later writers it seems that they preserved records of annual grain prices, unusual religious events and a list of the chief magistrates of the state as well as the notable events of the year including military victories. It is likely that the content of the entries expanded over time. The entries must have been quite short and preserved a bare outline of events rather than a detailed narration. The whole of the *Annales* was collected at the end of the second century BC and published. This made them easily accessible to later writers like Livy.

Military manuals contain some useful material.[15] The earliest known Latin manual, Cato's *On Military Matters,* written about 160, survives only in fragments. It does show some interest in the history of the Roman army and it seems to have dealt with practical military matters including military organization and battle formations. The extant manuals are all of Imperial date and present an interesting dichotomy. The majority of manuals dating from the early empire between the first and third centuries focus either on stratagems in the field or the role of the commander. They show little interest in the technical details of soldiering with few exceptions. The emphasis changes in the Late Empire and early Byzantine period. Vegetius' *On Military Matters* and the *Strategikon* ascribed to the Emperor Maurice are far more concerned with the practical aspects of war such as training, battle formations and armament. The reasons for such a change are not clear, but the more difficult military situation of the empire of the Late Empire may have contributed to the change of emphasis. These handbooks reflect the same attitude to warfare found in most historical narratives that also focus on the moral qualities of the commanders and their troops.[16]

Archaeology has made important contributions, especially for the early period. It has revealed two lists (in Latin, *fasti*) that are of crucial importance for the early army and for chronology. These lists, found at Rome and other cities, are a list of consuls starting with the first year of the Republic and a list of magistrates who had celebrated a triumph.[17] Both were set up towards the end of the first century under the Emperor Augustus in the Roman Forum. The consular list goes back to the beginning of the Republic and the list of triumphs starts with Rome's mythical founder Romulus. Both are fragmentary and their accuracy before the mid-fourth century is questionable. But it is striking that they agree with the historians, showing that by the end of the first century the Romans had developed a fixed picture of their history.[18]

Apart from the *fasti*, archaeology can be a useful aide, especially for the earliest period when reliable written sources are unavailable. Since the type of equipment an army uses bears a close relation to the formations it adopts, equipment can be used as basis for inferences about military tactics. Pictorial representations of equipment and of combat are especially helpful in reconstructing what was possible in ancient combat. Weapons finds can both confirm written descriptions and aid in understanding the use of such equipment in battle.

Archaeology is also helpful in providing information about defensive works which can be an aid to understanding the political situation in an area and the level of technical skill of its builders. It appears that in general Italian cities, including Rome, began to fortify themselves on a large scale only in the fourth and third centuries.[19] This was also the period of the Roman military conquest. At Rome there are traces of large-scale fortifications constructed in the fifth and fourth century. The most striking defensive work is the Servian Wall which the ancients thought had been built in the mid-sixth century but actually dates from the beginning of the fourth century. This is no accident. Traditionally the sack of Rome by the Gauls took place in 387 and Livy paints a picture of extensive devastation. In fact, a layer with extensive burning is visible in parts of Rome, but archaeologists have dated it to the sixth century. It is clear that Gallic sack did not lead to extensive destruction, but was more in the nature of a raid for booty, but it left behind a fear of the Gauls that was to influence later Roman relations with them. The fortification wall must be connected with the raid. It was an enormous project which showed that the city in this period was capable of mobilizing labour on a large scale. The walls enclosed an extensive area about 11km in length and 4.2km square in area. Of special importance in understanding the second century Roman army are a series of five Roman camps near the site of ancient Numantia in north central Spain.[20]

CHAPTER TWO

THE ARMY OF THE KINGS

Rome lay in northwestern Latium on the south bank of the Tiber, 19km from the river's mouth. It was situated on a boundary between Latium and Etruria, another fertile coastal plain north of the Tiber. Etruscan influences were to play an important role in Rome's early history. The site itself offered many advantages; it controlled an easy river crossing and was on the main north–south route in western Italy. The Tiber was navigable inland and offered the easiest east–west route in central Italy. Rome also lay near productive salt pans. These advantages were important, but they also presented problems; Rome was exposed to possible invasion from the north, south or east. The salt pans were important for trade but they brought conflict with neighbours who were eager to exploit them.

In origin Rome conformed to the pattern of other early settlements in Latium. It consisted of villages situated on a set of hills. All of the major hills were on the east bank of the river with only the Janiculum on the west. The two most important hills were the Palatine, which was the most densely settled of them all, and the Capitoline which was later to be an important religious centre. The plain below them, the future site of the Roman Forum, at this time still a low, marshy, half-flooded area.

The city of Rome was formed when these villages eventually became a single community. It was a long and slow process that led to a single urban centre. The impetus towards urbanization seems to have originally resulted from the influence of Greek colonies in the south. The Etruscans, influenced by contact with these colonies, began to urbanize by the late eighth century. They seem to have played the most important role in starting the process at Rome. It had a sizeable Etruscan population and was heavily influenced by Etruscan culture.[1]

Growth is visible archaeologically in the second half of the seventh century with the construction of comparatively sophisticated fortifications.[2] The Forum was drained and paved for the first time about 625.[3] Buildings made of stone appeared and were not only used for public monuments but also for private residences. Rome was urbanizing and creating a public space in the Forum that was to serve as a religious centre for the city. The monumentalization evident in these structures is striking evidence indicating the ability to mobilize labour on a large scale.[4] The evidence of Roman urbanization is paralleled by similar developments in other cities in Latium. The multiplication of inhabited sites with fortification walls indicates an increased sense of danger.[5]

The growing city was in Greek and Roman tradition ruled by a succession of seven kings. The historical basis of this tradition has received some support. In the Forum, the *Lapis Niger* or 'black stone' found in AD 1899 and dating from the second quarter of the sixth century is the earliest extant official document. It shows that Latin was the official language and that the writing and the carving of inscriptions was already in use at Rome. The Latin word for king (*rex*) appears on the Lapis. This find supports the Romans' view that their earliest form of government was kingship. Only the last three of the seven kings, Tarquin the Elder, Servius Tullius and Tarquin the Proud are likely to be historical and the stories about them may at least preserve some historical elements.

Although kingship appears to have been a frequent political form in early Italy, Roman kingship was unusual in being elective and not hereditary. The most basic attribute of the king was his *imperium*. It denoted the ability to exercise supreme command, especially in wartime. After the kings, it was used to specify the sum total of a magistrate's powers, both civil and military. It had a strong religious element, for *imperium* was joined with *auspicium* (the right to consult the will of the gods). This link is also manifest in the need for *imperium* to be conferred by religious rites, which signified that the holder, in this case the king, was acceptable to the gods. His council of advisors was the origin of Rome's senate.

Citizens who are labelled as patrician raise a particular problem. They appear after the transition to Republican government. During parts of the fifth and the fourth century they monopolized political and religious office. However, it is clear from the non-patrician names appearing in consular lists that this was not the case during the earliest days of the Republic or presumably during the monarchy. The position may have its origin in the status and power of the heads of leading families. Over time because of their power and influence they came to monopolize certain prerequisites especially of a religious nature.

The earliest Roman army was supposedly instituted by the mythical first king, Romulus. It rested on the universal obligation of male citizens to perform military service. Its organization was based on a system of three tribes: the Ramnenses, Luceres and Titienses. Each of these tribes was divided into ten units called *curiae* (singular *curia*), which were geographic groupings of clans, for a total of thirty units. The origin of these divisions of the citizen body is uncertain.

Each tribe had to raise 1,000 infantry and 100 cavalry. Each *curia* provided 100 infantry and 30 cavalry. The reliability of this information is uncertain and antiquarians supplemented their facts with their own inferences, as did historians. However, there is some supporting evidence. Division into threes and multiples of three are encountered in the later Roman army. For instance, in the army of the mid-second century there were sixty centuries arranged in three lines. Cavalry units consisted of thirty troopers and three officers.

There is more information about the cavalry in the regal period than about the infantry. In accounts of early battles, the cavalry usually plays the decisive role. This must surely be the result of the perennial association of the horse in combat with the elite in the Mediterranean world and elsewhere. That association was fostered not only by the advantages that the horse conferred in battle, but also by the wealth necessary to raise and support it.

The date when true cavalry – that is, cavalry fighting from horseback – began is unclear. Some scholars have argued that true cavalry only appeared as late as the Samnite wars of the last half of the fourth century, arguing that the pictorial representations of riders that we have as representing mounted infantry. In part, this is the result of a peculiar feature of our historical narratives of early battles. In most of them, at some point in the battle the cavalry dismounts to engage the enemy. True cavalry – fighting mounted – probably appeared around 600 in Rome and in Etruria as the result of Greek influence.[6] Significantly, the western Greek states, which were in most immediate contact with the Italic peoples, were especially strong in mounted formations.

The history of cavalry development before the mid-sixth century is confused and inconsistent. The 300 cavalry purportedly instituted by Romulus are called *celeres* in most of our sources; however, other writers claim that was a name for the king's bodyguard. The one explanation is not incompatible with the other. There were officers called *tribuni celerum* or 'tribunes of the *celeres*'.[7] This has suggested to some that the *celeres* were identical to Romulus' cavalry. This is of course not a conclusive argument, but it seems reasonable given the identical size and the upper class from which it was drawn that the king's bodyguard was also the early Roman cavalry arm. Interestingly, the cavalry component of the mid-second century legion also numbered 300.

A central problem is the chronology of changes to the cavalry. They are dated by some sources to the reign of King Tullus Hostilius (672–641), the third king of Rome, who is portrayed as extremely warlike, and by others to another king Tarquinius Priscus (615–579). Most scholars think that Tullus is unhistorical though some think that he did exist. The most important event of his reign, if he is a historical figure, is his successful war against Alba Longa (modern Castelgondalfo). It lay 19km southeast of Rome in the Alban Hills. It was considered the mother city of the Latins. Both Romulus and Remus came from its royal line, and it was a religious centre for the Latins including Rome. The thirty Latin peoples assembled there at the shrine of Jupiter Latiaris on the Alban Mount (Monte Cavo) to celebrate an annual festival.[8] Tullus is said to have destroyed the site and removed its population to Rome where he granted them citizenship. Their leaders were then incorporated into the Roman elite. Italian cities in general were open to the inclusion of new citizens, unlike their Greek counterparts. Many of the kings were also non-Romans. One often-cited example is that of Attus Clausus, a Sabine chief, who was driven out in factional fighting. He migrated to Rome in 504 with a band of his clients and was readily accepted into the elite and admitted to the Senate. It could be that in absorbing the population of Alba there were sufficient members of the elite to allow a doubling of the cavalry centuries to six from the original three.

The fifth king, Tarquinius Priscus, is said to have come to Rome from Etruscan Tarquinii (modern Tarquinia) to seek his fortune. He began and completed a number of building projects including the great temple of Jupiter Optimus Maximus ('The Greatest and Best') on the Capitoline Hill. There is an alternate tradition that it was his son, or more likely his grand-son, Tarquinius Superbus ('Proud') who completed it. Tarquin is said either to have doubled the number of men in each century so that they now totalled 600 or he doubled the entire force to 1,200 cavalry. The former seems more likely. There is evidence of a large increase in population that approximately coincides with the traditional dates for his reign. The bal-ance of probabilities makes it likely that it was Tarquinus who enlarged the cavalry and that by the end of his reign there were 600 cavalry organized in 6 centuries. There is also a tradition that the Romans possessed light cavalry, armed only with javelins and who wore no body armour. It seems unlikely that this was ever true, and there is no indication of any later unit of light cavalry. It also significant that in the later Roman army the light-armed troops were drawn from the poorer elements in the population, which was certainly not true of the cavalry of any period.

If the development of the early regal army is uncertain, its tacti-cal organization and command structure are even more so. The most obvious division was between cavalry and infantry. Presumably, the cavalry – as was the case later – was divided in two and stationed on the wings of the battle line. The numbers show a ten to one ratio in favour of infantry, which is typical of Mediterranean armies. The levy must have been carried out on a tribal basis. The later decimal organi-zation of the Roman army suggests that the 1,000 infantry provided by each tribe was divided into units of 100. This would account for the fact that the smallest administrative and tactical unit was called a century though it later never seems to have contained 100 men. This suggests that since each curia supplied 100 men, the men of the curia probably served together. Presumably, each group of 100 was commanded by a centurion. They would form a natural unit of organization since the men were living in the same area and many of them were probably kins-man. There is a modern parallel during the First World War: the British Secretary of State for War, Lord Kitchener, formed 'Pal's Battalions'. These units were enlisted with the promise that they could serve with their friends and relations.[9]

We have no knowledge about how the centuries were deployed on the battlefield. There may also have been other smaller units, as was the case with Greek and Macedonian armies, but we know nothing about them. The cavalry was probably divided into ten *turmae* (singular *turma*) as was the later Roman cavalry. These were units of thirty men in addition to a commanding officer, presumably the *tribunus celerum* with three subordinate officers, the *decuriones* (singular *decurio*), each in charge of a group of ten troopers.

At the highest level of command was the king who took part in military campaigns in person. Many of the campaigns, such as that of Tarquin against the Sabines, may be fictitious or have only a bare factual framework such as Tarquin fought a battle against the Sabines but nothing more.[10]

There is also evidence that the king used his family and friends to command armies on various campaigns.[11] Servius Tullius, the king who followed Tarquin on the throne, supposedly served as commander of Tarquin's auxiliary forces during the king's lifetime. Tarquin the Proud entrusted the control of the recently conquered city of Gabii to his son.[12] Friends and relatives would seem to be natural choices to command. There is no evidence of any formal system of overall command.

It is not clear whether the cavalry had a separate designated commander or commanders. In the Republic there was a commander called the master of the horse (*magister equitum*), appointed when a dictator had been elected. The name suggests that he commanded the cavalry, but this was not the case. The master of the horse acted as a general assistant to the dictator who was in overall command. Nevertheless, the title is suggestive; some scholars have argued that his office was as the representative of the corporate interests of the elite Romans who staffed the cavalry, but since he was chosen by the dictator or an earlier official who probably commanded the entire force called the *magister populi* ('leader of the army') and not elected by the cavalry this does not seem convincing explanation for the title. It seems more likely that he was the king's commander of the cavalry, that the office disappeared with the end of the monarchy, and was revived in an alternative form in the early Republic.

The evidence for the community's army before the mid-sixth century is scanty and often unreliable. In many areas the sources are inadequate. They often depend on hearsay, scanty records and family traditions. There is probably a basis in fact of the main outlines of army structure but little or no faith can be placed in the details.

The Roman army was not the only active military force. In many ways the king was more or less first among equals and members of the nobility were hard to impossible to control. There is tenuous evidence for what can be called a clan army. The Roman clan is called a *gens*.[13] It was a group of families linked by real or fictitious descent from a common male ancestor. It may have originated as early as the eighth century. Its core was provided by kin but its wider extension may have resulted from the growing power of local band chiefs whose military success allowed them to attach followers who as their clients were bound to them by bonds of mutual good faith (*fides*) and mutual obligations. It is likely that such groups provided aristocrats with the power base they needed to maintain their influence. For most of Roman history the family was and remained the most important social group.

The evidence for the use of the clan in early Roman warfare is sparse. Aristocrats controlling groups of dependants were common in antiquity. For instance, Caesar indicates that Gallic aristocrats could have enormous numbers of clients and that they could be used as a military force in internal disputes as well as in foreign warfare. The most striking example is that of a Helvetian noble Orgetorix who could muster 10,000 clients. Clients were bound to their elite patrons by various ties of which the most important was a social obligation binding a superior to an inferior through a mutual exchange of favours. Clients might be in debt to their noble patron or workers on his estates, or they might be young warriors looking for booty and social prestige. Although we do not have detailed evidence for the monarchy, the Roman situation seems similar.

There is one incident that centres on the actions of a clan army. The Fabian clan, one of the most aristocratic of all, played an important political role from the early fifth century until the end of the third century. This episode took place during one of the three wars between Etruscan Veii and Rome waged soon after the end of the monarchy. It is so close in time that it is likely that the same phenomenon took place under the kings. Veii was an Etruscan city that lay nearly 13km north of Rome on the other side of the Tiber. Unlike the raiding and tribal warfare that characterized Roman conflicts in other theatres, this war was fought by two large and powerful city-states against each other. The goal of each was to gain control of the enemy's possessions on the opposite bank, which would give complete control of the river. The conflict centred on Veii's control of the town of Fidenae on the southern or Roman bank of the Tiber. This gave Veii control of the Tiber and important routes to the coast and Italian interior.

The first war, from 483–474, ended in a stalemate. It was during that conflict that the battle on the Cremera (a small tributary of the Tiber) took place. Livy and Dionysius offer slightly different accounts, but the essential elements of the story are the same from both historians. Supposedly the state either had insufficient funds to carry on the war against Veii or was overburdened by fighting on a number of fronts. In 479 the senior member of the clan who had been consul the year before presented himself to the senate and offered to take over the burden of war against Veii. A total number of 306 Fabii, as well as 4,000–5,000 of their dependants and friends, accompanied them. They built a fort somewhere on the Cremera, probably close to its union with the Tiber and for two years waged successful warfare against the enemy, until in 477 the Fabii were ambushed and defeated. Of the 306 Fabii only one boy survived, who brought the news back to Rome and carried on the family name. The details of the story were heavily influenced by Greek accounts of Thermopylae and the 300 Spartans. The traditional date of the incident is 18 July 477. This is also the date of the most important Roman defeat in the early Republic, inflicted by a Gallic tribe at the battle of the Allia in 387. The number of clients and friends at the Cremera seems far too large and they are tangential to the story whose real focus is the Fabii. There is a strong possibility that the original account of the Cremera battle was originated by Rome's first historian, Fabius Pictor, a member of the *gens*. However, there is some support for the story. Down to 479, the Fabian clan had occupied a prominent place in the list of magistrates. A Fabius occupied one of the two consulships every year from 485 to 479. They disappear from the *fasti* and do not reappear until 467, which suggests an extraordinary change in fortune which might well be the result of the Cremera defeat.[14]

Another type of independent military force has come to light in recent years. In 1977 an inscribed statue base was found at the site of Satricum. The town was located on one of the main routes that connected Latium and Rome to the rich and fertile area of Campania to the south, situated close to Antium one of the earliest ports in Latium.

The inscription on the base is damaged and can be read in at least two ways. The most sensible interpretation is that it recorded a dedication by the *suodales* of Publius Valerius to war god Mars. The term *suodales* (singular *suodalis*) can be used either as a general term implying comrades or friends or more narrowly to signify members of a formal corporation or group. They are especially found at Rome in the titles of religious corporations. They seem all to have been public, no evidence has been found for private associations of this type. The first usage appears to cover sworn groups of comrades often assembled for military purposes who were bound to each other by an oath. Given the dedication to Mars there is a strong possibility that it is a dedication by such a warband to its leader. This is apparently another form of clan battle groups, based not on ties of kinship, but on voluntary association; nevertheless, it is likely that the Fabian group was also bound by such an oath. This would have applied to their clients and friends. Groups of this nature are widely attested in other cultures,[15] and it is important to remember that one of the most important functions of early warfare is the accumulation of wealth through booty won in battle.

There are no authentic descriptions of how early Roman armies fought. The historical sources say little about equipment and tactics as these are technical details that the writers consciously avoided. Their battle descriptions are full of invention which filled out whatever bare details they had in order to present a readable and attractive narrative. The situation improves towards the middle of the sixth century, but this was because of a specific event and after it trustworthy details are few and far between. The antiquarian writers offer only a little additional material. The only possible approach is to look at the archaeological finds of equipment and to try to use them to reconstruct aspects of warfare in this period.

The treatment of early warfare varies a great deal in Roman poets. It veers between the imitation of Greek heroic warfare and ideas about the lives of early men. The latter mentions that man's first arms were his hands, nails, teeth, stones, tree branches and fire. It portrays the early Roman warrior going into battle with fire-hardened stakes and without protective equipment. Such primitivism is linked to the writers' conception of the pristine morality of early Rome, poor in material goods, but with an uncorrupted morality. The writer contrasts these early Romans with their morally inferior contemporaries, but none of this rested on real knowledge of early fighting methods. Literary convention, evolutionary theory or moral purpose are the basic elements of the picture these poets present.[16]

The material evidence has to be treated with caution. The majority of the evidence comes from graves. But the number of weapons found varies over the period from about 1100 down to the second half of the sixth century when they disappear from burials in Latium and Rome. Variation in the number of finds over time can be due to a number of different causes. The evidence consists of two major types. There are finds of weapons and representations of weapons and equipment in the form of depictions in various media. However, such evidence has to be used with great caution. For instance, in the last quarter of the eighth century there is an increase in the number of military equipment finds. This could be the result of an increase in the frequency of warfare, but there might have been other reasons. The eighth century witnessed an expansion of trade and growing prosperity in the Mediterranean which in turn stimulated Italian manufacturing. An increase in manufactured goods of all types marks the period and it is just as likely that that is the cause behind the increase in weapons finds which could act as a display of wealth and status. The end of the practice of using weapons as grave goods in Latium and at Rome might be a sign of the lesser importance of warfare in this period. The literary sources depict the exact opposite. The appearance of particular weapons may be the result of particular funerary customs rather than their actual use in warfare. Miniature weapons are found in both male and female graves before the sixth century. Clearly, they were not used by women and have some other significance.

Depictions of combat present problems of their own. Is contemporary equipment depicted or are they depictions of weapons drawn from myth or imagination? There are pronounced Greek and Near Eastern influences on Etruscan art from the eighth century. How far can contemporary representations of arms and armour be taken to represent reality rather than the use of foreign artistic conventions?

Such considerations should never be neglected in evaluating archaeological evidence. Often such material allows us to see the range of possibilities rather than providing a definitive picture of contemporary weaponry and equipment.

There are only a few pieces of protective equipment from Rome for the period prior to 750. It may be that protective equipment was made of organic materials such as leather and has disintegrated over time. There is some support for the use of organic materials with the absence of metal in graves all over Latium in this period. This changes dramatically after 750 when there is a substantial increase in weapons finds. The Esquiline cemetery at Rome provides several examples of a pectoral or small roughly rectangular piece of metal with concave sides that probably was fixed to a corselet of leather or linen and held in place by straps. It was used to protect the middle of the chest. It has been suggested that its use was a mark of the elite in this phase. Some bronze shield bosses from Tomb 94 on the Esquiline hill, dating to 650, are also said to belong to this period. This tomb has also yielded a semi-circular metal cap-like helmet.

Offensive weapons are hardly more plentiful. In the earliest period only bronze spearheads are found of a type common across most of Italy. By the later eighth century the spearheads made the transition from bronze to iron and there is more variety in their sizes and shapes. Their size and weight suggest use as missile weapons. From the late eighth century, other types of offensive weapons begin to appear in the graves of the Esquiline cemetery. Among them is an antennae sword, a straight-bladed sword almost always made of bronze with spiral projections on each side of the hilt as a decoration. There are also daggers of the same form from the late eighth and second half of the seventh century. Moreover, a small number of knives and an axe have been found dating to the same time period.

Esquiline 94 also contained the remains of a two-wheeled chariot. Chariot remains are found in Etruria and at other sites in Latium besides Rome. They consist of two-wheeled and four-wheeled varieties. They are especially conspicuous in the seventh century and then disappear in the mid-sixth century. There is no evidence for their use in war. They are not mentioned by the historians, although they appear frequently in Latin poetry. The poems are too heavily influenced by Greek models to be of much use as a source. The burial of chariots in women's graves seems to point more towards their use as status symbols and they may have been associated with funeral processions; nevertheless, it remained associated with the greatest of Roman military spectacles, the triumph and so may originally have had some military use.[17]

The close ties of Rome to both southern Etruria and Latium allow us to include finds from those areas to supplement the meagre Roman material. In essence Rome was part of a cultural world to which Etruria belonged. But the city was also the product of Greek and Latin influences, and there is no evidence that it was simply a passive recipient of these influences.

It seems to have actively contributed to its own development. It formed part of a cultural horizon which included all of these elements.[18]

The material from Etruria is particularly rich. Early Iron Age defensive equipment of the tenth and ninth centuries is almost all made of bronze. The most striking helmet type was made in two pieces that were riveted together, topped by a pointed metal crest; this is a typical style in the ninth and eighth centuries, and is associated with the Villanovans who were predecessors of the Etruscans. Their culture seems to be ancestral to the Etruscans and was heavily influenced by the cultures of contemporary central Europe.[19] Another helmet type is a bronze helmet which is characteristic of southern Etruria. It is basically a semi-circular bell-shaped helmet. The final common type is a simple cap helmet with a smooth surface.

In Etruria as in Rome, there is no trace of metallic body armour except for the pectoral. However, in Etruria from the seventh century there is a circular form of pectoral in addition to the rectangular shape.

There is also evidence for two shield types. The first is an oval shield with a boss in the shape of a spindle and the second – which appears in the eighth century – has a round shape. The best examples of the latter are a series of small circular bronze shields with a central boss and metal central handgrip from Veii, which date from the third quarter of the eighth century. They are too small and too fragile to have been used in battle. They were probably used for ceremonial purposes. There is no reason to doubt that they are based on examples actually used in combat.

Swords are found from the ninth century onward. The most common type has a T-shaped pommel and a double-edged blade about 40cm in length. The antennae sword is also common and examples have been found at Rome as mentioned earlier. It was of varying length. Other sword types are found, but these are the dominant varieties. In addition, shorter swords and axes seem more prominent in this later period, which may point to a new style of combat.

In the later Iron Age there is a clear line of evolution in equipment from native types with the increasing influence of Greek hoplite armament. However, native types persisted and continued to evolve.

The metal of choice for protective equipment continued to be bronze. It is likely that organic materials like leather were still used extensively. About 700 a round pot helmet appears. By the second half of the sixth century the most widespread helmet type was the so-called Negau helmet, which had approximately the shape of a rounded cone and sat quite far up on the head. It remained in use at least until the end of the fourth century.

The pectoral continued to be used to protect the upper torso, but increasingly corselets based on Greek models become prominent both among finds and in the pictorial record. Presumably, they were expensive and so worn only by the elite. Greek shields also appear in this period, but are still used alongside native models of various shapes, including the Etruscan round shield, which differs from the Greek model in having a central handgrip. Also shown in pictorial representations is a rectangular shield that resembles the later Roman *scutum*. It appears in miniature in eighth century burials and on several warrior figurines. It is well represented on a set of *situlae* or bronze buckets from Bologna and Este in Etruria and dating to the sixth century. One of the types frequently portrayed is an oval shield with a central boss, presumably over its central handgrip.

Spearheads are the most common weapons finds as they are for all of the Iron Age period, although their forms and size now seem to indicate their use for thrusting spears rather than missile weapons. Swords tend to shorten and knives seem to have been used as thrusting weapons. Axes continue to appear including at least one example of a double bladed axe. Importantly, from about 700 the material used for offensive weaponry changed to iron.

Latium does not supply a great deal of comparative material. Miniature weapons are usual in early Iron Age graves, but disappear as they do at Rome in the seventh century. The pattern followed is heavily influenced by Etruscan models in terms of weapons, equipment and artistic motifs. The pectoral is common in the seventh and sixth centuries, followed by the adoption of Greek equipment. Offensive weapon types are either borrowed from Italian models or from the Greek colonies of southern Italy. The spear is the dominant offensive weapon. Swords, daggers and knives are found, their forms heavily influenced by Etruscan types. In the later seventh and sixth century, spearheads tend to become larger and heavier which suggests their use in thrusting weapons. Later the axe is occasionally found though not as often as in Etruria.

Cavalry, which appears in the seventh century, do not seem to have had specialized weapons. The round shield predominates along with spear and the sword in pictorial representations. Horse archers are also represented.

The arms and equipment of Rome and other Latin states were products of a larger cultural unit embracing Etruria. In this area metallic defensive armour before 600 was generally limited to helmets and pectorals. Presumably, most defensive equipment continued to be made from organic materials and have not survived. The use of metal was confined to those relatively well off and may have been a way to display status as well as for the battlefield. It is likely that only the elite were well-armed and the rest of the army functioned in a supporting role because of their inferior equipment.

Archaeological evidence is the only reliable source for reconstructing the earliest manner of fighting. In the early Iron Age period the spear predominates both the heavy thrusting variety and javelins. Swords are a later and, in general, secondary armament. Their presence in burials may be more indicative of their role as an expensive marker of status rather than as a crucial implement of war. The defensive equipment seems limited to the helmet of bronze and the pectoral. In addition a shield, probably of wood, perhaps with a metal umbo was probably the most important piece of defensive equipment. The paucity of remains at Rome itself remains the greatest obstacle to reconstructing early Roman warfare. Interestingly, at Rome, all of the spearheads found seem suited to missile weapons and not the thrusting spear. The rest of Latium also supports the notion of lightly armed troops. The general picture that emerges is one of close encounters, especially of members of the elite, combined with the extensive use of missile weapons. The heavy thrusting spear would argue for some sort of close order formation. It need not have been a very regular formation. The picture of small bands following a better equipped leader is perhaps represented by the combination of spear and sword in grave finds. It may have been this type of equipment that formed the basis of the early clan armies and warrior fellowships discussed above. Some have seen this weaponry as indicating an individualized approach to war. The prevalence at least in Etruria proper of the heavy thrusting spear would make some sort of massed formation likely. The disparity in armament between what appear to be the elite and the rest of the population would support the view that they were the most important element in battle.

The material evidence in Etruria for this period until approximately 600 shows no basic change in the types of weapons available, though it does indicate a greater variety of weapon types. Presumably the tactical organization implied is not any more complicated aside from the arrival of cavalry by 600. Their presence implies a more complicated command structure with the need to coordinate two different types of troops. But it may simply be that the elite arrived at battle on horseback and were capable of fighting either mounted or dismounted, and not as an organized body. The traces of the importance of cavalry, especially dismounted cavalry in the historians' accounts of early battles may or may or may not be a reflection of early practice.

Most wars may have been on a relatively small scale as the exploit of the Fabii indicates. Rather than the large-scale, set piece battles imagined by the ancient historians, it is more likely that early Roman warfare was characterized by raiding and small-scale skirmishing. The annalists portray the fifth century wars against the Aequi and Volsci as filled with pitched battles. However, a closer reading shows these continuous conflicts often consisted of just the kind of small-scale raiding and plundering expeditions characterized by the encounters fighting between small groups of warriors rather than the thousands envisioned by later writers.[20] Livy realized this and so characterizes the war-making of both the Volsci and Aequi as raiding rather than warfare.[21]

The Reforms of Servius Tullius

It seems that the organization and mode of fighting of the Roman army – as well as the basis of citizenship – underwent an important change in the middle of the sixth century. All of the sources associate this change with the sixth king, Servius Tullius. His dates are given as 578–534 and these dates appear to be approximately correct. They are supported by the archaeological evidence for the prosperous state of Rome in this period and by the spread of a new type of warfare based on the hoplite or heavily armed infantryman and closely associated with its development among Rome's neighbours in Etruria.

The historicity of Servius and his association with these reforms has been contested. His origins remain obscure. This may be due in part to the fact that he early became an important political symbol. By the first century AD he was viewed as the king who increased the power of the common people and as a key architect of Roman institutions. An exactly opposite view is found as well; he was seen as a conservative, a supporter of the rich and of the senate. Ideological considerations may be a part of the reason for the uncertainty about his origins that are visible in the ancient sources. One version of his personal history portrays him as Etruscan, but he is more likely to be of Latin origin. His name is Latin and it is related to the Latin word for slave (*servus*). He may have given rise to the legend that he was of servile birth. Tarquinius Priscus was militarily active and the sources associate Servius with him in a military capacity. It would not be surprising if the elective process and the influence of Tarquinius were the reason for his ascent to the kingship. Such a background would explain part of Servius' motives for the various reforms attributed to him and therefore supports his historicity.

The foundation of the new system he instituted was a census of all citizens and their property and then, based on that, the creation of a new army. The census of property became a means of assigning citizen rights and responsibilities. This was an important change from the existing system based on kinship and residence. Inherent in this reform was a new idea of citizenship. Rather than having an individual's political standing mediated through the power and standing of his kin group, the citizen now stood in a direct relationship to his community and was assigned his rights as an individual and not as a member of a group. In addition, Servius changed the existing tribal structure. He created four urban tribes and seventeen rural ones. Aspects of Servius' reforms have striking similarities to contemporary reforms in Greek southern Italy and in Greece itself.[22]

Cicero's *De Republica,* Dionysius and Livy provide accounts of the formation of a new centuriate assembly. It would in time become the most important of Roman assemblies. It is an assembly of the army in military units, the centuries, based on census valuations. It elected Rome's most important military commanders, the consuls, and issued declarations of war. These functions as well as its other powers point to its military origins. The description of Servius' reorganization of the assembly in all three writers is virtually identical except for some minor divergences which mostly concern the weaponry of the lower census classes. It is probable that the same antiquarian writer is behind all three accounts.[23]

With the addition of eighteen centuries of cavalry which were assigned to the first class, the infantry sitting in the assembly was divided into five classes according to their military equipment, which they had to supply as the state did not supply equipment until much later. The five classes were further subdivided into centuries that vary in number according to the property valuation of each class. The higher the property rating of each class the more expensive was its equipment. The class was also divided by age. Half of the centuries contained men aged 17 to 46 who formed the active field army and the other half included men over 46 who formed a reserve and could be called upon for service until they reached the age of 60. In addition to infantry centuries, there were centuries of engineers and musicians. Those citizens whose property rating fell below the minimum amount necessary for service in the legions were assigned to a single century. The total number of infantry centuries was 175. The organization is best presented in tabular form:[24]

Classes	Property Rating	Number of Centuries	Equipment
Class 1	100,000 and above asses	80	Round shield, breastplate, greaves, heavy thrusting spear and sword.
Class 2	75,000–100,000 asses	20	Helmet, rectangular or oval shield, greaves, heavy thrusting spear and sword.
Class 3	50,000–75,000 asses	20	Helmet, rectangular or oval shield, heavy thrusting spear and sword
Class 4	25,000–50,000 asses	20	Heavy thrusting spear and verutum (which seem to have been a small javelin).
Class 5	11,000–25,000 asses	30	Verutum and slings.
Engineers		2	
Musicians		2	
Those below the minimum census	Less than 11,000 asses	1	

Certain details found in all three authors are clearly anachronistic.[25] The property assessments are those of the mid-second century not the mid-sixth. There were certainly pre-weighed units of bronze in the mid-sixth but no proper coinage minted at Rome until bronze and silver were coined in the late fourth and early third centuries. The values given probably are those of the Second Punic War or somewhat later when the denarius Rome's first silver coin appeared valued at ten and then sixteen asses. Our best information comes from Polybius writing in the mid-second century. Based on his figures, it has been calculated that an ordinary legionary received 3 asses per day. However, food and clothing were deducted from it. What the actual value of the pay was is impossible to determine.[26]

In any case the census ratings are clearly impossible for the mid-sixth century as no coinage yet existed. In fact, the *as* evidently used was not introduced until 211. So the original source used for the reform must post-date that year. It is not impossible that the figures are recalculations in terms of the new coinage of earlier values and that this system of classes is far earlier. The tremendous stress on manpower produced by the Second Punic War might well have stimulated renewed interest in the system.

The system described seems incredibly complex and would make mobilization a terribly difficult procedure. It is far more likely that the original system was far simpler. There are hints in the sources that the army was divided into two types: heavy and light infantry. Some later writers mention a group called *classis,* a term usually limited to the first class. The other classes are designated *infra classem* ('below the *classis*'). The meaning of *classis* in early Latin is an army or military unit.[27] The differentiation between the first class and the others is due to their equipment. The first class is armed in the same manner as the contemporary heavy infantry whom the Greeks called hoplites and who appear in Greece about 650. These warriors were armed with heavy thrusting spears as their main offensive weapon and often with a short sword as their secondary armament. Their defensive equipment consisted of a cuirass, a metal helmet usually of bronze, and a new type of shield. The hoplite shield was their most distinctive piece of equipment; it was a large round shield, almost a metre in diameter, although examples as large as 1.2 metres have been found. It was extremely convex, so that it could be rested on the shoulder. It was made of a wooden core and covered in leather and rimmed with bronze. Later the entire shield was often faced with bronze.

This standard equipment corresponds to that of the first class in the Servian army. Hoplites fought in a rectangular formation, the phalanx. When the formation was closed up for battle each hoplite stood about half a metre from the man next to him. His left hand held his round shield that partially protected the right side of the hoplite to his left so as to form a wall of shields with spear points projecting from it. The Greek phalanx was normally drawn up in eight rows, although other depths are recorded.

When fighting other hoplites also arrayed the same way, the phalanxes moved to frontal contact with each other. What happened at that point is uncertain, but the fighting lasted until one side or the other broke.[28]

The phalanx seems to have evolved over an extended period. The deployment was far less uniform in the beginning and phalanxes initially contained light-armed and missile troops as well as heavy infantry. Its evolution proceeded by a progressive elimination of other arms so that it ended with the phalanx solely composed of heavy infantry. So little is known about the warfare of the sixth and early fifth centuries that all that can be said is that the process had ended by the mid-fifth century.[29]

Its spread to Italy appears to be linked to developments in Etruria at the end of the eighth century. There was an important cultural transformation in conjunction with increasing urbanization and social change: a substantial increase in luxury, visible in burials and in the large-scale importation of luxury objects from the eastern Mediterranean.

Accompanying these massive social and cultural changes was a phase of Etruscan expansion on land and sea. From the eighth century there is evidence for Etruscanizing elements in the culture of Campanian cities, although the chronology and the nature of Etruscan penetration is uncertain. There is no evidence that this was done in any unified or conscious manner. Rather, it seems to have been the work of individuals and small bands from different Etruscan cities. The Etruscans also expanded to the north into the Po valley. Their movement to the south was of particular significance for Rome because of the deep cultural impact it had. Rome of the seventh century was an open and ethnically fluid society in which Etruscans played an important role. It may even have had a bilingual elite.

The spread of this expansion and associated warfare in Italy must be traced through equipment finds and some pictorial art as the written sources are of no help. In central Italy most of the finds of defensive armour consist of native equipment such as the chest protector. Spearheads have been found, made of iron, as also are the spear butts. They display a range of sizes that could indicate the use of thrusting spears and javelins. The other major offensive weapon is the sword, made of iron and reproducing the characteristics of the Greek hoplite sword (a short iron sword whose blade widened towards its point). The Italian specimens are, however, two-edged rather than a Greek style single edge.

More difficult to assess is the evidence for the use of Greek hoplite equipment. Finds of Greek equipment are rare. The bulk of evidence for the use of hoplite equipment is pictorial and Etruscan. Despite these limitations it appears that the Etruscans began using such equipment from about the mid-seventh century, soon after its development in Greece. The earliest pictorial representations of what seem to be hoplites appear at the same time. From the beginning of the sixth century representations of hoplites become very frequent. Given the expense of hoplite equipment and the limited finds it would seem extremely doubtful that it was widely used. The evidence indicates that in northern Etruria at this period the use of hoplite armour was restricted, as expected, to the elite. It also appears that such equipment was adopted piecemeal. This may indicate that at least part of its reason for adoption was display and not for its military effectiveness, since the restriction of such equipment to a few warriors limits the effectiveness of the phalanx. In addition, given the small-scale nature of much of the warfare in this period, phalanx warfare is unlikely to have played a significant part. From the beginning of the sixth century representations of hoplites become very frequent. However, there is a greater diversity of equipment in Etruria than in Greece. This may be a reflection of the social and political system of Etruscan city-states, which was far more economically and socially stratified than the cities of the Greek mainland.

The evidence for hoplite equipment in this period at Rome is sparse. It consists of scattered pieces of equipment and some fragmentary representations of Greek equipment from which little can be inferred. There is some terracotta temple ornamentation with hoplite figures from around 600, but it is not clear whether it represents contemporary Roman equipment or is simply copied from Greek decoration. This is repeated throughout Latium. There is a significant general decline in the quality of grave goods in this period. Since in other ways it appears to be a time of substantial growth, this impoverishment of burials seems best explained as a deliberate change in the disposal of the dead. It may be that in this first period of monumental construction and urbanization in Latium, wealth that had formerly been deposited with the dead was now directed towards public building and display.

Given this paucity of data little can be deduced directly from the Roman material. In view of the general cultural similarities between Rome and southern Etruria there is every reason to expect that Roman warriors duplicated in their equipment and tactics the style of fighting prevalent in Etruria, and that the standard heavy infantry was composed at least in part of hoplites by the sixth century. This lends further support to seeing the Servian reforms as in part the creation of a hoplite army.[30]

The new centuriate assembly was far too complex to have ever functioned as an army; the simpler distinction between the first class as at least part of the hoplite phalanx, and the other classes as supporting and light infantry as found in some sources, makes much more sense. Several of the distinctions are clearly artificial and devised to justify the difference between the classes. The most striking distinction is that between class II and class III where the only difference is the presence or absence of greaves (shin protectors). Since the classes consisted of both junior and senior centuries the first class could field an army of 40 centuries or 4,000 men.

Classes II and III are more of a problem. They differ from class I mostly in the form of their shields, an oval or rectangular shield that the Romans called a *scutum*. This curved oblong shield with a central handgrip became the standard Roman shield in later centuries. The evidence for this Italian shield goes back to the eighth century, long before the Servian reforms.

The mixture of equipment is paralleled in the early Greek phalanx and in that case as well it must have been due to the fact that the soldiers bought their own equipment. The first class must have formed the front of the phalanx with its full complement of defensive equipment. The less heavily armed classes II and III must have formed the rear of the phalanx where the relative lightness of their equipment would have been less of a problem. The presence of all three classes in the phalanx is borne out by the organization of the latter legion. The number of centuries in the latter Roman legion was always sixty. The active centuries of the first three classes would also total sixty. In addition, when the Roman army evolved into a very different fighting force in the later fourth and early third centuries, it was organized in three lines although these were formed on very different principles. The number three of course can be found in the earliest Roman army, nonetheless, it seems to support the notion of the first three classes as forming the phalanx. It is possible that the original phalanx contained only the forty centuries of the first class and was later expanded to sixty when the other classes were included. This development may have happened soon after the introduction of the phalanx by the Servian reforms. It seems that one of the clear aims of the reforms was not only to broaden the idea of citizenship by basing it on wealth rather than kin ties, but also on creating a new decision-making body that embodied that principle and to increase the number of troops the city could field. If we assume the inclusion of the second and third classes took place either during the original reform or soon after, the army would have seen an increase of 50 per cent in its heavy infantry from 4,000 to 6,000 men.[31] Demographic calculations suggest for that period Rome possessed a territory of 510km square, which was far larger than any other city in Latium. Given modern estimates this would yield a citizen population of 20,000–30,000. Since in pre-modern societies about 29 per cent of the population consists of adult males this would yield a total of approximately 9,000 males eligible for military service. So the army of this period could not possibly have consisted of 6,000 hoplites given the distribution of wealth in a pre-modern society. If this is the case, the best solution is to assume that the centuries of the Servian army consisted of fewer than 100 men. This suggestion is supported by the fact that the Roman army never fielded an army with centuries consisting of exactly 100 men; the highest figure during and after the Republic was 80 soldiers per century. The Servian army may simply have taken over the unit of the century from the earlier tribal army where it may well have had a full complement of 100 men.

Eighteen centuries were assigned to the cavalry in the voting system of the centuriate assembly. However, the history of the cavalry during the regal period is the most confused of any part of the regal army. If it is accepted that by Tarquinius Priscus' reign the Roman army fielded 600 cavalry, this would lead to a tripling of Rome's cavalry strength. The number seems extraordinarily high. In most Mediterranean armies the ratio between infantry and cavalry was one to ten. For an infantry force of 6,000, an accompanying force of 1,800 cavalry would produce a ratio of approximately 3:1. It would also suggest that those wealthy enough to serve in the cavalry amounted to one-fifth of all males eligible for military service. This is an impossible number. It is more likely that the number of centuries was due to political rather than military reasons, to give more political power to the most elite citizens. This idea is supported by the claim in the sources that the cavalry received financial support from the state under Servius. This contradicts the general principal that each citizen was required to supply his own equipment. A total army of 6,000 infantry and 600 cavalry seems a reasonable total for Roman military strength in this period. It is important to remember that these are paper figures and do not necessarily represent the actual strength of the army at any one period or for any particular campaign.

The sources for political and military activity in this period must be assessed critically. This holds true especially in the domain of warfare, because of its close connection with the political and social standing of the elite who had a strong incentive to elaborate whatever facts survived in their favour as well as to glorify Rome. However, there is general agreement that by the end of the regal period Roman territory consisted of about a third of the total area of Latium. The next largest state was Tibur (modern Tivoli), which lay 30km northeast of Rome and was only slightly over a third of its size.

Whatever the military abilities of the individual kings and their commanders, Rome enjoyed certain advantages which in part explain her success. Perhaps the most important was her control of a vital Tiber crossing which allowed her to control a major north–south route giving her access into the Italian interior. The economic advantages of such a site are obvious and other peoples noticed it. There are traces of Sabine immigration from the northeast at Rome, and of Etruscan settlement too. The influx of newcomers allowed an increase in military strength, which in turn led to territorial expansion which allowed for more settlers and further expansion. It also must have given rise to acquisition of new skills and techniques, especially due to Etruscan immigration.

Additional support for Rome's dominance within Latium in this period is provided by a treaty between Rome and Carthage that the mid-second century Greek historian, Polybius, cites and dates it to the first year of the Republic (509). Although there has been debate as to the authenticity and date of this treaty, most scholars now accept it as genuine. It provides collaborative evidence for the situation in Latium at the end of the monarchy at Rome. In the treaty the Carthaginians were forbidden to harm certain peoples named as subject to Rome, as well as the remainder of the Latins. The parallels with the sections, which concern Carthaginian interests, make it clear that the Romans claimed a general supremacy over Latium.[32]

CHAPTER THREE

A TIME OF TROUBLES

At Rome, the end of the sixth and the beginning of the fifth centuries were marked by domestic turmoil and external threat. Internally, a coup d'état overthrew the monarchy and established a Republican form of government with strong oligarchic overtones. Externally, the disturbances that engulfed central Italy led to the appearance of serious new military threats.

The transition to the new form of government at Rome is obscured by a mass of myth and legend that makes it hard to separate fact from fiction. The ancient literary sources saw the change as the product of internal forces. The focus of these accounts is the last king of Rome, Tarquinius Superbus ('Tarquin the Proud'). The king's portrayal is clearly heavily influenced by traditional portraits of Greek tyrants: a ruthless tyrant whose equally ruthless son Sextus precipitated the expulsion of the king and his family because of his rape of the wife of a powerful nobleman. The outrage led to the formation of a coalition of powerful nobles who expelled the king and instituted a new form of government. This story has strong legendary elements. The role of the lust of an unjust and tyrannical member of the elite appears later in Roman history.[1] The Romans exhibited a penchant for explaining early constitutional change as the result of violation of the sanctity of the family. This reflects the ancient tendency to seek the cause of political and social change in individual actions and motives.

There is an alternative version of this change in the sources that seems both more plausible and more in keeping with general developments in central Italy. The area seems to have experienced a great deal of turmoil accompanied by extensive migration. For instance, in Etruria, a number of settlements, mostly smaller urban centres, were abandoned or destroyed as were palace centres at Acquarossa (near modern Viterbo) and Murlo. These towns were sacked at the end of the sixth century.[2] Pressure from the hill peoples surrounding the coastal plains increased the disruption.

In the context of these events we have a version of the fall of the monarchy at Rome that centred on an external attack on Rome by Lars Porsenna (the king of the Etruscan city of Clusium), who drove Tarquin and his family from the city, traditionally in 509. There is one Roman tradition found in Livy embroidering the story of his attack with all sorts of heroic actions by the Roman defenders that persuaded Porsenna to abandon his attack on the city and become a friend and ally.[3] An alternative version seems nearer the truth: that Porsenna did drive Tarquin out and in doing so captured and ruled Rome for a short time.[4] While in control of Rome he began to expand at the expense of the Latins. Finally, in 504 he sent his son Arruns who now governed Rome to fight a coalition of Latins and a Greek nobleman Aristodemus of Cumae. The battle at Aricia, the religious centre of the Latins, ended in the defeat of Arruns and the loss of Etruscan control of Rome.[5]

The kings were replaced by a college of two magistrates with equal powers, the consuls although the names of the majority of consuls of the first year of the Republic are fictitious.[6] These were annual magistrates each having equal power. They served one-year terms and could be re-elected to office.[7] Although they were given what in effect was the unlimited power of the kings, their actions were circumscribed by a limited term of office and the opposition of their colleagues.

As was the case for the kings, their power to execute the functions of their office was based on their *imperium*. They inherited the kings' *imperium* and the right to command military forces. They exercised jurisdiction, controlled public finances, maintained order, conducted the census, and selected the members of the senate.[8] It was with the appearance of the consulship that many scholars assume the regal army of 6,000 was now divided in two, with each consul commanding a legion of 3,000.[9] The consuls also possessed the right to ascertain the will of the gods through their right to take auspices.

From 447, two urban quaestors were elected by the tribal assembly to administer the state treasury as well as to perform certain judicial duties. Then in 421 two more quaestorships were created to serve as assistants to the consuls. A consul was always accompanied by a quaestor while on campaign. The latter's importance is made clear by the fact that at the centre of the Roman military camp, the quarters of the quaestor required a separate building adjoining the headquarters of the consul. In theory, the relationship of the consul to his quaestor paralleled that of a father to his son. His main duties were financial and logistic. He was in charge of the campaign treasury and saw to the provisioning of the army. But in practice he could be assigned any task. If the consul died or was incapacitated the quaestor assumed temporary command until the arrival of a replacement.

Legionary tribunes commanded individual legions. They came from equestrian and senatorial families; for the latter it was often the first step towards a political career. The sources claim that they originated under the kings and totalled three: one for each of the 1,000 infantry supplied by each of the three tribes. The Servian reforms rendered this system obsolete. They separated the tribunes from their tribes and assigned each of them to a legion. Originally there were probably three to each legion assuming that the early Republican legion consisted of 3,000 men. Later the standard number became six per legion, but the tribunes served in pairs with each pair serving for a third of the campaigning season. Down to 362, tribunes were selected by the consuls they were to campaign with. From 362 six were elected in the popular assembly, presumably three for each legion. Finally, in 311 the twenty-four tribunes of the four new legions levied each year were all elected. This step makes clear the increasing size of the army. We have almost no information on the duties of tribunes before the second century, but there is no reason to doubt that they performed the same duties as the later tribunes. Besides specific duties such as playing an important role in the military levy, tribunes selected the site for the daily marching camp and were responsible for aspects of guarding the camp and administering military justice. Among their duties as elected magistrates, they had the responsibility to support the health, interests and general welfare of their troops.

From sporadic references in Livy and elsewhere it is clear that the tribune did play a role in battle. We hear of tribunes setting the battle line in order, performing reconnaissance and making reports to the consul, sitting on the commander's military council, and commanding detachments.[10]

Traditionally in 501, although the date is not certain, a new office was created: the dictatorship. The fact that a dictator is described as fighting at the battle of Lacus Regillus in either in 499 or 496, makes it likely that the office was created around 500, perhaps as a response to growing problems with the Latin League and the pressure of the hill peoples from the Apennines. It was an unusual office. Unlike other magistrates, the dictator served alone. He had the power to nominate a subordinate magistrate, the master of the horse. The title of the dictator had been the master of the infantry; the fact that the commander of the infantry was superior to that of the cavalry is some support for a hoplite army at Rome at this time. In such an army, the cavalry, although prestigious, remained the less important arm.[11]

The consuls became the dictator's subordinates after his election. In some sense the dictator's office was a direct continuation of the king's. He was, at least in theory, in full control of the government. To avoid a return of monarchy, his term was limited to six months or the end of the task for which he had been elected. The military advantage of the dictator's undivided command was the important aspect of the office. However, dictators also performed other tasks as well as military command. They were used for certain religious ceremonies and in cases where internal disputes necessitated an arbiter.[12]

The period after 302 witnessed the gradual decline of the office, with the sources mentioning dictators only for 301, 249 and Fabius Maximus in 217. The last two appointments occurred in periods of severe crisis with a single theatre of operations dominating all of the others. The disappearance of the dictatorship seems to be the result of an attempt by the aristocracy to restrain the power of its members by limiting access to important offices. In addition, the development of new types of military commanders and the increase in the number of theatres where military campaigns were taking place reduced the need for an overall military commander. When the office was resurrected at the beginning of the first century it had radically changed its character.[13]

The end of the monarchy was also marked by a prolonged conflict, usually termed 'The Struggle of the Orders', which lasted for two centuries. It was a conflict between two groups within the citizen body that centred for the most part on two issues: the admittance of the excluded plebeians to the magistracies, and debt reform. By its end in the late fourth century a new elite had emerged along with substantial economic and political reform.

Defining each group is not easy. Tradition maintained that patrician status was a creation of the kings and was the exclusive privilege of certain clans. During parts of the fifth and fourth centuries, patricians monopolized political and religious office. However, it is clear from the non-patrician names appearing in the consular lists that this was not at first the case during the earliest days of the Republic. The patricians may have won their position because they were the heads of leading elite families. In time they came to monopolize certain privileges, especially of a religious nature. The most important was the right to take the auspices, without it one could not exercise military command.[14]

After 366, only twenty-one patrician clans are attested; another twelve are known before that date. Their limited number raises the question of how they could have resisted the pressure from the rest of the citizen body for so long. One reason may have been Roman relations of deference and dependence. The patricians became a closed aristocracy system.[15]

The plebeians formed a very diverse group. The easiest way to define it was that it consisted of all who were not patricians. They included both the rich and well-connected as well as the poorest of the poor. The range of wealth and status led to a division in the aims of the group. The wealthy plebeians wanted access to the senate and to office which would give them political power and status. Admission to the consulship was their most important goal as it opened up the prospect of military command, the surest route to prestige and political success.

The poor were hard pressed by debt and a scarcity of land. Food shortages also added to the plebeians' problems. They seem to have been particularly severe in the fifth century. It was probably exacerbated by the economic decline visible in central Italy in the first half of the century. There were a number of signs of this economic decline, including a general decline in the quantity and quality of Roman and Latin finds in this period. It is significant that though the sixth century opens with significant temple building, there is a hiatus after 484 continuing until the last third of the century.[16]

Pestilences that are normally caused by malnutrition appeared. Some outbreaks seem to have been extremely serious, such as one in 453 which resulted in the death of one of the consuls and his successor, as well as four tribunes of the plebs, and an unknown number of citizens. Supporting evidence for the reality of these outbreaks can be found in occasional references to Rome's inability to field military forces as a result of plague. In 463 Rome's allies requested help against a combined invasion of their lands by the Aequi and Volsci; the Senate responded that the city could not field an army because of the pestilence then raging.

There is also archaeological evidence that economic recession affected other areas of central Italy, though not universally. From the beginning of the fifth century north of the Tiber in southern and central Etruria, there is evidence for destruction and abandonment of a number of town sites. At the same time there are fewer temples and tombs and also their furnishings are far poorer than they were in the previous century. There is also a noticeable decline in local craft production. In part this may have been due to internal causes as the cities of the interior continued to flourish, but it fits well with the Roman situation and it is difficult not to see it as a part of the same phenomenon of the continuous warfare that affected the area south of the Tiber.

The first open resistance was a seccession, in reality a military mutiny, by the plebeians in 494. The causes of this seccession of the plebeians, which was essentially a military strike, were the pressure of debt, often caused by enemy raids, the burdens of military service and taxation. It was an action based on self-help, which was widely used in the absence of strong state institutions. The strike was a success that resulted in the creation of specifically plebeian officers, the tribunes of the plebs who would eventually be incorporated into the hierarchy of the state magistrates and whose role was to protect plebeians from oppression and to extend their civic rights.

Two further strikes took place in 449 and 287. It is probable that the details of the fifth century strikes were invented, although there is no reason to question the reality of the strikes themselves. We also hear frequently of tribunes obstructing levies in the hope of forcing the magistrates and Senate to accept their proposals. These tactics were to be repeated in the mid-second century for very different reasons.

The continuing crisis was solved in the mid-fourth century. In 367/6 a series of laws known as the Licinian-Sextian rogations were passed. One of the laws opened the consulship to the plebeians as well as reinstituting it as a regular magistracy. A further law was passed in 342 that required that one of the two consuls be a plebeian. The result of these measures was the development of a new patrician–plebeian nobility.

The demands of the lower stratum of the plebeian movement took longer to satisfy. The wealthy and powerful plebeians had provided leadership, and now they had been absorbed into the ruling elite. The plebeians' problems of debt and land hunger persisted. In fact, given the tiny size of recorded Roman holdings, they were intimately linked as cause and effect. The Licinian-Sextian laws had a provision to relieve some of the debt burden. It specified that as far as outstanding debts, the interest already paid should be deducted from the principal and the balance paid off in three years. Over the course of the fourth century other legislation was passed to further relieve the pressure of debt. The most serious imposition was *nexum,* which was a type of debt bondage. This was finally abolished in either 326 or 313. It was regarded as the most onerous burden that debt imposed.[17]

Another provision of the Licinian-Sextian laws limited the amount of public land any one citizen could hold. Public land seems to have been a feature of Roman economic life from the earliest times. Given the size of allotments the use of this land was vital to maintain subsistence farming. The rich had the wealth and pool of labour to exploit this land; the poor did not. Despite the laws on debt it was Roman expansion in Italy that solved the problem by greatly increasing the amount of public land that was available for distribution and use and so eased the pressure of debt and no doubt served as a major incentive.[18]

The fifth century was marked by the emergence of a new office, the military tribunate with consular powers. The office presents one of the most difficult problems in early Republican history. The tribunes appear as replacements for the consuls as the chief executive and military officers beginning in 444. Even the official title of these magistrates is uncertain. The office manifests striking variations in the number of office holders and in the frequency of its appearance. For instance, from 444–427 consuls alternate with three military tribunes; from 426–406 the alteration remains the same, but there were either three or four military tribunes; and from 405–367 there were almost always six consular tribunes.

Most aspects of the office are controversial. In part, this is due the ambiguous nature of evidence. The sources have no clear understanding of the institution and their narrative is often distorted by the backward projection of later political developments into the politics of the fifth and fourth centuries. Further difficulties result from the fact that the office disappeared after 367/6.[19]

In origin the consular military tribunes seem to have been the military tribunes of a legion invested with special powers. This is a reasonable theory in the light of the later history of the office. It is significant that in 362, within five years of the final disappearance of the office of military tribunes with consular powers, the tribunes of the legion who had earlier been selected by the consuls were elected by the people. This change can be seen as a concession to a popular demand for a greater voice in the choice of their magistrates, which they lost with the disappearance of the consular tribunes. The connection between these different types of tribunes is also supported by the fact that military tribunes later had general duties and were not linked to specific units within the legion.

As replacements for the consuls it might be expected that these magistrates would have had *imperium*. Many scholars have denied it. However, this seems an impossible position. How could the Roman state have functioned for extended periods without magistrates with *imperium,* or how could the military tribunes with consular powers have held independent command as they did? In addition, Livy provides clear evidence despite contrary interpretations that they were elected by the centuriate assembly, the same assembly that elected consuls and later other magistrates holding *imperium*. They must also have had the right to their own auspices, a right that was essential for military command and magisterial functions.

The major objection to the possession of full consular *imperium* by the tribunes is the absence of any record of triumphs celebrated by them. One late source claims that they did not possess the right to this supreme military distinction.[20] However, this evidence is of questionable value. The absence of consular tribunes from the list of those who had triumphed, set up at the end of the first century, is not as strong an objection as it might seem. There is a large gap precisely in the period when there were consular tribunes in office. In addition, it seems clear that during those years a serious military situation of the type that might lead to a triumph for a victorious commander was usually met either by the election of consuls or by the appointment of a dictator. A further point of some interest is that the record of the tribunes was less successful than that of the consuls. Especially in the early years of the new office, divided command and internal disputes often led to a lack of success on campaign. Given the limitations of our evidence, it seems more reasonable to accept that military tribunes had the right to triumph just as consuls and dictators acting under their own auspices did.

Perhaps the most difficult question is why the office existed at all. The ancient sources represent its creation as a stage in the struggle of plebeians for admission to the consulship. Livy claims that the tribunes of the plebs had brought their agitation to such a point that the levy could not proceed and in desperation the patricians agreed to the creation of this office, which would be open to plebeian candidates as a way of avoiding pollution of the consulship with non-patricians.[21] Against this explanation is that very few of the known consular tribunes have plebeian names. In addition, the strange variation of numbers and the alternation with consulship do not fit easily with a political explanation.

Livy introduces as an alternative explanation, which he does not support, that there were simply too many wars for two consuls to handle and so a new magistracy was required with more members to meet these pressing tasks.[22] However, there are serious problems in positing any relationship between military needs and the office of military tribune.

First, the decision to hold an election to the office would have taken place before the opening of the campaigning season and so the Senate, which appears to have made the decision each year on whether or not to appoint them, could not have completely known what the coming year's military demands were going to be. Second, the need for military leadership in critical situations was regularly met down to 406 by the appointment of consuls or a dictator. The varying numbers of tribunes also present a problem. The fluctuations do not seem to accord with the annalists' report of the dangers threatening Rome. Finally, the mostly dismal record that the military tribunes compiled in the field would have done nothing to recommend the continuation of the office for military reasons.

It has been suggested that the variations in time and numbers is to be explained not by a single cause but by the supposition that the office met a variety of needs over time. Nevertheless, in some years we have tribunes appointed but the annalistic record preserves nothing of note. The regularities in numbers of consular tribunes after 405 make an ad hoc explanation of the numbers unlikely. Growing administrative needs have also been used as an explanation for the institution of the office and it is true that when the consulate was restored the number of magistrates was increased. The fluctuating numbers are an objection to this explanation as they are to the one based on military needs.

In the end there is no clear solution as to why the Romans first used and then discarded this office. But two points stand out. Immediately before the introduction of consular military tribunes, a tribune of 445 passed a law that removed the barrier to intermarriage between patricians and plebeians, which had been put in place five years earlier. At the termination of the office in 367, the Licinian-Sextian laws formally opened the consulship to plebeians though in fact there seemed to have been no legal bar. Whatever the fictions in the historical record, it is hard not to see a connection with the struggle of the orders. The fact that so few plebeians were elected is less of an objection than it seems. The traditional methods used to attain electoral success were in patrician hands. No explanation can meet all of the problems that the history of this office engenders. The record is too tendentious and fragmentary to allow us to see clearly the factors at work. There are no definitive solutions, only possibilities.

The transition to the Republic was accompanied by external difficulties. The turmoil surrounding the expulsion of the last king affected the Latins who seem to have resented the dominance that Rome had acquired in the regal period. The Latins joined together to try to end or reduce that dominance. The sources name their main leader as Octavius Mamilius of Tusculum, the son-in-law of the last Tarquin, who was acting at the instigation and in the interests of his expelled father-in-law. This struggle was part of a wider-ranging conflict involving not only the Latins but the Etruscans as well. The crux was the Latins desire to be free of Roman dominance.

Lacus Regillus was the decisive engagement in this conflict. The sources offer two different dates for it, either 499 or 496 and there is too little evidence to decide between them. Livy and Dionysius are the main sources for the battle but they paint very different pictures of it. Livy presents us with a series of heroic encounters, not a battle narrative. Dionysius offers a more plausible picture. Of key interest is the fact that he uses the term phalanx to describe the Roman infantry formation.[23] The location of the battle is uncertain. It seems to have been fought in the hilly country near Tusculum. The Roman force was commanded by the dictator Postumius Albinus, with Titus Aebutius as his master of the horse. The decisive role in the battle is assigned by Livy and others to the Roman cavalry, who in the course of the struggle dismounted and fought on foot. The cavalry also plays a critical role in Dionysius' version. He does not mention that they dismounted to fight, rather in his version it is the cavalry charge of the dictator and the loss of their leaders that resulted in a rout of the Latins. The decisive role of the cavalry would seem to point to the fact that the term phalanx in Dionysius is not used to be specific of a particular formation, but rather simply to denote a densely packed infantry formation.[24]

Although the war with the Latins dragged on for another few years this victory paved the way for a settlement favourable to Rome. It was a bilateral agreement between Romans and Latins concluded by one of the consuls of 493, Spurius Cassius.[25] It provided for a perpetual peace among the signatories with a proviso that they were not to bring in foreign enemies or allow them passage through their territory. It also created a defensive alliance between Rome and the Latin League. In the event of war, it allowed for the equal sharing of any booty. However, later narratives in the sources contradict this term of the treaty. It also provided for the mutual settlement of commercial disputes. The addition of private rights in such a document is probably the result of an attempt by the Latins to safeguard them. One curious omission is the absence of any provision for the appointment of a commander for the League forces. Such an omission in a document concluding a military alliance is striking. However, there is a hint in another source about the procedure used in such cases.

> *The Latin peoples were accustomed to consult in common and manage the problem of military command by taking common counsel.*[26]

This seems to imply that commanders could be drawn both from Rome and the Latin states. When we do see the combined armies in action the commander is always Roman, but this may be that as a result of Rome's overwhelming position it became customary to appoint a Roman as the alliance's commander.[27] The settlement was a lasting one that endured until the dissolution of the League in 338.

In 486 the League was enlarged by the addition of a new group, the Hernici, on the same conditions as the existing members.[28] Little is known about the Hernici who inhabited the vast Trerus Valley (modern Sacco) to the southeast of Rome. They have left few material remains beyond fortification walls at some of their major sites. They seem to have had a league of their own under the leadership of the town of Agnania.[29] From 495 the Hernici had fought against the Romans until their defeat in 487. Despite this, the treaty of 486 recognized them as an equal partner. The change in Hernician policy seems to have been brought about by pressure from the same Apennine peoples who were causing troubles in Latium. Their addition to the alliance was important as their territory served as a buffer, separating the two main hill peoples, the Aequi and the Volsci.

The Hernici rendered effective aid to the Romans and had borne a heavy burden in the campaigns against the Aequi and Volsci. Their loyalty appears to have been undermined by various factors. First, it seems that they had profited far less than the Romans in the course of the fifth century wars and the very success of the coalition's wars made the danger of the Aequi and Volsci less threatening. As was the case of some of the Latin states, the Hernici seem to have been fearful of growing Roman dominance. After the 390s they too took the field in conjunction with various Latin states. Their defeat led to an uneasy relationship that again resulted in war in 362. Finally, in 306 they were defeated and later became so Latinized that their nature, language and culture disappeared.

A new threat to both Rome and Latium appears in the course of the 490s. The most immediate threat was the new pressure from the Sabellian hill peoples of central Italy who had begun to move into the lowland plains of central and southern Italy. This movement was far larger and more threatening than previous migration. It is part of a long-standing adversarial tension between mountain and lowland communities.[30]

> *For the Samnites used to live in villages in the mountains, and often made raids on the low country and the coastal districts. Living in the mountains and being wild, they despised the softer farmers of the plains who, as often happens, had developed a character in harmony with their surroundings.*

These peoples ringed Latium in a broad semicircle extending from the northeast to the Tyrrhenian Sea. The territory of the Sabines, who some ancient sources saw as the ancestors of the Sabellian peoples of the south, lay northeast of Rome and into the Apennine highlands above the Tiber River. The land of the Aequi extended south from Sabine country. They were concentrated on the upper Anio (a tributary of the Tiber) and in the Trerus valley close to the Hernici. To the southeast and south of Latium lay the territory of the most formidable of these tribes, the Volsci, who originally seemed to have had their centre in the Liris (modern Liri) valley.

We possess almost no information about the internal political organization of these peoples. Presumably, their highland settlements were organized in some sort of cantonal arrangement with village headmen and perhaps tribal assemblies. Their economy probably consisted of herding and mixed farming. The need for pasture for their animals must have meant that they had been in constant contact with the inhabitants of the plains. A common method of pasturing in ancient Italy – transhumance – required herders to move their animals up into the mountains in the summer and then down into the plains during the winter months. Infiltration and settlement in the plains must have been going on for centuries. In the southeast the hill peoples appear to have exerted growing pressure on the major Greek city of Tarentum (Taranto), the major port in southern Italy. They also expanded into the opposite direction where they created problems for the Greek cities of the western coast.[31]

What had been a constant interchange of people and goods between the plains and the mountains became an invasion that resulted in fighting for most of the fifth century and into the fourth century. The reasons for the movements of these Apennine people at the end of the sixth century are far from clear. The most frequent explanation offered has been that of over-population, but it does seem unlikely that all of these tribal groupings would suddenly have been affected by increasing population simultaneously. There were probably other factors that remain hidden from us. The waves of the movement seem often to have coincided with the rite of the Sacred Spring, which functioned as a sort of communal sacrifice to avert disaster. Everything born in the spring following the vow was to be sacrificed. However, children born at that season were not literally immolated. They were dedicated to the god of war and then on reaching adulthood were forced to leave the community and seek a new home. It seems likely that one function of the rite was to drain off excess population. Such practices led to constant small-scale warfare and raiding, although larger-scale expeditions could occasionally be mounted.

Our knowledge of the equipment of these fifth century warriors is limited. The most common finds of protective equipment are metal helmets and chest protectors, made of bronze and measuring 17–35cm in diameter. The chest protector was attached to a strap or metal band that ran over the shoulders to a back plate. This equipment is similar to contemporary defensive armament in Etruria and Latium. No shields have been found, suggesting that they were made of perishable materials.

Spearheads and butts were all made of iron, and display a range of sizes that point to their use for both javelins and thrusting spears. The other major offensive weapon was the sword. These were made of iron and reproduced the characteristics of the Greek hoplite sword, although they were two-edged.

More difficult to assess is the evidence for the use of Greek hoplite equipment. Finds of such equipment are rare, therefore the bulk of evidence for the use of hoplite equipment is pictorial. Given the expense of hoplite equipment and its circumscribed use at Rome, it would seem extremely doubtful that it was widely used. Given the small-scale nature of much of the fighting, phalanx fighting is unlikely to have played a significant role.

The ancient accounts of these wars seem to preserve a reliable outline of the events. There is even some acknowledgement by later writers that the large-scale battles of the earliest historians lack credibility. Livy stresses his perplexity about these wars:

> I have no doubt that, in addition to the overwhelming effect that must occur to those reading about these constant wars with the Volsci through the course of so many books the question will suggest itself which has occurred to me in my amazement while reading those writers who lived closer in time to these events: from what source did the Aequi and Volsci, defeated so many times, get their troops? What explanation can I give, since these early writers have passed over this matter in silence? It seems most probable that it was the result either of the intervals between the wars just as is now the case in Roman levies, that different age groups were drafted time and again for the frequent beginnings of wars or that the armies were not always enrolled from the same peoples, although it was always the same tribe that waged war or that there was a huge population of free males in those areas that now are a meagre seedbed for soldiers and are only kept from being a wasteland by the presence of gangs of Roman slaves.'[32]

Foundation dates and the locations of various Roman and Latin colonies yield a reasonable chronological outline. It seems that the tradition preserved the general outline of events as well as some significant episodes, but that annalists elaborated the details, which in many cases lack any historical foundation.

The wars of this period are very different from later Roman conflicts. While the latter often had political or expansionist aims, the primary goal of these struggles was the survival of the Roman state against what seem to have been unfavourable odds. The seriousness of the struggle is apparent from the internal political difficulties and the economic problems they caused. In addition, on Rome's northern border the fifth century was punctuated by a series of wars with the Etruscan city of Veii. The Sabines and Veii were the most direct threats to Rome. Roman territory was shielded in the east by the cities of eastern Latium from major direct raiding by the hill peoples. Over time the threat became more serious after the seizure of some of the major cities in that area by the tribes moved the frontier closer to Roman territory. In the southeast the Volsci's expansion exerted pressure in that area.[33]

The Sabine homeland lay to the northeast of Rome in the upper Tiber valley. It is important to note that for much of the fifth century most campaigning took place in a rather restricted area consisting of the immediate outskirts of the city and the Latin plain. Rome was still a local power. Its territory around 500 has been estimated as approximately 270km square. The sources claim that they played an important role in origins of Rome forming along with Latins and Etruscans a major element in the city's early population. Numa Pompilius, the second king of Rome, is assigned a Sabine origin in the sources.[34] Wars with them are mentioned under the kings.[35] Conflict with them continued under the early Republic with a series of battles between 505 and 500. These too are probably historical although once again some of the details cannot be true. These victories led to an advance by the Romans into the area between the Tiber and the Anio (modern Aniene) where it joins the Tiber just north of Rome. This must have fuelled additional conflict between the two peoples.

Migration and conflict with Rome was not ended, rather it seems to have intensified. In 460 we hear of a coup attempt by the Sabine Appius Herdonius with 4,000 followers that ended in disaster for Appius and his men. This again is probably historical event.[36] After 449 there are no further references in the sources to conflict for another 150 years. Finally, in the course of the Third Samnite War in 290 the Roman consul Manius Curius Dentatus conquered the Sabines and incorporated them into the Roman state as citizens, but without the vote. In 268 the lowland Sabines received full citizenship, while the upland communities had to wait until 241.[37]

The wars with the Aequi for the most part involved mutual raiding. The Algidus Pass (modern La Cava D'Agilio) around the eastern rim of the Alban crater figures prominently in the account of the Roman struggle with the Aequi. It was a crucial route between the valley of the Sacco River (also the Valle Latina) and the Tiber valley entering Latium near Tusculum. It was the scene of one of the famous legendary episodes in early Republican history, the most well-known battle in the war against the Aequi, the victory of Lucius Quinctius Cincinnatus who, during an emergency in 458, was summoned from the plough to assume the dictatorship. Within fifteen days he had gathered an army, marched against the Aequi, who were besieging a consul and his army camped in the pass and defeated them in a night battle and then forced them to pass under a yoke which was an open acknowledgement of their defeat and finally sold them into slavery. He triumphed, laid down his office, and returned to his plough.[38] The episode is hardly historical, certainly the details are not. If there was a major victory then there is no evidence in the sources. Within three years the Aequi were again in the field.

Cincinnatus may or may not have been a historical character.[39] More importantly, he was an exemplar of what the Romans considered to be the ideal citizen. It is the ideal of an agrarian aristocrat who, content in his poverty, responds to the call to save his fellow countryman.[40] After his total victory he humbly returns to his little farm. The importance of poverty as a way of avoiding the corruption of moral fibre that luxury brings is commonplace in Roman literature.[41]

The most important Roman battle against the Aequi was also fought at the Algidus Pass under the command of the dictator Aulus Postumius Tubertus in 431. Doubts have persisted concerning the historicity of the battle. Most have centred on the historicity of Tubertus' dictatorship. It is now generally accepted as historical.[42] A strong argument for the authenticity of the battle is that the campaigns that follow, which resulted in driving the Aequi out of the Algidus valley, only make sense on the assumption of a prior major victory.[43] Some details of the battle are on firmer ground than other incidents in the war.

By 418 the pass was garrisoned and closed to the Aequi. The Roman counteroffensive was no doubt intensified by the extent of the expansion of the Aequi into Latium plain. They seized control of the Latin cities of Praeneste, Pedum and Tibur, which lay at the eastern edge of the Latin plain. The Algidus battle ended the forward movement of the Aequi, they were slowly forced back into the Apennines. Fighting continued in a sporadic fashion until the 380s. By the beginning of the third century the Aequi had ceased to exist as an independent people.

The Volsci proved to be the most difficult of Rome's adversaries. It was to the Romans' advantage that most of the fighting took place in the area of southern Latium away from its own territory. The sources present a rather confused account of the fighting that is difficult to follow.

The Volsci occupied the southern half of Latium (the Pomptine plain from Antium to Terracina) as well as Velitrae, the Liris River Valley and the Monti Lepini, where they were neighbours of the Aequi. Linguistic evidence seems to point to their origin in the central Apennines. The economic effects of the conflict on Latium must have been severe as the Pomptine plain was a major grain-growing area and Antium (modern Anzio) the major seaport of Latium.

The brunt of most of the fighting during the fifth century fell on the Latins and Hernici. Most of the details are invented. A series of serious reverses took place in 490–488 when Volscians under Coriolanus, a renegade Roman commander, launched two devastating campaigns, the first near Praeneste and the second close to the coast.[44] The Volscians moved up the Latin Way, which passed through Mt. Algidus, conquering Corbio, Vetelia, Trebium, Labici and Pedum. From Pedum, Coriolanus approached Rome where he was turned back by the earnest entreaties of his wife and mother.

The figure of Coriolanus has been heavily overlaid by myth. Its elements are an eminent Roman who offends the people and is then driven into exile, returning at the head of the enemy to finally be deterred by ties of family and patriotism. It seems likely that there is a core of truth; it has been recently argued that Coriolanus was a real figure, a freelance with a retinue of followers who became the archetype of the disgruntled aristocrat. There is a parallel to the group mentioned on the Lapis Satricanus.[45]

As was the case with the Aequi and Sabines, most of the fighting must have consisted of raiding and small-scale encounters, but there were some important battles. In 431 they fought alongside the Aequi at the Algidus. This happened frequently, the sources indicate that the Aequi and Volsci often coordinated their attacks. In 423 Livy notes a defeat of a Roman army commanded by Gaius Sempronius Atratinus at the hands of Volsci at Verrugo.[46] It was probably located on one of the summits of the Alban Hills guarding the route that led through the Algidus passage and so was of strategic importance. It has been viewed as a fictional episode modelled on later battles, in particular the battle against Hannibal at the Trebia River in 218. However, the location makes sense as a reasonable site for such a battle. Once again, the details may be suspect but the fact that there was a battle is acceptable.[47]

Despite occasional defeats, Latin and Roman armies gradually drove the Volsci back. By the end of the fifth century they had made substantial progress in expelling the Volsci from Latium. In 406 Terracina was captured, but in general there is a decline in the number of campaigns against both the Aequi and Volsci. This seems to imply either that the fighting of the fifth century had exhausted these peoples or that the resistance they had encountered had convinced them that further expansion was impossible.[48]

Conflict resumed in 393 when Latin Satricum revolted from Rome. There were indications that the alliance with Rome – which had proved beneficial to many of the Latins in the fifth century – had now become problematic, probably because of Rome's military dominance and its designs on the Pomptine plain. The defections that took place did not involve all of the Latin allies. The most important Latin cities that fought Rome were Tibur and Praeneste on the eastern side of Latium, close to Aequian territory and under pressure from them. In 390 Rome was sacked by Gauls and although later writers exaggerated its effects, it did stimulate further opposition and gave hope to the Volsci. Those hopes were dashed in the next year in a decisive battle at Ad Maecium, perhaps a road station near the old Latin town of Lanuvium.[49] Though sharp fighting continued, Rome and its allies were able to advance and expel the Volsci from the Pomptine Plain. By 338 it was firmly in Roman hands. Much of the fighting centred on Satricum with Roman victories there in 386 and 385 against a coalition of Volsci, Hernici and Latins. By 350 the Volsci had been forced back to the extreme southeastern part of Latium and were under increasing pressure from the Samnites to the south. By 300 they had been absorbed culturally and had disappeared as a separate group.

The pattern of mutual raiding and small-scale actions mentioned above would seem to indicate that the Romans and their allies used varied formations and styles of fighting in the course of the conflicts. These could include small battle groups for hire or drawn by the opportunities for plunder, and Roman aristocrats at the head of family groups accompanied by their retainers defending their lands and augmenting their prestige or local villagers protecting their farms and flocks or launching retaliatory raids. At this level of conflict, open order fighting was likely the most common mode of combat. It is probable that there was a great variety of equipment depending on wealth and social status; some of this variation is visible in the classes of the Servian constitution. It is likely that hoplite equipment in whole or part was worn by the elite, and in the larger engagements hoplite warfare must have played a more prominent role. With the support of light-armed troops and cavalry they could have adapted to warfare in the mountains as well as the plains, as Alexander the Great's hoplites had done. It is perhaps best to see the combat of the period as consisting of a variety of fighting techniques and equipment. There is a parallel in the armies of early modern Europe: the standing armed forces of various kingdoms were only one element in a mix that included the retinues of nobles and mercenaries for hire by the state or other employers.[50]

Rome's victory in these wars was made possible by a number of factors. Despite occasional problems stemming from the pressure of the military levy, the Romans possessed the necessary reserves of manpower in conjunction with the Latins and the Hernici to deal with what turned out to be a century and half of attritional warfare. Rome's geographical position was also favourable: it was only in the north and northeast that Roman territory fronted on its enemies, and in the principal theatres of war against the Aequi and Volsci, it was the Latins and Hernici whose territory was directly menaced and who bore a heavier share of the fighting.

A significant factor in Rome's success was the planting of colonies at the strategic entry points to Latium from enemy territory. Early Latin and Roman colonization was ethnically based. The many colonies founded in the fifth and fourth centuries were technically Latin and founded with Rome as a participating member. Livy labels them Roman, but their legal status was Latin. The sources portray the Romans as acting unilaterally, which is probably a reflection of Roman predominance. The decision-making process is so obscured by our sources that it is impossible to reconstruct it. Certainly the Cassian treaty presupposes equality between Rome and the Latins and that must have been reflected in their common colonization projects, although it is clear that by the 480s Rome had the most significant role.

The colonies of the period such as Norba (492, situated on an easily defensible height), Signia (495, east of the Monti Lepini), Cora (494, on the other side of the same mountains as Velitrae, a formerly Volscian town on the southern slope of the Alban hills facing the Pomptine Plain) ringed the borders of Latium to the east and south. The sources make clear that the major motive for their founding was military. This was also the view of Romans in the first century. Cicero saw colonies as 'bastions of empire'.[51] From the first much was done to make the colonies defensible. They were given walls soon after their foundation. Such defences were probably necessary from the beginning as they were normally placed on land confiscated from defeated enemies.[52] Those Romans who joined the colonies still remained liable to military service, although now not as citizens, but as Latin allies. Thus the colonies had a further military purpose in that the land grants in the colonial allotments made many formerly poor citizens now liable for service in the legions. The possibility of bettering their lot must have made numerous citizens more than willing to fight given the prospect of a land grant.

It is important to note that the colonies could have more than a military purpose. The founding of a colony at Ardea by senatorial decree was done on the basis of a motion of both consuls of 442. The decision to found the colony according to Livy arose out of an unjust decision of the popular assembly in 446 about a local dispute between the cities of Ardea and Aricia that converted the holdings of the inhabitants of Ardea into Roman public land. Livy claims that, although the colony was publicly announced as directed against Volscian attacks, it was really a means to redress this unfair, although popular, decision. As a military motive, the colony served as a barrier on the southern approaches to Rome and as a defensive position against Volscian expansion. The civil strife in Ardea and the Volscian attacks in the following year illustrate the interweaving of both motives.[53]

A three-man commission elected by the assembly were in charge of the founding of the colony. These men were invested with *imperium* because a foundation was a quasi-military venture. Livy, our best source, seems to have used archival documents as the basis for his notices on colonial foundations. The colonies were self-administered and so nominally independent. Their largest burden was service in Rome's armies.

The colonies were sited at strategic points to protect Latium and to control territory. Labici, 19km southeast of Rome, was founded in 418 to exclude the Aequi from access to the Mount Algidus pass. In 383 a colony was established at Nepet, 40km northwest of Rome with a sister colony at Sutrium to block the route into central Etruria and southern Umbria, so as to guard against a possible Gallic threat.

In all, fourteen Latin colonies are known for the period down to 383/2, which was then followed by a hiatus that lasted for about forty years. Colonization was only resumed under Rome's control after its success in subjugating the Latins in the war of 340–338.[54]

All of our evidence focuses on the Roman role in colonial foundations which must have been emphasized after her victory over the Latins and the dissolution of the Latin League. Formally, the foundation of a colony was dependent on the passage of a law by the people, most likely in the centuriate assembly, since the colony always had a quasi-military aspect. The sources claim that the Senate had the major role on deciding on the founding, size and location of the colony. However, given that membership in the senate did not become regular until almost the end of the fourth century there is no reason to assume any overall continuity or plan in the location of colonies. The three-man commission must have been attractive to its members since service on it gave the commissioners an opportunity to enhance their prestige and distribute patronage. The Latin colonies could be sizeable enterprises. Later on they ranged in size from 1,500 to 6,000 settlers. A substantial proportion of these settlers were Roman citizens, but sizeable numbers came from populations that were neither Latin nor Roman. For example, at Ardea many of the local inhabitants, who were Rutulians, were enrolled in the new colony. Emigration for a Roman meant the loss of citizenship and taking the citizenship of the new foundation. However, Latin colonists did possess significant rights at Rome. They could contract formal legal marriages with Roman citizens, make legal contracts and carry on commercial activities. Significantly, they could, if they were willing, take up residence at Rome and thereby acquire Roman citizenship. The possibility of a return to Rome if the colony were less than a success must have been attractive. The land grants were in the Roman context substantial. They ranged in size from ten to thirty acres compared to the one and one-half acres allotted to members of the small number of contemporary strictly Roman colonies. Lots of this size would have allowed poorer Romans to qualify for service in the legions. This may also explain why the Roman government was willing to tolerate a substantial loss of manpower. What mattered in the end was not the total population of the city but the number that could be called upon to fight.

The colonies acted as permanent garrisons that controlled the vital strategic links that made Roman domination possible. They also allowed the Roman state to sizably increase its reserves of manpower. These reserves were to be vital factor in future Roman military success in Italy and overseas. The development of what is essence was a military road system linking Rome and the colonies from the late fourth century allowed Rome to respond quickly to internal and external threats.

There was also fighting on Rome's northern borders against the Etruscans, whose origins have long been a source of debate. Even in antiquity a series of different origins were suggested. The most plausible solution is that the Etruscans did not arrive in Italy as a coherent group but evolved in Italy from the pre-existing Villanovan communities.[55] The Villanovans are known exclusively from their archaeological remains. Fully developed Villanovan culture marks the opening of the Iron Age in Etruria. Their settlements were concentrated on defensible plateaus. Some were large.

At Caere, Tarquinia and Veii they numbered over 1,000 inhabitants. Living in village settlements the Villanovans had a simple economy based on agriculture and stock rising. The culture, which lasted from 900 to 700, was widely distributed; it is attested north of the Apennines and all over central Italy.

The metal resources of Etruria seem to have played a major role in attracting Greek colonists in the course of the eighth century. The founding of Greek colonies started perhaps around 770. The earliest settlements were located to provide easy access to Etruscan iron mines and in the rich farmlands of Campania, south of Latium. There were further colonial foundations in southern Italy including Sybaris, Naples and most importantly Tarentum (Taranto) during the rest of the century and into the following one. These colonies introduced the city-state into Italy whose organization and culture were to have a profound effect on Etruria. It is likely that the Greek foundations served as centres for the diffusion in Italy of Greek crafts and artistic techniques. It was also Greek cultural influence that led to the adaption of the Greek alphabet in Etruria and its eventual transmission to Rome.

Almost from the initial contacts changes are visible in Etruria. By the middle of the seventh century towns develop along with greater economic specialization, and the Etruscan imitations of local Greek craft styles appear. By the end of the century cities with monumental architecture are visible in the archaeological record. City-states on the Greek pattern appear.[56]

Eventually Etruria developed into a coherent cultural and linguistic area. It was bounded on the north and east by the Apennine Mountains, on the west by the Tyrrhenian Sea and on the south by the Tiber. The mining regions were concentrated in the north while the south and west were productive agricultural regions. The Etruscans also expanded outside of their heartland. To the south, probably from the late seventh century they established settlements in the fertile Campanian plain. To the north, perhaps at the same time the Etruscans expanded into the Po valley.

Despite a common language and cultural identity, the Etruscan cities appear to have rarely acted together. There is evidence for a league of twelve Etruscan cities that met at the as yet unidentified site of Fanum Voltumnae. Though some of the sources mention the league making political decisions and even the existence of a league army, the historical narrative depicts Etruscan cities taking independent military and political action and registers only temporary alliances between them.

By 500 most of the Etruscan cities seem to have been ruled by oligarchies whose members were embedded in close family units. The literary tradition mentions an earlier period when kings were the norm and Veii had a king as late as the 430s or 420s, but this appears to have been an exceptional situation. Given the scanty evidence available, these states seem to have been marked by sharp social and economic differences between the ruling elite and the rest of the population, which must have limited their military effectiveness.

We know almost nothing about Etruscan military practice beyond the type of tactical formation and equipment they used which paralleled the equipment of other Italian groups, although hoplite equipment seems more common among the Etruscan elite. Command appears to have been exercised by monarchs or their relatives. Presumably in oligarchical states the chief magistrates performed the same functions.

From the seventh century and perhaps earlier Greek writers mention a domination of the western Mediterranean by the Etruscans. It appears that the coastal cities had established naval fleets to support their merchant vessels. Archaeology has produced evidence of Etruscan activity as far west as Spain. They also established colonies on the eastern coast of Corsica in the late seventh and early sixth centuries. At an early but unknown date at least some of the Etruscan cities concluded a treaty of mutual aid with Carthage. Phoenician presence in Etruria is attested by the presence of religious dedications from the city of Caere (modern Cerveteri) dated about 500. About 600 BC, Greeks founded a colony at Massilia on the site of the modern city of Marseille. These Phocaeans, who came from Asia, were fleeing the Persian conquest of its Aegean coast. They were defeated by a coalition of Carthaginians and Etruscans, and driven out of Corsica. Etruscan naval supremacy in the Tyrhennian Sea was ended in 474 when they lost the naval battle of Cumae. This loss weakened Etruscan settlements in Campania, which were now isolated by both land and sea. By 400 they were forced out of Campania. In the Po valley the expansion of the Gauls into the valley from 400 gradually constricted the Etruscan area of settlement.

The initial conflict with the Etruscans was with the city of Veii. Unlike the situation confronting the Romans in other theatres, where she fought tribal groups, this war pitted large and successful city-states against each other Veii was situated on a high plateau in an extremely strong position. On all sides except the northwest the site was bounded by steep cliffs, and in addition surrounded by the Cremera River (Valchetta) on the western side, while a tributary of the Cremera protected the plateau on the east. It was only about 450 that these natural defences were supplemented by the construction of a defensive wall, perhaps as a result of Roman pressure.

Veii's territory was larger, healthier and more fertile than Rome's, measuring in the sixth century 349km square. North of the city there was an extensive series of rock-cut tunnels which seemed to have formed part of an elaborate drainage system which would later play a role in the city's fall to the Romans at the beginning of the fourth century. This system supported a dense occupation in the countryside. In the later sixth century Veii's wealth seems mainly to have rested on agriculture.

Like Rome the city lay along crucial routes. It commanded two routes that crossed the Tiber. Control of these allowed Veii to command the north–south traffic between Etruria and Latium as well controlling access to the coast and the Tiber salt pans. In the fifth century Rome disputed Veii's position in a struggle centred on the town of Fidenae which formed a bridgehead for Veii on the Roman bank of the river and it served as an easy crossing of the river. The sources claim that wars with Fidenae stretched back to the reign of Romulus, which is pure fiction. Later campaigns are mentioned under the kings some of which may well be historical. Supposedly Fidenae was refounded as a Roman colony in 498. Sixty years later, on advice from the king of Veii it defected from Rome and a war with Veii over Fidenae broke out in 437.

There were three fifth-century wars with Veii: 483–474, 437–425 and 406–396. The first war ended in a stalemate after the destruction of the Fabii at the Cremera in 478–477.[57] The details except for the episode of the Fabii seem to be mostly later invention. During the second war the crucial Roman success was the capture of Fidenae in 426. It eliminated Veii's bridgehead on the Tiber's southern bank.[58]

The third and final war was the result of Roman aggression. It was part of a more general aggressiveness that marked Rome's conduct in the later fifth century.[59] The Romans wanted to permanently end the threat from Veii and provide land for public distribution. Once again, the Veientanes failed to secure support from other Etruscan cities, in fact its near neighbour Caere seems to have been pro-Roman. Only the cities of Capena (north of the Tiber near Mt. Soracte [Monte Soratte]) and Etruscan Falerii came to her aid in 402, probably in fear of Roman expansion into their own territory. The climactic phase of the war was a ten-year siege of Veii. The narrative in our sources has been heavily influenced by Greek accounts of the siege of Troy,[60] and is likely to be unhistorical. The real chronology of the siege is unrecoverable, and it seems best to accept the traditional date for the fall of Veii in 396. Livy's account of the origin of the war seems a Roman patriotic fabrication.[61] Livy places the beginning of the siege in 405. This was a period of intense fighting with the Volsci and Veii hardly figures in the narrative. It seems more likely that the actual siege began in 403 when winter quarters were according to Livy erected for the first time to house the soldiers engaged in the siege of the city and eight military tribunes were elected for the first time.

The turning point came in 396 with the election of M. Furius Camillus as dictator. In Livy's account which is the only full narrative we have Camillus is portrayed as a second founder of Rome and as the commander appointed by fate.[62] Despite the accretion of legend around him there is no reason to doubt his historicity or the part he played in the war, his triumph after the fall of Veii or his role in later conflicts in the course of a career that spanned thirty-five years.[63] Veii's allies were also conquered.

The Rome's victories allowed the Roman frontier in Etruria to advance as far as Sutrium and Nepet, towns which Livy calls 'the gates and barriers of Etruria' and to strengthen it with the foundations of colonies there in the 390s and 380s.[64]

Many of the details of the siege are surely fabricated, most strikingly the use of tunnelling under the walls to capture the city. Veii situated on a rocky plateau offered little opportunity for tunneling. The fortifications were either provided by nature or where there was open ground a massive earthen rampart 20 metres in width and 5–6 metres high with a wall of solid stone emerging from it was constructed. These walls seem to date from the mid-fifth century and may indicate worsening relationship with Rome. However, to the north of the city there were an elaborate series of drainage tunnels some of which may have allowed access to the city and may have given rise to the tunnelling legend.

In Livy the final attack is marked by a dramatic religious rite carried out by the soon-to-be victorious Roman commander. Camillus prays that:

> *Under your divine leadership Pythian Apollo I go forth to destroy the city of Veii and I dedicate a tithe of the booty to you. At the same time, I pray to you Juno Regina who now cares for this city to follow us in our victory to our and soon-to-be your city, where a temple worthy of your majesty awaits you.*[65]

The rite here depicted was called by the Romans *evocatio*. It invited the guardian deity – in this case Juno, the queen of the gods – to abandon the city and so accept its destruction and take up a new abode at Rome.[66] The name Juno is a Roman equivalent of an Etruscan deity Uni, who was the queen of the gods in Etruscan mythology and a protecting deity. The rite is infrequently mentioned in the sources. Only two other instances of this rite are attested in Italy.[67]

The capture and destruction of Veii was of tremendous significance to Rome. The most obvious benefit was the addition of a large and fertile territory. The conquered land was distributed to individual citizens. By 387 four new tribes were created as a result of the expansion. This was made easier by the fact that Veii's territory was contiguous to Rome's. Possession of Veii's territory allowed the Romans to control the trade routes that ran north to south across the Tiber and northeast into the Apennine foothills and valleys. The expansion of Roman territory given the harsh conditions of the fifth century is remarkable. It was approximately 900 km^2 in 495 and had almost doubled to about 1,580 km^2 in 395.

Almost the entire population of Veii was enslaved. But some did escape the Roman net and were eventually enfranchised. It has been suggested that must have been the first instance of mass enslavement by Rome.[68] The fourth century seems to be a period when slavery on a large scale was being introduced into Rome and when it began to form an important part of the economy.[69] Since slaves were not eligible for military service this must have made Rome capable of more sustained economic production in periods of conflict.[70]

The prolonged siege had important military consequences. The first use of winter quarters was one. The normal campaigning season was from the late spring into the early autumn. Its boundaries were marked by religious ceremonies. In March at the opening of the campaigning season there were rites of purification for the army's weapons and the army itself. October, at the end of the campaigning season, was also marked by ceremonies to signal the end of fighting.[71] The consuls took office in March, until 151 when they started entering office in January. The rhythm of warfare was determined by the agricultural year: campaigns took place when most agricultural tasks were done and farmers were free from their labours. It was also limited by the need for food for both men and animals. Grain in the fields did not usually ripen before June. War preparations took place in the spring and the army was ready to march in the early summer.

The pressures of war could force a change. During the Peloponnesian War of 431–404 between Athens and Sparta, military operations took place throughout the year.[72] In both cases special circumstances made this possible. The increase in Rome's size and population allowed it to pursue the same path. The same held true for the Hellenistic kingdoms of the eastern Mediterranean whose financial resources were sufficient to engage in military campaigns throughout the year. At Rome as at Athens the introduction of military pay became a necessity once extended campaigning became possible.

Though some sources claim that pay for military service was introduced under the kings, a credible tradition, found in both Livy and Diodorus Siculus, links it to the last war against Veii, in 406.[73] Livy connects it to the struggle between patricians and plebeians and represents it as a concession granted by the Senate to the plebs. The historian interprets it as a way to relieve the economic pressure of military service on the less wealthy section of the population.[74] Some scholars have questioned the early date assigned to this reform on the basis of the lack of a coinage, which was not minted regularly at Rome until the early third century. Since pay could have been given in kind or uncoined bronze, this does not seem a compelling objection. Others would date the introduction of pay as late as the First Punic War, but this seems improbable given the number and size of earlier Roman armies. A date around 400 for some form of pay seems plausible.

The reform did not introduce pay as such, but rather compensation that allowed those who barely qualified for enrolment in the legions, to serve. There is no information on the amount paid or what it meant for different categories of citizens. It is best seen as a mechanism to allow the state to mobilize greater numbers of its citizens for military. Rome was under heavy military pressure in this period and the need to increase manpower must have been pressing. Such an increase might help to explain the relatively rapid recovery of Rome and its expansion in the course of the first half of the fourth century.[75]

Inextricably linked with the introduction of pay was the imposition of a method to pay for it: the *tributum*. It was not a tax in a formal sense, but rather a mandatory loan levied to meet military expenses including supplies and other necessities, which in theory would be repaid from war profits. Its specifically military nature is revealed by the fact that in the few years such as 347 when there were no military operations, the *tributum* was not levied, and by the few references to the *tributum* being repaid from war booty. There was a particularly striking example in 187 when a consul of 189 – Gnaeus Manlius Vulso – brought back so much booty from his victory that permission was asked of the Senate and granted by it to allow the booty to be used to pay off not only the expenses of the current war, but also arrears owed to citizens from previous levies of *tributum*. Not all citizens paid the *tributum*; those whose property was less than the minimum rating required for military service were exempt. In essence, it served to spread the military burden to all of those liable to military service including those not called up. The *tributum* seems to have been levied on the basis of tribes and centuries; they may have been responsible for collecting it and then turning it over to the state as there was no central state institution capable of doing so. It is clear from the sources that it was levied in proportion to a citizen's census rating and was a percentage of the total value of his property. The exact proportion is unclear though 0.1 per cent has been suggested as the rate. But the rate must have varied on the basis of expected military expenditures. The levy was confined to those actually eligible for military service and so the *proletarii* were exempt from it. How this was calculated is unknown. It has been suggested that the rich advanced the sums needed for a campaign and the *tributum* reimbursed them with the exception of their own assessment. The same sort of system must also have been used by the allies when they levied their own troops. The *tributum* came to an end in 167 when the booty from foreign conquests and provincial revenues allowed the state to carry on military operations without it. During the Republic, Rome never developed a permanent system of war financing.

The people whom the Romans called *Galli* or Gauls and the Greeks *Keltoi* or Celts impinged dramatically on Roman consciousness at the beginning of the fourth century. In 387 they sacked Rome and became an important psychological if not military factor in the Roman mind until the first third of the second century. The sack was not as serious as the Roman writers portrayed it but it did leave a psychological trauma out of all proportion to the event. The trauma was reinforced by events during the fourth and third century as the Romans conquered northern Italy. It was not until the end of the third and beginning of the second century that the conquest removed any possibility of a Gallic threat. During the first century it was Roman aggression in Gaul that reignited Gallo-Roman conflict. However, the attitudes that had been born during these conflicts and nurtured by their extended duration took much longer to be resolved. In the middle of the first century AD the Roman emperor Claudius had to argue for the admission to the senate of Gallic aristocrats from northern Gaul who were citizens, because of continuing prejudice against the Gauls.[76]

The Greeks had developed a set of standardized depictions of foreign peoples and places. Descriptions of various peoples covered a number of standard topics: such as location, geography, physical appearance, economy, manner of making war and psychological characteristics. Much of the material was made up of repeated commonplaces. The same descriptions were used to characterize a number of different peoples including the Gauls.

There is a particular set of attitudes visible in the descriptions of the peoples of northern Europe and they are used for both Celts and Germans whom the Greeks and Romans thought were closely related to each other. They were struck by their size and whiteness as compared to Mediterranean peoples. Cultural differences were always measured against a Greco-Roman standard which included cities, dress, various cultural practices and elite literacy. Any deviations from that norm were deemed inferior. Even those characteristics that were thought admirable in themselves, such as the warlike nature of the Celts, were balanced against negative traits such as lack of planning and extreme emotional reactions, especially in battle.

The Celts can best be characterized by their common language (related to Italic and ultimately to Latin) and their shared artistic traditions. At its greatest extent the area of Celtic culture stretched from the Atlantic to Asia Minor. The archaeological evidence as well as later Greco-Roman literary evidence points to a highly stratified society in which warriors had a central role. Elite burials are accompanied by the warriors' military equipment such as spears and swords, and religious dedications are often of military equipment. At the end of the second century, kings still seem to be frequent but later literary sources paint a picture of a social hierarchy in which warrior chiefs supported by bands of clients, sometimes of very large size, are the dominant political element.

The geographer Strabo writing under Augustus at the end of the first century mentions three groups of experts in Celtic society:[77]

Among all of the Gallic groups in general there are three classes of men who are especially esteemed: bards, seers and Druids. The bards are singers

> *and poets, the seers conduct sacred rites and study nature, and the Druids practise moral philosophy in addition to studying nature. The Druids are considered by them to be the most just of men and for that reason are trusted to decide private and public disputes. Previously they acted as arbitrators in warfare and stopped armies arrayed for battle from fighting. The Gauls especially turned over to their judgment cases involving murder.*

The basic economy of these Celtic communities was the typical ancient combination of stock raising and agriculture, with craft production in the characteristic forms of Celtic art. But raiding and mercenary service for various Mediterranean powers also played an important role as well.

Head-hunting is well attested in the literary sources as well as in Celtic art. Keeping parts of the enemy's body is a custom known in other areas of the ancient world. It is probably to be connected with the idea that possession of the head also gives control over the spirit of the enemy which can be used to enhance a warrior's power. The head was also a trophy serving as visible proof of the warrior's prowess:

> *After battle they hang the heads of their enemies from the necks of their horses and when they arrive home they nail them to the entrances to their houses.*[78]

Diodorus Siculus writing at about the same time that Caesar was campaigning in Gaul and Caesar himself give our most detailed description of Celtic military equipment.[79] Archaeological evidence can be used to correct and enhance their description. The Celtic shield appears to have been about a metre long and 60cm wide. It was constructed of wooden planks and covered with hide and had a central boss made in a variety of shapes. The most frequent shield shape is oval, but others are square or hexagonal. They resemble Italian shields. The archaeological evidence indicates that helmet use was restricted to elite groups. Helmets of bronze predominate in the examples found, but iron was also used. Celtic helmets also influenced Italian and Roman types. The helmets were often adorned with animal decoration to create more imposing and terrifying appearance. The most frequent types in northern Italy are variations of the 'jockey cap' type which is essentially a metal cap with a peak-like projection designed to protect the wearer's neck, and the Coolus type which has a more distinct and flattened peak. Both were also used by the Romans and other Italic peoples. Specimens of Gallic helmets have been found with sockets for attaching the projecting figures that Diodorus mentions.

The use of body armour is infrequent, which may be less a matter of style than of expense. The sources refer to a group of warriors called the *Gaesati* who made an impression on Greek and Roman writers. They seem to have belonged to a tribal group living in southern France. The references to them indicate that they served as mercenaries. They are often described as fighting naked, which may have been ritualistic. This implies that the other Gauls normally did not fight in this manner, and Diodorus clearly indicates that they wore clothing. In fact, there is archaeological and statuary evidence for chainmail by the third century. Celtic war trumpets appear on the famous silver Gundestrup cauldron from Denmark (dated to the first or second century) and actual examples have been found; they are animal-headed trumpets with movable jaws.[80]

The Celtic warrior who appears in the sources is primarily a swordsman. There are references to the great size and the inferior workmanship of Celtic swords. Polybius mentions the frequent bending of this sword in battle, which made its owner vulnerable to the short thrusts of which the Roman sword was capable.[81] Archaeological examples indicate that Celtic swords were, in fact, of high quality and there is no easy explanation for the bending or for the exaggeration of the length observed in Greco-Roman authors. There is an evolution visible in sword types from a cut-and-thrust to a slashing type which tends to be longer and wider than the earlier type.

That evolution may have something to do with the importance, at least by Caesar's time, of Celtic cavalry. The Romans were impressed by Celtic heavy cavalry; as was the case in other ancient armies, Celtic cavalry fought with javelins, which were thrown in volleys, and with the sword. In close combat the Celts dismounted and fought hand-to-hand. After the conquest of Gaul, Celtic cavalry units were drafted into the Roman army as elite units. Until the last quarter of the third century chariot units are attested. After that it is only the Celtic peoples of the British Isles that continued to use them. Although as Caesar discovered when he invaded Britain they could be quite effective, Cassivelaunus leading a coalition of Celtic tribes confronted Caesar with an army whose core consisted of 4,000 chariots.[82]

Remains of spears as much as 2.4 metres in length have been found. Also a variety of head types are attested including serrated ones. They have iron heads 45cm or more in length. These are too heavy to be used for javelins, so that there must have been Celtic spearmen as well as swordsmen in the battle line. Javelin heads are also extant. Arrowheads have also been found but in general there is little evidence for the use of the bow in battle.

The picture of the Gauls as simple warriors who thoughtlessly deploy for battle is part of the notion of the noble savage and is not borne out by the sources. The tactic that most impressed the Romans was the strength of the initial charge, which attempted to overwhelm the enemy. This was probably their most effective tactic against the densely packed mass formations they found among Mediterranean armies. However, such a charge meant that it was impossible for Celtic warriors to maintain formation and if it failed, it must have put them at a severe disadvantage against better organized opponents. The few descriptions we have of Romans and Celts in battle, including those of the Allia and Telamon as well as the later account of Caesar, display a grasp of tactics that contradicts Strabo's view.

The timing of the Celtic movement into northern Italy as far south as the Apennines is a matter of controversy. The ancient tradition presents us with two dates separated by two centuries, either around 600 or 400. There is limited evidence of a Celtic presence in northern Italy by late 400s. It seems likely that there had been constant Celtic movement into the area during the fifth century but that these were probably small-scale warrior bands. However, around 400, large-scale migrations began and resulted in extensive settlement by Gallic tribes in northern Italy.

At the entry of the Celts into northern Italy the Etruscans dominated the Po valley. Their control of the area evaporated under Celtic pressure. The migration probably unfolded in waves and Livy knows of at least four of them of which the most recent were the Senones who settled on the Adriatic coast. The most important tribes as far as the Romans were concerned were the Insubres north of the Po with their capital at Mediolanum (Milan), the Boii particularly noted for their savagery between the Po and the Apennines, the Cenomani centred on the Italian Lake District, and the Senones. Though these were the areas of major settlement it is clear from archaeological discoveries that the Celts penetrated, on at least a small scale, much farther south in peninsular Italy. The most southerly Celtic find is a helmet from Canosa in Apulia and we hear of Celtic bands operating even farther south. The initial migration was not the last; there was continued migration into Italy, northern Europe and parts of the eastern Mediterranean. It was only by the second century that the area of Celtic settlement in northern Europe and the Mediterranean began to contract especially under pressure from German-speaking peoples.

The first large-scale encounter of Gaul and Roman ended with the sack of Rome in 387. The Roman sources portray this as the result of a tribal migration, but it was more likely a mercenary band of Senones on its way to take service in southern Italy, most probably hired by Dionysius I, tyrant of Syracuse, and not averse to raiding and plundering along the way. During the fourth and third centuries, Gauls were employed as mercenary troops by major powers in Greece and also in the eastern Mediterranean. This would explain why the Celts were so far south as well and explains the absence in the sources of any reference to women and children accompanying them.

The initial battle with the Romans was fought at the Allia, a tributary of the Tiber that enters it about 18km from the city. Whatever the truth about the course of the battle, it was no doubt a disastrous reverse. Livy blames the commanders for the defeat.[83] They revealed their total incompetence, ignoring correct religious ritual and for not fortifying their camp.

Its date is certain, 18 July, which as a result became an ill-omened day on which no public business could be conducted.[84] As is usual in this period the details of the battle are unreliable. Even its exact location is a problem with some sources asserting that it took place on the left bank of the Tiber and others on the right bank of the river. Rome was sacked and despite Roman propaganda to the contrary the garrison on the Capitoline ransomed itself with a large payment of gold. The story of Rome's redemption from the attack is ascribed to Camillus, the conqueror of Veii. But the absence of any references to his victory in our earliest sources makes it likely that the victory was a face-saving legend.

Livy, Plutarch and other writers describe widespread burning and destruction which led to extensive rebuilding. However, no archaeological trace of such a burn level has been found. It seems that what the Gauls were interested in was moveable plunder, and once the Roman field force had been defeated, the lightly fortified city was a tempting target. The rapid recovery suggests the limited scope of the attack. Its psychological consequences were far more profound. The building of a strong fortification wall enclosing the seven hills of the city is only the most concrete manifestation of the anxiety caused by the attack.

Another legacy of the Roman defeat was most likely the *tumultus Gallicus*. It has been used to support the notion that a major thread in Roman foreign policy was a fear of the Gauls.[85] This seems unlikely. There was also a *tumultus Italicus*. The *tumultus* was essentially an emergency response to a militarily threatening situation. It led to the suspension of all state business, leave was cancelled and all eligible citizens were enrolled in the army. The fact that it was called in response to an Italian threat as well indicates it was the proximity of the threat that was at issue and not the fact that the Celts were involved.[86] This is not to deny that the defeat and sack produced an especial aversion to the Gauls – but they seem to have stimulated the Romans to an unusual ferocity.

CHAPTER FOUR

RECOVERY AND EXPANSION

The story of Rome's recovery after the Gallic attack focuses on Camillus, the conqueror of Veii. The details are clearly fabricated to compensate for the defeat of the Allia and the disgrace that resulted. Livy reports that the Romans holding out on the Capitoline Hill were finally driven by hunger to ransom the captured city. Camillus had been in exile after his victory over Veii because he was accused of embezzling part of the booty from Veii.[1] Livy portrays Camillus as the epitome of piety and patriotism, and claims that the real cause was his opposition to plebeians' agitation in 391. He spent his exile at the Latin colony of Ardea, a Latin colony south-west of Rome.[2]

Camillus is supposed to have rallied the people of Ardea and inflicted a stunning defeat on the Gauls.[3] This victory encouraged men from the surrounding towns as well as Roman settlers from Veii to join him. They then marched on Rome and arrived just when the Romans were paying their ransom to the Gauls and inflicted an overwhelming defeat on the northerners and so rescued Roman honour.[4]

Despite the fictional elements in Camillus' career there is no reason to doubt that some of his campaigns and victories are historical. In the wake of the Gallic sack, Rome very quickly began restoring its political and military position and went on the offensive continuing the expansionary policy it had pursued before the sack.[5] In 387 a reorganization of the territory that had formerly belonged to Veii was undertaken. Four new territorial tribes were added. The addition of this territory was of crucial importance in accelerating Rome's recovery. It more than doubled the land available for cultivation and settlement. A further indication of the quick revival was the construction of the so-called Servian Wall, which was actually constructed after the Gallic sack. It is a major achievement, built of stone quarried from Veii. The wall measures around 11km in length, and consists of large rectangular blocks. It shows that soon after the sack Rome was able to mobilize manpower and to find financing for building on a large-scale.[6] The Volsci were defeated near Lanuvium in 389 and then a victory was achieved at Satricum in 386 against a coalition of Hernici, Volsci and Latins.[7] The Aequi were also defeated in 388, all under the leadership of Camillus. They are not mentioned again until their revolt at the end of the century. To consolidate their control, the Romans founded colonies in Etruria at Sutrium and Nepet, 'the keys to Etruria', probably in 383.[8] To control the Volscians, colonies were founded at Satricum and Setia in 385 and 382 in formerly Volscian territory. Commissioners were appointed to settle colonists in the Pomptine Plain as well. Strong resistance from the Volsci delayed the final colonization of the area until the beginning of the 350s.

The drive to expand is clear in the Roman seizure and annexation of the important Latin town of Tusculum in 381, which had been one of the leaders of Latin resistance to Rome after the fall of the monarchy. The Latins had already allied with the Hernici and Aequi but after their failure they continued to struggle with Rome. The Cassian treaty which had regulated relations between Rome and its Latin allies had been allowed to lapse and an expansionist Rome had no wish to renew it. The war was waged not against a unified Latin enemy but with individual Latin cities. Some of the Latins remained allied to Rome. They still faced possible threats from the Apennine tribes, and Rome still seemed to offer a preferable option. There were prolonged hostilities provoked by Rome's expansion. It is surely no accident that the disaffection was a parallel to that of over a century before when a Rome weakened by the fall of the monarchy also found itself at war with the Latins. The Latins had hoped a weakened Rome could be defeated. They were wrong. They had now made the same mistake again. The important Latin town of Tusculum surrendered to Camillus, and the free inhabitants were given Roman citizenship, which was a wholly unprecedented step. The Tusculans would now be obligated to do military service and to pay the *tributum* as any other Roman citizen would, but they were left to manage their own affairs. However, they may not have been happy with their new status as they joined the Latin revolt against Rome in the 340s. As a device to bind the new citizens to Rome it seems not to have been especially successful at first, although it would later prove exceptionally useful. The Romans had created a new political entity, a *municipium*. It was a self-governing community of Roman citizens physically separated from Rome itself. It would later become a key means to bolster both the city's military manpower and to increase the funds necessary to support Rome's campaigns.

After the continual campaigns of the 380s, the years from 376 to 362 were a peaceful interlude that allowed Rome's focus to turn inward.[9] The struggle between patricians and plebeians intensified. The central issue was plebeian admission to the consulship. Much of the detail is later invention or projection backward from later events. The key date was 367/6 when the Licinian-Sextian rogations were passed, opening the consulship to plebeians. The first plebeian, Lucius Sextius, was consul in 366. Finally, in 342 the Genucian law made it mandatory that one of the two consuls be plebeian.[10] It was in 342 as well that a plebeian consul conducted an independent campaign.[11] By 337 all offices of consequence could be held by plebeians. What emerged was a new patrician-plebeian nobility that controlled Roman politics and commanded her armies. To a Roman outside the charmed circle of the new patrician-plebeian nobility, whose main concerns were debt and land, nothing had changed.[12] What is especially important as far as Rome's army was concerned was the continued importance of military service for the aristocracy. A political career still required at least ten years of service in the cavalry or as a military tribune to qualify to stand for the quaestorship, the lowest rung on the ladder of office. It meant, given the fairly constant warfare in the Republic, that most aristocrats had at least some military experience. It could, but did not necessarily, include battlefield command. Military tribunes are mentioned commanding detachments and junior senators serving as quaestors could command military units as well.

After 362, warfare resumed. The most important conflict was the continuation of war with the Latins. Rome's main Latin rival was Praeneste which was 37km southeast of Rome.[13] It surrendered in 354 after three years of continuous warfare. The defeat of Praeneste also brought with it the end of coalition of nine Latin towns against Rome.

Tibur seems to have been the more serious problem. Tibur allied with the Gauls in 361.[14] Before their alliance, the Gauls had confronted the Romans on the Anio. This confrontation was the setting of a famous single combat between the young Roman noble Titus Manlius Torquatus and an enormous Gaul who was guarding passage over a bridge. The combat ended in a victory for the Roman. Gauls customarily wore a torque or stiff metal neck ring, and Polybius mentions that even those Gauls who went into battle naked wore one, as was the case in this duel. Manlius took the slain Gaul's torque and so acquired his last name Torquatus ('the man with a torque').[15]

The incident is generally accepted as historical. The Roman fondness for single combat seems to date from the beginning of the city and it is last attested in 45. It is also found among the Gauls, which makes Livy's report more believable.[16] Polybius notes that such combat was a Roman custom.[17] It must have been striking to him; although the Greeks of the *Iliad* and later frequently fought in single combat, with the adoption of the phalanx the custom had generally disappeared. Roman single combat involved a formal challenge to the enemy as in the Torquatus episode. The custom was common in the ancient world. David and Goliath is an obvious example. It was a way to limit bloodshed. Given the importance of courage and aggression, essential to the Roman concept of manliness, its relative frequency is understandable. In addition, that display of manliness had a political and social dimension and eventually a religious aspect as well.[18] At Clastidium in northern Italy, Marcellus – who seems to have had a fondness for single combat – vowed a temple to Honour and Courage in 222, after his killing in single combat the king of the Insubrian Gauls Viridomar.[19]

Single combat could also lead to one of the greatest awards open to a Roman aristocrat, the *spolia opima*. These highest of spoils were a special class within the larger category of booty. They were the arms and equipment taken from a slain enemy commander and could only be won by the supreme Roman commander who killed him in single combat. Tradition records only three men as dedicators of these spoils, Romulus, Cornelius Cossus in a mid-fifth century war against Veii, and Marcellus mentioned above. The last two dedications are historical while the first by Romulus is a myth justifying the custom.[20]

The spoils were suspended from an oak frame, a practice which has parallels elsewhere in the Mediterranean and then dedicated in the temple of Jupiter Feretrius on the Capitoline Hill. The custom may have had its origin in warfare between aristocratic bands in the archaic period.

Sporadic encounters with the Gauls continued. In 358 a strong Gallic force encamped in eastern Latium was defeated by the Romans under the dictator Gaius Sulpicius Peticus. These may have been the Gauls who had concluded the alliance with Latin Tibur. If so, it must have been a serious blow to Tiburtine prospects. In 354, overwhelmed by superior force, Tibur surrendered. In the same year Praeneste also surrendered and with Tibur concluded peace with Rome.

The Gauls had been active even before their alliance with Tibur. Those who had sacked Rome were quickly enrolled as mercenaries by Dionysius I, the ruler of Syracuse,[21] who was engaged in a war with the Greek cities of southern Italy. But Rome and Latium continued to experience problems. There is some disagreement in our main sources about the number of Gallic attacks in the period that ended in the 330s. There were Roman victories over the Gauls in 350 and in the next year. Disaffected Latin cities refused to help in accordance with the treaty they had concluded with Rome in 358.[22] Despite the lack of help the Romans defeated the Gauls. The Gallic defeat must have been sufficiently serious since nothing is heard of them for almost three decades. Finally, in 331 a treaty was concluded with the tribe of the Senones on unknown terms.[23] However, the treaty was of very limited effect. The Senones were only one Gallic tribe, and there were many others. In a culture where raiding and the capture of spoils were important it should come as no surprise that a treaty to limit these activities had very little impact.

The Romans were also active in the north. War opened in 358 with Etruscan Tarquinii, which was joined by Falerii and Caere. The war against Tarquinii was marked by a particularly gruesome incident. In the forum of Tarquinii, 307 Roman prisoners of war were executed after a victory in 358.[24] In 355 the Romans retaliated by executing 358 Tarquinian nobles in the Forum at Rome. It is possible that the Etruscans acted out of religious motives.[25] The Romans too resorted to this practice on a number of occasions in the face of what they perceived to be severe threats. It was not until 97 that the Roman Senate passed a decree forbidding human sacrifice.[26] Livy is clear that this war involved setbacks for Rome and that might explain the intense animosity to which these executions attest. The war was ended by a series of truces and without gains on either side. The Romans were too preoccupied elsewhere to fight on and these cities were not a serious threat to them. The menace of Gallic raids and disaffection among the Latins may have made the war in Etruria seem relatively unimportant. Rome's relations with the Etruscan cities were peaceful from 351–311. The only major change came in 343 when Falerii asked for an alliance to replace their truce. The alliance does not seem to have involved any submission to Rome or admission of inferiority. The Romans probably concluded it to protect Sutrium and Nepet, which were exposed to Falerii. This too seems to have been due to the demands elsewhere as well as internal developments.[27]

In 341 a war broke out between Rome and her Latin allies as well as with unaligned Latin cities, which was to have immense consequences for the future. It entailed four years of very difficult fighting. Livy presents it as a demand for equality by the Latins but it is more probable that Roman expansion had placed too many demands on them and Rome's growing power seemed to point to the end of their independence.[28]

In 340 the Latins and their Campanian allies, along with the Sidicini, suffered twin defeats. The Sidicini had become involved because of a conflict with the Samnites. They had appealed for help to Rome and had received it, but in 341 the Romans had made an alliance with the Samnites at their expense. As a counter to this, the Sidicini allied with the Latins to fight Rome. One of the battles of 340 was fought at the Veseris River near Mount Vesuvius, the other at Trifanum, a town on the west coast between Minturnae and Sinuessa. Trifanum was not purely a Roman victory, as Samnite troops were also present on the Roman side.

The battle at the Veseris is one of the two occasions on which a Roman commander sacrificed himself in the cause of a Roman victory on the battlefield. This practice was called *devotio,* that is vowing oneself as a sacrifice to the gods for victory. It was done at the Veseris in 340 and again at the battle of Sentinum in 295. At the Veseris, it was the consul Publicus Decius Mus and at Sentinum it was his like-named son who was serving in the same office. A third *devotio* performed by a grandson is certainly not historical.[29] The father had been directed by a dream to sacrifice himself, while his son had been inspired by his father's action. The self-sacrifice was supposedly accompanied by a special prayer. The ritual devoted the consuls to the gods of the underworld and to Mother Earth as a sacrifice so that the gods would destroy the enemy army. The consuls then charged into the enemy army to meet their fate. There has been scepticism about the historicity of these acts. They stand isolated and limited to a single family. The mythic precedent of Horatius at the bridge might suggest the Decii were imitating Horatius' example.[30] It can be seen as a variant of the vow often made by a commander before battle to devote a temple or some other monument to a god or goddess, if he secured victory.[31]

The victories of 340 resulted in a lull and Rome used this time to punish its enemies by depriving them of a portion of their land. This was a standard consequence of defeat as Rome conquered Italy. Those who had remained loyal were rewarded, but the sources do not specify what the rewards were. In 343, Capuan envoys from the most powerful city in Campania came to the Roman senate to ask for an eternal treaty of friendship and mutual aid after a defeat by their enemies the Samnites.[32] After some hesitation because of an earlier treaty with the Samnites, they received what they sought. In return the aristocratic cavalry of Capua assisted the Romans and were now given certain economic privileges and an honorary citizenship without the vote.[33]

The next year fighting flared up again. It was to last until 338. When the war finally ended, Rome's treatment of the Latins set a precedent for future alliances and settlements. It was in many ways remarkably lenient, although some cities lost part of their territories, which became Roman public land. Some did receive harsher treatment depending on their conduct during the war, but none were destroyed or had their inhabitants sold into slavery.

Rome ended all mutual ties between the Latin cities and dissolved the Latin League. She concluded bilateral treaties with them whose only direct, but substantial, burden was the requirement that the cities provide troops to serve under Roman command and supply them while they were in the field. Because of close ethnic and historical ties these communities were given commercial privileges at Rome as well as the right to conclude legal marriages with Roman citizens and to move to Rome and become full citizens. These privileges set the Latins apart from other Roman allies and they remained a separate judicial category. The only exceptions were Tibur and Praeneste, which remained without these rights. Over time Latin status evolved from the mark of a particular ethnic group to a purely legal status that could be conferred on anyone, although restrictions were placed on some of its privileges. Some of the Latin communities were absorbed into the Roman citizen body although allowed local autonomy.[34]

Unusually at this early stage Roman citizenship was also given to several Volscian communities. This grant has been contested, but given the long history of interaction between Latins and Volscians it would not be surprising to find highly Latinized Volscian communities suitable for such a grant.[35]

In the north, further attempts were made to link cities more closely to Rome. At some point, perhaps after the sack, Etruscan Caere was granted a special status whose exact nature is disputed. It may have been a form of 'public hospitality' (*hospitium publicum*) or of citizenship without the vote. Public hospitality was a legal relationship. It was granted by Rome to another individual or state allowing the other state's citizens to reside at Rome, to conduct business and to engage in legal proceedings in Roman courts. Citizenship without the vote was at first not an attractive option. It entailed the burdens of citizenship without any potential benefits, nevertheless it was granted or imposed on a number of Latin cities. In non-Latin areas the Romans imposed citizenship without the vote including parts of Campania and Volscian towns.[36]

The Latin colonies founded by Rome after 338 made available another source of manpower. These colonists included both Romans and Latins. They were important in maintaining and increasing military manpower, offering a way to provide the property necessary for legionary service [37] With the acquisition of land through warfare over the next seventy years there was a substantial increase in colonization. Between 338–268, five citizen colonies and nineteen Latin colonies were founded.

The military functions of these colonies were complemented by the beginnings of the construction of a network of military roads which came to serve many other purposes. In 312 work began on the Via Appia, which originally ran from Rome to Capua, 212km away. It followed a coastal route through Latium before turning inland to Capua. It avoided some of the difficulties of the earlier Via Latina, an inland route that linked Rome to Latium and had been built in the 330s or 320s. It was a difficult route which passed through potentially hostile areas.[38] The Appia was the largest public work undertaken by the Roman state to this point. It was arrow-straight despite the natural obstacles in its way. Parts of it seem to have been paved although in the Republic most roads were constructed of compacted gravel.

Over the course of the third and second centuries the road system expanded, linking towns and colonies. It was a slow process. After the Via Appia it was not until the second half of the third century that projects on a similar scale were undertaken. In the second century the network expanded to the north and south to link Rome to its allies, allowing a rapid movement and concentration of troops all over Italy. This was especially true in the north where the early second century saw fighting against the Gauls. In addition to their military use, the roads served trade and commerce. These advantages led to a concentration of cities and population along the roads. The unifying effect of these roads was visible during Rome's war with her allies in 91–88; it was those peoples who lived along the roads that remained loyal to Rome.[39]

The Samnite Wars

By the mid-fourth century Rome's horizons were expanding. In 348 it concluded another treaty with Carthage.[40] It is a puzzling document with the Carthaginians offering little in return for the restrictions that the Romans agreed to place on themselves. It may be the potential for Carthage's help in supplying her armies that made the arrangement attractive, even if no direct military aid was contemplated. During the war against Pyrrhus another treaty between the two powers specified that Carthage would use her ships to transport Roman troops even though she would not necessarily join the fight.[41]

Of greater immediate significance was a treaty made six years before with the Samnites who inhabited the densely populated fertile upland valleys of the southern and central Apennines. In the end they were to prove Rome's fiercest and most dangerous opponents in Italy. It seems that the Samnites were impressed by Roman victories and perhaps anxious because of Rome's expansion.[42] Unfortunately the terms of the alliance are unknown. The Samnites appear to have rendered the Romans substantial aid in their war with the Latins.

The Samnites, who did not speak Latin but a dialect of a south Italian language called Oscan, were divided into tribal groups.[43] They also formed part of a widely distributed group of peoples called the Sabellians, which included the Volsci and Aequi. They lived in scattered villages with associated rural sanctuaries and hill forts which served as refuges in wartime. Their political organization was based on local groupings of villages, *pagi* (singular *pagus*). Each *pagus* had an elected magistrate, the *meddix tuticus,* who guided its fortunes. The office seems to have been dominated by a few families. The tribes were composed of these *pagi*. The number of tribes is usually given as four, but in fact, the number is uncertain. It has been thought there was some type of Pan-Samnite federation, but there is little evidence for it. It is more likely that the Samnite tribes banded together only in times of war when an overall commander with wide powers was elected by all of the tribes and who was assisted by a council of advisors. How the Samnite tribes coordinated their military organization in time of war is unknown. The sources name overall commanders, but have little information on the lower levels of command or organization.

The Samnites sustained themselves with a mixed economy of farming and stock raising. The economic base was simply not large enough to sustain them. There were few towns of any size, despite the dense population, so that emigration was a necessity. In the course of the fifth century, the Samnites gradually made their way into the adjacent lowlands with the result that most of the cities of central and southern Italy with the exception of the Greek colonies had substantial or majority Samnite populations. In the fifth century the Samnites had replaced the Etruscans at Capua and the Greeks at Cumae. Despite this change in the population traditional social and economic structures persisted and by the fourth century the lowland Samnites had fully assimilated with the existing population.[44] They also spread into the valleys of southern Italy and fought with the Greek cities of the south.

The ancient evidence for Samnite population movement stresses the role of the rite of the sacred spring in the process of migration. Through its use, Samnite villages expanded and produced new communities and tribal groupings. In essence, it was a religious act designed to respond to communal calamities and internal and external stresses. The ritual was a communal sacrifice to avert disaster. Everything born in the year following the vow had to be sacrificed. However, children born then were not literally killed. They were dedicated to the god of war and on reaching adulthood were forced to leave the community and seek a new home. This practice led to constant small-scale warfare and raiding.

Strabo, the first century geographer, provides an excellent summary of the rite, which applied not only to the Samnites but all of the hill peoples of the central and southern Apennines: [45]

> *The Sabines were at war with the Umbrians for a long time and made a vow, just as some Greeks do to dedicate everything born in the course of this year. After their victory they sacrificed some of them, and dedicated others. When a food shortage ensued, someone said that it was also necessary to dedicate the children born in that year; they did this and called the children born at that time sons of Mars. When they had reached adulthood the community sent them out to settle elsewhere with a bull as their guide. It came to rest in the country of the Opici,[46] who lived in villages scattered over their territory. They expelled the natives and settled there and sacrificed the bull to Mars, the god who had given them rule in accordance with the pronouncement of their prophets.*

Our knowledge of Samnite military equipment is very meagre. Livy's description of it does not match excavation finds. It seems likely that they did carry a form of long shield, which the Romans called a *scutum*, of either oval or rectangular form. However, Samnites are more frequently represented with a round shield and with helmets that appear to be based on Greek prototypes. They are frequently depicted with a broad leather belt covered in bronze, which must have served to protect their midsection, and sometimes with a breastplate in the form of a triple disc. They are also shown wearing two greaves and not the single greave in Livy's description. Their main offensive weapon appears to have been a javelin with throwing loops, but they also used the heavy thrusting spears.[47]

Romans and Samnites fought three wars. The first was from 343–341, the second from 327–304 and the third 298–291. A last desperate battle was fought against the Romans during the opening salvos of the Roman civil wars of the first century. On the afternoon of 11 November 82 at Colline Gate,[48] a fierce battle was fought by the Samnites and their Roman allies against Cornelius Sulla. The losses were heavy on both sides. After the battle the vindictive Sulla had the Samnites butchered. This ended any large-scale attempt to win their freedom from Rome.[49]

The Campanian plain lay just south of Latium, separated by mountains and rivers with steep banks that made movement out of Latium and into Campania difficult. Like Latium, Campania is a volcanic plain that extends from the Liris River in the north to the Silarus River (modern Sele) in the south. On the east, it is bounded by the Apennines and to the west by the Tyrrhenian Sea. Unlike Latium, its coasts have a number of good harbours and bays, among them Cumae, Naples and Puteoli and the Bay of Naples. The lands extending from the Volturnus River (the major Campanian River) in the north to the Sorrentine Peninsular in the south were particularly favoured by the elite in the late Republic and during the empire. A number of Roman nobles built villas along the Bay of Naples coast. Besides its natural beauty Campania was thought to be the most fertile area of Italy.[50]

By the middle of the fourth century Samnite groups were again on the move. They were now moving northwest towards the Liris River and the neighbouring mountains. The area had been controlled by the Volsci, but years of warfare with Rome and her allies had worn them down and they were not able to stem the influx. Expansion then turned west where the Samnite migration threatened Teanum Sidicinum, which gave access to Campania and controlled routes between Rome and Capua. Teanum belonged to the Sidicini. They were a Sabellian people so were related to the Samnite invaders.

In response to the invasion the Sidicini appealed to Capua. Capua was the richest and most important city in Campania. In the fourth century it was the head of a league of northern Campanian cities which probably fielded a joint army. But it was far from including all of the important Campanian cities, and, in fact, a rival league had also come into being. Capua had accepted the Sidicini's appeal. It fought two battles against the Samnites losing both of them. The Samnites then put Capua under siege.

In their desperation the Capuans appealed to the Roman Senate for aid. Given Rome's string of victories and aggressiveness it was the only real possibility that the Capuans had available. Livy reports a long speech by the Capuan envoys that amounts to an argument that they would be an invaluable ally once the Romans defeated the Samnites by adding their military forces and wealth as well their control in Campania to augment Roman strength.[51] The appeal was accepted after the Capuans surrendered themselves into the faith of the Roman people (*deditio*), which in theory placed them at the complete disposal of the Romans. Accepting the appeal raised a serious moral issue. The awkward fact was that the Romans had an alliance with the Samnites dating back to 354. This clearly was a violation of that treaty. Livy portrays the senators as moved by the plight of the Capuans. Accepting their *deditio* made the Capuans basically wards of Rome, so that in attacking them the Samnites were attacking Rome. Strategically, if the Samnites took Capua, it would open most of Campania to them and bring their forces to the borders of Latium. The war lasted from 343–341. The first year of the war saw a string of victories that resulted in triumphs for both of the consuls. The next year 342, serious internal political problems prevented any large-scale engagement. These problems were resolved by the end of the year. In 341, at the mere appearance of a Roman army, the Samnites sued for peace and were granted a renewal of their alliance with Rome as well as permission to attack the Sidicini. The looming Latin revolt must have persuaded the Romans to make peace at this point. Expansion could wait till later.

The war was a relatively minor affair. The Romans had other problems on their minds and the Samnites, given the lack of central organization, had problems mounting a combined offensive. It was Roman aggression that created the conditions for another conflict, on a much larger and more serious scale. The sources for this war and for succeeding periods are of a much higher quality than earlier Roman history.

A decade passed between the end of the Latin War in 338 and the outbreak of the Second Samnite War in 328. The relative peace of this period, broken only by a minor campaign, was probably devoted to the organization and assimilation necessary after the Latin War.

The situation began to change in 337 when the Sidicini, who had earlier abandoned their alliance with Rome and had fought against her in the Latin war, attacked the Aurunci. A group of the Aurunci, the Ausones, made common cause with the Sidicini. The Romans, worried about a possible alliance of the Sidicini with the Samnites, fought a war with the Sidicini and Ausones from 337 to 335. The Romans captured Cales and garrisoned it. In 334 a Latin colony was sent to the site with 2,500 settlers and their families.[52] It was located on some of the richest agricultural land in Italy. The colony had a strategic purpose. Cales commanded a strategic pass on the Via Latina between Rome and Capua. The foundation of a colony meant that an invasion of Latium from the south would be harder to mount.

In 328 a colony was founded at Fregellae at an important crossing point of the Liris River and the route to the coast. The colony sat on the southern bank of the Liris and therefore lay in a region that had recently overrun by the Samnites. Within a year the Samnites were once again at war with Rome.

Livy claims that the Samnites incited the population of Naples to attack the area of Campania controlled by the Romans and also brought about the revolt of several other cities. Naples or Neapolis ('New City') had been founded in the middle of the seventh century. It was situated on one of the two most important routes joining the coast to the interior, the other being the Tiber. One of the most northerly of the Greek colonies, it had retained its Greek character. In the early first century AD, Greek was still spoken there and the future emperor Claudius could spend time there dressing in the Greek manner.[53] Its nearby neighbour on the Bay of Naples, Puteoli, was founded as a colony in 194 and became the major overseas port for the Republic.

As was the case for many of the other Campanian cities, there was a struggle between the rich who formed the elite and the rest of the population. Contemporary Rome had many of the same problems. The plebs or general population favoured the Samnites, and the aristocrats Rome.[54] This fissure points to one of the most important elements in Rome's success in Italy and later as an empire. Its own aristocracy managed to establish strong ties with the aristocracies of other cities and states. They agreed to support Rome in return for Roman help in maintaining control at home.

Livy reports that Naples on its own initiative had begun harassing Romans living in Campania. In response to a Roman demand for redress, the Neapolitans sent back a defiant reply. The Romans then declared war on Naples and assembled an army to attack it.[55] The Romans also assembled a second army to deter the Samnites from intervening. A Samnite force of 4,000 and another 2,000 men from the important Campanian city of Nola had been admitted to the city. Most of this account seems fictitious and designed to exonerate the Romans from the charge of being responsible for the war. The colonization of Fregellae and now the attack on Naples provided legitimate grievances for the Samnites. Rome was expanding into territory which, if not Samnite, had at least been under Samnite influence. The Samnites were correct to fear that if they did not stop Roman expansion it would eventually threaten Samnium itself. Most Samnite expansion was directed towards areas like Apulia where there was no immediate Roman interest. The Samnites were not alone in their anxiety about Roman expansion. It was reported that Tarentum, the most important Greek city in southern Italy was sending help to the Neapolitans to aid in resistance to the Romans.[56] Naples was merely the catalyst that set the war in motion.

In 327 the city was placed under siege by the consul Quintus Publilius Philo. As the year drew to a close, Philo would have normally been recalled to Rome to hold elections and then to complete his term of office. Instead of interrupting operations until the next year's consuls were available, his command was extended into 326 to complete the siege, which seems to have been expected to end soon in a Roman success.[57] The extended command, a promagistracy, was designated a proconsulate, that is an office in which an individual acted in place of a consul. There are later instances of extended commands for the performance of specific tasks. Philo's extraordinary record of political and military achievement must have played a part in the decision. By the time of his promagistracy, he had already held the consulship twice and he was to go on to hold it twice more, a record which stood until the first century. He had been dictator, master of the horse and censor although of plebeian rank. He had an established reputation for military success. After his capture of Naples Philo celebrated the first triumph held by a proconsul. Until the extension of empire made prolongation of commands regular and necessary, proroguing of commands remained a device designed to deal with specific situations.

This marked the first time that this expedient, which would play a crucial role in the Roman command structure, was used. The number of annual magistrates was sufficient until Roman expansion created the need for additional commanders. Rome now had to field multiple armies at the same time. There were only three magistrates, the two consuls and a praetor, who were capable of independent military command. In addition, annual tenure was a further limitation. These limitations had been put in place as safeguards against the abuse of power; but in the face of increasing demands they had created a problem. One solution might have been to enlarge the number of offices that possessed *imperium*. Such a solution was attempted in the previous century with the creation of military tribunes with consular powers and found unacceptable. The need to retain commanders of demonstrated ability presented another dilemma. The elite's own interests dictated the need to maintain restricted access to the highest offices and so limit the possibility of outside competition as well as limiting the success of its own members to avoid a power imbalance among the members of the elite. Since military office was so vital to prestige and political success, it remained the area where restricted access was particularly important.

Though in theory the powers of the consuls in their military and civilian aspects were integral parts of their office, in practice by the mid-fifth century the idea had developed that a number of the consuls' tasks could be split off and assigned to other magistrates. Not only various duties, but the power of a magistracy was thought of as separable from the office. This was especially true of *imperium* because it was conferred separately. By continuing an official's power but not his office, the number of magistrates remained limited and barriers against outsiders could be maintained. Eventually, even those who held no office could be given *imperium* and command armies.

In 326, Naples fell to the Romans. The inhabitants were hard pressed by the siege and the pro-Roman faction betrayed the city and its Samnite garrison. Philo went on to celebrate the first triumph by a proconsul. There would be many more. The year was also marked by an open break with the Samnites. The Romans issued a declaration of war, and were joined by the Lucanians and Apulians.[58] The alliance with the Lucanians soon collapsed and they reverted to their alliance with the Samnites.[59]

Down to 321 the war was marked by Roman campaigns in and around Samnium. There is no record of any move by the Samnites against Roman territory. The campaigns of the first years of the war seem to have been directed against western Samnium and the Vestini in the Abruzzi region. Related by culture and language, they were important Samnite allies.

In 326 the first campaigns began in Samnium and the next year against the Vestini. Livy claims that both campaigns were a series of Roman victories. The Vestini were beaten in the field and then when their army dispersed after the defeat the Romans launched a series of assaults on their cities. Several of them were taken. In Samnium in 325 the Romans won a key victory at a district called Inbrinium, whose location is unknown. Another major victory followed in 322 at an unnamed location. The battles and Roman victories are historical but the descriptions of the battles are so generalized that they are for the most part unhistorical elaborations. Livy voices his own doubts about which Roman commanders won the victory:[60]

> It is difficult to decide which account or which authority to prefer. I believe that the true history has been falsified by funeral orations and lying inscriptions on the family busts, since each family appropriates to itself an imaginary record of noble deeds and official distinctions. It is, at all events, owing to this cause that so much confusion has been introduced into the records of private careers and public events. There is no writer of those times now extant who was contemporary with the events he relates and whose authority, therefore, can be depended upon.

Despite the defeat of 322, the Samnites took the field again in 321. Their main army encamped at Caudium, which lay about 18km southwest of Beneventum (Benevento) in Campania. Livy describes the entrapment of the Roman army in a pass he labels the Caudine Forks. The Samnites were supposed to have lured the Romans on by rumours that they were besieging Luceria in Apulia with all their forces. The consuls decided to move to its rescue. The shorter of two available routes to Luceria was chosen. It passed through the Caudine Forks, which had a narrow western entrance and then widened into a plain. On its eastern end it ran through another set of passes that were even narrower than the western end. Once in the pass the only way out was through one defile or the other. The Romans entered the pass, crossed its open section and were nearing the eastern defile when they found it had been blocked by the Samnites, whose warriors crowned the surrounding heights. Attempting to reach safety by retracing their steps the Romans found the western pass blocked as well, and the hills above the pass were also occupied by the Samnites. The Romans were trapped and were forced to surrender, by passing under a yoke of spears. It seems to have been a widespread custom that signified that those passing under the yoke were somehow equivalent to yoked animals and therefore no longer warriors.[61]

There are serious problems with Livy's account. Livy's description of the pass does not match the topography of any of the passes in the area. The traditional site is the pass that runs between the towns of Arienzo and Arpaia, but its topographical features do not correspond with Livy's description. It has been pointed out that Livy's geography and topography are in general quite weak.[62] Other sources imply there was a battle which was a Roman defeat.[63] The defeat was real although its exact circumstances are lost. One additional point is the utter lack of scouting the story implies. Scouts are never mentioned nor do the consuls incur criticism for their absence. It seems likely that the Romans invented the story of Samnite trickery to explain away what must have been a serious defeat.

To extricate their army, the consuls were forced to sign an agreement, probably a treaty that entailed the surrender of Fregellae and Cales.[64] Fighting seems to have died down and there were no major campaigns by either side until 316 when the Romans, disregarding the treaty, resumed fighting.

There are Roman victories in the sources between 321 and 316. The action seems to have focused on Campania and Apulia. In 320 there was a supposed defeat of the Samnites, which is probably invention but the seizing of Luceria seems authentic.[65] For the most part the campaigns down to 318 are fictions as is the supposed request by a few Samnite communities for a new treaty and the Roman grant of a two-year truce.[66]

The years from the Caudine Forks until the reopening of the war with the Samnites show evidence for an overall campaign plan. The Romans strengthened their position in Campania. In 318 they created two new tribes in southern Latium and astride the Via Appia in northern Campania.[67] They also campaigned in Apulia and Lucania. In Apulia they forced the surrender of several cities as they did in Lucania.[68] These actions seem to be part of a plan to cut Samnium off from any potential allies in preparation for a direct attack on it.

Livy claims that the Samnites chose to renew hostilities in 316. The Roman actions were probably understood as a prelude to an attack and they must have had to meet the threat before the Romans did any more damage. In 316, the first direct confrontation between the two adversaries took place at Saticula in Samnite territory.[69] A Samnite defeat allowed the Romans to besiege Saticula, which was taken in the following year. Sora had become a Roman colony in 345, but with the prospect of Samnite support the locals murdered the Roman colonists. The Samnites moved up to the city to try to lift the siege. The armies fought an engagement at the strategically important pass of Lautulae near Terracina in Latium, from which the Samnites emerged victorious. It is the first evidence for any operations by the Samnites in Latium.[70] The Samnites then advanced into Latium and devastated the coast as far north as Ardea. Despite the Samnite campaign the Romans achieved several successes in the following two years. The Romans continued to try to isolate Samnium and various Samnite peoples from each other. A string of colonies was established on its borders and on strategic internal routes of communications.[71] The Via Appia was begun in 312.[72] The Samnites were now encircled by Roman allies and, with the Via Appia, an important route into the heart of Samnium had been opened.

The period from 312 until the end of the war in 304 is for the most part poorly documented. One or two Samnite victories are recorded but the course of the war ran steadily against the Samnites. In 306 in response to further Roman incursions, they undertook an invasion of northern Campania where they captured the towns of Calatia and Dora. They may have been helped by the fact that the Romans were also engaged in campaigns against the Hernici and Anagnini which ended in success, and there were rumours of possible conflict in the north. The next year the Romans launched a full-scale invasion of Samnium. They inflicted a defeat on the Samnites at Tifernum and then captured the important and frequently fought over stronghold of Bovianum, the capital of the important Samnite tribe of the Pentri.[73] With the Romans in the heart of Samnium, the war was almost over. In 304 the Samnites submitted peace proposals. To test them one of the consuls Sempronius Sophus made a demonstration march through Samnium and, satisfied that the proposals were serious, recommended that they be accepted. Essentially, the treaties of 354 and 341 were reinstated after a war of twenty-two years.[74]

In 311, during the Samnite War but after the tide had shifted in Rome's favour, the colony at Sutrium was attacked by the Etruscans. There had been no war with the Etruscan cities since the 350s; with Rome distracted by events in central Italy there was no pressure to expand in Etruria. The Etruscan states kept the peace as well, so the attack of 311 was probably the result of increasing success against the Samnites. The Etruscans must have thought that it would be better to confront the Romans while they were still occupied than to wait for Samnite defeat and face an even stronger Rome. The Etruscans might well have felt that they would be next. Sutrium, a key point of entry to southern Etruria, was an obvious choice for an attack. Which of the Etruscans attacked is not clear. The sources simply mention the Etruscans with the explicit omission of Arretium. This is certainly incorrect: a unified Etruria did not exist. It was probably the states of central Etruria that mounted the attack.[75] According to Livy a bloody, but indecisive battle was fought outside Sutrium which he claims as a Roman victory. The fact that the Romans remained at Sutrium and nothing further happened in the course of the year indicates that the battle was at best a draw.[76] It is striking that the siege continued despite the supposed victory. In 310 the consul Fabius Maximus Rullianus advanced north through the Ciminian forest, which takes its name from the Ciminian mountains (Monti Cimini) and extends from the Tiber to the sea, blocking the route from southern to northern Etruria. Fabius then proceeded northeast to Umbria, finally reaching Camerinum in southern Umbria. There he concluded a treaty with the city that seems to have included a military alliance. He turned southwest to northern Etruria plundering and laying the area waste. He then concluded agreements with several cities. Livy mentions the treaties and adds that as a result of the ravaging the campaign created support for those Etruscans opposed to Rome in northern Etruria and Umbria.

The chronology of 308 and 309 presents problems as it is confused in both Livy and Diodorus. The campaign of 308 also involved the Marsi and Paeligni (northern neighbours of the Samnites). The entry of these peoples is further evidence for the growing apprehension that the expansion of Rome was causing in central Italy. Finally, a truce was concluded between the warring parties.

During the rest of 308, the focus of Roman campaigning turned to Umbria. The Umbrians in alliance with some Etruscan cities had now become openly hostile and had levied an army which was now in the field. A battle at Mevania (Bevagno) ended as usual in a Roman victory and the Umbrian cities submitted.

During the next few years resistance in the area bordering Latium was extinguished. In 306 the Hernici, perhaps seeing what the future held, revolted and joined the Samnites. The war's end came quickly. A surrender was negotiated with the Romans that conferred citizenship without the vote on the rebellious communities. Those who had remained quiet retained their original status as allies. In 304 it was the turn of the Aequi. In a campaign of fifty days the Romans attacked the Aequi, and overwhelmed them. They destroyed their hill towns and massacred the population. The lesson was not lost on other hill peoples of the Abruzzi region, who rushed to conclude treaties with the Romans. Roman control of the area was solidified by the planting of several colonies and the creation in 299 of two new tribes. Rome now dominated central Italy. It had extended its reach to the Adriatic in the north and now totally controlled Latium and the surrounding territory. The Samnites had in two wars shown that even if they could win a few battles, they were no match for the Romans. Already the Romans had shown interest in the south with an alliance with the Lucanians in 326 although it had broken down by 317.[77] It seemed now that no one power could stop them.

Tarentum, the major Greek city in the south was suspicious of Rome's future plans.[78] The Romans had begun interfering in Tarentum's sphere of interest, the Greek cities of the south. They had already done so in Naples and now they gave further evidence of their interest in the area. In 302 the Spartan mercenary commander Cleonymus – originally hired by Tarentum to fight the Lucanians – turned his attention elsewhere. He seized the Greek city of Thurii on the southwestern shore of the Gulf of Tarentum. He was either defeated in battle and forced back to his ships or left on his own so as not to come into conflict with Rome.[79]

The alternate versions, which involved who commanded the expedition and what actually happened, raise an important issue about the events of the Third Samnite War. As has been pointed out, Livy's account and presumably his sources register a greater degree of disagreement than is the case for the second war against the Samnites.[80] For the first time we have an inscription, an epitaph, for one of the participants, Lucius Cornelius Scipio Barbatus, consul in 298.[81] It too presents differences with Livy's account. What seems to have happened is that the third war took place within approximately a century of the beginning of historical writing in Rome. It was still within a period when oral tradition about the conflict would still be available to a historian. That would help to explain the abundance of information and the conflicting accounts. Families fighting for political position in the course of the third war would manipulate events to increase the importance of family members in the conduct of the war. Once again, the outline of the main events can be accepted.

From the end of the Second Samnite War there was minor fighting in Umbria and against some rebellious Aequi. In 302, a rebellion of the Etruscan cities began at Arretium due, according to Livy, to an internal struggle for power between aristocrats. At the same time the Marsi, angered by the presence of Roman colonists, rose and were quickly defeated. They renewed their treaties with Rome.

In 302 a Roman defeat by the Etruscans was quickly followed by a victory.[82] The Etruscans sought and were granted a two-year truce which was followed by a peace treaty in 300. In 299 the Etruscans planned war according to Livy. But an inopportune invasion by the Gauls, which reached as far as southern Etruria, made a war with Rome impossible. According to the second century Greek historian Polybius, the Gauls returned home laden with spoils from the raid.[83]

In 298, there were further troubles in Etruria. There was a battle at Volterrae and plundering in the territory around Falerii.[84] The Roman victories seem to have borne fruit. In the next year Livy records a general peace movement throughout Etruria. This led to a major change in the direction of Rome's military efforts. The key event was a treaty concluded between Rome and the Lucanians who had been at war with the Samnites. The treaty was followed by Roman demands that the Samnites withdraw from the territories of Rome's allies and from their frontier with the Lucanians. The first demand seems to indicate that they had already occupied parts of Lucania. If they accepted Roman demands they would once again be hemmed on the north and south and the loss of face would be damaging. Rome was once again engaged on multiple fronts. It was a clear demonstration of Roman power and resources.

One of the consuls Fabius Maximus Rullianus ravaged Samnium and captured the city of Cimetra while the other consul, after a victory over the Apulians, joined his colleague in laying waste to Samnite territory.[85] They continued to do so in the following year. The year was marked by a crucial development. A Samnite army evaded the Romans and made its way into Etruria. This was enough to set off a new Etruscan revolt. An agreement was reached with the Etruscans that they and the Samnites would jointly wage war against the Romans under the leadership of Gellius Egnatius, the Samnite commander, and in addition, they decided to seek help from Gallic mercenaries.[86] The allies added the Umbrians and Gauls to their coalition. This seems to have been the largest coalition formed in Italy to this point. [87]

In 295 the opposing forces met at Sentinum in Umbria. The Romans mustered a double consular army of four legions with 4,200 men each. In addition, there were probably an equal number of allies present, bringing the total strength of the army to around 34,000. It was the largest army the Romans had yet put into the field. The size of the force of Samnites and Gauls who faced them is unknown but given the fierceness and length of the struggle was probably about equal to the Romans.[88] Their army was not at full strength, as their Etruscan and Umbrian allies had declined to join them, instead being drawn away by a diversionary Roman attack in Etruria and defeated.[89]

Some of the details of the battle seem authentic. The consul Fabius Maximus was posted on the right with two legions while his colleague Decius Mus was posted on the left with the other two legions. The one wing of the allies would have formed up on the right of Fabius' legions and the other on the left of Decius'.[90] Livy claims that the contest initially remained evenly balanced and that Fabius on the right was purposely prolonging the struggle to wear down his opponents. He makes reference to the Gallic propensity to make a furious charge that if unsuccessful left the Gauls with less endurance to fight a prolonged battle.[91] He makes the same comment about the Samnites, but there is little evidence to support his statement.

Decius led a rash cavalry charge that almost cost the Romans the battle. The Roman cavalry was put to flight, which would have opened up the infantry's left flank to the Gallic cavalry. It was at this point that he devoted himself and the enemy to the infernal gods as his father was supposed to have done at the battle of the Veseris against the Latins.[92] The victory seems to have been due to Fabius. He first brought up his reserves to stabilize his line on the left wing and then sent allied cavalry and units from his legions to take the Samnites in the rear. That last manoeuvre resulted in the death of the Samnite commander and broke up the Samnite formation, which fled the field. The Gauls suffered the same fate. Whatever the moral value of Decius' *devotio,* it was the tactics of Fabius which decided the battle.

Livy supplies casualty figures for Sentinum. He claims that 8,700 were killed with the majority, as would be expected, falling on the left wing. The figures do not separate out allied and Roman casualties. The Samnites and Gauls lost 25,000 killed and 8,000 taken prisoner. It is far lower than some of the extraordinary and totally untrustworthy figures supplied by some other sources. Nonetheless, if the armies were approximately equal in size, Livy's figures would imply that the coalition army was almost completely wiped out. Although not impossible, it seems unlikely. The exact figure is irretrievable, but it would seem that a substantial number of coalition troops were either killed or captured.

Despite the massive defeat the war continued, albeit on a less intense level. The next few years were filled with fighting on multiple fronts. In Etruria there was fighting in the territories of Volsinii and Rusellae. The success of this campaign led to the making of another treaty with three important cities – Volsinii, Arretium and Perusia – although the continual resurgence of these towns after supposed Roman victories casts doubt on the narrative of an unbroken string of successes.[93] However, there was one important difference from earlier actions: for the first time a major city fell to the Romans.[94] Despite the treaty there was further fighting in 293, and by 292 major resistances in Etruria were over. There were noticeable differences in the treatment of northern and southern Etruria with treaties regulating relations in the north, while various degrees of incorporation and expropriation of land took place in the south. Rome was now firmly established in both Etruria and Umbria. The process of Romanization through colonization and finally by cultural assimilation seems to have been a long and slow process, it was only completed by the last century BC.

The war with the Samnites also continued. The consul Atilius Regulus marched into Samnium and sustained an initial defeat. In 293 the Romans inflicted a substantial defeat on the Samnites at Aquilonia.

Prior to the battle at Aquilonia (modern Agnone) in 293, Livy mentions a special Samnite ritual.[95] He describes the formation of an elite warrior band. An area was marked off in the Samnite camp to create a special enclosure, and a sacrifice was then performed following an old ritual. A summons then went out to all warriors of noble birth or who were distinguished by their military abilities. They were taken into the enclosure and forced to swear a terrible oath that bound them on pain of a curse on their families and themselves to be obedient to their commanders in all things and to slaughter all those they saw fleeing the battlefield. The commanding officer picked 10 of the men who had sworn the oath, and they picked 10 men who picked 10 others, and so on until they numbered 16,000. They were given beautiful armour and plumed helmets so that they would stand out from the other troops.[96]

It may well be that the Samnites created an elite force bound together by an oath. Such a procedure is common among Italian peoples including the Romans. When they were drafted Roman soldiers swore an oath to their commander which became mandatory from 216.[97] The oath had a religious basis and functioned as a ritual of initiation to promote group solidarity by invoking religious sanctions. The Romans considered military service to be a consecrated activity. The oath seems to have been considered as a necessary preliminary to any active military service. Without it the soldier was not permitted to use his weapons or to engage in fighting. It bound the soldier to follow the consuls against any enemies and not desert or act illegally, it also appears to have been valid only for the impending campaign and to the commanders of that campaign. Under new commanders the oath had to be repeated.[98]

Fighting continued in Samnium into 290, but the end of Livy's book 10 deprives us of detailed information about this period. We hear of one of the consuls of 292, Fabius Gurges, suffering a defeat but then with the help of his father serving as his legate securing a victory over the Samnites.[99] In 291 a further victorious campaign was followed in the next year by further successes and the end of the war. The Romans and Samnites concluded a treaty that significantly extended Rome's southern border to the Volturnus River and forced the Samnites to become allies. As a further assurance against Samnite resurgence the Romans founded a colony at Venusia in 291 to the rear of Samnium on territory taken from them.

Along with the conquest of Veii, the war marked a major turning point in Roman expansion in Italy. Sentinum was a battle of a magnitude greater than any that had gone before. In essence, it was the last chance for a successful coalition to be formed to counter the Romans in central Italy. The struggle with the Samnites was far from over and within little more than a decade Romans and Samnites would once again be fighting. However, no power in central Italy could now face Rome and win. She controlled a solid block of territory that extended from the Tyrrhenian coast to the Adriatic where the Latin colony of Hadria was founded probably between 290 and 286 in southern Picenum. Narnia in Umbria was established as a Roman strongpoint in 299. About the same time a citizen colony Sena Gallica was founded about 160km to the north on land confiscated from the Gauls as a result of their defeat at Sentinum. They served as anchors for Roman control on the Adriatic coast and Sena as a brake on the Sabines who had been defeated in 290, ending a long history of wars with Rome. The conquest may have had as one of its purposes the establishment of a territorial barrier between the Umbrians and Etruscans to the north and the Samnites to the south.[100] In 290 the Sabines received citizenship without the vote and full citizenship followed in 268.

The wars had been marked by changes in the Roman army.[101] In 311 the number of legions was doubled from two to four, with each consul now normally assigned a two-legion army plus allies which would constitute a force of about 16,000 men.[102] In addition, there was an increase in the number of elected military tribunes. They were first elected in 362 and totalled six. In 311 Livy notes that sixteen tribunes of the four legions were elected by popular vote. The remaining eight were nominated by the consul conducting the levy. The increase in legion numbers is clearly the result of the fighting on multiple fronts that the wars of this period involved. Livy represents the election of these tribunes as a popular victory but it must also have been the needs created by the formation of a larger army.

The larger more complicated force may also have benefited from the closer connection between the soldiers and the tribunes that election might bring.

The military demands of the period also had an important effect on the commanders. Three phenomena are noteworthy. The first was a far greater use of the proconsuls and legates. The most striking example is in 295, when five men were appointed as promagistrates. Legates were also appointed in record numbers. In 293 there were at least seven and possibly nine serving in the same year. The reasons are obvious as the demands of multi-front war intensified. The second development is in some ways the more striking, the repeated election of the same man as consul. For example, Quintus Fabius Maximus Rullianus, one of the victors of Sentinum served a total of five consulships over a thirty-year period. Third, *imperium* although a power that normally belonged to a magistrate was conferred on private citizens (*privatus*).

The war also seems to have led to the development of a navy on a very small scale. Rome's earliest attempts to deal with its naval needs reveal a persistent strand in her approach to the sea. Starting in the first half of the fifth century, Rome founded a series of small maritime colonies to provide coastal defence rather than establishing a naval force to police its shores.[103] This development illustrates clearly the Roman approach of dominating the sea by gaining possession of the land. Given the limited range of ancient warships, this was an effective policy. In 311 there was a change in policy when two minor magistrates, the *duoviri navales,* were appointed to command small squadrons of ten ships each, whose primary duty seems to have been to prevent piracy and coastal raiding. This should not have been a problem as far as the Samnites were concerned but it may have been a different matter once hostilities broke out with the Etruscans in the same year.[104] Many of the coastal states had a long history of seafaring and naval warfare. Their lack of importance and of naval warfare is clear from the intermittent nature of their appointment and their junior status. After 282 they cease to be appointed until 189 to 172 when they reappear on an irregular basis and then disappear forever. It seems likely that Rome's control of the Greek states of the south with their long maritime histories made the *duoviri* superfluous. In 267 four junior magistrates, the *quaestores classici,* were appointed to superintend Rome's new naval allies.

The years after the Third Samnite War were also filled with fighting in the north. Conflict continued in Etruria. By the mid-260s the wars there were over. The Etruscan communities were now bound to Rome by treaties of alliance, while Caere was given citizenship without the vote.

For a decade after their defeat at Sentinum, the Gauls seem to have remained relatively quiet. Ten years later the Senonian Gauls moved into Etruria and besieged Arretium. A Roman force sent to the city's aid was defeated and its commander, the praetor Metellus Denter, was killed. His successor, Curius Dentatus, sent an embassy to the Gauls to discuss an exchange of prisoners. This was unusual. At other times the Romans do not seem to have been overly concerned about Roman captives. The ambassadors were killed although Polybius, our single source omits to mention who killed them or why. The Romans then met the Gauls in battle and inflicted a serious defeat on them.[105] They confiscated part of their land and established the colony of Sena Gallica.

According to Polybius the Boii, another Gallic tribe, upset by the confiscation of land from the Senones had allied with the Etruscans. In 283 the combined force met the Roman forces at Lake Vadimon in Etruria about 80km north of Rome. Polybius claims that the Roman army under Cornelius Dolabella inflicted a crushing defeat, and in 282 the same coalition faced the Romans once again and were once again defeated. Polybius claims that the battle of 282 was fought by young and inexperienced troops. But the extent of the Roman victory at Vadimon is probably exaggerated. It was a defeat, not an annihilation.[106]

An intervention by the Romans occurred in the south in 285. The Greek city of Thurii asked for Roman help against the Lucanians. Rome's victories in central Italy and her distance from Thurii made her an attractive alternative to the only Greek power, Tarentum. Thurii, located on the western coast of the Gulf of Tarentum, had once been one of the most powerful of the Greek city-states. Her long struggle with Tarentum, now the dominant power in the region, dated to the previous century. The Greek city-states had in general been debilitated by the effects of external pressure from the local peoples and conflict with each other. They had also been through serious internal conflict in addition to economic decline. The local Italic peoples had gained ground at the Greeks' expense. By the first quarter of the fourth century the Greek cities had ceased to be first class powers. At first, Rome attempted to solve the matter by diplomacy since it had ties with the Lucanians. That might have seemed a feasible approach, but diplomacy brought no solution.[107] In 282, perhaps delayed by their commitments in the north, they turned to military force. The consul Fabricius Luscinus defeated an army of Samnites, Bruttians and Lucanians to ease the pressure on Thurii. He also left a garrison behind in the city.[108] The Roman victory brought appeals from other Greek cities, Croton, Rhegium and Locri for alliance and protection which Rome accepted. Her military successes in central Italy and now in the south made her an attractive protector, perhaps against Tarentum as well.[109]

Founded in 706 Tarentum, sited at the head of the gulf that still bears its name, was the only Spartan colony in Italy. The city's excellent harbour is still a major commercial and military port. It faced serious pressure from the natives over whom it won a series of victories during the fifth century. In 473, it suffered a heavy defeat in the war against the Messapians, a people composed of several tribes who had settled in what is modern day Calabria and Apulia. The defeat had serious internal repercussions, leading to the replacement of the city's aristocratic rulers by a democratic regime which maintained itself until the war with Rome.

The succeeding period was marked by the expansion and fortification of the city. Its growth continued into the fourth century when it reached its peak under the leadership of Archytas, the philosopher who led the city's forces to a series of victories. It also fought a number of wars with its Greek rivals and had by the 370s emerged as the single most powerful Greek state.

In the course of the fourth century the hill peoples pressed heavily on Tarentum and its fertile plain. The growing pressure of these Messapian and Lucanian peoples forced Tarentum to seek external military help. It called in commanders and additional forces from the Greek world outside of Italy. The last of these mercenary generals, King Alexander of Epirus, brother-in-law to Alexander the Great, had inflicted heavy losses on these hill peoples. The wars in Samnium also diverted their attention away from the Greeks.[110] However, despite this success the situation remained as dangerous as ever for Tarentum. It simply did not have the strength to master the problems that it faced.

As early as 331 and certainly by 303 a treaty existed between Rome and Tarentum prohibiting the Romans from sailing around the Lacinian Promontory, the exact site of which is uncertain but it was west of Tarentum near the city of Croton. The treaty was designed to keep the Romans out of Tarentine waters. The nervousness about Rome's aims and possible encroachment on the Tarentine sphere of influence is visible in 326 during the Roman siege of Naples at the opening of the Second Samnite War.[111] Rome's alliances with the Lucanians who were a formidable adversary also excited suspicion, and her relations with Thurii and the other Greek cities who had placed themselves under her protection, were direct incursions into Tarentum's sphere of influence.

The incident that led to the war between Rome and Tarentum came in 282. Roman ships appeared off Tarentum in direct contravention of the treaty. The Tarentines attacked them, sinking several. The Tarentines then marched on Rhegium and expelled the Roman garrison together with the aristocrats who had supported Rome. Despite being in the wrong, the Romans could not tolerate this blow to their prestige and sent an embassy in 282 or 281 to demand satisfaction. Not only were these demands rejected but the ambassador was insulted.[112] Given the disparity in strength between the two potential adversaries, the rejection of the embassy seems almost suicidal. But two things must be borne in mind; the first, was that it was likely that the Tarentines had found what they considered to be sufficient help to win a war with Rome; the second, that as a democracy it was violently opposed to the oligarchies the Romans had imposed on their Italian conquests. The Romans declared war and invaded Tarentine territory. They then drove the Tarentine army within the city walls.

In response the city did what it had done before and appealed for outside help to Pyrrhus of Epirus, with whom it had had previous contacts. Pyrrhus had been king of Epirus in the area of modern Albania, first from 306 when he was thirteen to 302, and then from 297 until his death in 272. He became involved in the disputed Macedonian succession and showed himself to be a successful military commander, although the impetuousness he displayed as a battlefield commander was later to lead to his death. That success led to his proclamation as king of Macedonia in 288. He held the throne until 284 when his co-ruler drove him out of Macedonia. Pyrrhus accepted the appeal for reasons of his own. He was fighting Ptolemy Ceraunus for the Macedonian throne when the call came from Tarentum. Success in Italy might give Pyrrhus the opportunity to establish a kingdom in Italy as a step to further conquests in Sicily and of Carthage. He made a treaty with Ceraunus in which he renounced his claim to the Macedonian throne in exchange for troops. He then set about a propaganda campaign to generate support in the Greek world portraying his expedition as a Hellenic crusade to protect Greeks against the western barbarians. He sent advance forces over under the two men: his advisor Cineas and his general Milo.

He arrived in Italy in May 280 with an army of 22,500 infantry, 3,000 cavalry and 20 elephants. Pyrrhus' elephants were the first to be used in battle in Italy and they initially created serious problems for the Romans who were unused to dealing with them; they later devised measures by which they successfully overcame the threat they presented.

From the death of Alexander in 323 until about 190, elephants played a subsidiary but important role in Western warfare. Both Indian and African elephants were used and the ancients regularly state that African elephants were smaller than Indian counterparts and were afraid to face the Indian elephants. In fact, the Ptolemies, the Macedonian rulers of Egypt and the chief source for the African elephants used the smaller of the two African species, the forest as opposed to the bush elephant. Both were smaller than their Indian relatives, and in modern times the bush species alone survives. The Ptolemies monopolized the supply of African elephants for warfare as for other purposes while the Seleucid dynasty, whose empire stretched from the coast of Asia Minor to northwestern India at its greatest extent, controlled the supply of Indian elephants. The number of elephants present at various major battles declined markedly in the course of the third century. They are difficult to breed in captivity and over-hunting was certainly a factor in the extinction of the African elephants. The numbers of Indian elephants also declined severely, but that seems to be due to the loss of the areas from which the Seleucids drew their supply.

In war the elephant's major function was to terrify the enemy and to wreak as much havoc as possible. They were used in three basic ways in battle: as a screen against cavalry, since untrained horses were unable to abide their smell; to attack infantry; and to break into towns or fortifications under siege. After 300, many of the larger elephants carried towers with two to four men armed with missile weapons. They were armoured and on occasion even the tips of their trunks were protected.

In most of these roles the elephant was not conspicuously successful. It was too vulnerable to missile attack and to elephant traps to be effective in siege warfare. In the case of infantry who had no experience fighting against them, they could be devastating; however, well-trained infantry could successfully deal with them and the elephants' tendency to stampede when panicked could wreak as much destruction among their friends as among their foes. Perhaps most importantly, the difficulties of supply, their unsuitability to the rigours of European winters, and the expense of maintaining them combined with their lack of effectiveness, finally ended their use in Western warfare and reduced them to a ceremonial role that the Romans retained.[113]

Pyrrhus' arrival would also compel the Romans to face a contemporary professional Hellenistic army for the first time. The phalanx remained its most important arm as it had for the Greek city-states and for the early Roman army. However, under Alexander the Great and his father Philip II, the phalanx underwent important changes.

Philip II continued the existing trend of lightening hoplite equipment by discarding the corselet and using a small shield suspended by a strap from the shoulder as protection for the upper body. The suspension of the shield was made necessary by his other crucial innovation: the *sarissa*. This was an 18-foot pike wielded in both hands that enormously increased the number of lethal spear points that the phalanx could present as well as increasing the range of its killing zone. And from the reign of Alexander, cavalry became a crucial element in victory on the battlefield for about seventy years (in the end the financial burden and the difficulty of procuring mounts undermined its importance). The phalanx became, as it had been earlier, the decisive arm on the battlefield.

The type of men who fought in the phalanx had also changed. In the Greek city-states of the fifth century and in the Roman army, the burden of military service had fallen on the state's citizens. In the Greek cities of the Hellenistic period, citizen levies still formed the core of the army, but they were often supplemented with mercenaries drawn from all over the Mediterranean and beyond. In two of the great kingdoms of the period – the Seleucid and the Ptolemaic in Egypt – and the smaller kingdom of Pergamum centred in northwestern Asia Minor, extensive numbers of mercenaries were employed and attempts were made to bind them to their employers by grants of land and other incentives. For the third of the major monarchies, the Antigonids in Macedonia, the availability of native Macedonian troops, who were sought by all of the Hellenistic kingdoms, resulted in the need for fewer mercenaries than elsewhere. Mercenaries in Macedonia were generally employed as specialist troops. Particularly famous were Cretan archers and Rhodian slingers. Pyrrhus' army would have probably consisted of native troops from Epirus with a contingent of Macedonian mercenaries, probably hired from contacts he had made while he was co-ruler of Macedonia.

Almost simultaneously with Pyrrhus' arrival there was a revolt against Rome in the south that included the Lucanians, Messapians, Bruttians and some Samnites. The revolt outlasted Pyrrhus' campaigns in Italy and did not end until the end of the 270s. Pyrrhus based himself at Tarentum, imposing a number of restrictions on the Tarentines, including the closing the theatres and gymnasia.[114]

The news of the revolt and of Pyrrhus' arrival brought a Roman army under the consul Valerius Laevinus south despite continuing troubles in Etruria and the Gallic threat. The Romans wanted to cut Pyrrhus off from Lucanian reinforcements. The Lucanians had been kept in check by the proconsul Aemilius Barbula who took up a position at Venusia. Pyrrhus encamped near Heraclea to wait for the reinforcements. He met the Romans at Heraclea located at the head of the gulf at the mouth of the Siris River. To gain time Pyrrhus sent envoys to Laevinus proposing a court of arbitration to judge Rome's dispute with Tarentum. Given the Roman preference for decisive victory and the loss of prestige, an arbitration – especially if it went against the Romans – was never likely to elicit a positive response.

Laevinus decided on battle. His army of about 30,000 Romans and allies outnumbered Pyrrhus' force and waiting any further might allow Pyrrhus to link up with Lucanian reinforcements. Laevinus sent his cavalry across the river, threatening Pyrrhus' centre, which pulled back allowing the legions to cross unhindered. The armies then directly attacked each other. Pyrrhus' phalanx, which he continually rallied, was pressed hard by the Romans and was in some difficulty. It was the king's elephants that decided the struggle. Pyrrhus had placed them on either wing and now launched them against the Roman cavalry. The untrained horses reacted as expected, and were thrown into a panic. The panicked cavalry opened up the Roman flanks to attack by Pyrrhus' cavalry. The legion, now also terrified by the elephants, broke and ran.

The victory had been a costly one for Pyrrhus. The Romans lost about 7,000 men with 1,800 captured, but the king's army had suffered about 4,000 casualties. The Romans could replace their losses easily, yet Pyrrhus could not. He had at best uncertain allies in Italy and more importantly the men he lost were highly trained fighters and not readily replaceable.[115]

The victory at Heraclea, like Hannibal's victory at Cannae, had immediate consequences in southern Italy; most of the region including some of the Greek cities that had joined the Romans came over to the king. The king, his army strengthened by reinforcements, now made his way north towards Rome along the Via Latina. He failed to take Naples and Capua, the two most important cities in southern Italy besides Tarentum. Meanwhile his troops alienated his allies by their plundering. What he expected to do at Rome once he got there remains uncertain. His army was not large enough to besiege a city of Rome's size and given the high casualties that ancient siege warfare entailed such an attempt would have been foolhardy. It is most likely that he was attempting to link up with the Etruscans and perhaps the Gauls to create a united front to face the Romans, to confront them with a coalition like the one that had fought at Sentinum. Hannibal, when a march on Rome was suggested to him after his success at Cannae, wisely refused, knowing he could accomplish little and that failure would weaken his position. When he finally did so five years later it was merely an unsuccessful feint to try to draw off the Romans from their siege of Capua.[116]

After his fruitless march on Rome, Pyrrhus turned back to Tarentum where he spent the winter of 280–279. A Roman embassy including three ex-consuls came to negotiate about the release of Roman prisoners of war. As a gesture of goodwill and to try to tempt the Romans into further negotiations, he promised to release all of his Roman prisoners without ransom. The prisoners were sent back to Rome accompanied by Cineas, who had been entrusted by the king with the further negotiations. The terms that Cineas offered which would have expelled the Romans from southern and most of central Italy, were simply unacceptable. The tradition claims that the Senate was inclined to accept these terms because of Rome's overextension, when a single senator – the blind Appius Claudius Caecus, the builder of the Appian Way – spoke out strongly against it. Apparently his eloquence (the speech continued to be read until the end of the first century) was enough to shift opinion against Pyrrhus' proposals.

With the failure of negotiations Pyrrhus prepared his army to fight on. He recruited mercenaries, mostly in southern Italy, and assembled the necessary financing for his army from the Greek cities during the winter. The additional mercenaries and allied troops brought his army to a total of 40,000 men which more than made up for the losses at Heraclea. In the spring of 279, Pyrrhus began his march north through Apulia, taking some minor towns with his goal being Samnium, which could serve as a base for a move into Latium. The Romans were aware of his movements and sent both consuls P. Decius Mus (the son of the consul who had given his life at Sentinum) and P. Sulpicius Saverrio to block him.

The armies came into contact at Asculum on the Aufidus River (Ascoli Satriano).[117] The countryside was poorly suited to Pyrrhus' army. It was a heavily wooded area and so problematic for elephants and cavalry, and more importantly the phalanx which needed a battlefield as level as possible to keep its formation as tightly massed as possible. Broken and wooded ground made that impossible.

Little can be said about the first day of battle except that it was fought in a wooded area that allowed the Romans to maintain their line. On the second day, Pyrrhus deployed his battle line on flatter and more favourable ground. Pyrrhus gave the Macedonian phalanx the prime place on the right wing, and next to them were mercenaries from Tarentum; next were troops from Ambracia in western Greece, then a unit of Tarentines with white shields, and then the Bruttians and Lucanians. In the middle of the line there were additional western Greeks, next to them various Greek mercenaries, and finally Samnites who formed the left wing. His cavalry was drawn from various Greek states and from the Samnites. He placed units of his Italian allies, who fought with sword and shield rather than the Macedonian pike, between the companies of the phalanx.[118] He divided the light-armed infantry and elephants into two groups and placed them on both wings, in a position slightly elevated above the plain. The king was with the royal bodyguard of 2,000 men outside of the battle line. This unit was to act as a reserve force.

He faced a double consular army of four legions and allies, probably about the same size as Pyrrhus' force.[119] Their allies were as usual attached to each legion and were placed on the wings. The consuls, as was usual, stationed their cavalry on the wings with the allies forming one wing and the Roman cavalry the other. Outside the line they stationed their light-armed troops and 300 wagons, which they had prepared for the battle with the elephants. These wagons had upright beams on which were mounted movable traverse poles that could be swung round quickly in any direction. On the ends of the poles there were either tridents or sword-like spikes or scythes. They also had cranes with grappling-irons. Many of the poles had grapnels wrapped in cloth that had been daubed with pitch, which were to be set on fire as soon as the elephants approached, at which time the troops were to rain blows on them to make them stampede. The wagons carried light-armed missile troops to bombard the animals and protect themselves.

The battle was a hard fought struggle by both sides. The cavalry of each army fought in its traditional fashion. The Romans dismounted when they encountered the enemy and fought on foot, while the Greeks charged, disengaged, wheeled about and charged once again.[120] The heavy infantry seems to have been engaged in an evenly matched struggle that went on for some time. At some point, the king's line was in trouble and so he sent his elephants forward to shore it up. In response the Romans sent forward the wagons they had prepared for just such an eventuality. For a while the wagons did their work and the elephants were halted, but a combination of missiles and light-armed infantry attacks drove the men who were in the wagons back onto their own lines, which they threw into disorder.

Despite this success the middle of the king's battle line, consisting of Italian troops including those from Tarentum, gave way. Pyrrhus sent some of his cavalry to stabilize the line, which they apparently did. A contingent of Roman allies from the city of Arpi, consisting of 4,000 infantry and 400 cavalry who had been sent to aid the consuls' army, appeared. By pure chance the road they were following came down in the rear of the king's army where they could see the battle. Discretion seems to have been the better part of valour in this instance and instead of attacking Pyrrhus' army, they attacked his camp. The camp was taken and burned to the ground. Pyrrhus, informed of what had happened, made a decision to keep his phalanx fighting the Romans, while he sent elephants and cavalry to the rescue, but it was too late by the time they arrived.

The troops who had been sent to rescue the camp now turned against the two legions who had advanced over the plain without waiting for their comrades, and were now exposed and vulnerable. Pyrrhus led a charge which disrupted the two legions, although he was wounded during it. The Romans sought refuge on a nearby height, which at least protected them from attack by the elephants and cavalry; however, they suffered heavy casualties from missile weapons. The king and the Roman consuls were informed of their predicament. Pyrrhus sent infantry and the Roman commanders horsemen. These forces collided and another phase of the battle began. As evening approached the king recalled his men as did the Roman consuls.

The toll of the struggle had been heavy: 6,000 Romans were dead and Pyrrhus lost about 3,500 men. It was a victory for the king, but it had been won at a heavy price. He then returned to a Tarentum that was finding his presence increasingly irksome. Once again, his Greeks must have sustained the majority of the casualties, as his Italian allies had fled the field. Given the difficulties he had in recruiting mercenaries, that must have been disheartening news. There was also bad news from Epirus: the death of the Macedonian king who was fighting a Gallic invasion now opened Epirus to invasion as well.

His Italian expedition seemed likely to end in a stalemate or worse. The Romans had made it clear that they were not going to concede defeat. However, the king's situation suddenly changed, and a much more attractive alternative appeared. He was offered the supreme command of the war against Carthage. Wars between Carthage, which occupied approximately the western half of Sicily, and the Greek city-states that were concentrated in the eastern half had been going on for several centuries. Syracuse, with its magnificent harbour on the southeast coast, had emerged as the most powerful Greek state and had the fight against the Carthaginians. Due to internal troubles, which had led seriously weakened it, Syracuse was no longer in position to fight. Its weakness was an open invitation to Carthage to press the attack. Carthage had recently concluded an agreement with the Romans that pledged each side to offer mutual military support. The Carthaginians must have feared that Pyrrhus would land in Sicily and lead the fight against them, and support for Rome offered the possibility that continued war with Rome would keep the king in Italy.[121] The offer to fight in Sicily was especially attractive to Pyrrhus as he had family ties to the island, which might facilitate his setting up the kingdom there that had eluded him in Italy. The island was immensely fertile and rich and could serve as a base for an invasion of Carthage's home territory, and perhaps even serve as a base for a renewed invasion of Italy.

In 278 Pyrrhus left for Sicily. He had been made king of Syracuse and appointed as commander of all the Greek forces in the island. At first his campaign went well and the Carthaginians were ready to conclude a peace agreement. However, his advisors and allies would settle for nothing less than complete Carthaginian withdrawal. It was an impossible demand. His support declined precipitously and his plans for further conquests fell apart; he abandoned Sicily and turned his eyes back to Italy.

The deteriorating situation in Italy required Pyrrhus' attention. In 277 the Romans had suffered a minor defeat in Samnium but quickly retrieved the situation. The major Greek city of Croton was lost to them and the Lucanians and Bruttians had suffered defeat at Roman hands. 276 brought no better news, with Roman triumphs recorded in Samnium, Bruttium and Lucania.[122]

In 276 Pyrrhus returned to Italy with more than 20,000 infantry and 3,000 cavalry as well as elephants, landing at Locri after suffering a defeat at the hands of a Carthaginian fleet. This force must have represented his total troop strength, as his Italian allies were either abandoning him or too busy with their own struggles against the Romans. He first tried to capture Rhegium at the toe of the Italian boot, but was frustrated by the garrison of Campanian mercenaries that held the city for Rome. Upon his retreat, his army was ambushed by another group of Campanian mercenaries whom he had already fought in Sicily: the Mamertini. The ambush was costly to Pyrrhus. He returned to Locri and began draining the city of money to recruit more mercenaries to replace his losses and to finance his conflict with Rome. The Romans also had their problems. The continuous warfare had exhausted and drained the citizen body and it was felt necessary for one of the consuls in charge of the levy to resort to threats for the first time in the history of the levy.

After successfully completing the levy, the consuls took up positions to try to prevent the king from marching on Rome. One stationed his army in Lucania to try to block the king's advance, or if that failed to cut his communications and supply route back to Locri and the south. The other consul took up a position near the town of Malventum in Apulia to block the king's advance north.

Pyrrhus, moving up along the route of the Via Appia, decided to try to defeat the Romans in detail. Leaving part of his army to meet an attack by the consul in Lucania he advanced against Curius Dentatus at Malventum. Given his numerical inferiority to the Roman army, which must have been about 50 per cent larger than his own army, he decided on a surprise attack. To carry it off he moved his troops into position during the night. Such a manoeuvre is always difficult for an army and such was the case for Pyrrhus' men. The troops, unfamiliar with the ground, became lost and confused. By the time they were in position and launched their attack it was too late. The Romans were ready for them and beat back the attempt. This failure was followed by the main battle in the plain known as the Campi Arusini, whose location is unknown. The Greek troops, exhausted by their nighttime advance and repulse earlier in the day, collapsed before a determined Roman advance. This time the elephants contributed to Pyrrhus' defeat. Using fire arrows, the Romans panicked them and drove them back on their own lines. While this was happening, the other consul defeated the Samnites and Lucanians ending any hope of reinforcements for the king.[123]

The king's losses are hard to gauge. All that can be said is he returned to Greece with 8,000 infantry and 500 cavalry. However, since his army had a high proportion of mercenaries the small number of men he brought back may have been, at least in part, the result of mercenaries looking for new employers as well as battlefield casualties. He left his son behind at Tarentum with a number of troops. It is hard to understand why he did so; he must now have realized that his Italian campaign was over and that Rome was simply too strong to defeat. It may be that despite this, he had still not given up hope. If his adventures in Greece and Macedonia turned out favourably he might have thought that he could assemble a strong enough force to renew the struggle. Despite some successes his career was ended in 272; during a battle in the streets of Argos a woman – frightened that the king meant harm to her son – threw down a roof tile that fatally injured him.

Pyrrhus' army was the first modern Hellenistic army the Romans encountered. It was commanded by a general who was a first class tactician and a brave man with a respect for the conventions of Hellenistic warfare, which emphasized chivalrous behaviour and a desire to avoid a fight to the finish when possible. He wanted to establish a kingdom in Italy to compensate for his losses in Macedonia and Greece and to act as a base to win back his losses there. His major mistake was to underestimate the resources Rome could put into the field and to not recognize that Rome was not bound by Hellenistic conventions. He also overestimated the ability of Rome's opponents in southern Italy to provide the aid he needed to win a war against the Romans.

It was this war that first brought Rome to the attention of the Hellenistic powers of the eastern Mediterranean. In 273 Ptolemy II Philadelphus, king of Egypt, sought Roman friendship. The friendship was granted and a return embassy was sent to Ptolemy headed by an eminent senator. Neither side seems to have gone beyond expressions of goodwill. As of yet Rome's conquests had all been west of the Adriatic, and except in southern Italy had not directly affected the Greek world.

In 272, the same year that the king was killed, Tarentum finally surrendered. Its resistance had only been possible because of Pyrrhus; without any further external aid, its cause was hopeless. In the next few years the Romans founded a series of colonies in the area. In 273 a colony was planted in Lucania at the formerly Greek city of Paestum. The Bruttians fared worse and lost a substantial portion of their forest land. Several Greek cities, including Heraclea, Thurii and Metapontum, became allies in 272. The peoples of Apulia and Messapia were also brought into the Roman alliance. In 268 the site of the last battle against Pyrrhus, Malventum became the colony of Beneventum, a more welcoming name.[124] In 269, the Romans once again defeated the Samnites and broke up their confederacy. The area was divided into a number of small units, each of which became Roman allies. Colonies were also founded north of Latium in Etruria. In the far north, as a bulwark against the Gauls, Arminium was founded in 268 on land confiscated from them. By 264 Rome had conquered all of peninsular Italy from where the Apennines curve westward towards the Tyrhennian Sea to the farthest tip of southern Rhegium.

CHAPTER FIVE

A NEW MODEL ARMY I

In the middle of the second century, the Greek soldier and historian Polybius, in an invaluable survey for his Greek readers, describes a Roman army as it probably existed between 220 and 170, although there are some anachronisms and mistakes in his account. The army he portrays is totally different from the Roman army that emerges from the description of the army reform of Servius Tullius.[1] In place of a Greek-style compact phalanx of heavily armed infantry whose main offensive weapon was the heavy thrusting spear, Polybius describes an army organized in what can be called a series of miniature phalanxes.

These miniature phalanxes were known as *manipuli* (singular *manipulus*). One meaning of the term is a sheaf or bundle and the metaphor has its origin in rural life, as would be natural in a society where the vast majority of people were farmers. The basic meaning of the term is 'a handful' and it is derived from the Latin term for hand, *manus*. By the first century, an agricultural explanation for its use was common; the poet Ovid, writing towards the middle of the first century claimed that the term was derived from a standard which consisted of a bundle of hay suspended from a long pole.[2] There is no other evidence for this standard and it seems more likely that the explanation of the term was part of a continuing Roman fixation on rural life and old-fashioned simplicity. The thirty maniples of heavy infantry were deployed in three separate lines of ten maniples each.[3] From front to back they were the *hastati, principes* and *triarii*. The names of the first two lines were troublesome even in antiquity. The ancient writers, including Varro (the greatest of Roman antiquaries writing in the first century), have no idea what the original meaning of these terms was. This would imply that they go back a very long way. The ancient writers seem to assume that the origin of the names lay in soldiers' equipment or age rather than in any tactical reason. The key problem was the fact that the *hastati* were at the front of the battle line, while the *principes* were stationed behind them. The normal assumption would be that, given their title, the *principes* should be the first line. Even more confusing was the fact that the *hastati* derived their name from the *hasta*, which is the normal term used for the heavy thrusting spear retained by the *triarii*.

The most reasonable solution to all of this is to assume that the name of the first line was derived from the weapons they used. *Hasta* was a term with a wider range of meaning than just heavy thrusting spears. It was also used for the javelin of the light-armed troops, the *hasta velitaris,* which was a version of the *pilum* used by the heavy infantry of the legion. Its use can be explained as due to the fact that the *hastati* were the first line to adopt the *pilum,* while the rest of the army retained the older weapons of the phalanx.

The *principes* are a second puzzle. In normal usage, the name should designate troops of the first line since the name means 'leaders' or 'those who come first'. The sources were confused by the name and postulated that somehow the *principes* had originally formed the first line of legion and that there had been a reversal of position for some reason with the *hastati*. Another possibility they suggested was that it meant men at the height of their powers. The problem with this explanation is that the other two lines derive their names from their weapons or their formation, not their physical condition. It has been convincingly suggested that they derive their name from the fact that the army began its evolution from phalanx to the manipular legion, after the *hastati* had made the transition, the *principes* were for a time the first line of the phalanx.[4]

The name of the third line, composed of older men who stood at the rear of the legion, is the easiest to explain. They were known as *triarii* or *pilani*. The title *triarii* was derived from their position as the third line of the legion. They were also known as *pilani* because they were deployed in columns not lines.

The maniples of the first two lines consisted of two centuries, each of 60 men for a total of 120 soldiers, while the two centuries of the third line each contained 30 men, with maniples of 60. The maniples of the two front lines had a rectangular formation like the hoplite phalanx that had preceded them and were armed with javelins and short swords, while the *triarii* of the third line were arranged in column and retained the heavy thrusting spear. These first two lines served as the striking force of the legion, while the older less mobile men of the *triarii* served as a reserve that would anchor the line and would only be used in emergencies. The new formation allowed the Romans to commit their troops in successive lines so that they had a reserve force of fresh troops to use as necessary. The difference that could make is clear from the battle at Sutrium in 311 which the Romans won against the Etruscans. The Etruscans fought in a compact mass – which sounds as if they used a phalanx – and after fighting off the Roman first line, they were defeated by the second line, which had not yet been committed to battle and so was fresh.[5] This army deployment had the advantages of being able to confront the enemy with reserve units. In addition, the maniples were able to operate independently.

The exact deployment of these maniples has been much debated as we have no explicit evidence about it, except for the fact that they were deployed in *quincunx* or chequerboard fashion before contact. The *principes* were deployed to the rear of the first line and between the gaps of the *hastati,* and the maniples of the *triarii* were similarly deployed behind the gaps of the line of the *principes*. Unlike the first two lines, the *triarii* would kneel with their left leg bent, resting their shields on their shoulders with the butt of their spears planted in the ground.[6]

The depth of maniple is uncertain, as is the position of the centuries within the maniple. Arguments have been made for placing the centuries in a maniple behind each other or side-to-side. Republican sources are unhelpful. The Jewish author Josephus in his work on the Jewish War of AD 66–70, in which he fought on the Jewish side, gives an account of the Emperor Vespasian's march into Galilee. He states that the legionaries marched in six columns. Although his description refers to the army of the first century AD, it is suggestive.[7] The maniples of the first two lines consisted of 120 men, so each century would consist of 60 men and would have made the transition from march to line simple, if the century was also 6 men deep. This would make it more likely that the centuries were arrayed side-by-side as too deep a line would be of no benefit for a unit fighting with the short sword. This view also gains some support from Polybius' remark that each maniple had two centurions. The senior commanded the right side of the maniple while the junior commanded on the left. It also seems likely that depth of the unit must have varied greatly depending on a host of variables such as the experience of the troops, the ground and the length of the opposing line. For instance, we know that at Cannae the maniples were formed up to a greater depth than usual and the intervals between them narrowed to give weight to the Roman advance.[8]

Did the deployment of the maniples change as they joined battle with the enemy? Were the gaps between them maintained or did they close up before contact? Although there have been scholars who have supported the view that the line closed up, this seems less likely than that the gaps were maintained when contact was made. First of all, the gaps between the maniples were not as dangerous as they might seem. If the enemy entered the gaps they would be exposed to attack on three sides, by the two adjacent maniples and in front by the maniples of the line behind the one they had penetrated. The troops on the flank of a maniple could turn to face the enemy, while its front line maintained contact with the enemy. Second, how could the maniples of a defeated line have disengaged and deployed behind the following line, if their line had become fused into a single formation? Officers on each side of the maniple would make little sense in the same circumstances. Also such a tactic would have defeated the whole purpose of a flexible manipular formation. It would have been a return to the phalanx at the moment that flexibility mattered the most.

The new tactical formation overcame many of the shortcomings of the phalanx. This comes out clearly in a comparison that Polybius makes between the manipular formation and the Macedonian phalanx. He accepts that in frontal encounters an unbroken phalanx with its projecting line of spears was in contemporary warfare irresistible. Plutarch in his life of Aemilius Paullus, the Roman commander at the battle of Pydna in 168, remarks on the psychological effect of an advancing phalanx:

> *When he (Paullus) saw that the rest of the Macedonian troops also were drawing their shields from their shoulders round in front of them, and with long spears set at one level were withstanding his shield-bearing troops, and saw too the strength of their interlocked shields and the fierceness of their onset, amazement and fear took possession of him, and he felt that he had never seen a sight more fearful; often in after times he used to speak of his emotions at that time and of what he saw.*[9]

After the battle Polybius provides an analysis of the advantages of the manipular formation over the phalanx.[10] It is significant that in all of the major encounters between phalanx and manipular legion the legion prevailed.

Paullus' reaction is hardly surprising. As developed by the Macedonians the phalanx had become a much more effective killing machine. In place of the 2.4 metre spear of the classical phalanx Philip II, Alexander's father, had introduced a much longer 4.8 metre pike known as the *sarissa,* which by the mid-second century was 6.4 metres long. This meant – as Polybius points out – that instead of the two or perhaps three spear points projecting from the shield wall of the phalanx, five spear points now confronted the attacker. Those behind the first five lines held their spears at a 45-degree angle to serve as protection against missile weapons and their pressure and solidity gave both weight and stability to the front line

But the phalanx is best suited for battle in a flat unbroken plain with few natural obstacles. The cohesiveness of the formation was vital to success on the battlefield, but Hellenistic armies were more flexible than Polybius implies. They fought in sections, as had the Greek armies before them. It was possible to lose on one wing and still win a battle.

Polybius overemphasizes the limitations of the phalanx. It fought successfully against a variety of peoples, often in irregular formations in a varied topography under Philip, and again under his son Alexander. The same was true of the armies of the Hellenistic kingdoms that arose after Alexander's death. Nevertheless, overall Polybius' analysis is correct. Given its equipment and formation, the phalanx had difficulty in responding to threats to its flanks and rear. In fact, it was the battle of Cynoscephalae in 197 that inspired this digression. An attack by the Macedonian phalanx's right wing during the battle forced the Roman line back, but the phalanx's left could not deploy properly and was thrown into confusion by Roman elephants. A military tribune detached twenty maniples from the Roman right and managed to march them behind the Macedonian line attack its rear.[11] This completed the rout of the enemy, and is a testimony to the flexibility of the Roman formation. Polybius stresses the Roman use of reserves because of the three lines. He also correctly emphasizes the maniples' ability to quickly adjust to threats from any direction and to launch attacks in any direction. One other problem should be mentioned in connection with the phalanx, especially when facing the Roman armies: if an opening could be forced in the wall of pikes, the Roman short sword could be used for close hand-to-hand combat far more effectively than Greek weapons could be used.

It is also important to realize that the three-line deployment on the battlefield was not rigid, and in the hands of a talented commander like Scipio Africanus, the flexibility of the manipular legion could be used to advantage. In 202, Scipio Africanus faced Hannibal at Zama, near Carthage, in the last battle of the Second Punic War. To counter Hannibal's 120 elephants, Scipio rearranged his maniples so that they were positioned one behind the other rather than deployed in the normal chequerboard fashion. The light-armed troops were stationed in the gaps between the maniples of the *hastati*. They were to bombard the elephants with their javelins; if they were forced back, they were to withdraw down the corridors or move to the side. In either case they were to continue throwing their missiles.[12] The tactic worked so well that eventually the elephants were driven back on the Carthaginians and wreaked havoc in their ranks. Later in the battle Scipio was able to reorganize his forces. He brought up the *principes* and the *triarii* into a single line with the *hastati* so as to match the length of Hannibal's front.[13] A commander of genius – like Scipio – illustrates the potential that the manipular formation possessed. Even in less capable hands, the standard deployment was capable of defeating most opponents. This is not to say that the Romans did not suffer a number of defeats. There are ninety-four known defeats during the Republic over a 500 year period.[14] Probably many more have been reworked as victories by Roman writers or are simply absent from our sources. It was not a foolproof formula but it worked most of the time.

It has recently been argued that it was not only the practical advantages of the manipular formation that led to its adoption by the Romans, but also its suitability to Roman male ideology. The most important quality a Roman male could display was his *virtus*, which is the origin of the English word 'virtue' but carried a very different meaning.[15] It is best translated as 'manliness', in the sense it denotes that conduct which characterizes ideal masculine behaviour.[16] *Virtus* was a broad enough concept to indicate two types of courage: the ability to display an unfaltering endurance, and a fierce aggression. Both were admired by the Romans, although aggression tended to be more highly valued. An early second century song of a wife expressing the importance to her of her husband's *virtus* points to an enduring Roman attitude:

> I want my man to be cried as a victor in war: that's enough for me.
> Virtus *is the greatest prize;* virtus *comes before everything, that's*

certain: liberty, safety, life, property and parents, homeland and children it guards and keeps safe. Virtus *has everything in it: who has* virtus *has everything good.*[17]

This supposition that Roman tactical dispositions mirrored a cultural belli-cosity rests on no evidence aside from Roman values and the open nature of the manipular system as opposed to the phalanx. However, if one looks at the image of the warrior king that pervades the ideology of the Greek kingdoms of the eastern Mediterranean, it is clear that the essence of king-ship was military victory.[18] Rome was not a special case. The emphasis on the *virtus* of common soldiers does seem especially Roman, but it is likely to have been due to the fact that Rome retained a citizen army and the Greek kingdoms made widespread use of mercenaries.[19] The circumstance that the system endured with modifications into the Imperial period has been used as further support for its moral and emotional fit with Roman morals and the achievement of status in Roman society. It seems more likely that the continued use of this formation had more to do with its effectiveness than its moral usefulness.

There was some recognition of the effectiveness of the Roman style of fighting in the Greek east. It has been argued that in the 160s both the Ptolemaic and Seleucid armies became Romanized, but the evi-dence for wholesale adoption of Roman equipment is very poor.[20] The best evidence is for the Ptolemaic army where there is an indication of administrative changes along Roman lines. It seems that there was Roman influence, but not a wholesale adoption of Roman equipment or fighting techniques.

As noted above, the change in tactical deployment was accompanied by a change in defensive and offensive armament. The circular hoplite shield (*clipeus*) placed a premium on protection.[21] Its peculiar grasping mecha-nism eased the problem of holding a heavy shield for long hours by dis-tributing the shield's weight along the length of the arm, and its convex design allowed the shield to be rested on the shoulder. However, it was not well suited for use outside the phalanx where the fighter's right side could be protected by the shield of the soldier to his right. Without that protec-tion, turning to face an enemy attacking from the right meant pivoting the whole of your body in that direction or awkwardly twisting to face a sud-den blow. Such a shield was unsuitable for the more open style of combat that the new formation required.[22]

The standard shield of the manipular legion during the Republic was an oval, convex shield, the *scutum,* held by a central handgrip. It seems to have descended from an old Italic shield type, first attested in Etruscan art in the mid-eighth century that spread throughout most of peninsular Italy. It seems to have passed through a series of shape changes begin-ning as circular, then leaf-shaped, and finally developing into the oval form used by Roman legionaries of the Republic. It also appears in the Celtic world as early as the fifth century. The shield's face had a *spina* or spine down the centre of the shield, and a central boss or *umbo* to protect the handgrip. There are some representations of the shield from the Republican period. There is a painting from a tomb on the Esquiline Hill in Rome dating from the late third or early second century. Part of the frieze shows a Marcus Fannius, perhaps the owner of the tomb, receiving something from the hand of a Q. Fabius. Right above this scene is a figure similar to Fannius. The figure has greaves, a loincloth and a cloak as well as an oval *scutum* and a plumed helmet.[23] The shield also appears on a monument, dedicated at Delphi by Aemilius Paullus to celebrate his victory over the Macedonian king Perseus at Pydna, in Thessaly, in 168. The third is an altar at Rome dedicated by Gaius Domitius Ahenobarbus in the late second or early first century. Given the perishable material from which shields were made, only one example has survived from antiquity. It is from the small town of Kasr el-Harit in the Fayum area in western Egypt. The date of the shield is uncertain and it may be as late as the reign of the Emperor Augustus at the end of the first century and the beginning of the first century AD, when the legions switched to a rectangular shield shape. It is 1.3 metres long and about 64cm wide. It is made of three laminated layers of birch planks. A central vertical layer was sandwiched between two horizontal layers and the layers were then glued together and covered with a layer of wool felt. It has a boss and spine, but they are made of wood not metal. The metal rim, which helped strengthen the shield against slashing blows, is also absent. The handgrip is horizontal rather than vertical. A reconstruction weighed 10kg, which is heavier than the round shield, but there is compensation in the fact that it would be considerably more useful in open formations as well as providing enhanced protection to compensate for the absence of a cuirass. It has been suggested that it was balanced against the shoulder during a charge and rested on the ground during close combat, functioning as a sort of wall.[24] The shield could also be used to bludgeon the enemy, as Livy makes clear in what seems to be a highly rhetorical but plausible description of a battle with the Umbrians in 308 during the Second Samnite War:

> *Whenever the fighting flared up the contest was fought not with swords, but with shields. The enemy was brought down by blows from the bosses of their shields...*[25]

The legionary also had additional protective equipment including a helmet, chest protector, and a single greave worn on the left leg. There is no definite evidence as to which helmet was used. The most common type in Italy and with examples from the fourth to the first century is a type known as the Montefortino, named after a town in east central Italy where the first example was discovered. The frequency of the finds and the obvious similarity to later known Roman helmets makes it a likely candidate to be the standard helmet of this period. It belongs to a large class of helmets resembling jockey caps with various additions, which were common in the Roman army of the Imperial period. All of these helmets are made of a bowl-shaped metal cap with neck guards at the back of the helmet. The neck guard increased in size over time, which is no doubt a result of the stooped stance the Romans used in battle. The bowl was of beaten copper and it frequently had a knob at the apex of the helmet so that feathers or a crest could be attached. Polybius mentions that the Romans used black or purple feathers. The feathers would have added height to the soldier, making him more impressive to the enemy and would also have aided in identifying him in the field.

The early models had triple-disk shape detachable cheek pieces, which were replaced by scallop-shaped cheek pieces in the third century. As was the case with all ancient helmets it had a liner. It seems to have been of Celtic origin, as is the case for some other pieces of Roman military equipment, such as mail. The helmets of the Montefortino type can be found in fifth century Celtic cemeteries in France and Austria. The Etruscans, who had close and unpleasant contact with the Celts, were probably the first to adopt the helmet. A tomb of an Etruscan warrior in Orvieto, of the first half of the fourth century, contained a hoplite shield, greaves, muscled cuirass, and a Montefortino helmet. The type then spread south.[26] It offered a reasonable level of protection and it was relatively cheap to produce.[27]

The construction of the Montefortino helmet gradually declined in quality over the course of the second century. Expansion into the Celtic world of continental Europe introduced other new helmet types. Instead of the copper construction of the Montefortino, new helmet types constructed of iron were introduced. The Montefortino was eventually superseded by the Coolus type which also had a Celtic origin, differing only in absence of an integral top knot. Its absence simplified the manufacturing process. The Coolus helmets also underwent changes, including a wider brim, the enlargement of the back peak and the addition of a brow peak. Two new types of helmets appear in the first century – the Agen and Port – which were also of iron construction. The Agen had a bulging cap with an oval profile and a brim, while the Port type had a similar bowl shape with a substantial neck guard riveted on.[28]

The *scutum* was supplemented by protection for the chest. Polybius mentions a chest protector, the *kardiophylax* ('heart guard') which in his time was a bronze plate covering and protecting the heart, which he states was 23cm square. It was worn over a linen tunic and its light weight must have made movement easier. The heart protector had a long history in Italy. The earliest evidence for it appears around 700 in Etruria. Its form varied with time and place, and it is found not only in Italy, but also Corsica,

Spain and southern France. It was often disk-shaped with either a single, double or triple disk configuration. Infantry with the highest rating were required to wear ring mail shirts, which of course offered superior protection.[29] All were attached by a strap or metal bands which were drawn over the shoulders and attached to a corresponding back plate. The higher standard of equipment was the result of the individual soldier supplying his own equipment until the first century.

In their descriptions of the manipular army, Livy and Polybius mention that the Roman legionary was protected by a greave or shin protector.[30] The greave had a long history in Greek hoplite warfare and was introduced into Italy with the rest of the hoplite panoply. It seems to have become popular in Etruria and central Italy during the sixth century. In both Greece and Italy there was a general replacement of the snap-on greave with greaves attached to the leg by laces. It is likely that the use of laces reduced the cost of the greaves because they did not have to exactly match the contours of the wearer's legs. Unlike the Greeks, the Roman soldier customarily wore only a single greave on his left shin. It was worn on that leg because it was extended forward in combat and so vulnerable to the enemy. They ceased being used in early first century.[31]

The legionary's offensive weapons consisted of a javelin and a short sword. Polybius provides the most detailed description of the javelin or *pilum*. As was the case with his earlier description of defensive equipment, his detailed account of Roman equipment is very unusual for an ancient historian. Such descriptions were usually left to technical manuals or antiquarian writers, while historians shied away from them as unsuited to the rhetorical rules of historical composition. This is not a universal rule, however, as the descriptions of the Servian army in Livy and Dionysius show. In fact, Livy does provide a detailed – if incorrect – description of the manipular legion in battle. Nonetheless, these passages are rare, and they seem to have been copied from some technical or antiquarian source. Although Livy and others writers project the use of the *pilum* into the regal period, this is unhistorical. It seems to be part of the general tendency to project back the manipular army into the earliest period of Roman history.

Polybius' material can be supplemented by archaeological finds at Telamon and Vulci in Etruria as well as the mid-second century Roman camps in Spain, especially at Numantia (near the modern city of Soria) and nearby Renieblas. The basic meaning of the word *pilum* is a pestle for grinding.

The *pilum* is basically a mass-produced javelin and the name was applied to various missile weapons. The *pilum* or a similar weapon must have been introduced in conjunction with manipular tactics. The weapon is of Italian origin and examples of similar weapons have been found in Italy dating from as early as the ninth century. The sources give various accounts of its origin, attributing it to the Samnites, Spanish tribes, Celts and Etruscans.

The strongest evidence is for a Spanish origin of a modified javelin type, but this is likely to have been a change in design and not a new weapon. The Romans were not active in Spain before the late third century; this is simply too late for the Spanish version to have been the original weapon of the manipular legion, which seems to have had its origin in the course of the fourth century. The first secure reference to its use by Roman forces is at the battle of Panormus in 251, against the Carthaginians during the First Punic War. This predates Roman involvement in Spain.[32] But it could well have been borrowed from the Spanish mercenaries that the Romans encountered during the First Punic War. It continued to be used in the Imperial period.

Polybius describes two variations of the *pilum,* a heavy and a light, saying that the troops carried both into battle. The heavier *pilum* weighed 4.5kg and the lighter 2kg. Polybius describes the iron head of the *pilum* as barbed, but various finds show that a pyramid-shaped head was also used. The wooden shafts were about 1.38 metres long while the head and its metal shaft were about the same length. The shaft of the metal head was driven into the wood for about half of its length and then riveted in place. This gave an overall length for both *pila* of approximately 2 metres, approximately the same length as a Greek hoplite spear. The finds, especially Spanish ones, indicate a much more varied construction. The shank of the head varies considerably in size, as does the head itself. Tangs range from 23cm to 1 metre in length. The lighter variety was usually socketed while the heavier was attached by the tang. In both cases the overall length of the weapon varied considerably, and Polybius gives an inaccurate impression of uniformity. The join was reinforced by rivets; Polybius stresses the strength of the join claiming that the metal would break before wood and metal separated.

There has been some debate about the existence and nature of the heavy *pilum.* Some reconstructions yield a weight of 9kg, which would have made it impossible to throw effectively. The best solution proposed is a tapering of the shank which could reduce the weight to 4.5kg. The best evidence for its effectiveness was its continued use in Imperial times.

The finds indicate that the *pilum* had a tendency to bend on impact making it impractical for the enemy to simply throw it back. One of the reforms attributed to the Roman general Marius was to reinforce this tendency by removing one of the metal rivets and replacing it with wooden rivets to make sure that the javelin would bend on impact.[33] But accounts of fighting after Marius mention the enemy returning them, so the date of this change must remain uncertain. A further reform in the *pilum* has been ascribed to Caesar, who supposedly left the metal shank untampered so that it would more easily bend on impact. There is absolutely no evidence for this.

The *pilum* had excellent penetrating power and the lighter *pilum* probably had a range of approximately 25–30 metres. The range of the heavy *pilum* would probably have been less than half that distance. The *pilum* was a substitute for other missile weapons. It was not until the mid-third century that the Romans used specialist troops such as archers from Crete and slingers from the Balearic Islands or Rhodes. Those types of weapons required lengthy training and a supporting cultural tradition. The *pilum* and other types of javelins required far less training and skill, and were far easier and cheaper to make.

There are few references to the use of the *pilum* in battle. The majority of references are simply to the fact that they were thrown before the Romans closed with the enemy. Caesar's account of the Gallic War and the Civil War provide the best evidence for its use and there is no reason to think there had been any substantial change in use over the centuries. But even Caesar's evidence is limited. He does not differentiate between the use of the light and heavy *pila* nor how the legionaries were deployed for their use.

Polybius implies that two *pila* were carried into battle by the *hastati* and *principes,* presumably one heavy and the other light. The prolonged exchange of missiles reported at some battles supports the idea that the soldier carried both and on occasion perhaps additional *pila*. At the decisive battle between Scipio Africanus and Hannibal at Zama in Carthaginian territory in 202, Livy mentions that Hannibal's elephants were subjected to a prolong bombardment by the Roman light-armed troops, and the *hastati* and *principes*.[34]

Given the short range of the *pila* they must have been thrown only as the formation closed with the enemy. It also must have been done in open order to provide room for each soldier to throw. After the release of the *pila* the maniple must have closed up for swordplay. This would still have allowed the line to build up some impetus before contact with the enemy. The *pilum* had significant penetrating power, which could be effective in disrupting a dense enemy formation. The effect of the *pilum* as a missile weapon is clear from a passage of Caesar's Gallic War describing a battle with the Celtic tribe of the Helvetii in 58:[35]

> *The soldiers from their elevated position easily broke the enemy phalanx by the discharge of their* pila. *After the enemy formation had been broken up, they drew their swords and attacked. The Gauls were severely hindered because the* pila *had passed through their shields and locked them together. When they bent the shanks they could not easily pull them out or easily fight with their left arms weighed down.*

Pila could also be used as thrusting weapons. In 48, at the battle of Pharsalus between Caesar and Pompey during the civil war, *pila* were used to attack cavalry. Caesar with a smaller cavalry force instructed some of his infantry to guard against a flanking attack by Pompey's cavalry by using their *pila* as heavy thrusting spears, thrusting at both the horses and their riders.[36]

Until about 120, the *triarii* retained a heavy thrusting spear as their main armament, presumably the same one that had been used by the phalanx. Parallel to Greek models, the spear had a spiked butt useful for planting the spear and as a secondary weapon if the point was broken off. The reason for its retention is not clear. The change after 120 does not seem to have made much difference. However, that change occurred in a very different army than the one of the middle Republic. In Polybius' period the *triarii* were composed of the oldest men. Given their age, they would not have had the physical stamina to meet the punishing demands that sword fighting required. It was easier to wield thrusting spears. They were the last ditch defence of the legion. Livy mentions that, if the first two lines failed, they would fall back behind the *triarii* who would close up and push forward as a phalanx. He cites the saying 'as far as the *triarii*' to mean that things were going badly.[37]

The most important offensive weapon of the manipular legion was the short, thrusting sword. The fullest description is again Polybius'. He comments on the strength of the blade and its suitability for use as both a stabbing and slashing weapon. He mentions that it was known as the 'Spanish sword'. This had led most scholars to assume that it was adopted during the First Punic War or Second Punic War when Rome came into contact with Celtiberian and other Spanish mercenaries. The second war is more likely as it saw extensive fighting in Spain. However, there is some evidence that the Romans were using what appears to be the same sword in the 220s, so it is possible it was taken over during the first conflict.

Until the last thirty years the evidence has been limited to sculpture and painting. However, examples have now turned up. One comes from the island of Delos in the central Aegean and probably dates to the sack of the island by pirates in 69. The other is of either late second or early first century date. They are similar to each other with a blade measuring about 76–78 cm long, with two parallel cutting edges. The blade is 5cm wide and has a sharp point. More than twenty examples in total have now been found at sites in Spain, France, Switzerland, Algeria and Israel. They are all about the same size as the two earlier examples. They are identical in form except that some have a slight inward curve near the hilt, which would have been made of bone or wood.[38] Found with the Delos sword were the remains of a charred wooden pommel and scabbard as well as suspension rings and buckles.[39] Normally the sword was worn on the right thigh. This type of sword remained in use until the mid-first century AD.

There is less certainty about the short sword in use before the adoption of the Spanish type. It was probably similar to the Etruscan short sword, which was made of iron and is related to types found in Greece.

In his description of the equipment of the legionary, Polybius strangely omits any mention of the dagger. It had a long history of use in Italy and was used by the legionaries in the Imperial period. Specimens have been found in second century camps in Spain. They are 15–20cm long with a central midrib and a waisted blade with a bulbous handle. Given their obvious uses in camp life as well as in battle, Polybius' silence is surprising. It may be that he was describing the normal kit of the soldier and daggers were brought along as personal items. Their appearance in the Imperial period may be the result of the increasing standardization of military equipment after the Emperor Augustus created a professional force. The dagger's origins may also lie in Spain. The well-known gravestone of a centurion found at Padua in northeastern Italy does have a representation of the centurion wearing a dagger. It is worn horizontally on his belt instead of in the normal fashion hanging from his right side. The gravestone has been dated to 43–42, but the date is not absolutely secure. It has been suggested that daggers were worn perhaps only by officers, but again this seems unlikely. If using a dagger was a personal choice, this would explain its presence.[40]

Fighting with a sword required far more training than with a heavy thrusting spear. There must have been a relatively prolonged training and we know the Romans did go to considerable trouble to train their troops in the Imperial period. We do have examples of overall weapons training, and more specifically of training with the sword during the Republic. It is important to bear in mind that most soldiers came from a rural background and their upbringing would have included work that would have kept them in good physical condition. The use of tools in civilian life for farm work would have helped to prepare them for the use of the weapons they would use in the military. There is no clear evidence for fixed courses of training. The duration and extent of the training depended on the commander's wishes. The training was carried out under the supervision of the military tribunes and centurions. What is clear is that training was regarded as an important activity. In 193, one of the consuls, Minucius Thermus, campaigning in Liguria in northwestern Italy, refused battle because his troops were newly recruited and had not had the time to be properly trained. The best evidence we have for some sort of fixed course of training is that Roman practice was known outside of Italy and admired. In 213, the Numidian king Syphax asked the Romans to provide him with a trainer. The Roman centurion Quintus Statorius was sent. The description provided by Livy gives us some idea of the content of this training:

> *Statorius conscripted the infantry from the abundant Numidian manpower and organized them as close as he could on the Roman model, teaching them to follow the standards in forming up as well as executing military drills and so accustoming them to fortifying and other normal military tasks that in a short time the king had equal confidence in his horse and foot.*[41]

The most detailed account we have is that of Scipio Africanus' method after his capture of New Carthage in Spain from the Carthaginians in 209.[42] He used the same procedures again on the eve of his invasion of North Africa in 205:

> *Remaining for some time at New Carthage [Scipio] constantly exercised his naval forces and gave the following instructions to the tribunes about the training of the army. On the first day, he ordered the soldiers to march three and one-half miles at the double carrying their arms. On the second day, he ordered them to polish, repair and examine their equipment in public. Then, on the following day, they were to stop working and rest. On the next day, some were to practice sword fighting with swords made of wood, covered in leather and with a button over the point, while others were to practice javelin-throwing with javelins which also had a button covering their points. On the fifth day they were to repeat the same set of exercises.*

A reform in training methods took place, probably in 105 or a little later. The consul P. Rutilius Rufus, facing a strong German enemy, introduced weapons instruction based on the practice of the gladiatorial schools.[43] Interestingly, gladiators were not especially effective on the battlefield.

The use of the sword had to be coordinated with the large heavy shield that the soldier carried into battle. This would have required fairly extensive space and Polybius claims that when hand-to-hand combat took place the maniple opened allowing each soldier a frontage of 1.8 metres. In comparison, the Greek and Hellenistic phalanxes closed up when engaging the enemy so that each hoplite stood 0.5 metres from the men on either side.[44] As contact was made, there must have been pushing and bashing with the shield. The men must then have stepped back so they would have enough space to use their swords.[45] The ideal Roman stance in sword fighting was for the legionary to stand sideways to the enemy, crouching behind his shield with his left foot forward, thus presenting the smallest target. The crouching position made the neck guard all the more important to protect against downward slashing blows. Although the short sword was capable of slashing, it was designed to stab at the enemy, which was considered more likely to deliver a fatal blow.[46]

In addition to the 3,000 heavy infantry, the manipular legion also included 1,200 light infantry drawn from those who did not meet the minimum census requirement to serve as heavy infantry; the lowest census class could not afford the more expensive equipment of the heavy infantry. This use of poorer citizens as light-armed troops was also the case in Greek armies. Again, it is important to stress that these figures are the paper strength of the legion. In the field, unless a special levy was held, the legions were probably far below this strength. At Pharsalus, in the confrontation between Caesar and Pompey in August 48, Caesar had an average legionary strength of 2,750 men.[47]

The name *velites,* which is probably derived from the Latin adjective *velox* ('swift'), is first attested in 211, although there were clearly light-armed troops in the Servian army. Other terms were used for such troops, although their meanings are not totally certain.[48] It is probable that they were known as *rorarii* (singular *rorarius*). The new title may be connected to a lowering of the census rating for legionary service, so a new term might have been thought appropriate.

Forty velites were assigned to each maniple according to Polybius.[49] However, this must have been only for administrative purposes. In battle narratives they operate separately from the heavy infantry, usually opening the battle as skirmishers to screen the deployment of the heavy infantry. If they were unsuccessful in dispersing the enemy's light-armed troops, they withdrew through the gaps in the maniples to the flanks of the army, to where the cavalry was normally stationed; from the mid-third century they often operated closely with the cavalry.[50] Strangely, the sources do not mention a commander of these troops, but one or several of the legionary centurions or their subordinates probably did so. For the most part, as was the case in Greek armies, they were not decisive on the battlefield. It was only when the enemy broke and pursuit began that their light equipment became an advantage.

Polybius describes the equipment of the light-armed troops:

> The youngest men are instructed to carry a sword, javelins and a round shield called the parma. The parma is strongly made and is of sufficient size to provide protection. It is round and three feet in diameter. They also wear an unadorned helmet and sometimes they cover it with a wolf-skin or something similar. They wear the skin to provide protection and as a distinguishing emblem so that those who energetically take risks on the battlefield are conspicuous. Their javelin has a wooden shaft three feet long and two inches wide. The head is four inches long and hammered out to such a fine point that is bent by its first impact and cannot be thrown back by the enemy.[51]

The main offensive weapon of the *velites* was the *hasta velitaris*. It had a shaft about one metre long, and a head 25–30 cm in length, designed to pierce shield and body protection. The *hasta velitaris* was similar to the light *pilum* of the heavy infantry; its development may have been influenced by Celtic or Samnite models. Livy claims that the *velites* carried seven of them into battle. There must have been some means of resupply, because we hear of repeated discharges of the missiles during battle. But the sources provide no information on this point. The *hasta velitaris* had an effective range of 40 metres and a maximum range of over 50 metres. There may have been a variant of the *hasta velitaris* which had a strap attached as a spear thrower to increase the distance of the throw.[52] Other types of missile weapons were also used by these troops; the sources mention the *gaesum* and the *verutum,* but we know little about them.

The round shield or *parma* was also employed by the cavalry. We have only literary descriptions and pictorial representations of it, as no actual examples have survived. Most likely it was made of a light material, wood or perhaps plaited willow branches, and covered with skin or felt. The *galea,* an unadorned helmet, may have been a leather or felt cap which would have been considerably cheaper to buy than the metal helmets of the heavy infantry. The use of a wolf skin covering on the helmet probably had more to do with telling Roman troops apart from the enemy rather than with marking out individuals for bravery.

The *velites* also carried a sword. It was the same Spanish sword as the one carried by the heavy infantry. Livy mentions the *velites* engaging the Macedonian light-armed troops in 199 during the Second Macedonian War.[53] They discharged their javelins and then closed with the enemy. It is only on rare occasions that the sources mention the *velites* engaging the enemy this way. It is hard to say anything more about their fighting methods. It has been claimed that they fought in a swarm.[54] However, swarms of men make excellent missile targets and so it seems more likely that they fought in an open order to take advantage of their speed.

The cavalry, as in all pre-modern armies, remained the preserve of the rich and well connected. Cavalrymen had to complete ten years' service to fulfill their military obligation and no-one could hold political office if they had not done so.[55] Such service reinforced the tie between military service and political standing and served as powerful incentive for the elite. After the war with Veii, the cavalry was expanded. It was now divided between those whose horses were granted by the state and those who paid for their own mounts.[56]

There were three hundred citizen cavalry in each legion. The cavalry was organized in squadrons called *turmae.* These in turn were divided into three units of ten men consisting of eight troopers and two officers. The officers were the *decurion,* who commanded the unit as a whole, and the *optio,* who acted as a second-in-command. One of the *decurions* commanded the *turma* as a whole.

Polybius provides a description of the cavalry's military equipment:

> *The equipment of the cavalry is now quite close to that of Greek cavalry. Earlier, they did not wear cuirasses, but went into battle without protection. That allowed them to dismount and mount quickly and effectively; but they were at risk in close encounters because they went unarmoured. Their lances were not useful to them for two reasons, they were thin and easily broken. Thus, they could not even be aimed and before they could fix the point of the lance in anyone, the weapons most often broke*

of themselves because of their own horse's movement. In addition, they were without butt-spikes and could be used to deliver only one blow with the point head of the lance. After their heads had been broken they were useless. They carried a shield made from ox-hide, in shape similar to the round bossed cakes that are used in sacrifices. They were of no use in attack because they lacked sufficient firmness. They peeled in the rain and rotted and, as unserviceable as they were before, they became at this point totally useless. Since the shields were shown by experience to be useless, they quickly adopted Greek cavalry equipment. The first blow of the lance head now became well-aimed and effective because the weapon was made to be both steady and strong; likewise, the additional use of the butt-spike was strong and forceful. It was the same story with the Greek shields which were well made and were constructed for effective use in attack and assault.[57]

Unfortunately, we cannot supplement or check Polybius' description of cavalry equipment as there is almost no archaeological evidence for it. However, given the general accuracy of Polybius's other accounts of Roman equipment, it seems reasonable to accept the overall accuracy of his description. His enumeration of the cavalry's armament before the change implies that it was a light – not a heavy – cavalry. The change to Greek equipment seems to mark the transition to a heavier cavalry. Unfortunately, Polybius does not specify the date when the change was made. Various dates have been proposed either during the Second Punic War or in the half-century following it. The Second Punic War seems a more likely period. As the Romans faced large and highly trained cavalry forces that inflicted a string of defeats on them, these may have served as a catalyst. The monument set up at Delphi by Aemilius Paullus, the Roman commander, to commemorate his victory over the Macedonian king Perseus, shows Roman cavalry wearing mail cuirasses.[58]

Greek cavalry of this period normally wore open-faced helmets, cuirasses, boots and occasionally a leather apron as thigh protection. It is probable, given the wealth of its members, that they wore the same mail corselet worn by the highest class of the infantry. Whether shields were used is uncertain. Earlier Greek treatises on cavalry recommended against its use because the writers felt it would impede the rider; apparently, this changed as Polybius claims it was normally carried. Certainly the Roman cavalry of this period did carry a shield about one metre in diameter. It was essentially a larger version of the round *parma* that the *velites* carried.

Surprisingly, there is no mention of a sword in Polybius's description. It is a strange omission. Contemporary Hellenistic Greek cavalry had it. Moreover, there was a long tradition among the Roman cavalry of dismounting to engage in sword fighting. We also know that Roman cavalry in the Imperial period employed the sword and that it was a normal part of the cavalryman's armament.[59] It is probable that the omission of a sword was mere inadvertence on Polybius' part.

The horse from which Greek and Roman cavalrymen fought was smaller than the massive warhorse of the medieval period. Size was not crucial. It was the horse's carrying capacity and endurance that really mattered. Smaller sizes could be advantageous, as small horses needed less food. It is interesting to note that in the nineteenth century wars between the American government and the tribes of the western plains, the smaller, sturdier horses of the Plains Indians had a decided advantage over the large thoroughbreds that the US cavalry took pride in and refused to abandon. As Bruce Vandervort notes:

> *If the US cavalry had been fighting a European enemy, the horses it prized so much might have done nicely, but warfare on the plains or in the mountains of the West was a different proposition. In that setting, the premium was on endurance, the capacity to cover a lot of ground and keep on doing it day after day, in pursuit of an elusive foe, and the 'American' horses the cavalry took such pride in lacked that kind of stamina.[60]*

The advantage in speed that a larger horse might have had was not a significant advantage. Ancient cavalry did not collide with other cavalry or infantry although accidents did, of course, happen. Horses will not crash into solid objects such as another horse or an infantryman. If heavy infantry kept their formation they could not be ridden down by a frontal attack. In cavalry fights, wheeling or formations opening to ride through each other were normal. The lack of effectiveness against formed up heavy infantry in most situations was a severe limitation.

The absence of stirrups also limited the ability of ancient cavalry to serve as shock cavalry. They seem to have been invented in India sometime during the last two centuries BC. However, they did not reach eastern Europe until around AD 600, and western Europe until the eighth century.[61] This is not to say that cavalry could not effectively wield their swords in the absence of stirrups, but it did make it more difficult as it meant that the horse had to be controlled with the rider's lower legs.[62]

A recent examination of the Roman cavalry saddle of the Imperial period has shown that by the first century AD, Roman cavalry were capable of using shock tactics. Since our evidence for cavalry equipment prior to the first century AD is almost nonexistent, there is no proof that the army of the Republican period used such a saddle. Greek cavalry did not. The Aemilius Paullus monument mentioned earlier shows cavalry operating without saddles, so the use of shock tactics must have been more limited. This may explain the preference for dismounting to fight. An example of this Roman practice is the cavalry encounter at the battle of Asculum against Pyrrhus in 279:

> *The cavalry of both armies was stationed on the wings and aware of those*
> *tactics in which they were superior to the enemy, they resorted to them.*
> *The Romans turned to hand-to-hand stationary fighting, while the Greeks*
> *to wheeling and flanking movements. When the Romans were pursued by*
> *the Greeks, the Romans wheeled their horses about, and reining them in*
> *would fight on foot. But the Greeks, when they saw the Romans turning*
> *to the right and wheeling through their own ranks, turned their horses to*
> *the front and applying their spurs charged the enemy.*[63]

In both Greek and Roman armies, cavalry were usually posted on the heavy infantry's wings. Their most frequent use was to drive off the enemy's cavalry and uncover the flanks of his infantry. This is exactly what happened at Cannae in 216, and again in the climactic battle against Hannibal at Zama in 202. They were used as a screen for the deployment of the infantry and to guard the army's flanks while marching. They were also employed on foraging parties and for scouting, although both Greek and Roman armies seem to have neglected scouting to a surprising degree. Once the enemy broke, the cavalry and light-armed infantry were extremely effective in pursuit.

The timing and the stages that marked the change from the phalanx to the manipular legion are absent from the historical record. The historians depict the manipular army of the middle Republic for all prior periods, even though at least some knew that the army had once been differently organized. This may be the result of the late development of history writing at Rome, which did not begin until the end of the third century. Basically, the army historians depict the army of Rome's first historian Fabius Pictor, who served in it and described it. Why the tradition ossified around this army is unknowable. The most that can be said is that it was this army that made possible the great victories against Carthage and Rome's expansion around the eastern Mediterranean and so must have enjoyed tremendous prestige. The references to earlier stages derived from antiquarian rather than historical tradition, as in the case of the Servian army. That tradition has left traces in our sources that do indicate an awareness of changes outside those found in historians' works.

The first is a fragment of a Greek text by an unknown author, now called *Ineditum Vaticanum,* which is quoted in two other writers.[64] It is from part of a work designed to illustrate a variety of maxims and adages and probably dates to the late first or second century AD on the basis of its language. The excerpt forms part of a description of a meeting between a Roman envoy called Kaeso and an unknown Carthaginian at the opening of the First Punic War in 264. Its basic theme – which seems to have been commonplace in Greek writing – was that as the Romans encountered new enemies, they were able to adopt the enemy's weapons and tactics and beat them at their own game.[65]

The Romans were well aware that borrowing, particularly from the Greeks in literary and artistic matters, had played a vital role in their culture. In these areas there tended to be imitation not competition. In the military sphere, which the Romans saw as particularly their own, competition was a natural attitude. The Roman Kaeso makes the argument that, even though the Carthaginians are supreme on the sea, the Romans will imitate and surpass them. As examples he cites Rome's adoption of the phalanx and hoplite equipment from the Etruscans, who were then defeated by the Romans fighting in the same way. He also claims that the Romans adopted Samnite equipment and cavalry techniques and then defeated them as well. Kaeso concludes, 'By emulating foreign arms we made subject to ourselves those who had a very high regard for themselves.'

The first century Roman historian Sallust also claims a Samnite origin for Roman equipment.[66] The same can be said of the *Ineditum Vaticanum*. The Romans did indeed borrow foreign equipment when they felt it was more effective. How the borrowing took place is not clear since each soldier equipped himself until the late second century. Also, we know little about Samnite military equipment. There have been finds of it and paintings of what seem to be Samnite warriors. The Samnites used metal helmets and the *kardiophylax* as the Romans did. They seem to have favoured a three-disk version. In addition, they are often shown with a broad leather belt covered with bronze, which must have served to protect their midsection. No shields have been found. It seems likely that they did carry a form of *scutum*, oval in shape, though Samnites are more frequently represented with a round shield and with helmet forms that seem to be based on Greek models with crests.[67] There is also evidence for the use of greaves, and some pictorial evidence for the use of hoplite equipment, but it is likely that given its expense this was confined to a small elite. Paintings confirm a variety of spearhead types, but there are no known representations of swords. However, they must have used one. There may indeed have been some borrowing, although the standard nature of these weapons and the regional variations in military equipment in Italy before its unification at the hands of the Romans tells against this. Of some significance is the fact that the Servian army already included soldiers armed with javelins among the light-armed soldiers and shields that the sources identify as a *scutum*. Except for the shield, manipular heavy equipment bears a strong resemblance to equipment of the light-armed troops of the Servian army. The Spanish sword provides an example of what might have happened. Basic native Roman equipment may have been influenced by comparable equipment found among other groups, but the influence did not lead to major change in fighting methods. Rather, what emerged was a refinement of existing types. The sources specifically have references to equipment, but say nothing about the adoption of new tactics.

The *Ineditum Vaticanum* also mentions that the Romans had hardly any cavalry, but were forced to fight on horseback in the course of the Samnite Wars. As has been pointed out, the homeland of the Samnites was mountainous which would hardly encourage the growth of a formidable cavalry force. In none of the battles recorded in Livy and Dionysius of Halicarnassus does the Samnite cavalry emerge victorious. The Romans had a long cavalry tradition, whatever its merits, dating back at least to the beginning of the Republic. In the sources allowing for their bias, the cavalry play a crucial role in many early battles. Certainly, there is nothing in either writer to indicate that Samnite cavalry differed in any significant way from Roman cavalry.[68] The only definite mention of a dramatic change in the equipment of the Roman cavalry is Polybius on the adoption of Greek cavalry equipment.[69] The basic issue is not the equipment *per se*, but the tactical formation of infantry maniples arranged in three lines that constituted the manipular army. There is no good evidence that the Samnites were organized in such a fashion. At the battle of Asculum, Polybius mentions that Pyrrhus interspersed between sections of his phalanx formations of Italian allies. The terms he uses to describe the Italian allied formations with Pyrrhus are not the same that he uses for a maniple, but an equivalent word, which is simply a variant of the word for maniple is used to describe the phalanx sections. Since one is a synonym for the other, it is likely that the one used for the Italian allies has no tactical significance.

There are hints in the tradition always centring on equipment that point to a change at a much earlier date. In connection with the introduction of pay during the war with Veii, Livy states that the introduction coincided with a transition from round shields (that is, hoplite shields) to manipular ones.[70]

> *The Romans had formerly used round shields; then, after they began to serve for pay, they changed from round to oblong shields; and their previous formation in phalanxes, like those of the Macedonian army, afterwards began to be a battle line formed in maniples, with the troops in the rear drawn up in several ranks.*

This description is part of Livy's prologue to the battle of the Veseris against the Latins in 340.[71] The account is of a fully operational manipular army. But his description includes a number of errors. It describes the legions as consisting of forty-five maniples, with fifteen in each of the three lines. The most troublesome part of the historian's description is his account of the third line. The total for the maniples of 189 men each bears no relation to any other evidence and the number of maniples is obviously wrong. The units he mentions as forming the rear of the third line must be incorrect. They are the *rorarii,* an early term for the *velites* which classifies these troops as light-armed, and the *accensi* who are normally not soldiers at all, but servants. It is striking that Livy places the *accensi,* whom he considers the weakest and least reliable troops, at the rear of the line. In contemporary Greek armies the troops at the rear were experienced men with a reputation for maintaining their position. They served to keep those in front from breaking and running to the rear. In all, it seems clear that Livy is describing an army whose organization and tactics he did not understand.[72] By his time, the army of the middle Republic had changed radically. There is evidence that the names of the lines no longer made sense in Livy's time.[73] Further, the digression seems to hang in mid-air. Given the fact that it opens with the claim that the change occurred sixty years before the chronological point at which he inserted it in his narrative, there seems to be clear disconnect between it and the rest of his narrative. There is nothing specific to the battle of the Veseris that would warrant its inclusion. It is also important to note that Livy presents the change as one in weaponry and not in tactics.

There is a vaguely similar tradition in Plutarch's life of Camillus (the hero of the siege of Veii) and the fourth century Gallic wars.[74] Plutarch reports that:

> *Seeing that the strength of the barbarians [Gauls] was in their swords which they wielded in a barbaric manner with no skill, slashing particu-larly at shoulders and heads, helmets were forged for the majority wholly of iron and polished on their circumference so that the swords would slip off or break and their shields were edged with bronze, as wood was not resistant enough, he instructed the soldiers on how to wield long javelins and how to slide them under or better deflect the swords of their enemies in receiving the blows.[75]*

Plutarch is a relatively late author, writing in the first century AD, so the worth of his testimony is questionable. We have no knowledge of where this passage came from. Interestingly, Plutarch's account of Camillus' actions places them at the same time as Livy's account of the legion. The claim that it was Camillus who was the author of these changes is most likely the result – as we can see in the cases of Marius and Caesar – of a famous name attracting developments thought to have occurred while he was active. The passage has a number of errors and is manifestly unfair to the Gauls. The most common helmet of the period was the Montefortino, which was made from a copper alloy, although there were some types of iron hel-mets. The edging of the shield is indeed correct, but it was still standard in Plutarch's time which would have made it easy to project such a shield into the past. The use of the javelins in the anecdote ignores the spears of the *triarii* and totally misunderstands their use in the Roman army in that period. It is as if Plutarch imagines a phalanx formation and not the triple line of the manipular legion. Whatever the origin of the passage, there is no reason to assign it any value.

There is no reason to think that the tactical transition to the manipular formation from the phalanx was accomplished all at once. After all, the new tactical system is so radically different that it seems hard to believe it was accomplished in a single step. The retention by the *triarii* of the spear characteristic of the phalanx implies a process of change over time. It was not until about 120 that all three lines were armed uniformly. There is a hint that the process of transition had already begun by the end of the fourth century and perhaps before. Dionysius of Halicarnassus, in his narration of the Pyrrhic War, probably at Beneventum in 275, mentions that:

> Those who fight in close combat with cavalry spears held in the middle
> with both hands and who usually save the day in battles are called
> principes *by the Romans.*[76]

Two-handed cavalry spears appear an unlikely weapon but, as Rawson points out, there is evidence for Hellenistic cavalry wielding the heavy two-handed Macedonian *sarissa* in battle.[77] It may be that Dionysius misunderstood his source and that the *principes* were still using the heavy thrusting spear of the phalanx. If the passage is accepted as historical, and there is good reason to do so, it would mean that in 275 only the first line of the legion was armed with *pilum* and sword as its main offensive weapons. There is further support for a change at least in the first line by this time. Plutarch's *Life of Pyrrhus* mentions that at Asculum the Romans were fighting fiercely with their swords.[78]

I would suggest the following reconstruction of the tactical change in the front line. It is unlikely to be the wars against the Samnites, as many have proposed, as a way of dealing with the open formations of the hill peoples. The Romans had from the fifth century fought the Aequi and the Volsci, who were also mountain peoples, with a phalanx. As pointed out above, the Macedonians with mixed forces like those of the Servian army had successfully fought and conquered peoples who did not fight in a phalanx in Greece and Asia.[79] This is not to say that the lighter equipment of the manipular formation was not an advantage, rather the argument is that the advantage was not in itself sufficient to bring about such a major change.

In the wake of the Gallic sack, Rome emerged as an aggressive power on a much larger scale than before. Just as importantly there were troubles with Rome's Latin allies. They were struggling to meet increased demands on their manpower. Rome responded to these pressures by increasing the number of legions it levied. In 362 the number of legions formed doubled to two and elections were introduced for military tribunes for six of the twelve tribunes in the two legions.[80] In 311, the total was now doubled again to four legions of about 16,000 each.[81] Two legions with allies would allow each consul to wage a campaign independently of the other. Given the number of active fronts this made sense. The need for greater military effort is also evident from 326 with the institution of the promagistracy. A further indication of the pressure that these wars exerted is the first levying of those classified as *capite censi*, that is those men who fell below the minimum census requirement legionary service. Such recruitment recurred at periods of particular danger.[82]

There is no certain information, but these increases in manpower may be associated with another change. The levy by centuries implicit in the Servian system was replaced by a system based on the tribes that spread the burden over a larger part of the male population. The burden on the first class would have been substantially lightened as well. Wealth still counted, but to a lesser degree than under the earlier system. Interestingly, in Polybius' discussion of the levy he mentions that the youngest and poorest were enrolled as light-armed soldiers, while those somewhat older were enrolled as *hastati*.[83] This implies that the difference between the two types of troops was for the most part based on age, and supports the idea that the *hastati* emerged from the light-armed units.

Some light may be shed on social changes in the army in this period by the events of 342. In the midst of the First Samnite War an internal military rebellion took place at Rome. The details have certainly been reworked, but the core facts of the incident seem to be authentic. After a victory over the Samnites, Roman troops were sent to garrison Capua and Suessa in Campania at these cities' request. Over the winter, disaffection began to spread among the garrison. A conspiracy developed which aimed to seize control of Capua. It was a town proverbial for its wealth. According to Livy, the soldiers contrasted the fertility and wealth of Capua with the arid and disease-ridden soil around Rome and their crushing burden of debt. Despite the rhetorical elaboration of these complaints by Livy, the events that followed provide some support for the reasons he gives for the revolt.[84] Eventually, the mutineers marched in battle formation to as close as 13km from Rome until they were stopped by the news that other forces were marching against them. A compromise was worked out; a number of laws were passed that formalized this agreement. Among the laws passed there is one that points to the social composition of the army. The Genucian Law made usury illegal.[85] The expansion of the levy to greater numbers drew in those on the margins who were heavily pressed by the problem of debt.

However, this expansion raised a further problem: how were these poorer men going to equip themselves? The solution was found in the equipment of the light-armed troops. As mentioned earlier, they used a javelin called the *hasta velitaris*.[86] Those who would form the *hastati* were equipped with a heavier version of the same weapon. The use of a larger, more protective shield now became both possible and necessary since speed of movement was no longer crucial. The addition of a metal helmet and chest protector were needed by troops engaged in close combat. Importantly, the new panoply was cheaper, probably by a substantial amount, than the hoplite equipment it replaced.

All of these factors would point to the second half of the fourth century – or even more likely the last two decades of the fourth century – for the change in the first line. We have no information on when the *principes* made the transition. It was certainly the case that by the Second Punic War of 218–202, the army had assumed the form it would have in Polybius' day. It seems possible that the catalyst for the change in the equipment of the second line was the First Punic War. Our sources for that war are mostly limited to Polybius. The major battles of the war were fought at sea and there were few land battles in the course of the war. One major encounter was the result of the Roman invasion of Carthaginian territory in North Africa in 256. After double victories, the Roman commander, Regulus, was defeated by the Carthaginians in 255 somewhere near the city of Carthage. Polybius' description of the deployment of his army 'many maniples deep' implies that the army was now wholly organized in this fashion.[87] There is a further reference to maniples at the siege of Panormus (Palermo) in 254.[88] Polybius certainly used Fabius Pictor and other early Roman historians but the First Punic War was about a half century in the past and so well within the period when documents for these historians (Roman) would have been available for an institution as important as the army. It seems that he used contemporary Greek sources as well which would not have been influenced by annalistic tradition about the nature of the Roman army. The war itself, although primarily naval, led to enormous losses so that there would have been increased pressure on Roman manpower resources which may have hastened the transition in the second line to manipular equipment and the new formation. The *triarii*'s deployment since they retained the heavy thrusting spear may have developed from the transition in the other two lines. They had to be brigaded in the same open formation to allow the other lines to retreat behind them. Whatever the exact steps may have been it seems that by the 220s the transition had been completed.

This leaves unanswered the question of who played the major role in these developments. The names of the individuals involved are lost forever. The essence of the reform was that it allowed each line to function as a reserve for the line in front. Unfortunately, there is no evidence on the origin of this formation or why it was adopted.

Recruitment and the Levy

The Roman army was a militia. Every male citizen could be called up for military service. It was a duty and privilege; service was linked to freeborn status. As in the Greek city-states, slaves were not liable for military service. Only in the direst emergencies were they drafted into the army, as they were in 216 in the aftermath of Cannae.[89] They seem to have been promised freedom in exchange for faithful service.[90] The prohibition against the drafting of slaves lasted until the early fifth century AD. It was also only in exceptional circumstances that freedmen were called, although in Imperial times they were eligible for service in the navy.[91]

The obligation to serve was based on census lists, which must have included a valuation of property and the names and ages of those living in the household. It was the basis of a citizen's rights and obligations. It determined a citizen's voting rights and status, his level of taxation and whether – and in what manner – he could be called up. Below a minimum level of wealth Roman citizens were not normally liable for military service. As with slaves, it was only at times of great danger that these poorer citizens were drafted. The first known instance came in 280 on the arrival of Pyrrhus in Italy.[92] They were drafted again during the First and Second Punic Wars, but there is no reference to their recruitment in the following years.

Men could be called up once they reached the age of 17 and remained liable for service in the field until the age of 46. After that, they could be called up for limited service until they turned 60. However, in extraordinary situations, those in the older group could be required to serve in the field. Cavalrymen who served in ten campaigns were legally exempt from further service, as were those in the legions who had fought in sixteen campaigns.

In all of these cases, exemptions for illness or other causes could be granted by the magistrate in charge of the levy (normally the consuls). Before an exemption could be granted, the consuls conducted an enquiry as to the merits of the case. What is less clear is how they handled the cases of men absent from Rome. Given the slowness of communication, it must often have been the case that if individuals were some distance away at the time of the levy summons, it is likely that they would not receive notice in time to return.

Certain magistrates could be granted exemptions. In 150 and again in 138, the tribunes asked the consuls who was presiding over the levy for Spain to grant them ten exemptions. The consuls refused and the tribunes briefly imprisoned them. This would have been a pressing issue as the war in Spain was extremely unpopular.[93] On the whole the system worked well, and given the manpower available, Rome had sufficient reserves to deal with draft evasion in normal times. For instance, during the Second Punic War, the censors of 214 discovered that among those who were eligible for service in the field army and had not served, there were no more than 2,000 men without a legitimate exemption or excuse.

The penalties for avoiding the draft could be very severe. Manius Curtius Dentatus, three times consul and a hero of the third war with the Samnites, found it imperative to order an emergency levy. One man selected in the levy failed to appear. The consul had his goods put up for auction. When in response the man appeared and appealed for help to the tribunes he ordered that not only the man's property, but he himself should be sold.[94] Loss of property was not an uncommon penalty and those who failed to assemble could be treated as deserters.[95] The most serious problem the consuls faced was appeals by individuals to a tribune as mentioned in the case of the consul Curius. In reaction to this problem, around 100 the levy was transferred from the Capitoline Hill to the Campus Martius, which had strong military associations but more importantly, was outside the jurisdiction of the plebeian tribunes.[96]

The Roman pool of potential recruits was unusually large for an ancient city-state. There are census figures preserved in the literary sources which are of uneven quality. Prior to 225, they seem to be of doubtful reliability; but from 225, they seem to be far more trustworthy. These figures are not exact but they do show overall consistency and so seem to have a factual basis.[97] For the last half of the second century the census figures vary between 380,000 and 400,000 men. There is some controversy as to what these figures represent. It seems likely that the figures count only the male population including those too poor to serve. Of these totals roughly three-quarters would be *iuniores* eligible for the field army, less those who fell below the census minimum. Even taking into account that a certain number of men would not be available for any particular levy, the numbers seem sufficient for an annual levy of four consular legions, totalling approximately 20,000 men. Even before this period, Rome was capable of putting far larger numbers in the field. In 212, the year of maximum effort during the Second Punic War, Rome could field a force of 25 legions normally of 4,200 infantry and 200 cavalry, with a theoretical total strength of 110,000 men. If the situation warranted it, the infantry of a legion could be increased to 5,000 and its cavalry to 300, making the paper strength for this number of legions 132,500.[98]

As a first step in the holding of a levy, the consuls were responsible for preparing an estimate of the men and money necessary for an approaching campaign and then submitting it to the Senate, which controlled the state's finances. The Senate then issued a decree approving the levy and allowing it to go forward. An edict was then published by the consuls, allowing thirty days for the enrolment to take place and requiring those drafted to assemble at Rome on a specific day.

The raising of men for the legions took place in two phases. The first was the actual levy and the second was the assignment of those selected to the appropriate legions. The sources claim that men were drafted on the basis of the centuries of the Servian system. This is plausible for the earliest period, although it is not clear how these individuals were assigned to their centuries. However, it was a cumbersome procedure which involved almost two hundred separate units. It also placed a far heavier burden on the wealthy as they staffed the majority of the centuries including the cavalry. The expansion of Roman territory and the formation of new tribes must have further complicated the process. At an unknown date the basis of the levy was changed from the century to the tribe. The early years of the First Punic War have been suggested as the time for this change. Given the increased demands for manpower and speedier mobilization in wartime, it is certainly a possibility.[99] This would also have borne less heavily on the wealthier citizens. In addition, the process was probably made easier by the introduction of military pay, probably at the beginning of the fourth century.[100] It is not unlikely that the system of drafting by tribes has its roots in the *tumultus* or emergency levy which involved the entire male citizen population. Its essence was speed, and drafting by tribes would have made for a much faster process.[101]

Polybius is our main source for the details of the levy. His account seems to be of the levy as it stood in the mid-second century, but there are problems with his account. The most striking is that he has the levy take place on the Capitoline Hill at Rome. By 218, the number of men eligible for service was already in the order of 100,000.[102] This number given exemptions and those already in service, is still too large to be accommodated in the space available. Also, Polybius' account assumes that each tribe had an equal number of potential recruits, which clearly cannot be the case. These and other difficulties point to the possibility that Polybius was not an eyewitness at a levy, but used a written account that had various errors. It has been suggested that he used a handbook for the military tribunes who played an important role in the process.[103] It is likely that he is not describing the initial levy, but rather the assignment of the draftees to various existing legions.[104] Certainly, it seems reasonable to assume that the actual levying of the troops took place not only at Rome but also in the towns and municipalities outside of the city and was overseen by local officials who then sent the men on to Rome.

After the levy a day was fixed for the men selected for service to assemble and receive their assignment to various legions.[105] The first stage of this process was the allocation of the twenty-four military tribunes to the four legions for this double consular army. The junior tribunes are assigned to their legions on the basis of the date they were elected or appointed.[106] The four first elected were assigned to the first legion, the next three to the second legion, the following four to the third legion and the remaining three to the fourth legion. The first two senior tribunes went to the first legion, the next three to the second legion, the next three to the third legion and the last two to the fourth legion.

Next the tribunes assigned to each legion assembled. The tribes were then summoned individually, their order determined by lot. The first to be chosen were the men destined for the cavalry of the legion who were by far the wealthiest group of recruits, although Polybius tells us that they had formerly been chosen last. First, four young men were selected from the tribe who were as similar in age and physical condition as possible. The tribunes of each legion chose one of them, beginning with the first legion. Then a second group of four was brought forward, but this time the selection process begins with the second legion. After this, another four were summoned and the first choice was made by the third legion. Finally, the process ended with the first choice of the fourth legion. The whole procedure began again, until all of the legions were assigned their full complement of men.

The process seems extraordinarily cumbersome and there must have been complaints and appeals that slowed the process. Added to this was the possibility before about 100 for the tribunes of the plebs to interfere and even try to suspend the entire process.[107] In 151, after news in Spain about the fierceness of the fighting reached Rome, there was a great reluctance to serve in newly raised legions destined for Spain. After a number of serious problems arose, including the temporary imprisonment of the consuls, the lot was introduced to determine which legions would serve in the Spanish theatre. This became a standard part of the levy.[108]

The legions raised this way were known as urban legions and in theory they were raised every time a campaign was in the offing, as the legions who had completed their campaigns were disbanded at the end of the season. In practice it is likely, especially once legions began serving outside Italy that not all four of them were raised in any one year, but probably one or two along with supplements for existing legions. In the last years of the Second Punic War the consuls were permitted to raise new legions for service in southern Italy along with supplements for existing legions.[109]

At the same time as the levy was taking place, the consuls issued an edict to allied communities, specifying the number of troops to be raised for the coming campaign. The total number of allied troops had already been set out in the edict of the Senate that had approved the war, named the commanders and their theatre or theatres of operation and authorized the raising of the appropriate number of legions. The senatorial edict also included the number of allied troops that had to be supplied based on the numbers in the *formula togatorum* or 'list of toga wearers', that is Rome's Italian allies, which likely specified the maximum number of soldiers that each ally had to provide. These numbers were probably computed on the basis of local census records. Given the variations in population and size of communities involved, there must have been a substantial difference in the numbers of soldiers each community was capable of providing. Most often allied forces appear as single ethnic units, but it seems likely that smaller towns must have pooled their limited sources and produced mixed units. The list was revised as conditions in the allied states changed.[110] At Rome they must have been assigned to their cohorts and for heavy infantry organized in *alae* (singular *ala*) or wings. The last step was probably the assignment of an allied *ala* to a particular legion.

It is likely that in the fifth and fourth century the majority of Roman recruits would have been farmers. There is contemporary Greek evidence that supports this view and there is no reason to think that Greek and Roman societies were economically different. The rhythms of the campaigning year reflect the cycle of the agricultural year. However, Roman military success and its expansionism in the later fourth century and after disrupted the relation of military service and the agricultural year. Nevertheless, the manpower of the army remained overwhelmingly rural. There is no doubt that the strains of military life increased but a reasonable argument can be made to show that, given the late age of marriage for Roman men (about 30), the need for their labour was not as important as it would have been for men with their own families.[111] The extension of Rome's empire outside of Italy from the end of the last quarter of the third century as well as economic pressure led to a gradual shift from a militia to a professional army. It was a slow process but it would be formally completed at the end of the first century under Augustus.[112]

In addition to the levy, volunteers were also raised by men who had a sufficient reputation and prestige to raise substantial forces. Although regulated by the state, these bands recall the followers of early warbands.[113] In 134 Scipio Aemilianus, the conqueror of Carthage, was able to raise 4,000 men for a campaign in Spain, a notoriously troubled theatre. He had been denied permission by the Senate to hold a levy. However, drawing on volunteers and clients, using his own fortune as well as those of his friends and supplementing these funds with gifts from various kings, he successfully defied the Senate.[114] Marius, elected consul in 107 and as rising military star, had been chosen by the popular assembly to carry on the war against the Numidian ruler Jugurtha, despite aristocratic opposition. The Senate allowed him only to levy a supplement to the existing army in Numidia. Substantial numbers of volunteers came forward. In general, during the second century there was less resistance to the draft, when service in the army involved operations in the relatively rich areas of the eastern Mediterranean than for the difficult fighting in Spain with little promise of booty. Recorded instances of opposition to the levy are recorded for Spain in the 150s and 130s. However, even in the eastern Mediterranean a difficult war with little progress could create problems. In 169 there was resistance to the levy for the war against the Macedonian king Perseus because of lack of progress and because the war was more difficult than the troops had been led to expect.[115]

The Oath

After his account of the completion of the levy, Polybius states that an oath was administered to the new recruits by the military tribunes. The tribunes selected one of the recruits whom they thought was suitable for the purpose and had him swear an oath that he would obey his officers and execute their orders as far as he was capable. Then the other men came forward in turn and took the oath simply by stating that they would do the same as the first man.[116]

Such an oath, which the Romans called a *sacramentum,* seems to have been common practice among Italic peoples. The oath was a religious act that served as a rite of initiation into a group and its religious character aided group cohesion and solidarity. In his account of the events of 293 during the Third Samnite War, Livy describes an oath and initiation ceremony meant to strengthen the resolve of the Samnite soldiers before their battle:

> *They were admitted into the enclosure one by one. As each was admitted he was led up to the altar, more like a victim than like one who was taking part in the service, and he was bound on oath not to divulge what he saw and heard in that place. He was compelled to swear a dreadful oath cursing himself, his family, and his clan, if he did not follow his commanders going into battle or if he fled from battle or did not at once kill anyone whom he saw fleeing.*[117]

Despite the rhetorical elaboration, Livy's description of the Samnite ceremony, whether true or not, captures the religious atmosphere of the oath and the dire consequences of violating it.

The oath was a vital part of Roman military service as well. In its absence, a soldier was not permitted to use his weapons or to engage in fighting. The oath was valid only for the coming campaign. When a new commander entered office, it was necessary to repeat it.

We have no text of the Republican oath. The surviving examples come from late in the Imperial period. We do have indirect evidence for the oath in the Republican period. Dionysius of Halicarnassus cites an oath that the citizens had supposedly sworn in 460 during the struggle between patricians and plebeians. To stop the obstructionism of the plebeian tribunes, the consul, the famous Cincinnatus, reminded the people that they had taken the military oath to follow the consuls in whatever wars they might designate and not desert or do anything contrary to the law.[118] It is not clear if this is the same oath that Polybius refers to; nevertheless, its basic provisions must be the same.

The oath seems to have evolved over time. Livy claims that the original oath was sworn to assemble on the day specified by the consuls, and not to depart without permission. He claims that the soldiers also swore among themselves not to desert or leave the battle line except in an emergency. Livy claims that, in 216 before the battle of Cannae the tribunes made this soldier's oath mandatory.[119] The oath that Dionysius ascribes to Cincinnatus over 200 years before Cannae contains the essential elements of the oath that Livy claims only became official in 216. It is hard to believe that no oath of this type existed until the end of the third century.

The oath sworn at the time of the levy was not the only oath that the soldiers swore. Polybius and the second century AD author Aulus Gellius record an oath connected with camp discipline. Polybius records that, after setting up camp, the tribunes administered an oath to all those in the camp, both slave and free, that they would not steal from the camp, and if they found anything, they would bring it to the tribunes.[120] Gellius' version, which claims to be a quotation, which he dates about 190, is rather different. For one thing, it applied not only to the camp, but to an area that extended 16km around it. For another, it has a curious provision that its prohibition against stealing would only apply to thefts worth more than a minimum amount and allowed the theft of military necessities. Anything above the minimum amount was to be brought to the consuls or their appointed representative or returned to the owner.[121] How all of these provisions were enforced is not clear.

It is important to note that the oath was not sworn to the state or to a head of state. In the conditions of civil war in 32, the future emperor Augustus had the citizens swear an oath to him personally.[122] This practice was followed under his successors at their accession and every year on the third of January, the army would swear allegiance to the emperor himself and not to their commanders.[123] By the Imperial period not only soldiers, but also civilians, swore an oath of personal loyalty to the emperor.

CHAPTER SIX

A NEW MODEL ARMY II

The change to the manipular formation was not accompanied by a modification in the Roman command structure, although the number of legions levied increased in years of high military activity, reaching twenty-five legions in 212 during the Second Punic War. This was a maximum number, but it is significant that the command structure was able to deal with it by a combination of increases in the number of junior magistracies such as the quaestorship and by the use of the promagistracy.[1]

The number of legions raised averaged nineteen during the war. It is true that Rome was involved in a desperate struggle with Carthage, but after her victory, the number of legions kept in service remained substantially higher than they had been before the outbreak of the war. Prior to 218 Rome had an average of three legions in the field each year. In the period after the war until the mid-second century, on average between eight and nine legions were in service every year.[2] In addition, starting with Sicily in 227, Rome began to develop a system of standing overseas commands, which would eventually become permanent provinces. These commands were usually for a year, which further taxed the system of available commanding officers. The appointment of senatorial legates brought some relief – not only to the need to multiply the number of available commanders, but also as a response to a serious weakness in the system. There was no automatic provision for a substitute commander when a consul or praetor was absent or incapacitated. Also with the growing variety of the theatres in which the army operated there was a need for commanders of special detachments of troops. Military tribunes could be used, but they had serious limitations. They were tied to specific legions and only two were active at a time. Further, they were often young men with limited military experience, probably not ready for an independent command. Although used sporadically earlier during the wars against the Samnites, it was not until the beginning of the second century that a permanent system of legates developed.[3] Further, just as was the case with the military tribunes, generals could assign any tasks to their legates.

Although the annalists mention them as important commanders as far back as the early Republic, this seems to be ahistorical. The Roman defeat at Cannae was so complete and the losses so catastrophic that it should be a good test of the presence or absence of legates in the Roman army. Livy records no legates in his list of casualties, which does include a number of senators.[4] It seems likely that it was not until the 190s that legates were routinely appointed. Certainly by the mid-second century they appear as normal military officers.

Initially, legates could sometimes be equites, but it became the norm for them to hold senatorial rank, and even men who had held the consulship are mentioned later serving as legates. For junior senators, the holding of a legateship opened a faster and surer path to political advancement. Eventually, it led to a decline in the importance of the military tribunate which had once been a significant path to important commands.

When the legateship became a standing office the method of appointment changed. Prior to that point, the appointment had been at the discretion of the magistrate in command. It now became a prerogative of the Senate. The legates were appointed at the beginning of the political year, which down to 151 began in March and after that in January, when the Senate assigned commands to regular magistrates. This may seem to be an attempt to limit the magistrates' power but apparently it was not. The legates were appointed after consultation with the magistrates. The need for the two to work closely together seems to have been the key factor in giving so much power over the appointment to the commander. Disagreement among consuls provided an example of what could happen when, as at Cannae and later at Arausio in 105, two consuls were operating jointly, but were of different minds about what course of action to pursue.

During the century after the office became regular, legates were used only overseas on campaigns or as assistants to provincial governors. With the outbreak of the war between Rome and some of its allies in 90, and in the civil wars of the 80s, legates were used in Italy. By the 50s Caesar appears to regularly use legates in Gaul. In 54, under the pressure of a poor harvest in Gaul, Caesar was forced to disperse his forces in a series of camps. Each of these was under the command of one of his legates who was also in charge of the surrounding area.

A good idea of the type of duties that could be assigned to legates can be gathered from a passage in Livy describing Lucius Aemilius Paullus' campaign in Macedonia in 168 and 167:

> *First of all, he requested the Senate to send legates to inspect the army and fleet, and to report back, based on first-hand knowledge of what military and naval forces were required. In addition, they were to find out what they could about the king's forces, how much territory the enemy controlled and how much was controlled by Rome; whether the Romans were encamped in difficult country or had cleared all the passes and reached level ground; which allies were loyal, which were doubtful and waiting on events, and who were openly hostile. Further, they were to ascertain the amount of supplies assembled and land and sea resupply routes. Finally, what the results were of this year's land and sea campaign.*[5]

In 67, Pompey the Great received a command against the pirates who were infesting the Mediterranean. Their large fleets had created a standing menace to commerce and property. In 73, they had interfered with the grain supply of Rome itself. They had even landed on the coast of Italy and carried off two Roman praetors and their entourages. Pirates had captured and held to ransom the young Julius Caesar when he left Rome to pursue his studies on the island of Rhodes. He was able to raise the ransom and was later to return and avenge his captivity by executing the pirates.[6] Starting in 101, the Senate had appointed various commanders to fight the pirates but none of these expeditions were entirely successful. Pompey's command included the power to nominate twenty-four legates. Unusually, these legates were given *imperium* equal to that of a propraetor. This grant would allow them to operate independently of Pompey. Given the size of the area of operations this was a necessity.[7] The use of independent legates is also attested in provincial government. In 55, Pompey received control of Spain for a five-year period; he remained in Rome while his legates governed the province.[8] The assignment of *imperium* to a legate would under the Empire become the normal way to appoint provincial governors and army commanders who acted as deputies for the emperor.

The sixty centurions of the legion formed a vital link between the high command and the ordinary legionary. They commanded and fought with their centuries and maniples, and their experience as fighters and leaders allowed the rather loose chain command in the Roman army to operate effectively. This was especially true during the Republic, as the men who commanded Rome's legions at the highest level had until the last century BC some military experience of one sort or another, but lacked any formal training. An example is provided by the famous orator Cicero. As a young man he had served in 90 and 89 on the staff of Gnaeus Pompeius Strabo during the Social War. This was the sum total of his military experience until he became the governor of Cilicia in 51, a post which he held for a year. As governor he won a victory over some rebellious mountain peoples for which he applied to the Senate for military honours and was granted them. Cicero was probably unusually averse to leaving Rome and to military command. But given changes in elite military service, especially in the last century BC, he was probably not exceptional.[9]

Centurions were the equivalent of modern non-commissioned officers. Their name implies that they had at one time commanded units of 100 men; the early regal army with its decimal organization may be where the term originated. A rigid social barrier separated these men from higher command during the Republic. However, in the Empire that barrier fell away. In the Imperial period service as the leading centurion of a legion could be followed by promotion to equestrian rank, which opened up service in elite units posted in Rome. These posts could serve as a springboard to higher administrative posts.

In Polybius' discussion of the annual levy of four legions at Rome, the military tribunes selected ten men from each of the three lines of the legions to serve as prior or senior centurions and then another thirty to serve as posterior or junior centurions for each legion. Although patronage as well as merit played an important role in the selection of these men, they were all drawn from the pool of ordinary soldiers and were men of proven military experience. The recruits would have known or heard about these men and it would have greatly weakened their morale to see unfit men placed in these positions that were vital to their well-being.

The century remained an important administrative unit, however the maniple became the standard tactical unit. It was under the command of both the prior and posterior centurions. Polybius states that the prior centurion commanded the right side of the maniple while the posterior was in charge of the left. The prior was in command of the entire maniple, while the posterior acted as his assistant and replaced him if he became incapacitated.[10]

Each centurion was assisted by a junior officer, the *optio*. He was chosen by the centurion he served with and seems to have acted as a general assistant. The Greek term that Polybius uses to translate the Latin term *optio* implies that in battle formations the *optio* was stationed at the rear of the century.[11] *Optiones* are also found in cavalry units.[12]

The centurions of the legions were arranged in a hierarchy. The centurions of the rear line – the *triarii* – were the most senior, then came the centurions of the *principes* with those of the *hastati* being the most junior. Within the lines seniority increased as one moved from left to right. In addition, each prior centurion was senior to each posterior centurion within the same maniple. This meant that the posterior centurion of the leftmost maniple of the *hastati* was the most junior centurion in the legion, while the prior centurion of the rightmost maniple of the *triarii* was the most senior. This centurion was also known as the *primus pilus* from the column formation of the *triarii*. Unlike the other centurions of the legion, the *primus pilus* was a member of the general's war council. The prestigious post lasted only for a year until the legion was disbanded at the end of the campaigning season.

The seniority of the centurions of the *triarii* may seem surprising, as the *triarii* were posted to the rear of the legion and saw the least action in the course of a campaign. The *triarii* were only used when the whole legion was in danger of being routed. However, that meant that these centurions were normally not committed to combat and so could issue orders to other centurions and rally the men to their front. The right side in both the Greek and Roman battle lines was always superior to the left. In part this was based on a superstitious belief that right was superior to left, but it also rested on more practical considerations. The right was the more dangerous side of a battle line. It was the unshielded side and so the most vulnerable.

It was also reflected in the fact that the senior centurion commanded the right side of the maniple.

The question of promotion of centurions has generated a great deal of controversy over the question of whether there was a formal system during the Republic. Even in the Empire when we know such a system did exist, we are unsure how it functioned. A complicating factor is that until the Romans maintained large-scale military forces outside of Italy, the legions were – except during wartime – dissolved at the end of the campaigning season and levied once again for the following year. Further, there is little evidence of the question of promotion. In instances where promotions are mentioned, we hear most about promotion to the centurionate not in it. In these cases, it is because of valour, endurance and aggressiveness in battle.[13]

A good example is provided by an attack by 2,000 German cavalry in 53 on the camp of Caesar's legate, Quintus Cicero the brother of Marcus. The camp held out but a foraging party was attacked on its way back to the camp. Some, as they were trying to escape, were caught by the Germans and annihilated. Caesar mentions that some of their centurions had been transferred from other legions and promoted because of their courage. He claims that they died fighting because they did not want to lose their reputation for valour.[14] That meant an ordinary soldier could, if his commander noticed his courage, have hopes of promotion. Caesar in his account of a battle in northeastern Gaul in 57, describes a dangerous moment for the Twelfth Legion, when its ranks had become disordered. After a courageous centurion had restored the line, Caesar says that the men fought with renewed vigour:

> The enemy attack was slowed as each man, no matter how desperate his situation was, wanted to do all that he could in the sight of his commander.[15]

Caesar also makes a rare mention of promotion within the centurionate. The same passage of Caesar, mentioned above concerning the German attack of 53, indicates that some of the centurions who died in the attack had been transferred from other legions and promoted to higher rank because of their courage.[16] Another example is that of the centurion Marcus Cassius Scaeva in the civil war between Pompey and Caesar. In early 48, Pompey had managed to cross the Adriatic and established himself at Dyrrachium (modern Durrës in Albania). Caesar, hoping to force him into a decisive battle, blockaded him with his smaller force. The blockade was not wholly successful as Caesar could not cut Pompey off on the seaward side and began to suffer severe supply difficulties. Pompey launched a major attack to try to end Caesar's blockade on the landward side and was repulsed with heavy losses. The attack on one fort had been intense. The soldiers claimed that more than 30,000 arrows had been shot into the fort.

No soldier had remained unwounded and four of the centurions from a single unit posted there had been permanently blinded. Caesar was shown Scarva's shield, which had 120 holes in it. On account of his actions Caesar presented him with a substantial cash bonus and after publicly praising him, promoted him from a centurion of the eighth cohort to the leading centurion of the legion.[17] There was general agreement that it was mostly through his efforts that the fort had been saved. So both promotion within a legion and transference to another legion at the same rank or above seem to have been normal. Lack of courage could easily end a centurion's career.

Such promotion brought both material and social rewards. Polybius states that a centurion's pay was double that of an ordinary legionary.[18] It had probably risen to five times legionary pay by the 40s.[19] Centurions also received a larger share of booty. Although there is no direct evidence, it is likely that the *primi ordines,* whose membership is never clearly defined, but probably included the centurions of the three maniples forming the right side of the line, received higher pay. They certainly did so in the Imperial army. In addition, the general could give military decorations for displays of courage. They enhanced the centurions standing within the army and in society.[20] As one scholar has remarked:

> *It is no surprise, then, that these awards were fiercely competed for by both soldiers and officers, simultaneously drawing from and encouraging a competitive atmosphere that was a hallmark of Roman warfare and a major motivating factor in the legions of the Republic and Principate.*[21]

Polybius' remarks on the qualities that the Romans expected of their centurions:

> *[The Romans] want their centurions to be not so much bold or risk takers, but rather wish them to be capable of command, steady and controlled. They do not so much want them to attack or to open the battle, but to hold fast even when the battle goes against them and they are hard pressed, and to be ready to die at their post.*[22]

Polybius' portrait is not totally accurate. Certainly steadiness and not panicking were crucial to maintaining the integrity of the maniple and the battle line. Self-discipline was a key part of the qualities that a successful centurion needed. It can be thought of as a passive courage, reactive to developments. A marked feature of Caesar's Gallic War is the number of passages devoted to aggressive exploits of centurions, what can be called active courage. Especially striking is his portrait of Sextus Baculus, who Caesar presents as a paradigm of military virtue and courage. Even though wounded, he reforms his unit at the height of a battle.[23] In 56 during an attack in his camp by the Gauls, he and the military tribune Gaius Volusenus advised the legate in charge of their camp that the only hope for salvation lay in a sudden sortie. It turned out successfully and the Gauls were routed.[24] In 53, although ill, he again saved a camp from destruction. Snatching weapons from some troops standing nearby, he took up a position at the camp's gate and rallied the other centurions so that they held off an attack long enough for the rest of the troops to rally.[25] However, this was the active courage which the Romans characterized as *ferocia* or a fierce, courageous spirit. Again, Caesar provides an example. While narrating an attack on the camp of Quintus Cicero by the Gallic Nervii in 54, Caesar inserts the story of two centurions, Titus Pullo and Lucius Vorenus. These men had a long-standing rivalry with each other. When the attack of the Nervii on the camp was at its height, Pullo taunted Vorenus about his personal bravery and decided to launch an attack by himself outside the camp rampart in what was a clear display of his superiority in bravery to his fellow centurion and his *ferocia*. Vorenus followed. The men were almost killed, but successfully made their way back into the camp and were greeted with great praise.[26] The fact that Caesar chose to narrate this action and that the men, after unnecessarily risking their lives were praised for their action, show the importance to the Romans of the aggressive, potentially reckless courage that was expected of a centurion. He could set his men an example and boost morale.

The tasks of the centurion extended beyond the battlefield. After leadership in combat, his next most important responsibility was maintaining discipline. It is no accident that the tombstones of late Republican and Imperial centurions show the individual with a sword at his left side and holding the *vitis*, or vine cane, with which he inflicted corporal punishment. It was such an integral part of the centurion's office that the *vitis* could stand for the office itself.[27]

Centurions often had a reputation for enforcing a savage discipline. In AD 14 the centurion Lucilius was killed in the course of a mutiny. He had earned the nickname *cedo alterum* or 'bring another' for the ferocity of the whippings he administered:

When one broke he demanded another in a loud voice.[28]

In the Imperial period centurions were usually instructed by their superior officers to carry out the punishment they had decided on, and it seems likely the same situation prevailed under the Republic. The types of punishments were to a great extent at the officer's or centurion's discretion. During his siege of the city of Numantia in Spain in 134, Scipio Aemilianus had soldiers beaten for falling behind on the march.[29] Those who abandoned their posts were beaten, as were soldiers who lost equipment.[30] Centurions had other tasks as well. They were routinely involved in selecting camping sites. In 57 Caesar sent his scouts and centurions ahead of his army to select a camp site.[31] They also had administrative tasks that required a competency in both reading and writing. As with other officers, centurions could be used in any capacity that their superior officers saw fit. They remained the vital link between the small number of senior officers in Roman armies and the ordinary soldiers. Their expertise made it possible that even a commander with little experience could win victories.

Logistics are crucial to the functioning of any army. The phrase 'an army marches on its stomach' may be hackneyed but it encapsulates a crucial truth: unless an army is sufficiently provisioned it cannot fight or engage in military operations.[32] Without supplies, sickness and desertion destroy armies. Since the nineteenth century, the term 'logistics' has been used to designate this vital function. It embraces all aspects of both supply and movement. Latin has terms for various aspects of logistics, but no all-embracing term. This difference highlights the much more abstract understanding of these functions in modern military thinking.[33]

Studying Roman logistics is further complicated by the fact that the sources – in accordance with their avoidance of technical detail – rarely supply information on the normal functioning of the Roman system. It is only in situations when the system broke down or an unusual event occurred that logistical matters are mentioned. To compensate for the lack of evidence much has to be inferred from analogy with modern practice, basic human and animal requirements and various other physical variables. Despite these limitations a general picture of Roman practice in the middle and late Republic can be constructed mostly from information drawn from Livy and Polybius.

In any study of supply, terrain plays a crucial role – for instance, whether it is mountainous or level – along with the availability of food, forage, firewood and especially water. All of these factors played a much larger role in ancient warfare as the technology which has solved some of these logistical problems did not then exist. Muscle power – whether human or animal – played the crucial role in transportation on land, while wind and muscle power did so on water.

The Mediterranean region where most of the campaigns took place during the Republic presents its own special problems.[34] The terrain is often rocky and hilly and there are substantial mountain chains – such as the Apennines in Italy and the Pindus in Greece – which hinder movement. Such conditions created problems for supply trains. Wagons, commonly used to transport supplies in northern Europe, were often a liability in the Mediterranean and had to be replaced by pack animals although this limited carrying capacity. Whenever possible the Romans sited their supply bases on rivers or at seaports, since transport by water was often quicker, cheaper and able to carry far larger quantities of supply.

Climate was also a difficulty. Rivers and streams are often not navigable for their entire length and many dried up during the summer. With the minimal amount of rainfall in many regions, harvests in the Mediterranean often vary tremendously from year to year and make it necessary to import food from outside the area. The need for food and fodder for animals meant that the campaigning season followed the agricultural cycle. Campaigns were normally conducted from the late spring or early summer to sometime in the autumn. Later, towards the end of the Republic, when the Romans campaigned in northern Europe, some of these constraints were lifted, but others appeared. Special problems also arose when the Romans began campaigning in dry regions of the Near East.

Food, forage and firewood amounted to about 90 per cent of the total weight of army supplies.[35] The amount of food required by the legions of the middle and late Republic is especially hard to estimate because of variations in the size of the legions. If we accept Polybius' figures of 4,200 for a normal and 5,000 for an augmented legion, we still encounter the additional problem that we have no figures for average personal consumption. We must use modern figures adjusted for change in physical size, and ideas about what constituted an acceptable diet. Based on these calculations the level of consumption can probably be put at an average of 3,000 calories per day as a normal ration, although armies could operate on far less for extended periods if they had to do so.

Basic ration figures are provided by Polybius and although he is writing about the mid-second century, there is no reason to assume any significant changes during the Republic. He only mentions the grain ration, which would have constituted the main source of nutrition and bulk in any ancient Mediterranean diet. The generally accepted equivalent would be about 0.9kg of wheat per day. It was normally in the form of unmilled grain, which the soldiers milled and baked for themselves.[36] The grain was ground with a stone hand mill carried by the unit's pack animals. It supplied about 60–70 per cent of their total calories per day. Barley was normally used only as a punishment ration, although it was eaten in civilian life. The grain ration was deducted from the soldier's pay.[37] The rest of the diet consisted of meat (primarily beef or pork), legumes, olive oil, cheese and salt. Water, diluted wine and vinegar were the normal drinks. The army strictly controlled the daily meal schedule of two meals per day. The ill or wounded were given special diets. The elite who provided the higher officers of the legion continued to eat food appropriate to their aristocratic status. In his life of Marius, Plutarch mentions the simple lifestyle of this general, pointing out that the Roman soldier was pleased to see his commander eating the bread that the common soldiers also ate, and sleeping on a simple pallet.[38] In addition to the soldiers, about 500 servants accompanied the legion and they too had to be fed.

Another supply problem was presented by the camp followers, who included women and merchants, and could be found accompanying most armies. It has been estimated that the ratio of camp followers to the troops was one to three. In early modern Europe, camp followers might number anywhere from 50–150 per cent of the number of combatants.[39] Roman armies used slaves and civilians for logistical support. They were particularly important for the cavalry. One source mentions one for every cavalryman.[40] The slaves appear to have been owned by both private soldiers and the state. By the second century they were armed and were used to defend the camp. They also performed useful services such as foraging and helping to fortify camps. A number of women also followed the army; they performed valuable services in food preparation and laundry, as well as providing companionship for the troops.

Army buying power attracted private merchants who accompanied the army with their wagons and sold to the army as a whole as well as to individual soldiers. The Latin terms of *calo* and *lixa* are used to describe them. They seem to have also functioned as servants or performed various supplementary tasks such as cooking or selling food and various items to the troops. They bought booty – especially slaves – from the soldiers. The difference between these individuals and the merchants who sometimes followed the army is unclear. It is possible that the distinction rested on the scale of the enterprise with the merchant conducting business on a larger scale. The camp followers could hinder army movements; when the troops formed up for battle, the baggage and the camp followers were moved to the rear of the army. Since they were stationed with the baggage that the enemy viewed as a source of booty and often were unarmed, they were far more vulnerable than the soldiers they accompanied. Despite the valuable services they performed, camp followers had to provide for their own needs.

The 300 cavalry that accompanied every legion were a substantial drain on supplies. Polybius informs us that the cavalry was given a monthly ration three times the amount of wheat given to the infantry.[41] In addition, they received 272kg of barley to feed their horses. The increased wheat ration was due to the fact that each cavalryman had two servants to look after in addition to his own needs.

The animals that accompanied the legion substantially increased the need for supplies. In addition to cavalry horses and remounts, which totalled approximately 500 horses, pack animals had to be fed. This limited the distance that the army could march without additional supplies. It has been estimated that each legion had required about 1,000 pack animals including a baggage train for each maniple; an army of about 40,000 men would include the standard consular force of two legions. An equal number of allies and servants would require 4,000 horses and 3,500 pack animals.[42] The animals required grain, straw and pasturage. Pasturage would have been available locally in most areas, but the army had to provide about 13.5kg of fodder per day per horse. Fodder accounted for the largest part of the weight of the legion's supplies.

The quaestor attached to each army supervised its supplies. However by the late Republic, the quaestor was often replaced in this role by any individual the commander thought suitable for the job. In 52 the Gallic Carnutes attacked the town of Cenabum (modern Orléans) where Caesar had established his major supply base.[43] They took the town, destroyed the base and in the process killed Fufius Cita, a man of equestrian rank, who oversaw Caesar's grain supply.

The troops also carried baggage of their own. Their heavy pack included arms, equipment and rations. It may have weighed close to 45kg by the end of the second century, when Marius – in an attempt to decrease the size of the baggage train – further burdened the soldier's pack, having him carry more of his own equipment. The troops were nicknamed Marius' mules.[44] The weight seems excessive, but has been tested on modern troops and found to be manageable.[45] The sources supply a number of figures for the amount of rations that the soldier carried. We know that Athenian hoplites were ordered to bring three days' rations when they set out on expedition.[46] It has been calculated that soldiers could and did often carry rations for about seventeen days based on the weight of other equipment that they carried.[47] When speed was necessary, units were sent out *expeditus,* that is without the normal heavy baggage.[48]

Armies can obtain supplies in various ways. Foraging, requisitioning, plundering and supplies brought from home are all possibilities. Armies could not survive only by foraging and plundering in their local area.[49] The need was especially acute when, as in the course of a siege, an army had to remain in one place. Normally armies that did not move would starve. Foraging was necessary for certain needs such as fodder, water and firewood, but the Romans rarely were able to meet all of their cereal requirements this way. Foraging required sending out large forces, which could seriously weaken the army left behind. Caesar routinely sent out a force of at least one and sometimes several legions accompanied by cavalry and light-armed infantry as protection against enemy attack. Plundering, although in theory an organized activity, could not ensure the army's food supply. It was rare than an area was rich enough to fill the army's needs for any length of time. Local supplies were also not available during various times of the year. Ripened grain would be in the fields for a short time and often the enemy did his best to remove all such cereals to a place of safety before the enemy attacked. The agricultural cycle in the Mediterranean was simply too uncertain to be relied upon. As the local area was denuded of food the foragers had to range farther and farther afield which opened them up to attacks by the enemy. Caesar's legate Quintus Cicero sent out a foraging party in the winter of 52. They were surprised by Gallic cavalry and a number of men were lost.[50]

Polybius claimed that one reason for the success of Rome's wars was due to its ability to provide its troops with abundant supplies.[51] To accomplish this, the Romans had two systematic methods. First, they requisitioned supplies from the neighbourhood or allies. The supplies were either gathered by soldiers or brought in by the local population, who had to bear the cost of transport. This method of supply was crucial for all pre-modern armies, given the limitations of ancient transport. In 199, during a campaign in Illyria on the northwestern border of Macedonia, the proconsul Sulpicius Galba had been able to keep his army in one area because of its fertility, but with the approach of winter he had to withdraw due to a lack of supplies.

An additional source of supply was provided by Roman allies outside of Italy. In 216 Hiero II, the king of Syracuse, sent by ship a significant amount of supplies including about 2,200 tons of wheat and 1,400 tons of barley to the Roman armies operating against the Carthaginians.[52] When the Romans were preparing for war against the Seleucid king Antiochus III, Massinissa, the king of Numidia, offered grain to meet Rome's requirements.[53]

The second method was to bring in supplies from outside the theatre of operations. It seems likely that the Roman system depended on two types of bases, an operational base that served as a major conduit and storage area for an entire theatre of operations and a local, tactical base within the area of operations that moved as the army changed its location. The operational base seems to be an innovation of the First Punic War. There is no earlier evidence for its existence.[54] It was normally located in a population centre, located either on a coast or on a navigable river. For example, in narrating the events of 212 during the Second Punic War, Livy describes the preparations for the siege of Capua. In any siege action, the army would have to remain stationary for a prolonged period. Grain supplies were collected at the city of Casilinum around 3km north of Capua, at the mouth the Volturnus River. A fort was built and garrisoned, commanding the coast and the river as well. They stockpiled grain at Casilinum which had been brought from Sardinia and Etruria to feed the army over the winter.[55] Freighters in operation during the Republic were in the range of 100 to 200 tons. It seems that some fifteen or twenty ships of this size were required.

The tactical base was supplied by pack animals and wagons. For much of the work of transport the Romans were able to rely on local populations. The distance between the tactical base and army in the field was limited, most significantly by the animals used to transport the supplies. They would need to be fed, both on the way to the troops and then back to the base. One modern study made on the basis of northern European campaigns in pre-modern era, estimates that the distance between a tactical base and an army could vary between about 95km and 160km, depending on the mode of transport. However, northern European armies were able to use wagons, which can carry far more than the pack animals that the Romans most often used. Nonetheless, the Romans were capable of transporting supplies by land over substantial distances. During the Third Macedonian War (149–146) they set up an operating base at Ambracia on the Gulf of Actium where they stationed a fleet to act as an escort for supply ships making for Ambracia.[56] They then moved supplies by land across the Balkans to Larissa in Thessaly, a distance of some 96km over mountainous terrain.[57] The expansion of the empire in the course of the Republic allowed the Romans to lessen the burden of transport as they gained control of more areas close to their theatres of operations. But some theatres of operations presented severe difficulties. The most difficult were the desert campaigns. They added the need to carry water, which added substantially to the weight the supply train had to carry. All of these methods were used by the Romans either singly or in combination depending on the circumstances they encountered in the field.

It has long been thought that grain transportation had been carried out by associations of private contractors of equestrian status, the *publican,* who bid on state contracts. This was certainly the case for the city of Rome after grain distributions to the population of Rome became regular towards the end of the second century.[58] However, it has been convincingly argued that the major burden was borne by the state itself, although the contractors did supply other items such as horses and uniforms. The Senate provided the funding and the actual provisioning, after which military personnel did the actual transporting and distribution of the supplies. After a conquest, the burden was shifted to the defeated enemy, who was now responsible for provisioning Roman forces serving as a garrison.

The addition of the provinces of Sicily and Sardinia after 227 probably eased the supply problem for armies active in the West and lessened the burden on the state. Both were rich grain growing areas which by the final third of the second century were also involved in providing grain for Rome itself.

The Allies

When Roman armies marched out to battle they were not alone. A crucial factor in Rome's success was her ability to mobilize vast reserves of manpower. Even enormous losses were sustainable. It has been estimated that during the Second Punic War (218–201) the Romans lost 120,000 citizens; nevertheless despite this Rome was able to field large armies in a number of theatres.[59] Part of this ability depended on Rome's generous policy of enfranchisement of foreigners, but as importantly on Rome's development of a wide-ranging system of alliances that encompassed all of Italy south of a line drawn from Arminium (modern Rimini) on the Adriatic to Pisa on the Tyrrhenian Sea. Polybius and other sources report details of the census taken to assess Roman and allied resources on the eve of the Gallic invasion of 225. The numbers indicate that the Romans had 250,000 infantry and 23,000 cavalry while Roman allies could put 330,000 infantry and 33,000 cavalry into the field. Velleius Paterculus, writing in the early Imperial period, claimed that Rome's allies supplied two-thirds of Roman armies.[60] This figure is too high. Apart from a spike in numbers at the end of the third century, when the allies did compose close to two-thirds of Roman armies, until the end of the Republic they numbered between 50–60 per cent of total Roman forces.[61]

The links between Rome and its allies varied enormously. The various alliances were created in a piecemeal fashion as Rome's Italian conquests expanded. Such variation was in part intentional. For instance, after its victory over the Latin League in 338, the Romans had disbanded the league and concluded bilateral treaties with its former members in an effort to sever the ties that bound the Latins to each other. Some were treaties between equals, while others recognized Rome as the senior partner. The central point of all of these treaties is that these allies should supply manpower for Rome's armies and support them while they were on campaign.[62] This system of alliances seems to have taken shape in the late fourth and early third century. The settlement with the Latins mentioned earlier seems to have served as a template for Rome's future alliances. Because of ethnic and historical links to Rome these communities were given additional rights that included commercial privileges at Rome, the right to conclude legal marriages with Roman citizens and the ability to migrate to Rome, settle there and become full Roman citizens. In the course of the second century this last right was restricted. The expansion of the empire had made new benefits available to citizens serving as an incentive to restrict access to citizenship. These privileges set the Latins apart from other Roman allies. During the empire Latin status lost its ethnic component and became simply a legal status open to all regardless of origin. By 265 the broader system of alliances covered all of peninsular Italy.

There was no central deliberative body nor was there a centralized executive. Rome's overwhelming preponderance meant that all power lay in her hands. This does not mean that the allies were bound to Rome simply by the threat of force. Rome cemented its ties to the local elites through a mutual exchange of benefits.[63] They were the crucial element in Rome's ability to control its allies. It is revealing that when the Social War between Rome and its allies broke out in 90, it was the local elites that precipitated the revolt. They were bound to the Roman elite by ties of friendship, marriage, kinship, patronage and by mutual self-interest. From a very early period the Roman elite had followed the Italic pattern of admitting foreign aristocrats to elite status.[64] This meant that branches of the same family could be resident both at Rome and in other Italian cities. Often these local elites appointed Roman senators as patrons to represent their interests at Rome or to provide help in disputes with other towns. Rome could even protect these elites against their own lower classes. In 265 the aristocracy of the Etruscan city of Volsinii was overthrown by its clients and slaves.

In response they called in the Romans. A Roman army laid siege and captured Volsinii. The Romans re-established the local nobility in power.[65] The absence of centralization among the allies allowed the local communities more latitude to manage their own affairs.

Although military demands were at times heavy, there were some advantages for allied soldiers. It seems likely that they were less burdened by military service than Roman citizens. While on campaign their food was provided without charge, unlike the rations provided to Roman citizens who had them deducted from their pay. They were entitled to a share of the booty, although they received a smaller amount than Roman soldiers did.

Probably from the Second Punic War, if not earlier, the Senate passed a decree each year setting out the state's military needs for the year. It authorized the raising of legions and specified theatres of operations as well the commanders for those theatres. Part of the decree specified how many allied troops would be needed. The consuls then issued an edict to the allied communities, stating how many men each community would have to provide for the coming year. The required numbers were based on a list that the sources call the *formula togatorum* ('the list of toga wearers'). The list, which was probably arranged geographically, set forth the military obligations of Rome's Italian allies in a particular year and so must have been revised annually. It specified how many men each ally had to contribute for the annual levy and so its basis must have been the total number of men of military age each ally had available and must have been based on the allies' own census lists. The consuls calculated what the total contribution of the allies should be for the campaigning year; this was then divided by the total number of men available and a percentage arrived at. This percentage then was the proportion of its available men that each community had to provide.[66] Polybius notes that in each allied community a levy is held by the local magistrates. An oath was then administered to the men and a commander and paymaster were appointed. The function of these commanders is unclear since they do not appear in the sources. The paymaster must be the equivalent to the Roman quaestor, and like the quaestor must have handled all financial matters. The differences in size and economies in each of the allied states must have led to a great deal of variation in the numbers each state had to provide. The sources mention these allied units with ethnic designations, but the smaller communities must have pooled their limited resources and produced mixed units. They were probably brigaded with each other on the basis of geographical proximity and ethnic similarity.

Allied units were organized in a different manner than the legions. The basic unit was the cohort of 400–600 men instead of the maniple. The Greek city of Rhegium, either in 282 or 280, asked the Romans for a garrison to protect it against the neighbouring peoples and Tarentum. Rome sent a force of 800 Campanians and 400 Sidicini under the command of Decius, a Campanian. This would imply that the cohort organization was already in place by the beginning of the third century.[67] This may have functioned more as an administrative than tactical unit although the Romans were later to use it as the basis for the organization of the legions.[68] Centuries and maniples are not mentioned, but they surely existed. Their existence would have made administrative matters such as food distribution easier as they already existed within the legions. There is also no evidence for the Roman division of the battle line into three parts but again the fact that they operated in conjunction with the legion makes it likely that they were also structured in the same way on the battlefield. It seems likely that allied military organization developed over time. Dionysius, in a passage describing the Roman deployment at Asculum, mentions that the allied forces were posted separately between the legions.[69] This mirrors Polybius' account of Pyrrhus' deployment of Italian allies. He posted alternating units of Italians equipped with their own equipment and hoplites in his battle order.[70] By the battle of Magnesia (in Asia Minor) against Antiochus III in 190, Livy describes the allied formations as indistinguishable from Roman ones. Whether light-armed troops were attached to the allied maniples as the *velites* were to the Roman is unknown. At the end of the second century we hear of a cohort of Paeligni from the central Italian Abruzzo region who were equipped with weapons similar to those of the *velites*. It may be that some allied cohorts had specialized functions, perhaps based on their native weaponry. It also presents the possibility that light-armed troops were brigaded in separate cohorts.[71]

Each consular army would have two *alae* or wings of ten cohorts each, with an *ala* assigned to each legion. The allied troops were normally deployed on the flanks of the legions.

In addition to supplying infantry, the allies were also responsible for supplying a force of cavalry three times the size of the Roman contingent.[72] In this period a consular army of two legions would have had 600 cavalry, the allies had to provide an additional 1,800. Cavalry service was expensive and this requirement shifted the burden for fielding the majority of cavalry on to the allies. Allied organization mirrored that of the Roman cavalry. They were organized in *alae*; each *ala* of 300 was subdivided into five double *turmae* of 60 men each. The cavalry does not appear to have been homogeneous, but was a mixed unit combining the troopers of different communities.

The consuls selected one-fifth of the allies' infantry and one-third of their cavalry to serve as *extraordinarii* or 'select' troops on the basis of their fitness. How this was done is not specified. Perhaps a record was kept of previous service and this was used as a basis for selection. In camp these troops bivouacked separately. Their quarters were located so that they could defend the most important part of the camp, which contained the headquarters of the consul and quaestor. On the march they were posted in exposed positions. This implies a high degree of confidence in their loyalty and abilities. What is not clear is why the Romans had such confidence.

Overall command of the allies was entrusted to Roman officers, the *praefecti sociorum* or 'prefects of the allies'. These seem to have been men of equestrian background. Six were assigned to each legion.[73] Their duties paralleled that of the military tribunes who also numbered six, but unlike the tribunes, they were all appointed by the consul. It was they who picked the *extraordinarii*. They rotated duties, as did the military tribunes. Officers from the allied communities, perhaps those appointed as the units were selected, acted as subordinates to the *praefecti*.

Not all of the allies supplied land forces; a portion of them supplied ships and their crews. These were primarily the Greek states of southern Italy that had a strong maritime tradition. It used to be thought that they were placed in a separate category but there is no evidence for this. There is no reason to think that their treaties with Rome were any different than those of the other allies. It is probable that all the treaties simply specified all the available forces and left it to the Romans to decide whether land or naval forces were going to be called up. It is probable that – just as in the case of the land allies – the Romans specified the number of ships, crews and supplies that had to be provided. At first, it seems the naval forces were commanded by quaestors; four were appointed in 267. But as Roman naval forces grew in size fleets began to be commanded by praetors and finally by consuls and proconsuls. Smaller squadrons could be commanded by equestrian prefects. At times the pressure on naval allies must have been intense. The standard warships of the period carried substantial crews. Although estimates differ, they required perhaps 300 rowers and an additional 40 men to serve as marines. However, it is not clear how many of the crew, whether rowers or marines, were drawn from the naval allies. It is reasonably certain that those who occupied the technical positions aboard ship were naval allies. The naval component of Rome's armed forces tended to atrophy after the First Punic War as the focus of Roman attention and effort turned back to her land forces.

In battle the allied *alae* were stationed on the right and left wings of the battle line. Livy makes their position clear at the battle of Magnesia:

> There were two Roman legions and two [alae] composed of the allies and those of the Latin name. Each of these units had 5,400 men. The Romans held the centre of the line and the allies were on the wings. The standards of the hastati were in front, behind them were those of the principes, and those of the triarii closed up the rear.

On the other hand, the allied cavalry was usually stationed on one wing while the Roman occupied the opposite flank. It is possible that by the mid-fourth century the Latins were equipped in Roman fashion. Livy in his discussion of the battle of the Veseris during the war with the Latins mentions that the Roman and Latin forces facing each other were equipped in the same way and used the same battle formation.[74] Since the Latins were closely related to and were neighbours of the Romans, it seems likely that they adopted Roman equipment or some variation of it. The same can probably be said of tactical formations quite early on. The process of adoption by Rome's allies of Roman military methods must have been made easier since their native fighting techniques were in many cases quite similar to Roman ones. For instance, *scutum*-like shields can be found among a number of Italic peoples as well as among the Gauls. The similarities would have made the commander's task easier.

The figures that we possess for casualties show that the allies suffered disproportionately high casualties, because the Roman commanders were more willing to risk their lives than those of their fellow citizens. There are also indications of rivalry between Roman and allied forces – not always with positive results. Although the danger was the same, the benefits that allied soldiers enjoyed were less than those of their Roman comrades. This must have created an additional spur to rivalry and anger on the part of the allies. Also their communities must have found it difficult to supply their troops for the incessant campaigns the Romans fought.

Some indication of the difficulties these communities encountered, although an extreme instance, came during the Second Punic War. In 209, twelve of the thirty Latin colonies informed the Romans that they could no longer furnish men or supplies for the Roman war effort. Only three years earlier the Romans had fielded twenty-five legions, which meant that an equal or greater number of allies were on active campaign. The number of legions for the period 209–206 fell to an average of 11, which still meant that approximately 55,000 allied troops were in service. It is significant that by this point the war had shifted in Rome's favour, which made the Roman reaction to the refusal all the more likely to be harsh. Despite this, the colonies refused and this shows that the exhaustion was real. The Romans still had other pressing matters in Spain and Italy and the colonies were not dealt with until 204.

Unlike the other allies, the Latin colonies do not seem to have had a treaty obligation to support Rome militarily; the requirement was an automatic consequence of the foundation of the colony. Livy's narrative reveals some important points.[75] The angry senate instructed the consuls to summon the magistrates of the recalcitrant cities and to demand that they supply double the number of infantry that they had previously contributed, as well as 120 cavalry each. Further, they stipulated that if a city could not supply a requisite number of cavalry, it could compensate by supplying three infantrymen for every cavalry trooper. Other penalties were imposed, directed at the local aristocracies. The emphasis on punishment of these elites reveals the sense of betrayal that the Roman senators must have felt at the conduct of men like themselves. The incident reveals how overwhelmingly dominant Rome's power was in Italy now that it had recovered from Hannibal's invasion. It also illustrates Rome's control of local government.[76] The imposition of a census on this community along Roman lines is one aspect of the growing Romanization of Italy. Usually, it was voluntary on both sides. Service in Rome's armies must have been a major force for assimilation.

CHAPTER SEVEN

THE ARMY ON CAMPAIGN I

At Rome, as in most ancient states, warfare was enmeshed in a set of religious rituals and celebrations that attempted to bring success in war by invoking the aid of the gods. At Rome, to win the favour of the gods it was crucial to prove that a war was morally justified. It was also important to the Romans to appear to be acting with just cause in the eyes of non-Romans. Such morally acceptable causes were usually based on self-defence or righting a wrong inflicted by another party on Rome. Polybius makes this clear; in a fragment of text, he mentions that:

> *The Romans take special care not to seem to have been the ones to have begun unjust actions, nor to be attacking their neighbours when they undertook wars, but to appear to be acting in self-defence and to be entering on wars out of necessity.*[1]

This was not a real concern, although it is clear that what constituted a just cause tended to be interpreted quite liberally. Nonetheless, the concept of the just war which went back to both Greek and Roman sources was more than just a cloak to hide unjust actions.[2] It seems to have had at least some real validity. Perhaps the best formulation of the Roman concept of the just war is Cicero's in his treatise on duties, written in the autumn of 44, in a difficult and dangerous political situation after Caesar's assassination in March:

> *In a republic it is especially important that we maintain the laws of war. There are two types of disputes, the one involves discussion, the other force. Since the first is unique to man and the second to beasts, we ought to resort to the second only if the first is not available. Wars ought to be undertaken so that we can live free from injury. After victory those individuals who were neither cruel nor inhumane in war ought to be spared.*[3]

For the Romans the concept of just war had two aspects, the human and the divine. They developed a religious process to try to guarantee that the gods would favour them because of the justness of their cause.

One or more of a college of priests called the fetial priests or *fetiales* was sent on an embassy to the offending party. Reciting an oath, the priest invoked Jupiter to guarantee that Roman demands were justified. This oath was recited four times: at the enemy's borders, and to the first man the envoy met after he crossed into enemy territory, at the city gate and in the city's forum, usually the enemy's capital. Part of the oath demanded that the enemy offer adequate compensation. At the end of thirty-three days, if there had been no satisfactory response, the envoy called upon Jupiter, Janus and other gods to witness that the Romans had been refused their rights and returned to Rome.[4] After the Senate had been consulted and war agreed upon, the *fetiales* carried a blood-coloured spear with its point tipped with iron or fire hardened to the frontier. One of the priests recited formulas and declared war in the presence of at least three adults. Then the spear was thrown into enemy territory as the first act of war. Much of the procedure has been questioned by modern scholars, but in the period when Rome's wars were local, it was feasible and in line with Roman conscientiousness about such matters.[5] By the first half of the-third century, the *fetiales* had been replaced by an embassy under a legate, perhaps because of distance as the empire expanded. They still maintained a role in maintaining and repudiating treaties.

From the third century, if not earlier, declaring war had become essentially secular. In theory, the assembly of the people, in this case the centuriate assembly, was the body responsible for the declaration of war, but in practice it was a much more varied process. The full formal procedure started with senatorial approval. After the Senate voted for war, the consuls were instructed by the Senate to sacrifice for a successful outcome. If the sacrifices were favourable, priests known as *haruspices,* who were experts in divination and interpreting various natural signs, were consulted. If they too reported favourable omens, the matter was then submitted by the consul to the assembly. On other occasions formal procedure was neglected. It seems that the key part of the decision-making process belonged to the Senate. [6]

The making of war involved religious rites and ceremonies. The religious observances concerned with war were concentrated in the early spring and summer when the campaigning season began. The main cycle of rites opened on 1 March with a war dance by the Salian priests of Mars, who were dressed in military attire (some of which was clearly archaic, like their figure-eight shields and long old-fashioned lances). Their prayers invoked Mars, and also Jupiter, and Janus.[7] On 23 February and then again on 14 March, the Equirria which was also associated with Mars and held on the Campus Martius was held. It has been suggested that its purpose was to purify the cavalry horses before the opening of the campaigning season.[8] On 23 March and then again 23 May, the Tubilustrium was held to purify and consecrate the war trumpets. It was also dedicated to Mars. At the same time the Salian priests danced through the city.[9]

At the close of the military season in the autumn, the ritual of the October horse was held. The horse was put to death. He was the right-hand horse of the chariot, which had won the chariot race held on the Campus Martius, which was associated with the army and warfare.

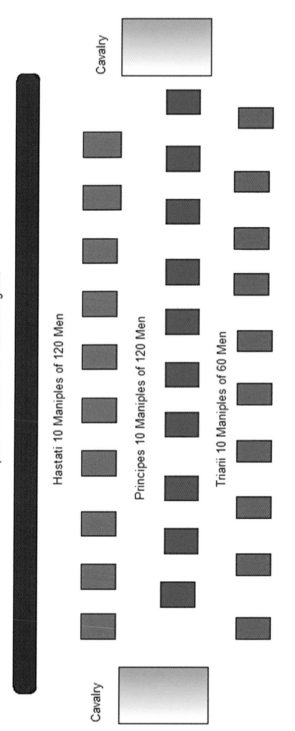

The manipular legion deployed for battle, with the screen of *velites* closest to the enemy. (Copyright: the author)

A *veles*, 3rd century BC. He is armed with a number of light javelins with which to harass enemy troops and a sword (*gladius*) for close defence. His only defensive equipment is the small, round *parma* shield, though the wolf-pelt headdress may also offer some protection. (Copyright: Philip Sidnell)

A *triarius* of the 3rd century BC. He is well protected with a mail shirt, Montefortino helmet, long *scutum* shield, and a single bronze greave protecting his left (leading) shin. (Copyright: Philip Sidnell)

A *princeps* of the 3rd century BC. Like the *triarius* he is protected by a *scutum*, Montefortino helmet and one greave, but wears a pectoral on his chest rather than the more expensive mail shirt. He is throwing an early form of *pilum*.
(Copyright: Philip Sidnell)

This *hastatus*, equipped just like the *princeps*, has already thrown his *pila* and drawn his *gladius*, ready to close with the enemy.
(Copyright: Philip Sidnell)

Roman *eques*. This relief from the forum in Rome (a later copy of a Republican original) depicts Marcus Curtius deliberately riding to his death in a chasm. The hero, well protected by a helmet, Hellenistic-style cuirass and a round shield, is armed with a spear wielded overarm.
(Courtesy of Lalupa via Wikipedia)

This figure from the so-called 'Altar of Domitius Ahenobarbus' (late 2nd century BC) is thought to represent Mars but his dress and equipment reflect that of a Roman officer such as a military tribune. He wears an Etrusco-Corinthian helmet and Hellenistic style cuirass with double row of *pteruges* and is armed with spear, round shield and sword worn on his left side.
(The Louvre, Paris. Photo by Jastrow, via Wikipedia)

Roman infantry and cavalryman on the 'Altar of Domitius Ahenobarbus' (late 2nd century BC). Note the mail shirts, the Boeotian helmet of the *eques* and the details of the *scuta* (shields): the horizontal grip and the central boss and spine.
(The Louvre, Paris. Photos copyright of Michael Taylor, used with his kind permission)

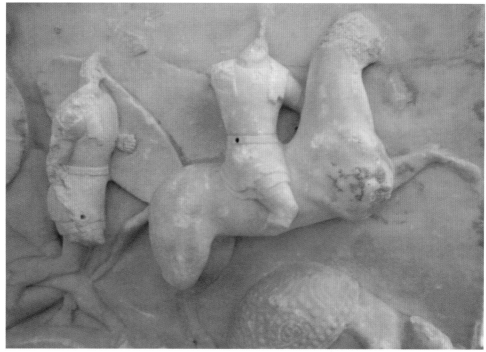

Figures from the victory monument commemorating the victory of Lucius Aemilius Paullus over Perseus of Macedon at Pydna in 168 BC. Above, a Roman cavalryman and legionary, both in mail shirts with shoulder reinforcements, advancing over a fallen Macedonian phalangite. Below, a Roman legionary defends himself against Macedonian cavalry; the scutum's horizontal grip is clearly shown.
(Both images copyright of Michael Taylor, used with his kind permission)

Montefortino helmet of a Republican soldier, now in the British Museum. The knob at the top was used for affixing plumes. Note the substantial cheek pieces.
(Photo copyright of Philip Matyszak, used with his kind permission)

A replica pilum head made by Southern Swords (www.southernswords.co.uk). The pyramidal head was designed to pierce an opponent's shield then be difficult to extract, especially as the shank would bend on impact.
(Photo copyright of Southern Swords)

Roman infantry helmet found in Dorset and now in the British Museum. Note the projecting neck guard
(Photo copyright of Malgosia Matyszak, used with her kind permission)

Drawing of a gladius and scabbard of the late-Republican period (circa 70 BC), now in Delos Museum.

(Copyright M C Bishop, used with his kind permission)

30cm

0

Replica Roman gladius and scabbard by Southern Swords.

(photo copyright of Southern Swords, www.southernswords.co.uk)

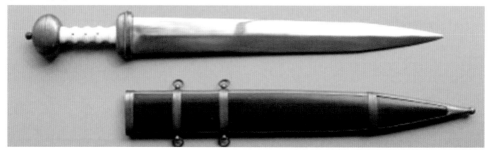

He was sacrificed on an altar to Mars. The head and tail were cut off, and then carried to Regia, originally the king's residence. While it was being transported, the horse's blood was allowed to flow in the Forum. The head then became the object of a contest between the people of two districts of the city; the victors nailed the head to the wall of the Regia. The other ritual that signalled the end of the campaigning season was the Armilustrium, held on 19 October. It included another festival dedicated to Mars, where sacrifices were performed and the war trumpets blown on the Aventine Hill at a location called Armilustrium. The Salii purified the army's weapons by dancing with their shields, presumably removing the infection that killing brought.

The campaign itself was enmeshed in religious ritual. Before the consul or praetor set out on campaign, he performed a lustration or purification of his army. These lustrations were repeated in the course of the campaign, especially before engaging in battle.[10] The sources do not supply the details of lustrations, but they were probably similar to those of the fleet. In his account of Octavian's attack on one of Pompey's sons in Sicily, Appian recounts the procedure:

> *Altars are built on the shore, and members of the fleet are ranged around them in a circle of ships, keeping a profound silence. Priests offer the sacrifice at the water's edge, and carry the expiatory offerings in skiffs three times round the fleet. The generals sail with them, calling upon the gods to turn the bad omens against the victims instead of the fleet. Then, cutting up the entrails, they throw a part of them into the sea, and put the remainder on the altars and burn them, while the troops chant in unison.[11]*

Obviously, there must have been differences, but the sacrifices and the involvement of the commanders must have had their parallels in the army ritual.

Before leaving Rome the commander took auspices on Capitoline Hill to see if the gods were favourable to the campaign. The gods signalled their favour in two ways: through sought signs – through sacrifice and divination – or through natural events such as the flights of birds or lightning, which were read according to a standard set of rules. Neglecting to perform the ceremony or ignoring the results could bring disaster. The army of Gaius Flaminius, one of the consuls of 217, was ambushed and destroyed at Lake Trasimene in Etruria. The disastrous defeat was attributed to Flaminius' willful omission of the auspices. Among the omissions were the failure to take the auspices before his army marched out of the city, his repeated failure to attend to the auspices and unfavourable omens before the battle.[12] A more famous incident concerns the taking of auspices before a naval battle in the First Punic War. In 249, the consul Appius Claudius launched a naval attack on the Carthaginian-held port of Drepana in Sicily. The sacred chickens used for auspices before a battle would not eat the grain given to them, which would have been a favourable sign. After repeated attempts, Claudius ordered the sacred chickens to be thrown overboard with the words, 'If they won't eat, let them drink.'[13] The daily construction of the military marching camp, or later of any permanent camp, also involved religious ritual. Auspices had to be taken before a camp could be built. However, promagistrates did not have the right to take auspices and with the proliferation of military and governmental commands held by promagistrates, the use of auspices on campaigns gradually disappeared. By the mid-first century Cicero could claim that auspices were no longer taken while on campaign.[14]

Victory in battle was followed by another ritual. Enemy arms were collected from the battlefield and then burned as a sacrifice. Various gods and goddesses are recorded as recipients. The rite is last attested at the beginning of the first century.[15] Further rituals were performed on the return of the army, especially after a significant victory.[16]

Once the religious formalities had been completed, the army marched out of the city accompanied by its baggage train. The correct marching formation was a vital aspect of a general's competence. However, it presented its own problems. The Romans had developed a series of standard formations, but the choice among them was to a great extent determined by three factors: the terrain to be crossed, the supply situation and the proximity of the enemy. Speeds varied as a function of the terrain, the condition of the men and the speed of the baggage train. Polybius offers a description of the standard marching formations, but omits a number of variations that are mentioned in other sources.[17]

The standard formation used, when there was room and no immediate threat of enemy attack, placed the legions in the centre of the column with allied formations in front and behind them. The cavalry of the *extraordinarii* formed the vanguard with their infantry immediately behind them. Next in line came the right *ala* of the allied troops. These units were then followed by their baggage. After them marched the first Roman legion with its baggage immediately behind it; the second legion came next in the same formation with the baggage of the left behind it. The other allied wing formed the rear of the main column. The rest of the cavalry sometimes marched to the rear of the unit to which it was assigned and sometimes on the side of the column, keeping the baggage animals from straying and also offering them protection. The order of march was designed to allow an easy transition from marching column to battle line. The battle line usually had the legions in the centre and the allies on the wings, a formation mirrored in the marching formation. The looser deployment of the cavalry was possible because their speed of movement allowed them to move into formation quickly. If there was a threat of an attack on the rear of the column, the *extraordinarii* formed the rear of the column. Each day the legions and the allies changed position so that they could share the fresh food and water.

Polybius also describes the formation used if there was a threat of attack. If there was sufficient open ground the three lines of the legion, the maniples of the *hastati, principes* and *triarii* of each legion, marched in parallel columns with the baggage to the front. This was the case for all of the legions. If some immediate danger presented itself, they turned left or right towards the enemy and then disengaged from the baggage. At times, the *hastati* had to wheel about depending on the direction of the enemy. In this way they shielded the baggage and protected its attendants.

If the Republican marching formation was similar to the Roman army of the first century AD, the men would have normally marched six abreast.[18] This would suggest that a maniple's depth in battle formation was the same. This would also mean that they marched in maniples and so it is probable that the maniples of each line followed one another so that the maniples of the *hastati* marched first, then those of the *principes* and finally those of the *triarii*. This would allow for a fairly simple transition from column to line.

The position of the baggage train on the line of march was of great importance, given its vulnerability. When an enemy attack was imminent, if there was sufficient space available, the army marched in a square formation with the baggage and non-combatants placed inside the square.[19] The square could be used in the absence of the baggage train as an all-around defence, but it had weaknesses. In his disastrous expedition against the Parthians in 53, Crassus changed his marching formation into a square with cavalry placed at each corner so that all of the infantry would have cavalry support. However, the square offered no protection against the repeated missile attacks that were to destroy his army at Carrhae in northern Syria.[20] There were other formations possible depending on circumstances. In 57, Caesar had invaded the territory of the Belgae, who constituted the Gallic tribes of northeastern Gaul. Moving to engage one of them, the Nervii, he knew that they were close and to his front so he moved his baggage to the rear of his column, guarded by two locally conscripted legions.[21] If the terrain was unfavourable or the number of troops too large, the army could be divided into multiple columns. In 53, Caesar attacked the Gallic Menapii who lived between the Scheldt and the Meuse. He set out with five lightly equipped legions and divided his army into three columns, one under his own command – which probably consisted of three legions – while one legion each was assigned to two of his legates. The separation into three columns was an excellent tactical move. There was no reason to expect his army to be met by a large enemy force. The division's purpose was to spread devastation as widely as possible and to block the Menapii's likely escape routes from their difficult and swampy territory.[22] Further evidence on the flexibility of the march formation is provided by the arrangement that the new commander Caecilius Metellus adopted on his arrival in Africa in 109:

> *Metellus, acting as if the enemy was present, proceeded with his column*
> *well protected. He scouted the country far and wide. He believed that the*
> *signs of surrender were only a ruse and that the enemy was looking for a*
> *place to ambush him. He headed the column of cohorts ready for action,*
> *with a select group of slingers and archers. The rear of the column was in*
> *the hands of his legate Gaius Marius with the cavalry, while on the flanks*
> *he had assigned auxiliary cavalry to the military tribunes and prefects of*
> *the cohorts. Mixed in with them were light-armed troops to repulse the*
> *enemy horse wherever it should appear.*[23]

A baggage train necessarily slows down the speed of the march. It has been suggested that a large Roman army could make 16–24km per day, although smaller forces, especially those not hindered by a baggage train, could march substantially farther. For instance, the fourth century writer Vegetius prescribes a march rate of 32km per day for an individual soldier and a forced march of around 38.5km.[24] In 54, on orders from Caesar, his legate Crassus covered 40km in somewhat more than 10 hours, but this was with a single legion. Smaller units can move more quickly than larger ones. Furthermore, the baggage train created problems if it was attacked while on the march. Polybius notes the train's vularonerability to cavalry attack in flat country.[25] Often, when speed was crucial and the enemy near, columns were sent out without their baggage, but of course this left the baggage train vulnerable to attack even if guards were left with it, as they normally were.

Until the last century of the Republic, Roman scouting was not terribly effective. The ambush at the Caudine Forks in 321 during the Second Samnite War and Hannibal's ambush of Flaminius' army at Lake Trasimene in 217 were in part made possible by inadequate scouting.[26] Scipio Africanus was an early exception to this neglect of scouting.[27] Since scouting was the prerogative of the general, the use of scouts varied widely. Polybius was alert to the need to scout the enemy's territory. In his assessment of Hannibal's crossing of the Alps, he notes that only the most incompetent of generals would not know the roads and the territory he was marching through, his enemy and whether the campaign was feasible. The growing awareness of the necessity of scouting by the last century is evident from Caesar's conduct in Gaul. In his first major confrontation in Gaul with the Helvetii, his scouts brought back the news that the enemy was encamped about 11km away from his own camp. Caesar then sent forward additional scouts to reconnoiter the hill behind their camp. He was planning to secretly station troops there and then have them fall upon the rear of the Gauls during the battle. The scouting was successful and led to a victorious conclusion to the battle.[28] But at times, even Caesar would neglect to scout sufficiently. The next year in his campaign among the Belgae, at the critical battle against the Nervii, Caesar was surprised by a sudden attack by the main body of the enemy who had been hiding in nearby woods. The battle almost ended in a Roman defeat. Much of the blame for the surprise rests with Caesar. Although the Nervii had done what they could to create difficulties for Roman scouts, Caesar stresses that he knew where the Nervii were and it is hard to believe that over 400,000 men could remain undiscovered, even if they were hidden in the woods across the river.[29]

On the march, cavalry and light-armed infantry were assigned scouting duties. They probably advanced no farther than 13km from the main body given the limitations in communications. It would have not only been time consuming to pass the information to the main column if the scouts advanced farther, but it would also have been likely that by the time they had informed the commander of the situation it would have changed sufficiently to negate the value of their information.[30] Problems in communication were not the only obstacle to effective scouting. Unfavouruable terrain and adverse atmospheric conditions also served to limit its usefulness.

There was also the need to gather what has been called strategic intelligence before going on campaign. As mentioned earlier, when Aemilius Paullus received the command against the Macedonian king Perseus in 168, he dispatched legates to investigate the army's logistical situation, including its overland and seaborne supply lines, the strength of the enemy, and potential Roman allies, neutrals and enemies.[31] Caesar supplies an example of the gathering of this kind of general intelligence about the peoples and area he was intending to campaign in. Before his invasion of Britain in 55, he set out to learn what he could about the people, places, harbours and routes in the island. He claims that there was general ignorance about Britain in Gaul. Even the traders he consulted could supply him with little information, though one has to wonder if some of this ignorance was feigned. As soon as his plans became known, traders relayed the information to the Britons. He was forced to send out one of his military tribunes, Gaius Volusenus, with a warship to reconnoitre the coast.[32]

There was no systematic means of gathering intelligence. For instance, when Cicero took over his governorship of Cilicia in 51 he was ignorant of the state of his province, as well as the crossing of the Parthians over the Euphrates, both of which posed a major threat to his province. He only learned of their crossing from a client prince whom he did not fully trust. Roman governors often had to depend on what they could glean from fellow governors, client kings and local elites. On campaign, in addition to the commander's own scouting, prisoners of war, deserters or encounters with locals were used as sources of information.[33]

It was the standard Roman practice to encamp at the end of the day's march. Of course, it was not an invariable rule. The same Caecilius Metellus who had taken up the command against Jugurtha and had carefully sent out scouts, criticized his predecessors for failing to routinely fortify their camps as they should have.[34]

Polybius offers us a detailed picture of the Roman camp, but there are some uncertainties about his description. For instance, there has long been a dispute over whether the camp is for a consular army of two legions or describes one-half of a camp of a double consular army of four legions. The other sources, given their lack of interest in technical detail, do not allow us to check his accuracy. Some archaeological evidence can be used to supplement Polybius. During the long wars in Spain in the second century, the Romans constructed a series of camps in northeastern Spain at Renieblas, near the ancient Celtiberian city of Numantia (close to modern Burgos). They date from the 150s to the 80s; however, of special interest is the third camp which has been identified as that of Quintus Fulvius Nobilior, consul in 153, who in that year unsuccessfully campaigned against the Celtiberians. The date of the camp is about contemporary with Polybius' description so it can act to some extent as a check on his account.

There is more information for the Imperial period. We have a treatise by Pseudo-Hyginus, *On the Fortification of Camps* and Vegetius' *On the Military Institutions of the Romans*.[35] The author of the Pseudo-Hyginus text is unknown, as is its date. It could range anywhere from the late first to the third century AD. However, some of its details can be collaborated from excavations of Imperial camps.[36] In this period there are traces of marching camps particularly in Britain, but Republican evidence is very limited. Since these camps were built only for very temporary use and constructed of perishable materials, it is hardly surprising that there are few remains. Until the late first century, camps were usually built of such materials. This was especially true for the Republican period when legions were raised annually and disbanded at the end of the campaigning season. However, there were exceptions. Nobilior's camp was built of stone, presumably because it was to be occupied over the winter of 153/152. The Latin term for a winter camp is *castra hiberna*. Unlike the marching camps, it had 1-metre thick walls of stone and these camps as well as the later Imperial ones show that the Romans were not limited by a set plan.[37] Although the structures of the camp were the same, the camps were constructed to take advantage of the local topography and in accordance with campaign needs. Despite the large number of camps of the Imperial period excavated, no two are identical. There is no secure information on the origin of Roman methods of camp construction. It has been suggested that the layout of a camp was heavily influenced by contemporary town planning, which stressed grid layouts.[38]

Campsites were selected by the military tribunes. The site was chosen with a number of prerequisites in mind. The site should offer a good view in all directions. Only in totally flat land would it be located in a plain. Gentle elevations were chosen, that allowed easier and quicker access in and out of the camp. This preference and the advantages it brought are clear from an account in Caesar of an attack by the Gallic Venelli during Caesar's campaign against the coastal Veneti in 56. The Venelli had surrendered to a legate of Caesar the year before, but over the winter had thought better of their decision. The leader of the Venelli, Viridovix, exercised a general command over those tribes that had rebelled and assembled a sizeable army. Caesar's legate, Titurius Sabinus, had entered the territory of the Venelli to bring the rebel army to battle. It is interesting that Caesar claims that Sabinus had located his camp wisely. The camp was situated on a hill that sloped up gradually for 0.8km. The Gauls rushed the camp carrying brush to fill up the ditch, but their run uphill winded them. The Romans made sorties from two of the gates, which allowed them to attack the enemy from multiple directions, and the Gauls fled. Both the site of the camp and its construction brought the Romans important advantages.[39] The camp also should be located to provide easy access to water, wood and fodder.

Construction was carried out under the tribunes' overall supervision with the work of construction overseen by centurions. The troops whose quarters were closest to a particular side of the camp were responsible for construction of that part of the camp. The general pattern was rectangular but the characteristics of the site influenced the camp's shape.[40] To lay out their camps, the Romans developed a specialist corps of surveyors. In fact, the Romans were the first to create surveying manuals. It was one of the few literary genres they did not borrow from the Greeks. Both the legions and the allied units took part in the work of construction. In cases when danger threatened, part of the legionary and allied forces would stand guard in front of those who were employed in construction. In his campaign against the Nervii in 57, Caesar decided to construct a camp near the River Sambre. Knowing the Nervii were on the other bank of the river, he sent his cavalry and light-armed troops across to act as a screen for the six legions building the camp.[41]

The fortifications were relatively simple and consisted of three parts.[42] First a ditch was excavated (the *fossa*) around the camp's perimeter. It was usually 1 metre deep and 1.5 metres wide. Then an elevated walkway (the *agger*) was constructed out of the turfs excavated from the ditch. Finally, wooden stakes were driven into the top of the *agger* to create a palisade. These stakes were carried along in the baggage train, until the first century when the legionaries carried stakes in their packs. A large open space was left around the perimeter of the camp to allow additional soldiers and animals to be brought into the camp, for quick mobilization in case of an attack as well as for protection against missile weapons. Polybius' figures for the size of the camp yields a square approximately 610 metres per side. Adding the other double legion camp to it results in a rectangle of approximately 1460 metres by 610 metres.

The heart of the camp was formed by the *praetoria* or commander's tent, the quaestor's quarters, the *quaestoria* and the forum which was an open space in front of the officers' quarters that was used for a variety of activities. To the left and right of these quarters were the tents of the veterans, *extraordinarii* and volunteers. These were laid out in a line with the *praetoria* which stood at the centre. The ends of the line were formed by tents for veterans, and select legionary and allied troops. To the front of this line ran the *Via Principalis* which terminated in two gates the *Porta Principalis Dextra* and *Sinistra* (or right and left). It was so named because the tents of the commanding general and his officers lay along it. The tents of the legates, military tribunes and prefects of the allies fronted the *praetorium* on the *Via Principalis*. Across the *Principalis* were the tents of the legions and the allies. They were arranged so that they duplicated the position of the legions and the allies in the battle line with the allied tents on the two sides and the legions in between. The tents were bisected by another street the *Via Quintana* which led to two further gates, the *Porta Quintana Dextra* and *Sinistra*. The wall to the rear of those tents was broken by another gate, the *Porta Decumana*. Finally, behind the praetorium were the tents of the rest of the *extraordinarii,* both cavalry and infantry and any foreign troops. These units were divided into two parts bisected by the *Via Praetoria,* which would in a two legion camp have led to the *Porta Praetoria*. In the four legion camp, two legion camps were placed back to back. It has been estimated that construction of a two legion camp would have taken about three hours and could have been completed in an afternoon after a morning march.

Camp defences were not especially strong. It appears that when camping in safe territory the outer defences might be omitted. However, clearly this was not the case in enemy territory. In such a situation the gates were fortified. These defences consisted of an obstacle erected in the middle of the gate, a ditch or curving extensions of the walls from both sides, so that an attacker would be forced to turn and expose his unshielded side to the defenders.

These marching camps were only meant as temporary bases and shelter and not for permanent occupation of territory. They did provide at least a minimum of security and allowed time to respond to attacks. It also could serve as a base for offensive action. The winter of 54/53 was a hard one in Gaul, and a poor harvest added to Roman difficulties. Caesar had to encamp his legions separately because of the limited supply of food. The Gauls saw an opportunity to rebel because of the separation of the camps, and attacks were launched on the camps. One was successful, the others were not. An attack on Quintus Cicero's, the brother of Marcus, camp in northeastern Gaul had failed, but it was now under siege by the Nervii. Caesar went to its relief with two legions. The Gauls learned of Caesar's approach and set out to ambush him. Quintus warned Caesar of the enemy's approach and the general halted his march. He then built a camp in an advantageous spot. Caesar claims that he narrowed the paths around walls, and around and through the camp interior, to give the impression that he had a smaller force. It is interesting to note that the Gauls were so familiar with Roman camp construction that they could estimate the size of a force by the area of the camp. Caesars' plan was to lure the Gauls on so that they would fight near his camp. In anticipation he had the rampart heightened and the gate was barricaded with turfs. The men were withdrawn from the rampart and the Gauls bombarded the camp with missiles unhindered. His ruse succeeded. The Romans issued from all the camp gates at once, along with their cavalry. The unsuspecting Gauls were immediately routed and fled without putting up further resistance.[43] The camp also lessened the problem of deserters, which plagued all pre-modern armies. It also served as a symbolic display of Roman discipline both for the troops and for the foreigners.

The effect on at least some foreigners is clear from Polybius' comparison of Greek and Roman marching camps:

> *In this matter the Romans seem to be pursuing a course of convenience opposite to that of the Greeks. The latter think that the most important point in encamping is to adapt to the natural strength of a place, because in the first place they shirk from the labour of entrenching and, secondly, because they do not consider man-made fortifications superior to the natural strength of a position. So they are compelled to constantly change the form of their camp in accordance with the natural configuration of the ground and to have to move units to unsuitable positions, and the result is that individuals and units are uncertain of their location in the camp. On the other hand, the Romans prefer the fatigue of entrenching and other defensive works because of the convenience of having a single form of camp, familiar to all.*[44]

Polybius' preference for the Roman camp is understandable. Certainly the marching camps of the classical Athenians seem to have been rather unimpressive. The housing for the troops varied as materials and building styles were personal preferences. Their siting was haphazard, as was their interior layout. They might or might not be fortified. The Spartan camp was, as might be expected, of more regular construction, with a preference for a round form of camp.[45] Nonetheless, Polybius is too dismissive. We have literary evidence that Greek commanders did at times fortify their camps. For instance, in 480 Gelon, the tyrant of Syracuse, constructed a fortified camp with ditch and palisade in a war against the Carthaginians.[46] Nevertheless, the general pattern seems to conform to Athenian camp construction with an absence of fortifications. Alexander the Great did not normally fortify his camp. At Gaugamela in 330 he did so, because he wanted to leave the army's baggage as well as his sick and wounded there.[47]

The building and functioning of the camp also served as tools to instill discipline in recruits and to maintain it through the closely regulated routine of the camps. Its construction required coordination, ordered effort and a degree of standardization, as did marching drill.[48] Vegetius stresses the importance of entrenching camps, not just for the safety it would bring but also for the discipline and teamwork it would instill in recruits. The training value that the Romans ascribed to digging and construction is clear from an anecdote about Scipio Aemilianus who captured the city of Numantia in 133. To discipline his troops, he had them dig ditches and construct camps daily and then demolish them.[49]

Within the camp a strict disciplinary regime was enforced. However, since it depended on the particular commander this must have varied a great deal. When Caecilius Metellus took over command in the Jugurthine War he found the army in utter disarray. One of the signs of it was soldiers wandering from camp as they pleased.[50] One of the measures he took to restore discipline was frequent camp construction as Scipio had done a little more than two decades earlier.[51]

Polybius provides the fullest account of camp discipline.[52] The tribunes played the major role as they did in camp construction. Once the camp was completed, they gathered all the men in camp including slaves and administered an oath. The oath bound the men to refrain from theft and to bring anything they found to the tribunes. They then issued orders to the centurions of two maniples of the *hastati* and *principes* in each legion to take care of the grounds in front of their tents. Three of the remaining maniples of these two lines were assigned to each of the six tribunes of the legion. The *triarii*, presumably because of their longer service, were exempt from this duty. Each of the three maniples attended the tribunes in turn and were assigned to perform various services. Polybius mentions that they levelled the ground for his tent and pitched it; they also fenced in any baggage that needed protection. Given other pre-modern armies, it is likely that the tribunes brought along substantial amounts of baggage and so this was a necessary task. Further, each maniple including the *triarii* were required to provide a guard for the horses of the cavalry unit camped behind them. Each maniple in turn mounted guard around the consul's tent.

The tribunes also served as a channel of communication. At the consul's tent they received their orders and then passed them on to the centurions and decurions. Another crucial function they performed was the provision of the night watchword. They chose a soldier from the tenth maniple of each line of infantry and a trooper from the cavalry who was exempted from guard duty to meet the tribune at sunset to receive the night's watchword, which was written down on a wooden tablet. He then returned to his quarters and informed the senior centurion of the watchword and it was then passed on from maniple to maniple. The tablet was returned to the tribune, so that he knew that the watchword had made the rounds. Guards were appointed from the infantry and the cavalry to keep watch over them. If the guards failed in their duty, they suffered severe punishment.[53]

We know little of the religion of the army during the Republic. A remark by Dionysius of Halicarnassus in connection with a mutiny in the fifth century – which may be legendary – mentions that the standards were considered holy.[54] There is no reason to doubt that the camp had a religious dimension as did other aspects of warfare. This seems to have been especially true of the legionary standards, including unit standards such as those for the maniples. Once a campsite was selected the first task was to mark the site by thrusting the standards into the ground. In the Imperial period each camp had a shrine, which served as the centre for the religious life of the camp, the *sacellum,* in which the standards of the legion were kept. There is no reason to doubt that the same practice was true of the Republic, although we lack evidence for it. Certainly, the standards later played a central role in the religious life of the soldiers and of their camp. They were present at all rituals. Oaths were sworn before them and they appeared in all parades.[55] Seneca, writing in the first century, saw the cult of the standards as embodying discipline, loyalty and tradition.[56] One might also add unit cohesion. The gods of the Roman state were worshipped in camp as well.

In the introduction to his history of the rise of Rome, Polybius justifies his choice of topic by citing Rome's astonishingly successful development of an empire based on both direct and indirect control that encompassed much of the Mediterranean coast of Europe and had expanded to into parts of Asia and North Africa:

> For who is so thoughtless or indifferent as not to want to know how and under what political system, the Romans in less than fifty-three years have succeeded in subjecting nearly the whole inhabited world to their rule – a thing unique in history.[57]

Rome's extraordinary expansion was not without its setbacks. There were almost a hundred known defeats and perhaps many more passed over by our pro-Roman sources. Two of those defeats were disasters of the first magnitude: Hannibal's victory at Cannae in 216 and the Roman defeat by the Germanic Cimbri at Arausio (Orange) in 105. However, in these cases – as in all the others – the end result was a Roman victory.

The wars in the western half of the Mediterranean began with Carthage, but changed character after her defeat. Rome faced wars against tribes and coalitions of peoples, some with few urban centres. Often, as in Spain, their opponents possessed weapons as good or better than Roman ones. Much of the conflict in Spain was fought as guerilla war, a type of war as difficult to master for the Romans as it is for modern armies. It took them two centuries to pacify the Iberian Peninsula. After the end of Carthage as a major power at the end of the third century, it was only in the conflicts with migrating German tribes at the end of the second and beginning of the first century that Rome faced a serious threat. In general, these groups fought in much looser and more open formation than the Romans did. They were also more difficult to subdue, because unlike the kingdoms of the eastern Mediterranean, these groups had few or no urban centres and they often lacked a central authority whose capture would lead to the surrender of the entire state.

The East was more heavily urbanized than the West, and was to remain so throughout antiquity. During the Republic it was mostly divided among three major kingdoms. These states had emerged out of the wars that followed Alexander the Great's death in 323 and continued until about 280.[58] Antigonid Macedonia with parts of Greece was the most homogeneous of the three kingdoms. To its east was the largest and most heterogeneous kingdom, the Seleucid, which at its greatest extent stretched from the western seaboard of Asia Minor to northwestern India. Finally, the Ptolemaic monarchy in Egypt, which included parts of modern Libya and Syria along with the Aegean islands. It was the richest of the three, with the most easily defended borders. A lesser kingdom, that of the Attalids, centred at Pergamum in northwestern Asia Minor, had emerged from the Seleucid kingdom in the late 260s, played an important role in Rome's eastward expansion. Almost all of the rulers and most of the elites were of Macedonian or Greek extraction. These monarchies relied on an elaborate and bureaucratically structured administrative arm necessary for the infinitely larger and politically, socially, and ethnically more complex territories than those of the older Greek city-states. The island of Rhodes remained a significant naval power because of its importance as a trading centre. In Greece the major powers of the classical period such as Athens, Sparta and Thebes were no longer of military significance. Instead, as a response to pressures in the classical period and then to the growth of the monarchies, states emerged that could wield power on a much larger scale. Two of these, the Achaean League in the Peloponnese, and the Aetolian League in central Greece, were to play important roles in the period of Rome's eastern wars.

All of the successor states that emerged from Alexander's conquests shared certain common features. They were hereditary monarchies in which, except for certain traditional prerogatives in Macedonia, the king was in theory absolute. The kings acted in accordance with a common ideology of kingship. Its most important element was a preoccupation with, and a need for, success in warfare. In every case for which we have evidence, the title and status of a king was acquired through military action. This had obvious implications. If royal status was achieved through struggle and victory, it would have to be maintained through continued success in war. If royal status could be acquired by any member of the elite, the example could be imitated by others, so where exactly did the process stop? One way to interpret the political history of the period is to see it as a struggle by those who had achieved royal status, partly to hold on to that status and power and to maintain control of their territories and to keep the membership of the 'royal club' as restricted as possible.[59]

Their armies were, with the exception of Macedonia, mostly composed of professionals and mercenaries drawn from all over the Mediterranean. These monarchies' wealth (especially in Egypt), their bureaucracies and their large populations allowed them to raise armies of substantial size. In the period immediately from Alexander's death to the early third century, major battles appear to have been fought by armies of about 40,000 infantry and 5,000–6,000 cavalry. By the mid-third century, the armies of the Seleucids and the Ptolemies in Egypt had grown enormously. For major campaigns both sides could put roughly between 70,000–80,000 men in the field. At the battle of Raphia in 217 between Antiochus III and Ptolemy IV, the armies of both sides totalled over 140,000 troops. European armies remained smaller, with the Macedonian kingdom typically fielding between 25,000–35,000 troops.

All of these states employed the phalanx. As a result of Macedonian developments its basic equipment differed from the phalanxes of classical Greece; in place of the 2.4 metre thrusting spear, the troops carried a pike called the *sarissa,* which in Polybius' day was 6.4 metres long, as their main weapon. The increase in length allowed the spear points of the first five rows of the phalanx to project beyond the front of the phalanx and so increased its killing power. As a secondary armament, the infantry carried a short sword as it had done in the classical period. It was about 45cm long with a single edge, primarily for slashing. The increase in length meant that the pike had to be held in two hands. This led to the abandonment of the heavy hoplite shield and its replacement with a much smaller shield about 60cm in diameter with a central handgrip (which was hung by a strap around the neck when not in use). There were still hoplites with traditional equipment, but they no longer formed the core of the infantry. In the early third century a new type of shield appears, the *thureos,* which was oval in shape and seems to have been used by more mobile troops who could fight with missile weapons as well as at close quarters and probably was adopted as a result of Celtic influence. There is some evidence that, in the mid-second century, the armies of the Seleucids and Ptolemies may have equipped soldiers in the Roman fashion, but the evidence for this is not compelling, although such a development is not unlikely. Pyrrhus had already used Italian units at Asculum and his victory may have provided some impetus for such a development.[60]

The trend among Hellenistic infantry had been towards reducing the weight of body armour, especially in the rear ranks of the phalanx, to increase mobility. The armour of the cavalry developed in the opposite direction. They adopted more body armour, particularly the muscle cuirass and large round shields from the early third century.

Despite the large number of troops and formidable power of a frontal attack by the phalanx, the armies of the Hellenistic monarchies were relatively easy to defeat in set piece battles. In the aftermath of his account of the defeat of the Macedonian king Philip V in the battle of Cynoscephalae in 197, Polybius supplies an analysis of the weakness of the phalanx in comparison to the manipular legion.[61] He stresses the phalanx's irresistible frontal attack. Aemilius Paullus' reaction at the battle of Pydna against the Macedonian king Perseus in 168 allows us to understand what Polybius meant:

> *As the attack began, Aemilius came up and found that the Macedonian battalions had already planted the tips of their long spears in the shields of the Romans, who were prevented from reaching them with their swords. When he saw that the rest of the Macedonian troops, also were drawing their shields from their shoulders round in front of them, and having levelled their* sarissas *were withstanding his troops, and when he saw the strength of their interlocked shields and the fierceness of their onrush, amazement and fear took possession of him. He felt that he had never seen a sight more terrifying.[62]*

As terrifying as the onrush of the phalanx might be it suffered, as Polybius points out, from serious weaknesses. To be at its most effective it needed level ground without obstacles such as creeks or trees, because a crucial element in its success was its cohesion. This was vital for maintaining an unbroken wall of shields. He points out that it lacked the mobility necessary to deal with an enemy who refused to engage in a set piece battle, but essentially fought a guerilla war. One of the most important points the historian makes is the absence of a reserve, since the strength of the formation depended on mass at the point of impact. Breaking it up into smaller detachments made it far less effective. The Roman system of miniature phalanxes (the maniples) armed with javelin and sword was a far more effective fighting formation, although it should be borne in mind that the *triarii* retained the thrusting spear until the end of the second century. Such units could be detached from the main battle line to surround the enemy. Its weapons allowed it to be far more effective on its own. It also was better in resisting flank and rear attacks. Maniples on the flanks or in the rear of the legion could quickly turn to face attacks from any direction.

It is true that in all of the major battles between the manipular army and the phalanx the legion emerged victorious, but Polybius exaggerates the weakness of the eastern armies by highlighting the phalanx. These armies had troops that could operate independently, particularly the light-armed infantrymen and those carrying the *thureos* type of shield. Alexander's army had been consistently victorious in the East and later Hellenistic monarchs like Antiochus III continued to be so.

War in the West

Telamon

In 232 the tribune Gaius Flaminius, who was to die as consul in the ambush of his army at Lake Trasimene in 217, carried a new land law that distributed additional land to poorer citizens individually. The land called the Ager Gallicus lay between the colony of Sena Gallica (Senigallia) and Ravenna and had been taken from the Senonian Gauls. The measure excited a great deal of resistance at the time among his political enemies and their hatred distorted the picture of Flaminius in later historians. These portrayed him as a forerunner of the later agrarian reformers of the late second and first centuries who were seen as having done much to destroy the Republic. It seems that the resistance to both the tribune and to his proposals had more to do with his bringing it forward outside of normal channels than with the content of the measure. The most reasonable explanation for it was as a military measure to provide additional security, by establishing colonists behind the existing frontier with the Gauls, and also to assure there would be a jumping-off point for Roman forces moving into Gallic territory.[63] There is some evidence for aggressive Roman intentions. Already in 241 the Romans launched an offensive into Gallic territory and repeated it in 238 and in 237. An attack by the Gallic Boii on the colony at Arminium in this period was part of a short-lived and unsuccessful counteroffensive that resulted in the confiscation of a sizeable portion of Boian territory.[64] The Romans were expanding into the northeastern Italy and the Gauls were surely aware of this.

Polybius claims that Flaminius' measure led to the Gallic invasion of 225 that ended in the battle of Telamon. The problem with such an explanation is the seven-year gap between Flaminius' legislation and the outbreak of the war. However, it seems likely it was one step among others that contributed to the feeling among the Gauls of the Po valley that sooner or later the Romans would advance into their lands and displace or exterminate them. That fear was, in fact, to be realized. In the first thirty years of the second century the Romans were to push north and subjugate all of Italy between the Apennines and Alps. It is probable that Celtic fear of Rome finally created a Gallic coalition that felt itself capable of challenging Rome.[65]

The tension between Roman and Celt came to a head in the pivotal battle at Telamon, today the village of modern Telamon in Tuscany, which lies near the mouth of the Oso River where it flows out into the Tyrrhenian Sea. The Gauls had succeeded in building an alliance of the four major Celtic tribes of the middle and upper Po valley; the Senones, the Boii, Insubres and the Taurisci. In addition, they hired Gaesati, Celtic mercenaries from beyond the Alps.[66] The army in total consisted of 50,000 foot and 20,000 cavalry and chariots. This was the last time that chariots were used in warfare on the European continent. After Telamon, only the Celts of the British Isles continued to use them. The movement of this enormous army was not hidden. The Romans had been hearing for months of the Celtic preparations for an invasion and had prepared a response, raising legions that were stronger than usual and gathering supplies as well as summoning their allies, who must have been as worried by the invasion as the Romans were. In all, ten legions were levied. Of these, eight were for use in Italy, two for each of the consuls and a reserve army of four legions was stationed at Rome. Each of these enlarged legions consisted of 5,200 infantry and 300 cavalry. In addition, Polybius reports that 30,000 allied infantry and an additional 2,000 cavalry were raised.[67]

On learning of the march of the Celtic army, the Romans stationed one of the consuls, Lucius Aemilius Pappus, at Arminium (Rimini) on the Adriatic coast and sent a praetor with allied troops to the borders of Etruria.[68] Polybius claims that 4,000 Sabines and Etruscans and 50,000 infantry were with the praetor. The figure seems far too large; the infantry alone would be equal in numbers to two consular armies. Normally, praetors commanded a force of a single legion and allies and this, perhaps reinforced given the impending danger, seems a more reasonable size of the praetor's army. The other consul, Gaius Atilius Regulus, had already been sent south to campaign in Sardinia. In all, at Telamon the Romans had 3,200 cavalry to the Gauls' 20,000.

The Gauls' crossing of the Apennines took place without difficulties. They overran Etruria without opposition. Advancing as far as Clusium, they discovered that the praetor was approaching with his troops. In response, they moved north and engaged him in a battle that ended in a Roman defeat with heavy casualties. Pappus learning of the disaster brought his army up to the Gallic camp. His arrival precipitated a retreat of the Gauls northwards along the coastal road. They had had such success that they were too encumbered by booty to be able to fight effectively. While they were retreating, the other consul Regulus arrived by sea at Pisa with his army from Sardinia and began making his way south to Rome. By a chance encounter with Gallic foragers, he learned that the Gauls were nearby and aware of his colleague to the south, he saw the possibility of catching the Gauls between the two armies. He then set his troops in motion towards the Gauls, seizing a hill that overlooked the road which the Gauls would have to take.

The Gauls were at first unaware of Regulus' arrival, and thought the cavalry on the hill was from the other consul's army. Mobilizing their own cavalry, they charged the Romans on the hill. Capturing some prisoners, they learned that they were facing two consular armies, one behind them and the other to their front. Despite the claims of their enemies that the Gauls possessed little tactical skill or interest, they formed up so that their army faced both ways. Meanwhile Pappus' army had finally discovered from the fighting on the hill that Regulus' army was now engaged with the Gauls. Seeing this they formed their battle line and advanced to engage the Gauls. In the meantime, the Gauls had also formed up facing in two directions. The Gaesati and the Insubres turned to face Pappus' force, which was coming up behind them, and the Taurisci and Boii confronting Regulus' force to their front. Their cavalry, wagons and chariots were stationed on the wings. They placed their booty on a nearby hill under guard.

The fighting was at first confined to the hill where a furious cavalry engagement took place in which Regulus lost his life. His head was taken as a trophy.[69] The Roman cavalry finally overcame their opponents and gained control of the hill.

The battle now turned into an infantry engagement which would decide the outcome of the struggle. Polybius notes that the Romans were terrified by the good order of their enemy, their war cries and the blare of their trumpets and horns.[70] The notion that the Celts exclusively relied on an undisciplined charge, which if it failed ended any hope of victory, was a product of ethnic prejudice and not observation.[71]

The infantry phase opened with the advance of the Roman light-armed troops. Their effect on the Gauls was far more serious than was usual. The naked Gaesati who occupied the front ranks were vulnerable to missile weapons since they were without protective equipment. The missile attack was devastating; many, unable to maintain their position, rushed upon the Roman ranks and died. Others retreated, throwing the ranks of the men behind them into confusion. The Gaesati were now a spent force. The Insubres, Taurisci and Boii now closed with the Roman maniples and a hard struggle ensued. The Gauls were outmatched in discipline and equipment, but they held their ground despite their losses. Polybius goes out of his way to praise their courage.[72] He also remarks on the superior protection that the *scutum* offered and claims that the Roman swords were more effective, since the Gauls' swords were only good for slashing. This last assertion is not borne out by the archaeological evidence and other literary sources. The Gallic swords of this period were primarily slashing weapons, but some types could be used for stabbing as well.[73] The Roman cavalry that had gained possession of the hill attacked the Gauls from higher ground, and on their flanks as they charged down the hill. The pressure from all sides was too much. Nonetheless, the Gallic infantry held their ground and were cut down where they stood, while their cavalry fled the field.

40,000 Gauls were killed and not less than 10,000 taken prisoner. Their leaders made their escape with a few followers and then committed suicide.[74] The spoils captured from the Gauls were sent to Rome, while the property looted by them was returned to its owners. The army then went on to attack one of the main tribes in the Gallic coalition – the Boii – and compelled them to submit. The tide had turned. Never again would a combined force of Gauls of this magnitude threaten Roman Italy. The events of 225 inaugurated a series of campaigns that by about 170 had subjugated the whole of the Po valley and established Roman control as far as the foothills of the Alps.

The First Punic War

The most serious wars that the Romans fought during the Republic were with the North African city of Carthage.[75] It had been founded in the last third of the ninth century by colonists from Tyre in Phoenicia, one of the major ports in the eastern Mediterranean, as part of a general expansion of Phoenician settlement and trade into the western Mediterranean. It was also one of the largest and most powerful cities in the Mediterranean. It has been estimated that its population by the fourth century had reached between 100,000 and 250,000.

Carthage's commercial success was the crucial factor in its growth. The city was located on a triangular peninsula projecting into the western side of the Gulf of Tunis. The gulf provided a sheltered anchorage and the site of Carthage had naturally strong defences, as the Romans found during their siege of Carthage in the mid-second century. The city's great prosperity was based on its rich agricultural hinterland, commercial success in trading its own products and as a transit point for the goods of others. It was not only trade with the coasts of the western Mediterranean, but also with the peoples in its North African hinterland. Its expanding territory was productive and river valleys – the Bagradas to the north and the Catadas to the south – provided access to inland trade. It dwarfed all other trading centres in the western Mediterranean.

Carthage had won a considerable empire that extended along the North African coast from Cyrenaica in the east to the Atlantic Ocean. It included the Cape Bon peninsula and the fertile valley of the Bagradas (the modern Oued Medjerda). The area's inhabitants were Libyans (modern Berbers). Carthaginian expansion in North Africa reached its greatest extent in the fourth century, and resulted in it gaining control of a number of important coastal towns including Utica and Hadrumentum (modern Sousse). These towns were inhabited by a mixture of native Libyans and Phoenician colonists. All of these peoples paid tribute and taxes to the Carthaginians as well as serving in her army.

Carthage had extended its influence outside of Africa. Commercial needs led to her taking over the earlier Phoenician foundations of Gades and Tartessos in southern Spain, the latter being a major entrepôt for trade with the Iberian interior. Carthage's possessions in Spain included mines, especially one producing tin which was in short supply in the

Mediterranean. Her interests in Spain remained purely commercial until after the First Punic War.[76] The Carthaginians also controlled Sardinia and Corsica.

The richest prize of all was Sicily, which was eventually to lead to conflict with Rome. The Carthaginians established their dominance in western Sicily in the last half of the sixth century by taking over existing Phoenician colonies, such as Panormus (Palermo) and Motya. Their presence in Sicily brought them into conflict with the Greek colonies in the eastern half of the island, some of which dated to the latter half of the eighth century. Among these, Syracuse on southeastern coast emerged as the strongest opponent. It built up an empire of its own and led the struggle with Carthage. The conflict lasted until the coming of Rome. Neither side could permanently alter the balance of power, victory alternated with defeat and expansion with contraction.

Our sources offer little on the organization and equipment of Carthage's armed forces. They seem to have mostly consisted of mercenaries, troops drawn from subject peoples and allies such as the Numidian kingdoms. The most effective troops seem to have been the African infantry, armed and fighting in the manner of other Hellenistic armies. The procedure for levying troops is unknown, although given the extent of the empire, it seems likely that cities or rural peoples were given a quota to fill. After the levy finished, the units were probably sent to a central assembly point. Light-armed troops who fought with a small shield and javelins much like their Roman counterparts were also levied, and proved no more successful. Among the cavalry, Numidian light horse were the most effective and after the war served with the Romans. Celtic mercenaries were also employed by Carthage, as they were by the Hellenistic monarchies

After the end of the First Punic War in 241, which resulted in the loss of Sicily and then Sardinia, the Carthaginians initiated a period of expansion in Spain under the command of the Barcids, the family of Hannibal. Large Spanish contingents were drafted into Carthaginian forces. At least some Spanish troops probably served as mercenaries before this period, but they now served as conscripts or as allies. At the opening of the Second Punic War, after Hannibal's invasion of Italy, Celtic tribes served as allies, after he made contact with them in northern Italy.[77] Mercenaries continued to be used as well. One of the most difficult wars that Carthage faced had been the conflict with its mercenary forces and Libyan conscripts who had served in Sicily, when she tried to disband them after the end of the First Punic War. They had not been paid for a very long time. When they had been brought back to North Africa to be dismissed with no prospect of receiving their back wages in full, they revolted and were joined by many of Carthage's Libyan subjects who had been oppressed by heavy taxes and conscription. Brought together by their grievances, the mercenaries and the North Africans fought one of the most savage wars of antiquity with no quarter given or asked. Polybius called it the Truceless War, a title which was well merited. The four-year war ended in 237 with the extermination of the mercenaries.[78] In certain circumstances such as the battle of Zama in 202, Carthaginian citizens also served, although they were more usually to be found in the fleet.

The Carthaginians used both heavy and light cavalry. They were drawn from Spanish, Celtic, and Numidian sources, although citizens served as well. For the most part, the cavalry was of high quality. One of the keys to victory for Scipio Africanus in his final victory over Hannibal was the presence on the Roman side of overwhelming numbers of light Numidian cavalry.

Elephants were also used. They were controlled by a driver in a howdah and carried light infantry armed with javelins. Their most effective use was in the charge, which if successful would destroy the cohesion of the opposing infantry. In addition, untrained horses could not abide their smell.

The exact method of appointment for senior commanders is unknown. By the Second Punic War (218–201) there is some evidence that a commander could be appointed by the troops he led. This is the method used in Hannibal's case, but that may have been due to the fact that the army was in Spain far from home, and in a difficult situation. An additional factor that probably contributed to his appointment was the fact that since the army's arrival, it had always been commanded by a member of his family. As opposed to the yearly tenure of a Roman consul, Carthaginian generals served either for an unlimited period or until they had completed their task. However, failure could entail not only loss of command but also severe punishment, including crucifixion. This must have given them the opportunity to form close ties with their troops. Roman commands were prolonged by the promagistracy, but that was an additional appointment that allowed the continuation of command on slightly different terms. Given the mixed composition of Carthaginian armies, issuing commands and developing cohesion must have been difficult tasks. There is a close parallel in the problems faced by the Austro-Hungarians during the First World War, as their armies were polyglot and units were affected by ethnic animosities.[79]

Roman and Carthaginian ways of making war were very different. The states of the ancient Mediterranean existed in a state of continuous anarchy. War was a normal part of life. Between 274 and 168 the Ptolemies and the Seleucids fought a total of six wars over the possession of Syria and Palestine. The Macedonians were involved in a series of wars in Greece and in Illyria and in Asia Minor.[80] Although constant, this warfare was for the most part limited. It did not aim at the annihilation of the enemy, but either through projecting overwhelming power or by destroying his ability to resist and compel him to make peace on reasonable terms. Carthage approached war this way. Rome did not; she was prepared to fight, but only so long as gains outweighed losses and was ready to compromise to obtain peace. The Romans approached war as a struggle to the finish. Their approach to war was offensive and they continued to attack until the enemy was beaten into submission. It was only then, when they could dictate terms that negotiations would begin. One of the Carthage's weaknesses in both the First Punic War and the Second Punic War was her inability to understand the Roman approach to warfare. Despite staggering losses in their wars against Carthage, the Romans continued to fight on. The same attitude was already clear in their war against Pyrrhus. After they had suffered substantial losses and two defeats they refused to negotiate with the king and fought on until they were victorious.[81]

Carthaginian contact with Italy and specifically the area around Rome predated direct dealings with Rome. They allied with the Etruscans to stop Greek piracy. In 540, in conjunction with the Etruscans they defeated a Greek fleet off Alalia (Aleria) in Corsica. There is evidence for trading connections with Etruria as well. At Pyrgi, one of the ports of the Etruscan city of Caere, we have a dedication in both Punic and Etruscan by a local ruler to commemorate the help he received in his ascent to power from the Phoenician goddess Astarte.

These facts provide a context for their earliest known treaty with Rome. It dates to 509, the first year of the Republic. This was followed by further treaties in the mid-fourth century and in the 270s. They established a recognized a sphere of interest for each. At this point, their interests were different so that there was no cause for a major clash between the two.

It was Rome's war with Tarentum and its victory over Pyrrhus along with Carthaginian victories in Sicily that dramatically changed the relationship between the two. Rome's domination of southern Italy brought her to the narrow straits that separated the toe of Italy from Sicily. The Straits of Messina is only about 3km wide. In Sicily, Carthage's string of victories had brought her to the straits as well. In 264 she was able to throw a garrison into Messana (Messina on the Sicilian side of the strait). After Pyrrhus' departure from Sicily in 275, Carthage was able to reconstitute its position in eastern Sicily. Messana had been taken over by a group of Campanian mercenaries, the Mamertini or sons of Mars. Defeated in battle by Syracuse, they asked for Carthaginian help and Carthage garrisoned Messana at their request.[82] The geographical proximity of Messana and Rome's relationship to the southern Italian Greek cities raised the possibility of a conflict with Carthage.

The Mamertini had seized control of Messana in the 280s. The city was a strategic prize, as its possession along with that of Rhegium across the straits would give any power the ability to close the straits. Syracuse also played an important role in these events. Its ruler, Hiero, had finally succeeded in bottling up the Mamertini in Messana after his victory over them at the battle of the Longanus River in 269 and had placed Messana under siege. This placed him in direct opposition to Carthage. However, as has been recently suggested there is no evidence to show that Carthage at any time planned to dominate the whole of Sicily. The garrison at Messana could be viewed as a way to make sure the straits remained open to her shipping and nothing more. With the Carthaginians firmly in place, Hiero withdrew. Relieved of immediate pressure, a dispute broke out in the city over the presence of the Carthaginian garrison. Those who wanted its removal appealed to Rome.

The Senate was divided on how to respond to the appeal. They had had previous experience with the Mamertini. During the war against Pyrrhus, Rhegium had appealed for Roman aid. The Romans had sent a garrison of Campanian mercenaries. These eventually expelled or killed the townspeople with the help of the Mamertini. The war delayed a response, but after the war with Pyrrhus had ended, the Romans sent a force that retook the city and executed the surviving mercenaries.[83] Given this background, it is hardly surprising that the Senate deadlocked on the appeal and referred the appeal to the assembly. In the assembly one of the consuls of 264 argued for action on the basis that Carthage was a potential threat and held out the lure of the immense booty to be won. The assembly authorized him to accept the appeal. It is unlikely that at this stage Rome or for that matter Carthage envisioned anything more than a localized conflict. Neither recognized that, given the Roman attitude towards war, there would be no chance of a compromise before one or the other side was totally defeated.

By 263, the Romans had captured Messana and Hiero – realizing the magnitude of Roman strength – concluded a treaty with them. He was to be a valuable ally until his death in 215. The Carthaginian command of the sea made supplying Roman forces vulnerable to shortages. Supplies from Syracuse were an important contribution to the Roman war effort. Late in 262, the Romans attacked the main Punic base in Sicily at Agrigentum (Agrigento) in southwestern Sicily. After a difficult siege in which supplies from Hiero played an important part, they captured it the next year. The sacking of the city and the selling of its inhabitants into slavery antagonized many of the Sicilian cities, who then threw in their lot with the Carthaginians.

Polybius claims it was this development that led to the Roman decision to expel the Carthaginians from Sicily. Given the strength of the Carthaginian war fleet which numbered about 200 vessels, it must have been clear that the only way the Romans could do so was by the construction of a major war fleet. They proceeded to do so and amazingly the fleet won its first important victory at Mylae in northeastern Sicily in 260. In 256 an attempt was made to win the war by an invasion of Carthage's own territory in North Africa, but it ended in disaster. The rest of the war consisted of naval battles in which the Romans mostly emerged victorious. In Sicily they conducted a number of sieges but could not entirely expel the Carthaginians. Finally, at the Aegates Islands (modern Egadi) off the western coast of Sicily in 242 a naval victory at last exhausted Carthage's ability to resist. It surrendered and a peace treaty was concluded.[84]

The Second Punic War

The origins of the Second Punic War are closely tied to the results of the first. The war had deprived Carthage both of Sicily and of an effective war fleet. Relations with Rome worsened further in 238, when the Romans seized Sardinia and Corsica while Carthage was fighting for its life against its mercenaries in the Truceless War.

Drawn by Spain's mines and potential manpower, the Carthaginians began to extend their presence in Spain and intervene militarily for the first time. In 239, Hamilcar Barca and his son Hannibal landed in Spain. Hamilcar and his son-in-law Hasdrubal had already emerged as virtual rulers of Carthage in the wake of the First Punic War and the Truceless War.[85] Hamilcar initiated a policy of expansion in southern and southeastern Spain, where the Carthaginians had had a presence for centuries. His successes came to an end in late 229 or early 228, when he drowned in a stream, perhaps the Segura in southeastern Spain, while on campaign.[86] He was immediately succeeded by Hasdrubal, who continued his policy of expansion, pushing the boundaries of the Carthaginian empire to the north and founding the city of New Carthage (Cartagena) on Spain's east coast as the new capital of Punic Spain. Sometime between 228 and 225, Hasdrubal concluded an agreement with Rome, the Ebro Treaty, whose provisions are far from clear. It limited Carthaginian military action to Spain south of the Ebro River. This would imply that the Romans conceded a free hand to the Carthaginians south of the river. At this point Carthage's empire still lay considerably south of the Ebro line, but it at least provided some security to Rome that Hasdrubal would not move north where he could potentially threaten northern Italy and southern France. In fact, there is no evidence that he contemplated any such move. However, Rome faced a major threat from the Gauls, which was finally ended at the Battle of Telamon in 225, and probably wanted as much assurance as it could get that there would be no distractions.[87] In addition, it was Carthaginian expansion in Spain that concerned the city of Massilia, a longtime ally of Rome which was heavily involved in trade. It had a trading port at Emporion (modern Ampurias) in Spain and perhaps another one near Malaga on the south coast. Its trading interests gave it a strong incentive to block or limit Carthaginian expansion to the north. In 221 Hasdrubal was murdered in a private dispute. He was succeeded by Hamilcar's son Hannibal, whose selection was ratified by the army in Spain and then by the home government.

Hannibal continued the expansion initiated under his father. Within a year central Spain had been brought under control. It seems likely that at this point he became interested in the additional resources such expansion would bring. There was no indication at this point that Rome had any interest in Spain, so a clash with it seemed unlikely. The move north ran into a problem. The native town of Saguntum (modern Sagunto) lies about 29km south of Valencia near the coast. More importantly it lay about 160km south of the Ebro River. It seems to have had some prior relationship with Rome, but why Rome entered into it is not clear.[88] There was an internal struggle in Saguntum between pro-Punic and pro-Roman factions. The pro-Roman faction appealed to Rome and the Romans responded by entering into an informal relationship with Saguntum based on the Roman concept of *fides* or trust. It was a moral not a legal bond, but it was nonetheless theoretically binding.[89] The obligations inherent in this bond tended to be ill-defined and much was left to discretion, especially that of the stronger party. Nevertheless, the Romans saw it as giving them the right to intervene, if they chose to do so.

By 220 the Saguntines were fearful of an attack by Hannibal and appealed to Rome. The Romans sent an embassy with the instructions to warn off Hannibal from assaulting Saguntum. The sudden interest shown by the Romans may have been the result of the end of the Gallic threat and perhaps some pressure exerted by Massilia, which probably saw her interests threatened. It may have had commercial relations with Saguntum, which would be jeopardized by Carthaginian control.[90] Hannibal's claim was that Saguntum had attacked tribes friendly to Carthage. He launched an attack in the early spring of 219. The city fell after a siege of eight months. Oddly, no Roman support materialized, which seems to imply that Rome was only interested in Saguntum as a political tool. Finally, in March 218 an embassy was sent to Carthage to demand the surrender of Hannibal because of his taking of Saguntum, accompanied by the threat to declare war if this was not done. The Carthaginians refused and after a hiatus of twenty years, once again the two sides found themselves at war.

Why both sides decided on war so quickly is not immediately clear. The first war had been a long, gruelling and exhausting contest. It may be that the Romans thought that a declaration of war would cause Carthage to back down as it had in 239, after the Romans had seized Sardinia during the revolt of Carthaginian mercenaries on the island. At worst, they thought that if war broke out they could confine it to Spain as the first war had, for the most part, been confined to Sicily. In addition, during the first war they had regularly beaten the Carthaginians. They felt that their superior resources would wear Carthage down as they had in the first war. It would serve as the conclusive demonstration of Roman superiority and as a warning of what Carthage's fate might be.

Hannibal's response to Roman demands may have been determined by the same considerations. Rome's position on Saguntum limited his freedom of operations in an area it had earlier recognized as under Punic control, and it made clear that Rome was ready to interfere where and when it chose to do so. It must have weighed on his mind that twenty years before, Rome had blatantly and unjustly seized Sardinia and Corsica. He could not trust them. The future was, of course, uncertain but judging by past behaviour, it seemed likely that sooner or later Carthage would once again have to fight the Romans. His success in expanding Carthaginian control in Spain made it more likely that the conflict would begin in Spain. He must have thought that his successful campaigning in Spain had enabled him to amass significant resources, both those he had ready to hand and those he could assemble in the future, and gave him a reasonable chance of success. The speed at which he assembled his forces suggests he had already thought deeply about the possibility of war with Rome and had devised a plan for it.

In devising this plan, Hannibal had to take into consideration two problems that would face Carthage in any conflict with Rome outside of North Africa. The first was a result of the First Punic War, which had begun with Carthaginian domination of the seas. As war began, Carthage probably had a fleet of 200 warships and Rome had only an insignificant naval force. Now the roles were reverse; Carthage's losses in war and the confiscation of her remaining warships at the end of it had given Rome an overwhelming advantage at sea. That meant that if his plan involved an invasion of Italy, only a land route was practical. It also meant that any supplies and reinforcements he might need would have to come by land as well. Second, was that a campaign in Spain would turn into a battle of attrition as had happened in Sicily during the first war. Rome's superior manpower would prevail in the end. Victory would only be possible if Hannibal could destroy the sources of that manpower. The most important source was Rome's Italian allies. If he could sever the ties that bound them to Rome, he would have an immeasurable advantage that might decide the outcome of the war. This could only be done by attacking these allies, and by a swift and victorious campaign as well as exploiting their grievances, persuade them that they had more to gain by breaking their ties to Rome than in serving in her armies. The hostility of the Gauls of northern Italy to Rome increased his chance of success; they could provide a safe base after the descent of his army from the Alps and augment his manpower.

An invasion by way of the Alps was a daring idea, but faced serious difficulties. First, there would be the need to leave garrisons behind in Spain, and once over the Pyrenees Hannibal's army might well have to fight its way across southern Gaul. The crossing of the Alps was certain to claim a toll in men and animals, and once he arrived on the north Italian plain he would be dependent on local resources for the majority of his supplies and reinforcements. There was the possibility of further reinforcements from Spain, but these reinforcements would also have to face the same perils to reach Italy.

Hannibal began his march in June, 218 with 90,000 infantry, 12,000 cavalry and 37 elephants. The garrisons and crossings of the mountains did indeed take a heavy toll. He finally arrived in Italy in October with 20,000 infantry and 6,000 cavalry. Only one elephant survived and it would soon be lost.

Publilius Cornelius Scipio, one of the consuls of 218, had been assigned the campaign against Hannibal. He initially set out for Spain, but learning that Hannibal had already left, tried to intercept him in southern Gaul. The attempt was a failure and so he returned to northern Italy to confront Hannibal there. Scipio's position became more complicated when he also faced a Gallic rising that may have been instigated by Carthaginian agents. He initially met Hannibal at the Ticinus River, a tributary joining the Po near Ticinum (Pavia). The battle was essentially a cavalry action that the Carthaginians won, inflicting heavy casualties, and the consul himself was wounded during the battle.

Scipio at first withdrew eastwards towards his camp; he was wounded and worried about the Gallic uprising. However, at the news of Hannibal's advance to the Trebia, another tributary of the Po, he crossed the river and built a camp on its eastern bank. These events finally forced the Senate to take action. The other consul, Tiberius Sempronius Longus, was summoned back from Sicily to face the danger at home. He arrived there in December 218 and joined Scipio and his army. Hannibal now faced a force of four legions and allies and was heavily outnumbered. He soundly defeated Longus' army by driving away the enemy's cavalry and then surrounding the legions. It was a rehearsal for the great battle at Cannae two years later. The Romans suffered heavy casualties amounting to half of their army.

Wintering north of the Apennines, Hannibal crossed them in the spring of 217. The Roman consuls had taken up positions to oppose him. One consul, Gnaeus Servilius Geminus, had been posted along the road into Etruria that ran along the west coast; the other, Gaius Flaminius, was at Arretium (Arezzo) in Etruria to meet Hannibal if he crossed directly over the Apennines, which he did in May. At Lake Trasimene (Lago Trasimeno) in central Etruria, Hannibal ambushed Flaminius and his army. The ambush was successful and Flaminius' army was destroyed and the consul killed. Six thousand Romans broke through, only to be taken prisoner and sold into slavery.[91]

The defeats at the Trebia and Lake Trasimene had undermined Roman confidence to a degree not previously seen. In emergency, a dictator, Quintus Fabius Maximus, was appointed. He was a reasonable choice. He had been twice consul and had command experience. He was later to hold a fifth consulship and to reconquer Tarentum from Hannibal in 209. During his first consulship in 233, he had celebrated a triumph over the Ligurian peoples of northwestern Italy. His master of the horse was Marcus Minucius Rufus. It was not a happy combination. Since direct confrontation on the battlefield had failed, Fabius adopted a strategy of attrition. Closely following Hannibal's army, he wore it down through small engagements, denied it supplies and intimidated potential Carthaginian allies. The strategy, despite the successes it had, went against the Roman approach to warfare. It is hardly surprising that a strong faction at Rome advocated returning to the offensive. Fabius' master of the horse, who was in favour of an aggressive strategy, was made co-dictator with Fabius and their different views complicated the campaign until Fabius, had to come to Minucius' rescue in one of his engagements with Hannibal. Fabius was now in sole command. His strategy remained in place until the end of 217 when he laid down his office. Whatever other effects it might have had, it did allow Rome the time to recuperate and to prepare for a decisive battle in the new year.

The Battle of Cannae

The two new consuls for 216, Gaius Terentius Varro and Lucius Aemilius Paullus, took office after a hotly contested election. At issue was the future conduct of the war. Was Fabius' strategy of attrition to continue or was Hannibal to be met in battle, this time with overwhelming force? Despite the serious defeats there was a strong feeling that it was necessary to fight Hannibal once again. Besides ideology, the presence of a victorious Carthaginian army in the heart of Roman Italy was a standing invitation to allies who had been forced into the Roman alliance to break away and join Hannibal. It was true that no allies had gone over to Hannibal, but the longer he remained undefeated, the likelier that possibility became.

New legions were enrolled. The sources differ over numbers, but it is likely that the new legions were of increased size with 5,000 heavy infantry and 300 cavalry.[92] In addition to the new legions, a further four legions were stationed in southern Italy at Gerunium, a town in Apulia. The eight legions, plus an equal number of allies, would total about 80,000 infantry and 6,000 cavalry. Of these, probably 2,400 were Roman cavalry and the rest allied. The army contained an unusually high number of senators and equestrians, which was an indication of the attraction of fighting and the understanding that this battle was to be the decisive one. The determination to prevail is evident in Livy's report that an oath that had been informally sworn by the troops was now administered by the tribunes; the soldier swore he would never break ranks, except to rearm or to rescue a fellow citizen.[93] Despite their determination and enthusiasm, the troops had serious deficiencies. They lacked the training to fight effectively. The consuls did their best, but they could not compensate for absence of prior battle experience, training and the lack of coordination between units because of their lack of prior service together. The end result was that despite their superior numbers, they would enter battle at a serious disadvantage compared to Hannibal's battle-hardened veterans.

Probably in June when the crops were ripe in the fields, Hannibal – who was camped opposite the Romans at Gerunium – moved south to Cannae, which served as a Roman supply base about 96km away. Polybius claims his motive was to try to compel the Romans to fight.[94] Other sources assert that the reason for the move was his lack of supplies. This would be hardly surprising since his force had remained stationary for a long period and without an adequate source of supplies. His provisions were probably near exhaustion.

Cannae was located on the modern Monte di Canne. It lay on the right bank of the Aufidus (Ofanto) River, on a hill approximately 8km from the river's mouth.[95] At the time of Hannibal's arrival, the town had already been razed, but supplies were still stored there. The position offered a commanding view of the surrounding area. There was a series of hills on the south side of the river in addition to the one Cannae was located on, but on the north the land was flat and good cavalry country.

The size of the Punic army has been the subject of much debate. Polybius and Livy claim that Hannibal had 40,000 infantry and 10,000 cavalry. However, this figure probably includes light-armed troops as well, who would be far less significant on the battlefield. A reasonable estimate would be 28,000–30,000 heavy infantry and 10,000 horsemen, who were also divided into heavy and light units. The majority of his heavy infantry consisted of Gauls, Spaniards and Libyans. The Africans were his most experienced and steadiest troops; many were armed in the Roman fashion with weapons recovered from earlier battles. This may have led to some confusion during the fight.

Paullus and Varro joined the forces at Gerunium. The combined army then marched south following Hannibal to Cannae, arriving there in late July. All of the surviving accounts fix the blame for the disaster at Cannae on Varro.[96] But as has been pointed out, the decision for open battle had already been taken. Paullus was extraordinarily well connected. He was Scipio Africanus' father-in-law and the grandfather of Scipio Aemilianus. Varro was a man without a distinguished pedigree with no prior military experience, but Paullus had no prior familiarity with warfare on this scale either. In fact, no Roman commander had. The vote of thanks he received from the Senate after the battle as well as the fact that he was given important posts in later years tells against the view that he was held responsible for what happened. It seems clear that the sources reflect an attempt by Paullus' supporters and descendants to shift the blame for the disaster on to Varro. The joint operations, with command alternating daily, were a source of confusion and irritation to both men.

Hannibal, arriving first, camped on the south bank of the river for several weeks. On the second day of their march the Romans came in sight of the enemy camp, which was situated about 5km away. Paullus refused to immediately engage which made sense. His army must have been tired from the march and he had to construct a camp for his troops, which he did on the northern bank of the Aufidus. He found the ground unsatisfactory and the army seems to have needed further supplies. Hannibal had access to supplies from Cannae, but how the Romans – especially given the size of their force – were provisioned is unclear.

Paullus sent a third of his army across the Aufidus and had a fortified camp constructed on the south side of the river as well, about 1.5km from the Carthaginian camp, near the ford his army had used. Dividing one's forces in the face of the enemy was extremely unusual and counter to the normal military doctrine, which advised keeping an army together in such a situation. It may have been an attempt to deprive Hannibal's army of supplies and to give his own men easier access to them that led to the construction of the second camp.[97] It does, however, undermine the view that he was reluctant to engage Hannibal. Such a move might provoke Hannibal either to move or to fight. The latter is the more likely choice as simply compelling him to move would accomplish little, but increase his supply difficulties but not necessarily lead to a fight. In fact, there were a series of indecisive skirmishes before the main battle took place.

The date of the battle, 2 August, is secure but the location of the battle-field has been a perennial problem. Our best source, Polybius, indicates that the battle was fought on the right or southeastern bank where Cannae was located. There still remains the problem of where on the right bank the battle was fought. Unfortunately, the river – which has several tributaries and a winding course – has changed its course many times since antiquity. The battle could have been fought east or west of the smaller Roman camp and there is no way given the changes in course that the issue can be resolved.

The Roman command alternated daily. Supposedly on Varro's day of command he decided on an immediate battle. He moved the troops out of both camps and had those from the larger camp ford the Aufidus. After both groups had assembled, he drew up his battle line, placing the troops from each camp beside each other. The combined army faced south according to Polybius.[98] He stationed the Roman cavalry on the right of his line next to the river and on his left he placed his allied horse, while stationing his light-armed infantry in front, presumably masking his deployment. Polybius claims that he had 80,000 infantry and 6,000 cavalry in his battle line. These are the total numbers of troops with which the campaign began; however, there had been skirmishing and troops who must have been detached on various duties. The figures are probably too large. The battle line seems to have been drawn up in the standard three-line formation. However, the maniples were formed to a greater depth and had smaller intervals between them. The maniples' ability to maneuver independently was one of the main advantages. Varro's dispositions would seem to have reduced that possibility, but they were reasonable in the light of the lack of training and cohesion of his men, who had previously formed two separate armies. In this case, cohesion was probably the more important requirement. It is also likely he saw his best chance of victory in delivering a massive forward push that would break the enemy line before the Carthaginian cavalry could drive off the Roman cavalry and bare the infantry's flanks. Such a break-through had occurred in the battle of the Trebia in 218. Paullus was in command with the 2,400 Roman cavalry on the right wing, while Varro led the 3,600 allied cavalry on the left. The proconsul Servilius was in charge of the infantry that perhaps numbered 55,000–60,000 men. The allocation of commands stressed the importance of the cavalry on the wings maintaining their position as long as they could, while the infantry delivered the decisive blow.

Hannibal, on the basis of past experience and, perhaps, as a result of good intelligence, had anticipated the Roman battle plan and arranged his army to meet it. He placed his Numidian cavalry, perhaps 3,000–4,000 men on his right, opposite the allied cavalry; on his left he stationed his Gallic and Spanish horse, numbering 6,000–7,000. These forces in total were more than twice as large as the enemy's cavalry. The most innovative aspect of his plan was the deployment of his infantry. His 10,000 African infantry, armed in the Roman manner, were arranged in two parallel columns behind the ends of his infantry line. The 22,000 Gallic and Spanish infantry formed the centre.[99] He moved this centre forward to create a convex bulge in the line facing the Romans. It has been suggested that the units were arranged in echelon, but it seems more likely that they were formed in line given Polybius's description.[100] He designed the formation to channel and slow the advance of the Roman infantry while his cavalry drove off the Roman horse and then attacked the Roman rear. As the Romans moved forward between the columns of African infantry, these columns would turn inward and attack the flanks of the advancing legions. The final result would be the complete encirclement of the Roman army and its crushing defeat.

The battle opened with the usual useless skirmishing of the light-armed infantry of both sides. The real battle opened with an attack by the Spanish and Celtic cavalry on the Roman cavalry on the Roman right. Overwhelmed by the enemy's numbers, the Roman cavalry was crushed and driven off. Meanwhile, the Roman began to relentlessly push the Spanish and Celtic infantry in the centre backwards with its superior weight. The fighting was concentrated as Hannibal intended in the middle of the line. The Romans, having pushed the centre of Hannibal's line back far enough, were crowded together and now vulnerable to the African infantry on both their flanks. In the narrow space, the maniples were forced together and the units began to lose their cohesion. The African columns turned inward towards the Roman flanks and began to attack them. Meanwhile, the Numidian cavalry on the right attacked the allied cavalry on the Roman left. According to Polybius, their attack did not result in a great deal of loss to either side, but it kept the enemy cavalry occupied and so essentially out of the battle. Finally, the Spanish and Celtic cavalry returned from pursuing the Roman cavalry, and bore down upon the rear of the allied cavalry. Seeing the approach of the enemy cavalry, the allied troopers turned and fled the field. The Numidians were detailed to pursue them, while the heavier cavalry from the Carthaginian left wing fell upon the rear of the Roman infantry. For Polybius, the cavalry was the key to Hannibal's victory:

> At this battle [Cannae] and in earlier actions their cavalry was crucial to the Carthaginians. This made it clear to posterity that it is better to give battle with half as many infantry as the enemy, but to have an overwhelming superiority in cavalry than to go into battle evenly matched in all respects.[101]

An exaggerated judgement, but in this case he was right.

There was constant fighting on the periphery of the Roman formation. Men were being killed, while the survivors were forced back into an ever-tighter formation, so that in the end many of them lacked the room to use their weapons. The Roman casualties were enormous. Polybius notes that about seventy cavalry made their way to Venusia (Venosa) near the headwaters of the Aufidus. About 300 more found refuge in the surrounding area. The remainder of the army – 70,000 – died in battle. Ten thousand infantry were taken prisoner away from the battlefield and a further 3,000 managed to flee to nearby cities. These figures are too large for the army that Polybius claims began the battle. Livy's figures are rather different, even though he is heavily dependent on Polybius for his account of the battle. Livy has a total of 17,000 infantry escaping the battlefield – 10,000 to the smaller camp which was closer and 7,000 to the larger camp on the other side of the river – and 19,300 captured by Hannibal.[102] His figures of 45,500 infantry and 2,700 horses killed seem more plausible than Polybius' version.[103]

The losses among the elite were severe. They included twenty-nine military tribunes, two quaestors and men who had served as consuls, praetors and aediles: Paullus, Servilius (the proconsul who had commanded the centre), M. Minucius (who had been a master of the horse and a consul) and eighty senators or men who held offices that would have given them senatorial rank.[104]

Carthaginian casualties were substantial. Polybius claims that 4,000 Celts and 1,500 Spaniards and Libyan infantry died. In addition, 2,000 cavalry or about 20 per cent of the cavalry were lost.

The Battle of Ilipa

In addition to Italy, Spain was the other major theatre of war before the Roman invasion of Africa in 204. It was crucial to the success of the Carthaginian war effort in Italy. Despite the defeat at Cannae and the loss of some of her allies in southern Italy, the core of the Roman alliance stood firm. If the Romans could cut the Carthaginian lifeline to Italy, it might be possible to slowly weaken Hannibal, so that what could not so far be accomplished by battle could be brought about by attrition.

The Romans had sent Publius Cornelius Scipio, one of the consuls of 218, to Spain to intercept Hannibal, but he had failed to do so. The two had finally met in northern Italy and their encounter had ended in two Roman defeats. The wounded consul had sent the greater part of his forces to Spain under his brother Gnaeus' command. His brother had scored one success after another. In 217, Publius was sent to join him. The string of successes continued. In 214 or 213 as a result of a revolt by a Numidian king in Africa, some Punic troops were recalled to Africa and this further weakened Carthaginian resistance and so opened southern Spain to attack.

The situation in Africa gradually quietened and the diversion of troops to Spain from other theatres allowed the Carthaginians to field three separate armies under three different commanders. To face these multiple threats, the brothers split their forces. Celtiberian mercenaries in Gnaeus' army were persuaded by the Carthaginians to desert, and without sufficient manpower he was forced to withdraw. The Carthaginians finally caught up with Gnaeus, he was killed and his army annihilated. Publius was also cut off and his army destroyed. He too was killed in the battle. Only a remnant of Roman forces survived the disaster. The Romans retained only a narrow coastal strip north of Ebro. The arrival of reinforcements, under the consul Claudius Nero in 210, allowed the Romans to consolidate their position north of the river.

Publius' son, also named Publius (236–183), had fought alongside his father at the Ticinus in 218 and then served as military tribune at Cannae. Scipio would be a suitable replacement to avenge his father and uncle, and to re-establish Roman power in Spain. Italy remained the theatre of the war where senior commanders were needed; Scipio's inexperience as a commander would be less of a liability in Spain.

Scipio sailed to Spain in 210 and established his base at Tarraco (modern Tarragona). Over the winter, he organized his forces and devised a daring campaign for 209. He decided to strike directly at the main Carthaginian supply base in Spain at New Carthage (modern Cartagena). The three Carthaginian armies in Spain were too widely dispersed to come to its aid, and it was held by a weak garrison of 1,000 troops. Its capture, besides depriving the Carthaginians of their major supply base, would give the Romans the best port on the east coast of Spain and facilitate operations both in the south and in the interior. After several attempts to storm the town, he staged a diversion while sending a scaling party to attack the undefended wall on the lagoon side. The town fell, yielding an immense amount of booty and supplies.

In preparation for the campaign of 208, Scipio trained his troops rigorously. This training was vital to the innovative tactics he was to employ in all of his future campaigns. In 208 he defeated Hannibal's brother Hasdrubal at Baecula (modern Bailen), north of the Baetis River (Guadalquivir).

The next year was spent in gaining control of the Celtiberian recruiting areas that fed the Carthaginian armies in central Spain, and at the same time protecting his western flank. The remaining Carthaginian general, another Hasdrubal, had retreated to Gades (Cadiz) in the extreme south under pressure from Scipio. However, it was vital for Hasdrubal to fight Scipio; if he could not defeat him, all hope of supporting Hannibal in Italy would be lost.

Early in 206 Hasdrubal and Mago, another of Hannibal's brothers, advanced north from Gades to Ilipa (probably modern Alcala del Rio), which lies a few kilometres north of Seville, and encamped there with a force of 50,000 infantry, 4,500 cavalry and 32 elephants.[105] His camp stood on high ground fronted by a broad open plain.

Scipio moved to engage them. His army probably numbered 45,000 infantry and 3,000 cavalry of whom just over half were Romans or Italian allies. The rest were Spanish troops whom Scipio did not fully trust, but he had no choice but to use them.

When Scipio was encamping on a low range of hills across the plain, the Carthaginians delivered a cavalry attack which was beaten off. The next few days were taken up with an attempt by both sides to draw the other into battle on terrain of their own choosing. There were skirmishes between the cavalry and light-armed troops of both sides. Finally, a full-scale battle developed.

This battle is, perhaps, the most tactically innovative of any of Scipio's battles. He noticed how Hasdrubal deployed his forces on the days leading up to the battle. The deployment was always the same. He placed his African troops in the centre of his line and his Spanish troops with his elephants and cavalry on his wings. Scipio placed his own Roman troops in the centre of his line with his Spanish contingents on his wings. In this way he mirrored to the Carthaginian arrangement.

On the day of the battle, Scipio marched out of camp at sunrise to the middle of the plain. He then changed the deployment of his troops. A screen of light-armed infantry and cavalry prevented Hasdrubal from observing Scipio's changing deployment. The Roman commander now placed his Spanish units in the centre of his line, while his Roman troops formed both the wings. Once his men were in place he sent forward his cavalry and light-armed infantry to launch a missile attack on the enemy camp. As often happened, their skirmishing was without a decisive result. Scipio received these troops back into his ranks through the gaps between the maniples and placed them behind both of his wings with the *velites* in front and the cavalry behind. He then made straight for the enemy line and when he was about 1km from the enemy he instructed his Spanish troops to continue their advance and ordered the infantry and cavalry on his right to turn to the right, and those on the left wing to turn to the left. Scipio, who was on the right wing, took the three leading squadrons of cavalry, placing them in front of three maniples and their associated *velites*. His commanders on the left wing did the same. With these units he marched to the right until he extended his line beyond the enemy's on his right, while they did the same in the left. He now outflanked both ends of the Carthaginian battle line. He then wheeled his units on the right to the left, while the units on the left wheeled to the right; all of these formations then advanced directly on the enemy. While all of this was happening, the Spaniards in the centre were advancing slowly and still some distance from contact when Scipio attacked the wings of the enemy, which led to a total rout.

Scipio's manoeuvre with the troops on his wings was an unusually complex one to carry out in the middle of a battle. It could easily have led to a loss of cohesion, which would have fatally weakened his line. That it could be carried out is the result of the tremendous emphasis he placed on training his men. It also is indicative of the restoration of morale among Roman forces that he had achieved. Polybius' description is somewhat confusing. It seems likely that what Scipio did was not simply a movement of three maniples plus associated light-armed infantry and cavalry, but of the entire left and right wings of the army where the Roman troops were stationed. In the first phase the right wing turned to the right and the left wing to the left and marched parallel to the Carthaginian line until they reached a point either at the end of the Carthaginian line or more likely some way beyond it. They advanced in column until close to the enemy line when they wheeled into line, so that the infantry was on the inside and the cavalry and light-armed troops formed the end of the line. These movements, as complicated as they are, must have been executed quickly to forestall any attempt by Hasdrubal to change his formation. Their position at the ends of the line allowed the cavalry and light-armed infantry to operate together as they had done since the fourth century, and to protect the other infantry against a flank attack by the Carthaginian cavalry.

In the battle, the elephants created havoc on all sides, and did as much damage to their own side as they did to the Romans. Maddened by the Roman missile attacks, they struck out wherever they could. The infantry on the Carthaginian wings fought well, knowing the fate of the struggle rested with them. But as the heat of the day advanced, they weakened. Many had formed up without breakfast and were inadequately rested. The African troops, who were the elite of the army, were unable to come to their aid because of the advancing Spanish. Under the unrelenting pressure they were slowly forced back and then gave way as they made for the heights where their camp lay. The Romans pressed on, but luckily for the Carthaginians a heavy downpour began which forced the Romans to end their pursuit.

The battle displayed Scipio as the most innovative Roman tactician of the war. He had mastered Hannibal's methods. This is especially clear in his rearrangement of his forces before the decisive encounter. Hannibal had utilized the psychology of his opponents against them; Scipio did this at Ilipa, taking advantage of the pattern that Hasdrubal kept repeating in his troop deployment. The handling of his troops under the pressure of battle was unmatched by any other Roman commander in the war. The battle ended the Carthaginian presence in Spain and any hope of Hannibal's that he might be reinforced. Four years later Hannibal and Scipio would face each at Zama in North Africa. It was a hard battle but in the end Scipio prevailed and the war ended.

CHAPTER EIGHT

THE ARMY ON CAMPAIGN II

War in the East

Rome's involvement in the eastern Mediterranean was at first tentative, and probably the result of pressure from her Italian allies. The situation in the lands bordering the Adriatic Sea was unstable. The Illyrians, who inhabited the northwestern part of the Balkan Peninsula, had a long history of attempts to expand to the south and east. They had repeatedly invaded Macedonia and were, in the second half of the third century, expanding along the northern and eastern coasts of the Adriatic. They began raiding to the south as far as the Straits of Otranto and had even plundered the coast of southern Italy. As a result of this raiding and Illyrian expansion, the problem of piracy had grown significantly worse, damaging the interests of Italian traders. Particularly significant was the capture and sacking of the important city of Phoenice in Epirus by the Illyrians; this resulted in the death or capture of a number of Italian traders. A Roman embassy sent to deal with these problems was poorly treated and, to make matters worse, the ship carrying the embassy home was attacked by pirates and members of the embassy – including a senator – were killed.[1] The complaints of the Italians, the disrespect shown the embassy culminating in the murder of a senator, and perhaps memories of Pyrrhus' invasion from across the Adriatic led to a declaration of war.

The first Illyrian War opened in 229 and ended within a year. Rome employed overwhelming force, including a fleet of 200 ships and a consular army of 22,000 troops. The settlement that ended the war restricted the activities of the Illyrians, ended the threat of piracy and reduced the size of their kingdom. To curtail the possibility of future problems, the Romans installed a client ruler and established a protectorate on the Balkan side of the sea. They then withdrew their forces completely.[2] There is no hint of any Roman presence east of the Adriatic after the end of the war.

A decade later, in 219, a second Illyrian War broke out. Its origin seems to lie in the conduct of the Roman client Demetrius, who the Romans put in power after the first war. He was aggressive in expanding his possessions, diminishing Roman influence and threatening the settlement of 229. As the second Ilyrian War began, Hannibal was causing trouble in Spain. To resolve the situation in the Adriatic as quickly as possible, the Romans once again resorted to overwhelming force. Both of the consuls of 219 were sent against Demetrius, who had drawn close to Philip V of Macedon.

It was a relationship that was to have consequences in the future. Once again, the war was over within a year. Demetrius was defeated after the capture of his capital, removed and the situation returned to what it had been after the first war. There was no expansion of Roman control. The native kingdoms were left intact; Rome's attention was directed elsewhere.

The First Macedonian War (215–210)

Rome's first serious involvement in the east came in 215 when Philip V made an alliance with Hannibal. The origins of the alliance and the conflict that followed lay in the ambitions of the young king who had come to the throne in 221 aged 17. He had been at war in Greece with the Aetolian League, the major power in central Greece; however, in 217 he made peace with it. It seems that his ambitions for expansion now turned westwards towards Illyria. He may have done so because he saw that Rome was fully engaged with Hannibal in Italy. It was the only power that could stand in his way. The Roman defeat at Cannae seemed to indicate that it was on the verge of collapse. He began negotiations with Hannibal and a treaty of alliance was concluded. It committed both sides to an offensive alliance directed against Rome, which on the conclusion of the war, would become defensive.[3]

The Romans sent a small force to deal with Philip; they were too preoccupied with Hannibal to do more. In 212 or 211 they concluded an alliance with the Aetolian League. Cities and territories captured from Philip and his allies would be given to the Aetolians, while the Romans would receive the portable booty. The alliance had important benefits for the Romans. The Aetolians probably had the most effective cavalry force in Greece, and were to render striking service in the Second Macedonian War and later. The two contracting partners were represented as equal and the treaty was to last until Philip was defeated, but neither of these two propositions was true.

Firstly, as Rome advanced into the eastern Mediterranean, it became clear that she was the dominant partner no matter what terms were specified in the various treaties of alliance. Secondly, the Roman approach to alliances was pragmatic. When it became clear that Philip was no longer a threat, they abandoned the Aetolians and left them to extricate themselves as best they could. They concluded the treaty of Phoenice with Philip in 205 that ended Roman involvement. Rome retained control of certain areas in Illyria, but in general, Philip kept his conquests. More important in the long run was the suspicion of Philip that the treaty and war engendered in the minds of Roman senators.

The Second Macedonian War (200–196)

Rome had developed friendly relations with the kingdom of Pergamum in northwestern Asia Minor and the island of Rhodes, the major Greek naval power in the Aegean during the Second Punic War. Both warned the Senate that Philip V and the Seleucid king Antiochus III had concluded a treaty of alliance aimed at dismembering the Ptolemaic monarchy in Egypt during the winter of 203–202.[4] A number of wars over the possession of Syria had marked relations between the Seleucids and the Ptolemies. The succession to the throne of Egypt of the six-year-old Ptolemy V, and the weakness of the Egyptian government, opened up the prospect that Antiochus could permanently remove a rival. Antiochus advanced south and drove the Ptolemies out of Syria and Palestine and then set about organizing his gains. In 202 Philip began campaigning in the north Aegean. In the next year his campaigns began to excite alarm. He captured a number of cities belonging to the Aetolian League. He then went on to take a number of islands with ties to the Rhodians, and defeated the Rhodian navy in a sea battle. He also became embroiled in a war against Pergamum in Asia Minor and campaigned in southern Asia Minor against some of Rhodes' mainland possessions. By 201 Philip was pressing hard on both states and there seemed to be no Greek power that could help them.

They turned to Rome, which had now concluded the Second Punic War and was for the moment at peace. It was a natural development. Pergamum had given military support to Rome during the first war against Carthage, and Rhodes had helped to negotiate the end to that war. Embassies came to the Senate from both states, as well as from numerous other Greek states including Athens – whose territory had been invaded by Philip – to ask for protection against him. They received a speedy response from the Senate. An embassy was sent to Philip to demand he stop his aggression against the Greeks and offer compensation as determined by tribunal for his offences against Pergamum.[5]

The Roman embassy was merely a propaganda ploy. When the new consuls took office, one of them, Publius Sulpicius Galba, received Macedonia as his province. He was instructed to present a motion to the centuriate assembly for a declaration of war against Philip. Astonishingly, for the only recorded time, the assembly turned down the motion when a tribune argued against it on the grounds of exhaustion from the war against Carthage. However, the prospect of booty and the exemption of certain categories from the draft soon resulted in a reversal and war was voted.[6] The Senate's attitude seems to have been the result of resentment of Philip for his alliance with Hannibal and a desire to stabilize the situation in Greece, while at the same time presenting Rome as a beneficent power interested in protecting the Greeks from Macedonian domination. There is no reason at this point to see any more far-reaching aims behind Rome's conduct.

The first two years of the war were marked by manoeuvring by both sides without a decisive battle taking place. In the summer of 199, the Aetolian League joined Rome in the war against Philip. Two years earlier he had attacked and taken territory that belonged to it; the Aetolians, with Rome in the field against Philip, now had an opportunity to retake it. In addition, the Aetolians – famous for their plundering activity – were attracted by the possibilities of booty that the fight against Philip offered. What appeared to be developing into a successful invasion of Macedonia offered an opportunity to enter the war on the winning side, but the invasion bogged down and in their battle with Philip the Aetolians suffered a serious defeat.

The arrival in 198 of a new commander, Titus Quinctius Flamininus, changed the situation dramatically. He developed his attack on Macedonia from the southwest moving up through Thessaly. He slowly drove Philip out of Thessaly and back to the borders of Macedonia. But the going was difficult as Philip had garrisoned a number of towns, and Flamininus consumed most of campaigning season capturing them. Finally, at Atrax in Thessaly he was unable to take the town and was forced to go into winter quarters. But Roman successes brought the Achaean League, the major power in the Peloponnese, into the coalition against Philip. Flamininus' command was extended for 197, and he now intended to bring about a decisive battle.

To deal with Flamininus, Philip had two possibilities: he could defend the passes from Thessaly into Macedonia, or go on the offensive. The first possibility was impractical. There were too many passes to defend, as the Greek alliance had discovered in 480 when they hoped to stop the Persians at the Vale of Tempe. If Philip failed to mount an adequate defence, he would expose himself to further loss of territory. The other course was more attractive. If he met the Romans in battle and defeated them, he might change the course of the war, although the results of Hannibal's victories at the outset of the Second Punic War might have given him pause. A victory might make new converts to the Roman cause rethink their alliances, or perhaps opt for neutrality. It also might lead to serious negotiations with the Romans in which he might protect both his kingdom and his influence in Greece. Given the disparity of resources and the relentless character of Roman war-making, this was not a promising course, but the king had little choice.

The Battle of Cynoscephalae[7]

In late March of 197 Philip marched south to Dium in southern Macedonia, where he began training his new recruits for the coming battle. At the same time, Flamininus resumed his policy of gradual conquest. He moved north into Thessaly, where he received significant aid from his Greek allies, including 6,000 foot and 400 horse from the Aetolians and a further 2,000 cavalry from other Greek states. He now had 26,000 men, including his two legions and Italian allies, along with 8,000 Greek infantry and 2,400 cavalry. Perhaps 4,500 of the Greeks were posted to garrison duty, so his field force amounted to approximately 21,500 infantry and 2,400 cavalry as well as an unknown number of elephants.

Flamininus marched north with the object of isolating the Macedonian strongpoint at Demetrias.[8] He had hoped to take the important town of Phthiotic Thebes by treachery, but was forced to besiege it. During the siege, news arrived that Philip had entered Thessaly. Flamininus advanced north towards Pherae to engage him and encamped about 9.5km south of the town. Philip, having learned that Flamininus was at Phthiotic Thebes, marched south and then east along the Thessalian plain and encamped about 5.5km to the north of Pherae. He had with him an army about equal in size to Flamininus'. His most reliable troops were the 16,000 Macedonians who formed his phalanx. In addition, he had 2,000 light-armed peltasts,[9] 2,000 Thracians, and 2,000 Illyrians, as well as a mixed force of 1,500 mercenaries and 2,000 cavalry. The following day, advance forces of both armies came into contact at a pass between Thebes and Pherae. A skirmish developed involving cavalry and light-armed infantry, and Philip's forces were driven back. No major engagement took place, as both sides decided that the area around Pherae had too many obstructions for them to easily deploy. The next day, the king marched west to his base at Scotussa to resupply and to find suitable ground for the battle. Flamininus, knowing of Philip's move, also marched towards Scotussa, hoping to ravage the fields before Philip's men could forage. Three days of parallel marching ensued, with the two armies separated by the hills of Cynoscephalae and unaware of each other; a lack of effective scouting was the norm in Greek and Roman armies in this period.[10]

A thick fog hindered visibility early on the day of the battle, which probably occurred in the neighbourhood of Scotussa. Despite the heavy fog, Philip marched southeast on the morning of the battle. He sought to reach the plain of Pharsalus where there was flat land suitable for a phalanx. But he could continue his march only for a few kilometres. The fog was too dense and it was dangerous to cross Cynoscephalae in such low visibility. He halted on the north side of the hills and sent out a reconnaissance force consisting of 1,500 infantry and 700–800 cavalry. Flamininus too, hindered by the fog, sent out a small party of 250 cavalry and 1,000 light-armed troops.

The battle started from an accidental encounter. A fight broke out between the two scouting parties which blundered into each other; almost three decades later, the major battle of Philip's son Perseus in his war with Rome began in a similar fashion.[11] On the Roman side, 500 cavalry, mostly Aetolian, and 2,000 light-armed troops came up in support as the fight was nearing the Roman camp, an additional 700–800 cavalry and 3,000 foot drove the Macedonians back.

Philip had not planned for a battle and many of his troops were out foraging. He must, at this point, have decided to risk a full-scale engagement.

The reason why is not clear. Typically, the phalanx needed level ground to operate effectively and it is rather surprising that Philip chose to engage on broken ground at Cynoscephalae. It seems that the pressure of the situation pushed him forward as he brought support to his beleaguered vanguard. He may also have thought that the advantage of attacking from higher ground would balance the absence of a level field. It is even harder to understand his decision to advance with only his right wing fully deployed. Troops were recalled and sent immediately to the heights in support. The whole of the Thessalian and Macedonian cavalry and all the Thracian soldiers – now at least 3,500 infantry and 1,400 cavalry – were engaged.

The fog had begun to lift which increased visibility. Flamininus marched his men out of camp in the southern section of the valley, which was less than 2.5km wide from east to west. The consul was commanding the left wing, where the cavalry fighting was especially fierce, and his light-armed troops were giving way before the charge of the right wing of Philip's phalanx as it attacked downhill. The encounter between the two armies was fierce. Philip drove back the Roman left. However, his centre was still some distance away and his left had just crested the hill and was visible on the heights. Flamininius, seeing the perilous situation on the left, moved his right forward to engage Philip's centre with his elephants in the van. The consul had deployed them there because there were fewer obstacles in their way. The Macedonians were in disarray and had not yet formed from column into line. At the Roman attack the Macedonian centre lost cohesion and began to melt away. Most of the Roman right pursued the fleeing Macedonians cutting them down as they fled.

One of the military tribunes stationed with the Roman right wing, seeing both the predicament of the Roman left and the disintegration of the Macedonians, detached twenty maniples from the right wing and led them behind the Macedonian right and fell upon its rear. The long spears of the phalanx made it almost impossible to turn to face the new threat. The Macedonian right began to collapse, which allowed the Roman troops to their front to attack as well. The Macedonians were being assaulted from both the front and rear and they were in an impossible situation. Their formation fell apart and each man fled as best he could.

Philip, seeing the outcome of the battle, assembled what troops he could and made his escape. Flamininus moved uphill with his men in pursuit of the survivors from the Macedonian centre. As he reached the hill he saw the Macedonian left, which had just reached the summit. The Macedonians raised their spears: a sign of surrender. Flamininus, learning the meaning of the gesture, tried to halt his men, but before he could do so some of the troops at the front of his formation attacked, cutting down those Macedonians closest to them. The rest fled, abandoning their equipment.

The battle illustrates a common occurrence in ancient set-piece battles: the victory of one part of the battle line and the failure of its other parts. In this case, both the Roman and Macedonian right wings were successful, while their left wings were defeated and the Macedonian centre was forced back. This battle was one of the few known instances in which a military tribune acted independently on the battlefield. Finally, the battle illustrates the much greater flexibility of the Roman formation compared with the rigidity of the phalanx, as Polybius' subsequent discussion points out.[12] According to his figures, the Macedonians lost 8,000 killed and 5,000 captured, while the Romans lost 700. The figures are hard to accept as they stand; the Roman casualties seem too low. The Roman left had suffered heavily in the course of the main battle, so it is hard to believe that Roman casualties could have been as few as Polybius reports. It is not clear whether the figure includes the fighting on the hill before the main battle, and whether allies such as the Aetolians are included in this figure.

In 196 Philip and the Romans concluded a peace treaty. It must have been obvious to Philip that he did not have the manpower to continue. The Romans were not interested at this point in acquiring territory east of the Adriatic. There were good reasons to accept a settlement that would end the threat of Philip's expansive polices, but maintain the integrity of the Macedonian kingdom. Macedonia would still be able to form a buffer against northern tribes, as it had often done in the past. In addition, the Seleucid king Antiochus III had returned from his campaign on the eastern borders of his kingdom. He had shown himself an energetic and able campaigner and was now looking to recover former Seleucid territory in the west. If he decided to do so, Rome might well be involved in another eastern war. Philip had to give up all territory outside of Macedonia. However, his kingdom remained intact. The Aetolian League – who were a long-time adversary of Macedonia and had been abandoned by Rome during the First Macedonian War – was disappointed once again. It had wanted to invade Philip's kingdom, plunder and dismember it. Its dissatisfaction was to have important consequences.

The dominant power in the Balkans was now Rome, although it exercised its power indirectly through the threat of possible military intervention. The settlement distributed the spoils of the war – the territories lost by Philip – among the Greek states that had supported Rome, so that no one Greek power was strong enough to challenge Rome's dominance. That dominance received no concrete expression and in 194 the Senate, acting on an earlier proclamation of 196, evacuated all Roman troops from the Balkans.

The War Against Antiochus III

Antiochus III (c.242–187) had come to the throne in 222. The kingdom he inherited was beset by rebellions, both in the west in Asia Minor and in the east in Persia and Mesopotamia. In addition, the Ptolemies had detached much of southern Syria from the Seleucid kingdom. By 197 he was able to overcome these rebellions and re-establish his power in Asia Minor and the east. His attempts to retake Syrian territory controlled by Egypt were less successful. He was defeated in a great battle at Raphia (modern Rafah) in southern Gaza in 217. However, he did regain important Seleucid possessions in northern Syria and annexed Egyptian possessions in southern Asia Minor.

Antiochus' initial contacts with Rome had been friendly. At the start of the war against Philip, the Romans had treated Antiochus as a friend and had met with him in 200. In 198 Antiochus was engaged in fighting with Rome's ally, the kingdom of Pergamum. When the Romans asked him to break off the fighting, Antiochus agreed and in return was rewarded with honorary decrees. In the spring of 196 he crossed over to Thrace and re-established Seleucid control there. That step altered his relationship with Rome. Rome's settlement after the Macedonian war had included the slogan of freedom for the Greeks. On that basis the Romans demanded that Antiochus evacuate Europe and those cities conquered from Philip or Ptolemy. Further, they demanded that he must leave all Greek cities free and not cross over to Europe in the future. No threat of military action was made at this point.

Antiochus was not willing to accept such terms. He saw them as an unacceptable intrusion in his affairs by the Romans. Both sides had differing aims and interests. The Romans wanted to prevent the king from gaining control of the cities on the western coast of Asia Minor and also to keep him out of the Balkans. These were aims that complemented each other. The absence of naval bases on the coast of Asia Minor would hinder any attempt to expand into Greece. In 196, Antiochus had an enormous fleet and army. He also had a spectacular record of military success that had earned him the title of 'The Great'. The king had firm historical claims to the coasts of Asia Minor and Thrace. The atmosphere of suspicion and tension only deepened with the arrival of Hannibal at Antiochus' court. He had been elected one of the chief magistrates of Carthage, probably in 196, and instituted a number of successful reforms that angered his political opponents in the aristocracy. To escape possible danger, he went into self-imposed exile and found his way to Antiochus' court.

The end of the war against Philip had left the Aetolians extremely dissatisfied. They felt that the Romans had once again treated them unfairly, given the important contribution they had made to victory. With the continuing tension between Rome and Antiochus, they thought they had found a solution to their problem with Rome. In 192 they invited Antiochus to free the Greeks and to act as an arbiter between them and the Romans.

It appears that Antiochus was less well informed on the situation in Greece than one would expect. The Aetolians falsely persuaded him that there was strong anti-Roman feeling in Greece and that he would be warmly welcomed, if he decided to land in Greece. Antiochus accepted the invitation. It may be that he had decided that there was no alternative to a conflict with Rome. Her demands were dictates that no independent power could tolerate. The invitation from the Aetolians offered him a chance to fight the Romans outside his own territories with – he hoped – useful allies. It seems clear that it was Rome's mistaken view of Antiochus' intentions that led to a war that nobody wanted.

In the autumn of 192 Antiochus began ferrying his army of 10,000 infantry, 500 cavalry and 6 elephants over to Europe. It was far too small to engage Roman armies with their enormous manpower reserves; its size was an indication that the king expected to find substantial military support in Greece. Except for the Aetolian League, the king's hopes of support were disappointed. By the end of 192 he had obtained only minimal backing. Antiochus had little success in Greece. Despite the Roman evacuation, there was dissatisfaction among the Greek states, but his army was too small to attract much support. He had some successes in Euboea and Thessaly and liberated a few towns. In 190, a consular army under Acilius Glabrio crossed over to Greece and in a series of battles culminating in a final encounter at Thermopylae, forced Antiochus to evacuate Greece and return to Asia. Glabrio did not pursue him as he needed time to settle the situation in Greece. The Aetolians were still hostile. The campaign against them continued. Under Roman pressure the Aetolians asked to negotiate and surrendered; the Romans treated them so harshly that they renewed their resistance. Finally, in 189 they surrendered to Fulvius Nobilior, who had succeeded Glabrio. The terms were harsh: a large indemnity, restrictions placed on who could be a league member and the Aetolians were to have the same friends and enemies as the Roman people and preserve the empire of the Roman people without fraud. This is the first recorded instance of this requirement.

The Battle of Magnesia

In 190 the command against Antiochus was given to the consul Lucius Scipio, the brother of Africanus, who had served as a legate for his brother in the Second Punic War. Africanus accompanied the army as a legate of his brother, reversing the roles they had played in the war against Carthage. Much of the year was consumed by affairs in Greece. It was not until October that Lucius and his army crossed over to Asia. Antiochus' experience in Greece must have weakened his confidence. He tried to gain allies in Asia Minor, but with no success. He entered into negotiations with the Romans, but their demands would have resulted in his total loss of Asia Minor as well as access to the Aegean. He had no alternative but to continue the war.

Antiochus mobilized his forces at his base at Sardis in western Asia Minor. He assembled an army with 60,000 infantry, 12,000 cavalry and 54 elephants. The key unit of his phalanx was an elite formation called the Silver Shields (from the colour of their shields). They had originated under Alexander and continued as an elite unit under the Seleucids.[13] His cavalry included Dahae horsemen from central Asia, and 6,000 cataphracts. The cataphract was unusual not only in being armoured from head to toe, but also in riding an armoured mount.[14] His equipment was of central Asian origin; his main weapon was a long, heavy lance, although he often carried a bow as well. His horse was usually protected by a metal breastplate. Antiochus also had light cavalry and scythed chariots.

He marched northwest to confront a much smaller Roman army advancing southeast from Pergamum. That army consisted of 27,600 infantry, 2,800 cavalry and 16 elephants. Among the infantry formations were 3,000 Greek hoplites and peltasts from Pergamum and Achaea, and smaller units of other Greek troops. The cavalry under Eumenes, the king of Pergamum, numbered 3,000, of which 800 were from Pergamum.

The two armies encamped opposite each other in a plain northeast of the town of Magnesia ad Sipylum (near modern Manisa in western Turkey). The confrontation took place at an unusually late time of year: December 190.[15] It is likely that Lucius Scipio was hoping to win a decisive victory before his term of office expired at the end of the month. The area is bounded on three sides by rivers, the Hermos to the south, the Phrygios to the west and north but was open to the east. The Romans camped west of the river and then crossed over to its east bank and deployed in the narrowest part of the terrain's horseshoe. Deploying there minimized the danger to the Roman flanks from Antiochus' superior numbers, as well as his superiority in cavalry.

The Roman battle order was unusual in its deployment of cavalry. Almost all of it was stationed on its right wing, only 4 *turmae* or 120 troopers on its left. The generals must have hoped that the river would protect their left, and so stationed almost all of their cavalry as well the Greek cavalry on the right to prevent an outflanking movement by Antiochus. The Roman infantry and the allied *ala* on the left were commanded by the legate Domitius Ahenobarbus, while Lucius Scipio commanded the right legion and allied *ala*. His brother Africanus lay ill.

Antiochus' force was somewhat smaller as a result of leaving 7,000 troops behind to guard his camp. He positioned his phalanx in the middle of his line drawn up thirty-two deep rather than the usual sixteen. The king separated the phalanx units from each other, placing two elephants in front of each of the units to hold the gaps. Mercenary contingents guarded the phalanx's flanks. It may be that Antiochus was influenced by what had happened at Cynoscephalae seven years before, when the Romans had attacked the rear and flanks of Philip's phalanx. It seems probable that the unusual depth was a way of guarding against a Roman breakthrough in the centre, which had happened several times at Trebia and Cannae during the Second Punic War. It also seems to point to a battle plan in which the Romans would be held in front by the phalanx, while Antiochus' superior cavalry and his light-armed infantry would outflank and roll up the Roman line.

The battle opened with a charge by Antiochus's army on both flanks. On the right, the cataphracts and part of the phalanx broke the left legion and drove it back to the Roman camp. The military tribune Aemilius Lepidus rallied the men and prevented Antiochus' troops from taking the camp or returning to the battle. On the king's left, the battle developed very differently. Before the scythed chariots could be launched into battle, Eumenes' light-armed troops swarmed all over the chariots and bombarded them. The retreating chariots were thrown into disarray and fled the field. Eumenes ordered an attack by all of his cavalry in massed squadrons against the cataphracts. The assault opened a gap between the left wing and the rest of the army. Antiochus' light infantry and the cavalry now panicked and fled back to camp.

There was no longer any chance that the king's left would outflank the Roman right. What was worse was that the left flank of the phalanx was now exposed as Eumenes' light-armed troops attacked the troops shielding it and the elephants to its front. The phalanx and the elephants were held in front by the right Roman legion and allies while being attacked on its left flank by cavalry and light infantry. The phalanx formed into a tight square that the Roman infantry could not penetrate, and resisted for some time. Finally, after a prolonged bombardment by missiles, the elephants posted to the front panicked and broke up the phalanx. That signalled the effective end of the battle.

Livy puts the Seleucid casualties at 50,000 foot, and 3,000 cavalry, while 1,400 men and 15 elephants were captured.[16] Appian has a lower figure, stating that the total of captured, wounded and killed was 50,000, but he does not vouch for it. Neither figure seems likely. It is probable that the number was far lower. It is noticeable that neither historian mentions those who escaped. Given the size of Antiochus' army and the much smaller force of the victors, it seems probable that a substantial number of the king's men did manage to save themselves. Livy gives Roman casualties as 300 infantry, 24 cavalry and 25 soldiers from Eumenes' troops. Appian's figures for Roman losses are virtually identical to Livy's.[17] These seem too low. Nonetheless, given the course of the battle there is no doubt that the king's army suffered very heavily in comparison to the Romans.

After returning from his partially victorious right wing, Antiochus saw that the battle was lost and fled to Sardis. There he entered into negotiations with the Romans. Their demands were the same as they had been earlier. The king must evacuate all territory north and west of the Taurus

Mountains and pay an enormous war indemnity. These terms meant that the king was forced out of Asia Minor. It is clear that the Romans had no desire to directly control any territory in Asia Minor. Their interest was in safeguarding the Balkans and Italy's security. The evacuated territory was turned over to their allies, Pergamum and Rhodes.

The End of Macedonia

Even after Philip was defeated, Macedonia remained the most powerful state in the Balkans. The defeat reduced him to the status of a Roman client. During the war against Antiochus, he had cooperated with Rome and had expected a reward. It was not forthcoming. Rome was still suspicious of him and would do nothing that might increase his strength. He had unilaterally occupied some territory, but had been forced out by Rome and once again confined within his own borders. In an attempt to placate the Romans, Philip sent his younger son to Rome to answer complaints against him by other Greek states. The Romans found the son, Demetrius, a compliant tool who could be used to govern Macedonia in Rome's interests. They even encouraged Demetrius to hope that he might supplant his father on the throne. This set him at odds with his elder brother Perseus, who would normally have succeeded to the throne. The situation within the royal family deteriorated to such a point that Philip openly declared that Demetrias was trying to kill him. His suspicions were heightened by Perseus' manoeuvres against his younger son. Philip imprisoned Demetrius and then had him executed. The act increased Roman suspicions of both father and son.

In 179 Philip died and Perseus came to the throne. He sent to Rome a request for a renewal of friendship and assent to his succession, which were granted. Perseus' marriage into the Seleucid royal house raised the spectre of an alliance of Macedonia with the Seleucids, although none was contemplated. Increasing the climate of distrust were measures that Perseus took to alleviate internal problems in Macedonia. He recalled those exiled for various offences or for crimes against the throne. He declared an amnesty for debtors to eradicate discontent among those Macedonians, overwhelmed by debt, who had fled to Greece.[18] The result was that the poor in many Greek states began to see him as their champion. This was particularly upsetting for the Romans as they favoured the upper classes. His popularity in Greece was unwelcome to Rome – which saw itself as the major patron of the Greek states – and also to Eumenes of Pergamum who was also interested in being seen as a benefactor of the Greeks. Eumenes did all he could to injure Perseus. He journeyed to Rome. While there he addressed the Senate portraying Perseus as secretly plotting to fight the war against Rome that Philip had not lived to launch.

The result of all this was that by the late summer of 172, the Senate had decided on war. However, it was not until the next year that a formal declaration of war was issued. An embassy was sent to the Greek states to try to win support for the war and it was decided to send an advance force across the Adriatic to prevent the king from closing the passes through the Pindus Mountains into Macedonia and Thessaly. The disparity in human and material resources between the two adversaries made the eventual result a foregone conclusion.

In 171, the consul Publius Licinius Crassus was sent to open the campaign against Perseus with two legions and allies. Since he had no alternative, Perseus began mobilizing his own forces and marched into Thessaly. His cavalry encountered Crassus' at Callinicus, near the important town of Larissa, and decisively defeated it. The king, hoping this defeat might have convinced the Romans that the cost of victory would be high, immediately asked for peace. The Romans responded with a demand for unconditional surrender, which was obviously unacceptable. The Greeks, despite their experience with the Romans, still did not understand the Roman attitude to war-making which demanded nothing less than the absolute submission of their opponent. In the Greek East – as had been the case with Carthage – war-making was viewed as a means to attain a set of limited political goals.

Aulus Hostilius Mancinus, consul in 170, achieved little. In 169, Quintus Marcius Philippus was more successful. He combined astute diplomacy with a strong offensive against Perseus. He was able to force his way into Macedonia, and by the end of his term in office in December, the Roman army was encamped on the banks of the Elpeus River (which flows from Mt Olympus southeastwards into the Thermaic Gulf). The advance opened southern Macedonia to attack.

Lucius Aemilius Paullus, one of the consuls of 168, was given the command against Perseus. He had already been consul in 182 when he had fought the Ligurians in northwest Italy, and in the following year as proconsul he continued his campaign. He had also fought in Spain. He was granted substantial reinforcements and a strengthened fleet for his campaign in Macedonia. The arrival of the consul together with his praetor, Gnaeus Octavius, induced Perseus to strengthen his defences against the impending attack. Troops were sent to strengthen coastal defences and reinforcements were dispatched to the pass that ran through Pythium and Petra, to stop any attempt to turn the king's position on the Elpeus River. He also reinforced his defences at the Elpeus, which at this time of the year was dry. The town of Dium, which lay to his rear, functioned as a supply base. The king probably hoped that, although he could not win a war with Rome, in the long run he might be able to draw out the conflict until the Romans tired of it and would conclude an acceptable peace.

Paullus, whose army was now camped south of the Elpeus, decided correctly that Perseus' position on the Elpeus was impervious to direct assault.

The best hope for success lay in an attempt to turn the king's position. Paullus dispatched a military tribune, Scipio Nasica Corculum, with a force of 8,200 cavalry and infantry. He successfully surprised the garrison and turned the pass. The figures for the garrison that appear in our two major sources Plutarch and Livy seemed inflated. It is probable that they depended on Scipio's own account in Greek of his actions.[19] The turning of the pass forced Perseus from his position on the Elpeus and he retreated northwards.

The Battle of Pydna

The exact location where Perseus deployed his army is a matter of dispute. The most likely place is south of the city of Pydna, where there is a plain and ridges that fit Plutarch's description of the battlefield. In addition, two streams flow through the site that could be the minor obstacles mentioned in Plutarch and Livy. Both Livy and Plutarch depend on Polybius, whose own account has survived only in fragments, and the memoir of Scipio. These are the major accounts, although some additional information of varying quality can be found in other sources.

The exact date of the battle, 22 June 168, is fixed by the mention of a lunar eclipse.[20] Polybius claims that the eclipse heartened the Romans because it was interpreted as portending the eclipse of the king.[21] The three days of skirmishing prior to the battle must then have taken place on the 19–21 June.

The figures for the numbers of troops involved are uncertain. Plutarch claims that the Macedonian army consisted of 40,000 infantry and 4,000 cavalry; Livy that 20,000 Macedonians were killed in battle and 11,000 were captured. Plutarch supplies a higher casualty figure of 25,000 killed. Both authors' numbers are compatible with Plutarch's figures assuming that troops had been detached to guard the camp and assigned to other duties. At Magnesia, Antiochus had assigned 7,000 as a camp guard.[22] Perhaps 21,000 formed the phalanx, while the rest would have consisted of light-armed fighters and various specialist troops such as peltasts. They would have been stationed on the wings of the phalanx. Paullus' army consisted of two legions and allies, which normally would have totalled about 20,000 men. But Livy specifically mentions that Paullus had received substantial reinforcements. These were presumably supplements to the existing army that Paullus took over from the commander of the year before. So perhaps 25,000 legionaries and allies is a possible figure. In addition, Paullus had contingents from the Greek allies. Given the absence of any reference to the disparity of forces and the absence of any fear of outflanking, it is likely that the armies were roughly equal in size.

The Macedonians deployed facing southwest while the Romans faced northeast. The Macedonian left consisted of the Royal Guard, 10,000 Thracians, mercenaries and Paeonians.[23] In the centre was the phalanx divided into two units: the Silver Shields on the right and the Bronze Shields on the left. The rest of the right wing consisted of mixed troops totalling 10,000 and 3,000 cavalry directly under the king's command. The cavalry was positioned on the right of the line since the phalanx's right was unprotected by natural barriers.

Aemilius, who was a deeply religious man, ordered sacrifices to be made before the battle to see if the gods were favourable. During the morning of the day of battle, he sacrificed twenty oxen to Hercules, seeking a favourable omen for the coming struggle. Finally, on the twenty-first sacrifice, an omen appeared indicating victory, if he stood on the defensive. He then vowed 100 oxen and games in honour of the gods after he had defeated the king. He gave the order for the army to deploy.

The Roman line was arranged in the usual manner with the two legions in the centre opposite the phalanx, and the Italian allies on the flanks of the legions. Unfortunately, we do not possess a detailed account of the Roman order of battle. Livy's text might have supplied it, but it has gaps. But he does mention that the Greek allies and the elephants were on the Roman right. Strangely, there is no mention of the Roman cavalry at this point or in any of the battle narratives. They must have been in their usual position on the wings of the infantry. The sources mention that all of Perseus' cavalry escaped, which implies that the Roman cavalry was of little importance during the battle, but given the Macedonian casualty figures it must have played an important role in pursuit.

The battle began by accident. Plutarch gives two versions of which the more likely is that the king's Thracian troops attacked draft animals carrying forage back to the Roman camp. They were counterattacked by a unit of 700 Ligurians. As the fight continued, more men joined from both sides until a general engagement developed. The Macedonian line advanced at great speed to the attack. As the Romans moved to meet it, they were stopped by the *sarissas* of the royal guard, and the phalanx – fixing their spear points in the Roman shields – kept the legionaries from using their swords to break into the phalanx. Plutarch reports, on the basis of Polybius' lost account, that Paullus was struck with amazement and fear at the sight of the phalanx in action.[24]

The struggle with the phalanx continued. One of the allied Italian units, the Paeligni, made an attack on it which ended in disaster. The unit's commander hurled one of its standards into the phalanx, and to avoid the terrible disgrace of a captured standard, the unit rushed to rescue it and suffered severe losses.[25] Another allied unit tried the same tactic with the same results. Gradually, the Roman line was forced back. In pushing the Romans back, the Macedonians encountered broken ground and as the struggle continued their progress was uneven, with parts of their line pushing further forward than others. This created gaps in the formation. It was these gaps that decided the outcome of the battle. Paullus, dividing up his army into smaller units, sent them into these gaps. According to Livy, it was the second legion that finally broke the phalanx.[26] Once the phalanx had lost its cohesion, the results were fatal. It could not respond to a multitude of attacks coming from all directions. The gaps also exacerbated another problem. If the phalanx was attacked from the front and closed up, the shorter Roman swords could not reach the hoplites; however, once the enemy was inside the killing zone of the spears, the men of the phalanx had only a weak secondary armament which was no match for the *scutum* and the Spanish sword of the legionaries. Some of the hoplites, in their desperation, fled to the Aeson river where they were cut down by ships' crews.

Macedonian casualties must have been heavy once the phalanx disintegrated. Plutarch claims that 25,000 died; Livy 20,000 dead and 11,000 captured. Both report extraordinary low figures for Roman casualties. Plutarch claims Roman deaths numbered either 80 or 100, while Livy states that they numbered 100, but that many were wounded.[27] The same pattern is also present at Cynoscephalae and Magnesia. Further, there is no accounting of the wounded, some of whom must have died of their wounds.

Perseus survived the battle; pro-Roman sources claimed he had conducted himself disgracefully.[28] The truth can never be known. He surrendered and was imprisoned at Rome. The Macedonian monarchy was extinguished and Macedonia was divided into four weak republics. The Romans attempted to isolate them from each other by forbidding intermarriage and economic relations between them. They also closed the gold and silver mines that had been an important source of the king's wealth. They now collected the taxes previously due to the king, but only half of what the king had collected. All of these measures were designed to make sure that Macedonia would never again be a threat. The settlement was a failure. Within twenty years, revolt had broken out and a pretender tried to reestablish the monarchy. A definitive solution only came in 146, when Macedonia became a Roman province. The aftermath of Pydna also marked a turn to a harsher Roman attitude to the Greeks. They were no longer needed.

Siege Warfare

Little is known about the early history of siege warfare at Rome. The key development in both Greece and Rome was the development of siege machinery. Livy describes a number of sieges of the fifth and fourth centuries, but the factual basis for these descriptions is probably tiny and artistic elaboration is a significant part of his narrative. An example is the siege of Veii.[29] Before the invention of siege machinery, the methods available – especially to heavy infantry – were few in number.

Although forts and other relatively small fortifications such as Roman marching camps could be subject to sieges, the most important sieges involved cities. The quickest method was by a direct assault, but the presence of fortifications, which had grown in sophistication, usually precluded the success of such an assault. Generally, if it succeeded, the assault often had an element of surprise in its favour or it faced a garrison that was too weak to defend the walls adequately. In 209, a major factor in Scipio Africanus' capture of New Carthage was the small numbers of defenders who numbered 1,000 mercenaries and 2,000 citizens.[30] Mining operations, as at Veii in 396, offered another possibility. Treachery was also a significant factor in the capture of a city. In a mid-fourth century handbook on siege warfare by the Greek Aeneas Tacticus, numerous chapters are devoted to protecting the city against betrayal.[31] Finally, blockade and starvation were the surest method, but also the costliest in terms of time and casualties. In general, some combination of these methods were used.

The advantage lay with the defence. Greek improvements in fortification had spread throughout the Mediterranean. City ramparts took advantage of any natural protection a site provided. Brick construction was, where possible, replaced by stone. Fortification walls incorporated turnings to provide flanking fire against attackers and gates were defended by curtain walls for the same reason. Perhaps, as a result of borrowing from the Near East, towers were added to the walls to provide flanking fire and to partition off sections, so that if one section fell to attackers, the defenders would still have protection. By the end of the fourth and the beginning of the third century city fortifications, especially in the eastern Mediterranean, had become more elaborate. The increasing premium placed on an active defence led to the incorporation of trenches, crenellations and postern gates. These last were hidden gates in the wall from which sorties or escapes could be made.

The first developments that began the transformation of siege warfare also started in the Near East. There, the most highly skilled practitioners and developers of new techniques were the Assyrians. Siege machines appear in Assyrian reliefs: ramps, towers, tunnels and wheeled wicker-covered machines usually with a domed turret and with an iron-tipped beam (they presumably functioned as battering rams).[32] The knowledge of these techniques was passed on to the Persians, who were equally proficient in siege warfare and probably through them to the Greeks.

However, there was another route of transmission through the Phoenicians who had had experience with Assyrian siege techniques in the Near East and passed them onto the colonists they sent out to the western Mediterranean. At the end of the fifth century, a ruthless and capable tyrant, Dionysius I (c.432–367,) had seized control of Syracuse. At that time, it was the most important and powerful of the Greek cities in Sicily. The impetus for the development of mechanization in siege warfare seems to have been the result of preparations for a war with Carthage which broke out in 397 and ended in 392. The Carthaginians employed the full range of siege machines developed in the Near East, but it was the Greeks, and specifically Dionysius, who carried mechanization further by developing machines that could propel missiles of a size and at a speed that far exceeded what had previously been possible.[33]

Dionysius was responsive to new technologies and had the wealth to support their development. According to Diodorus Siculus, in anticipation of warfare with Carthage, Dionysius assembled a team of craftsmen from Sicily, Greece, Italy and from Carthaginian territory in 399. He claims that it was at this point that the catapult was invented. The first catapult design was what the Greeks called a 'belly-shooter', which was basically an enlarged crossbow, cocked by the operator placing his stomach into a groove, bracing the stock and pulling back on the string. The cocking mechanism was improved by the addition of a winch to pull back the string. By the end of the fourth century, probably at the court of Philip II, the torsion catapult was developed. This was a major step forward. It was powered by springs made of hair or sinew, which were wound up to store energy and then released. It could hurl objects further and faster than the belly-shooter and its release of energy was more controlled, allowing for far higher accuracy.

There is no mention of the use of such machines by the Romans until the First Punic War. In 258 they retook the rebellious town of Camarina on the southeastern coast of Sicily with battering rams and used artillery during the war against the town of Motya in western Sicily. The machines in both cases were borrowed from Syracuse. The Greeks used catapults, towers and other devices to clear the defenders from the walls, so that the besiegers could approach the walls more safely with the goal of breaching them and forcing an entrance into the city. By the time of the war against Hannibal, the Romans were routinely using siege machines borrowed from the Greeks, but their approach to their use was very different.

Roman siege methods appear during the First Punic War. They are mentioned for the first time at the siege of Agrigentum, the main Carthaginian base in Sicily in 262. It was much more labour intensive than the typical Greek siege method. Forts and camps were constructed around the periphery of the city walls at locations that controlled the surrounding countryside. These strongpoints were connected by a system of trenches and ramparts that cut the city off from its hinterland and were designed to starve the inhabitants. Agrigentum also provides the first evidence for a contravallation to defend against a relieving force. The most sophisticated example of such a siege fortification is that of Caesar's at the siege of Alesia in southern France in 52. He had a continuous siege wall over 16km in length constructed to close off Alesia; the construction of the wall varied from place to place, taking advantage of the local topography. Along the perimeter of the siege wall twenty-three forts were built to serve as garrison points to guard against unexpected sorties. The circumvallation was fronted by ditches and eleven camps were constructed along the perimeter of the wall. A contravallation was constructed that stretched for nearly 21km, mostly along the surrounding heights. It was also fronted by ditches. Towers were built along the wall and booby traps were dug in front of it. The final century BC was also a period when the techniques learned in siege warfare were applied to field fortifications.

The siege of Agrigentum was a failure, although it was captured after the Carthaginians suffered defeat in open battle. But Roman methods in this case were typical of their procedures during the rest of the Republican period. If possible, an initial attempt was made to carry the city by storm. If that failed, a circumvallation was built, and if necessary a contravallation. These barriers could be either single or double. Artillery was then used to clear the defenders from the walls so that a ramp could be built up to the height of the walls and mining operations could be carried out. Battering rams with a protective covering to protect the troops were employed at the gates to try to force a way in and also as a way to create a breach in the city walls.

Although the Romans used the full range of siege equipment available during the course of the third century and after, siege artillery played a secondary role. In Greek sieges the role of these machines was far more prominent. It is possible that the difference had its origin in the different types of armies fielded by Rome and the Hellenistic kingdoms. Mechanization of siege engines was the product of professional expertise. Dionysius had assembled craftsman from all over the Mediterranean, and Philip II had professional experts who were crucial to the development of the torsion catapult. Hellenistic armies were for the most part composed of professionals. Among them were skilled technicians who were in charge of the army siege train and oversaw the construction of artillery and other siege engines in the field. Roman armies had neither the expertise nor the continuity of the Greek armies. They were composed of annual levies with no special expertise in siege warfare. They could and did hire experts, but the constant turnover militated against the building of a core of professional specialists. In the Imperial period when Rome fielded professional armies, they regularly included siege trains and the professionals needed to build and maintain them.

During the Republic, almost all reported sieges were offensive operations, so we know little about what measures the Roman took to defend cities or fortified sites. It was only during the civil war period of the first century that we have accounts of Romans defending rather than attacking fortified positions. The majority of these descriptions are cursory. The only extended description is Caesar's account of his siege of Pompey's base at Dyrrachium (Durres in modern day Albania) in the spring of 48. After Caesar's arrival, Pompey had refused battle and withdrawn to his base at Dyrrachium. Caesar began a siege in an attempt to force Pompey to fight. As Caesar himself remarks, it was an unusual siege as it involved a larger force being besieged by a smaller one. Caesar built a series of fortifications to restrict the area from which Pompey could draw his supplies. This was especially hard on the large force of cavalry in Pompey's army. They needed to forage for their mounts, and the fortifications also had the advantage for Caesar of closing in Pompey's cavalry, so that they could not harass Caesar's own foraging parties. Caesar hoped that it would pressure Pompey to fight as remaining idle would damage his reputation.

In an attempt to thwart Caesar, Pompey built his own fortifications to protect his access to supplies. In addition, Pompey hoped to force Caesar to so extend his fortifications that he could no longer adequately garrison them. Caesar faced additional problems. Pompey had access to a port so that he could use his fleet to obtain supplies, and if he chose, he could land troops in Caesar's rear. The besieger faced a more difficult supply situation than did the besieged. The siege was finally lifted when, after weeks of ineffective skirmishing, Pompey launched a strong attack on a gap in Caesars's defences where they approached the coast. Unusually in this case, both the defenders and the attackers used fortifications.

The siege of Dyrrachium highlights a major problem: the difficulty of supplying a besieging army. Caesar's situation was made worse by the fact that he started the siege during the winter. Unlike Pompey with his access to supplies by sea, Caesar's camp was inland on a high hill, so that his army was limited to foraging in the surrounding countryside. Even if an army was mobile, in most cases foraging was insufficient to fully supply its needs. This was especially true in infertile or desert environments. The problem was compounded in the case of besieging armies. The surrounding territory would often be exhausted quickly. Foraging parties would need to move further from their base, which increased the time spent foraging and made the foragers more vulnerable to attack. At the siege of Agrigentum in 262, which lasted in total for seven months, the Roman army was without an external supply system and had to disperse to gather wheat; the Carthaginians, seeing an opportunity, attacked the foraging parties and almost captured the Roman camp.[34] At Dyrrachium, Caesar's army had serious supply problems. He had almost no wheat available, which was the basis of the Roman military and civilian diet. Although barley, vegetables and meat were obtainable, they were insufficient to sustain his men for an extended period, especially in winter.[35] It was not just food for the troops, but forage and grain for the horses. In certain conditions water could be an issue as well. The most effective way to deal with these problems was to set up a supply system which allowed these supplies to be drawn from a wider area. As mentioned earlier this is exactly what the Romans did, often depending on nearby or distant allies for supplies. At Dyrrachium with his fleet, Pompey was able to draw on supplies from Asia and other areas of the east under his control. In addition to food, wood and stone for use as building materials were also important, and given their weight, presented special logistical problems especially when they had to be moved some distance.

Finally, the presence of thousands of men in close quarters presented sanitary problems. Often they were not solved, and dysentery and other diseases quickly took a serious toll of the besiegers. For instance, disease broke out in the consul Marcellus' army besieging Syracuse in 212. Again, during the third and final war with Carthage, disease broke out in the army of the consul Censorinus besieging Carthage. Other instances can be adduced. It was a constant danger for both the besiegers and the besieged.[36]

The easiest outcome of the siege for a commander was the surrender of the city without the need for a costly assault. However, the troops probably preferred an assault as this offered them the opportunity to plunder. The Romans expected the inhabitants of the city to ask for surrender terms. A general would offer to spare the city, if it surrendered before the first battering ram touched the walls. For instance, in 57 attacking a town of the Belgic tribe of the Atuatucae, Caesar gave them the option of surrendering before the ram touched their walls.[37] Such a surrender was what the Romans called *deditio in fidem* ('unconditional surrender'). Even if the city surrendered, it would not necessarily escape sack and massacre.[38] However, if the siege was carried to conclusion, the results could be horrific. Polybius records the conclusion of the successful siege of New Carthage by Scipio Africanus in 209:

> *When Scipio thought that a sufficient number of troops had entered [the city] he sent most of them, as is the Roman custom, against the inhabitants of the city with orders to kill all they encountered, sparing none, and not to start pillaging until the signal was given. They do this, I think, to inspire terror, so that when towns are taken by the Romans one may often see not only the corpses of human beings, but dogs cut in half, and the dismembered limbs of other animals, and on this occasion such scenes were very many owing to the numbers of those in the place. Scipio himself, with about a thousand men, proceeded to the citadel. On his approach Mago at first attempted to resist, but afterwards, when he saw that the city had undoubtedly been captured, he sent a message begging for his life and surrendered the citadel. After this, upon the signal being given, the massacre ceased and they began pillaging.*[39]

Often the massacre was restricted to adult males who were capable of resistance, but occasionally – as in this example – all living beings were included. According to Polybius this was to terrorize other Spanish towns into surrendering. Usually, rape accompanied the looting and slaughter. Although Polybius ascribes the horrors of the sack of New Carthage to a conscious act of will by Scipio, in many cases once the men were let loose inside a city that had caused them extensive casualties, the commander could not exercise control until his men's anger and greed subsided.

The Experience of Battle

Reconstructing the experience of soldiers and their officers in ancient battle is extremely difficult. John Keagan in his book *The Face of Battle* was the first to focus on this problem.[40] In it he focused on the experience of soldiers at three famous battles: Agincourt, Waterloo and the first day of the Somme. His work has had a significant impact on the study of ancient warfare. In the years since its publication, there have been a number of studies that have applied his techniques to the study of ancient warfare.[41] However, there are serious obstacles to understanding what the experience was. The first is the difficulty in reconstructing battle as a whole.

The literary sources that provide battle narratives are often imprecise about the topography of the battlefield. For instance, there has been controversy about whether Cannae was fought on the right or left bank of the Aufidus River due to the lack of detail in Polybius' account of the battle. The same imprecision is also a problem in the troop numbers found in the ancient sources. The commander had no war staff to draw up and record whatever plans were adopted. There was no expert observer, and battle was and is chaotic. Even an expert observer would only have seen a small part of the battlefield. There is a further problem in analyzing ancient battles and that is the type of sources that are extant. Except for the accounts of Polybius, Caesar and Ammianus Marcellinus in the fourth century AD, our sources were written by men without direct experience of battle. Even if they had access to eyewitness accounts, such as Scipio Corculum's letter about his exploits in the war against Perseus, their lack of experience sometimes led to misinterpretations and mistakes.

There is a further problem. Major battles in the ancient world were battles of mass. That is, the combat was for the most part close order hand-to-hand fighting of great numbers of men. The experience of the light-armed infantry and cavalry must have been quite different. However, with the appearance and then the domination of the battlefield by firepower, such a formation became suicidal by the mid-nineteenth century. As Keagan pointed out, dispersal was the only way to survive on modern battle-fields.[42] Because of this development, the nature of modern battle is so different from the ancient one that we have no comparable experience. Although groups exist that recreate ancient warfare, they cannot replicate one of its most important aspects: the threat and presence of death on the battlefield. Perhaps the greatest obstacle to understanding the experience of the average soldier is the absence of his voice. It is not until the First World War that we have numerous memoirs written by lower rank officers and common soldiers.

Despite all of these obstacles, it is possible to at least partially construct a model of the experience of battle for the Roman soldier. Several factors must be taken into account. First, the need to look at cultural expectations of conduct in battle. What did Romans think constituted courageous conduct in battle? For example, Caesar praises his centurions highly, in particular the centurion Sextus Baculus. Caesar presents him as a paradigm of military virtue and courage. Even though wounded, he reforms his unit during the battle against the Nervii in 57. In 53, although ill, he saved a camp from destruction. Snatching weapons from some troops standing nearby, he took up a position at the camp's gate and rallied the other centurions to hold off an attack long enough for the rest of the troops to mobilize. There was also an active courage which the Romans characterize as *ferocia* or a 'fierce courageous spirit'. Caesar provides an example. While narrating an attack on the camp of Quintus Cicero, Caesar inserts the story of two centurions, Titus Pullo and Lucius Vorenus. These men had a long-standing rivalry with each other. When the attack of the Nervii was at its most intense, Pullo taunted Vorenus about his bravery and decided to launch an attack outside the rampart in what was a clear display of his superiority in bravery and his *ferocia*. Vorenus followed. The men were almost killed, but finally made their way back into the camp and were greeted with great acclaim. The display of such courage or *virtus* was the most highly valued characteristic of a warrior.[43] This model of courage was probably the most important cultural influence on the soldier. There were also personal ties that affected the soldier's feeling and conduct. The Roman custom of camping in a unit (*contubernium*) of eight soldiers helped forge and then strengthen personal ties between the men. The factors promoting bravery in battle were counterbalanced by fear. Where the balance was struck varied from soldier to soldier. Training must also have played a role in building confidence. At Cannae the consuls made their maniples deeper than normal because of the inexperience of their troops.[44]

Alongside intangible influences on the way men felt and acted in battle were physical limitations. The limits of human endurance played a strong role in how the troops experienced battle. Service in the field included men from the ages of 17 to 46. The effect of aging on endurance and strength must have made itself felt given the athletic character of ancient warfare. It seems likely that the older men at the extreme rear of the line probably never expected to do more than watch younger men fighting. Livy's account of the functioning of the manipular formation in battle mentions that the rear maniples, the *triarii,* consisting of older men, only fought when the army was in desperate straits. Since the campaigning season ran from the late spring through the summer, the heat of Mediterranean battlefields must have been an important factor for the legionaries in particular with their heavy equipment, less so for the light-armed troops. But even for those troops, the dryness and the heat could produce heat exhaustion and clouds of dust that obscured their vision and choked them. The physical exertion of pushing, slashing and thrusting – as well as holding up a shield that by one estimate weighed 10kg – must have necessitated frequent pauses for rest.

The length of a battle also affected the troops. Some encounters, such as Pydna, lasted only for about an hour, but others could go on for much longer. During the opening phase of the civil war in Spain, a battle fought at Ilerda between Caesar and Pompey's lieutenants continued for about five hours.[45] The second battle at Bedriacum, during the civil war of AD 68–69, lasted through the darkness of an autumn night.[46] Courage, confidence, fear, heat and equipment must all have conditioned how men who were not professional soldiers, but members of a militia, imagined and experienced the struggle of battle.

In a set-piece battle the commander's role was crucial. A good commander was expected to try to manoeuvre the enemy onto a battlefield that gave his own army the advantage.[47] It was also crucial for the general to be able to effectively deploy his troops and manoeuvre his men. To counter the superiority of Pompey's cavalry on his left wing at Pharsalus, Caesar took six units from his reserve and deployed them at an oblique angle to his line with instructions to use their *pila* as thrusting spears to drive off the Pompeian cavalry. The deployment worked.[48] Caesar again provides an excellent example of the use of manoeuvre. By a series of manoeuvres that cut off the Pompeian forces in Spain from their communication and supply links, he defeated them without a major battle.[49] The other side of the general's role was a psychological one. He needed to inspire his troops and reinforce their loyalty. Ancient historians routinely begin their description of a battle with a speech by the commander to inspire his men. With large armies, clearly the commander could not have been heard by all of his men. However, it is likely that the substance of the commander's speech was passed down to the unit commanders who then directly addressed their men.

A traditional method to create a bond between the general and his men was for the commander to share his troops' hardships. Gaius Marius, the most successful commander at the beginning of the first century, openly shared his troops privations. Equally important was the commander's displays of courage in the course of the battle. In the classical period, Greek commanders fought in the front line; once the opposing armies met in the absence of reserves or multiple lines, there was little else that the commander could do except to provide a moral example. With the development of these formations, a commander had to remove himself from the front line so as to keep control of uncommitted units. Nonetheless, commanders could and did intervene in the thick of the fighting when defeat threatened. Caesar, in a battle against the Nervii in 57, illustrates both aspects of the commander's role. On the right of his line the men had become crowded together and were impeding each other. Also, a number of centurions had been killed leaving the men leaderless. Caesar moved forward, and since he had come up without his shield, he snatched one from a soldier in the rear ranks and made his way to the front. There he ordered the men to advance and open ranks so that they could use their weapons effectively. These actions, especially the appearance of their commander, restored his men's morale.[50]

The equipment of the legionaries, both the protective equipment (except for the shield) and offensive weapons were made of iron. The use of iron rather than bronze enhanced both the protective power of defensive equipment and the offensive power of the troops' weapons, although this may have led to an increase in the weight the soldier carried compared with bronze equipment.[51] The shield added considerable weight, probably around 9kg. The sword was a minimal addition to the soldier's load, but he went into battle normally carrying heavy and light *pila*, which must have impeded his movement before he discharged them at the enemy. On a hot Mediterranean summer's day, even walking must have been exhausting. But until the first century much equipment was carried by the legion's wagons and pack animals.

The Battle

The battle usually opened with skirmishing between light-armed troops. This fighting was never decisive, but it screened the deployment of the main battle line. Often simultaneously the cavalry also engaged the enemy. Unlike the light-armed troops, cavalry engagement could be decisive. At both Zama and Magnesia, the success of the cavalry brought victory.

However, the key to victory was almost always the heavy infantry. The maniples they were formed up in were flexible and mobile. The flanking that Scipio Africanus achieved at Ilipa would have been impossible without the manipular formation. The organization of the maniple or later the cohort could be altered to some extent according to circumstances. It could be deepened or positioned at an angle to the main battle line as Caesar did with the larger cohort unit at Pharsalus.[52] The Roman approach to combat was not to wait on the defensive, but to move forward to the attack. In his account of Pharsalus, Caesar criticizes Pompey for keeping his legions on the defensive. He claims that waiting on the defensive robs the troops of their élan.

As the line moved forward to engage the enemy, spacing was important, so that the line would move as a whole and each of the maniples would keep formation. The centurions of each maniple, with some help from the military tribunes, were essential to keeping the troops in formation. Each soldier probably occupied a space of 1.8 metres measured from the left shoulder of the man to his right to the right shoulder of the man to his left. This would leave him enough space to use his sword.[53] This was wider than the hoplite line, but men using swords needed more room to use their weapons. When the line was about 28 metres from the enemy, it halted so that the troops could release their light *pila* at this distance and then again at 14 metres to throw their heavy ones. It has been suggested that the rear ranks might have retained their *pila*. There is some evidence for prolonged missile exchanges that supports this thesis.[54]

Once missiles had been discharged, the line moved forward at a charge. Sometimes the enemy collapsed at this point, but more often, he stood his ground. The initial charge must have ended in an attempt to butt the enemy with the soldier's shield and its projecting metal umbo to try to unbalance the enemy so that the legionary could use his sword. If the initial attempt to break into the enemy formation failed, as it must usually had done, the legionaries turned to swordplay. The standard stance that the legionary assumed was as far as possible to turn so that only the left side of his body was offered to the enemy. Given the size of his shield, he could then crouch behind it, while stabbing and slashing with his sword held in his right hand. It implies that the men behind the front line could not have been intentionally pushing the men in that line forward. It seems likely that what happened once the lines of both sides had separated a little from each other was that individual combats broke out along the line involving one or more soldiers. The fight could not have been continuous, given the weight of equipment that a Roman soldier laboured under, as well as the exertion that prolonged use of the sword must have required. There must have been pauses for men to rest where the distance from the men of the opposing line was wide enough to provide security. It was an opportunity for the men to hurl insults at the enemy to encourage their comrades.[55] At that point, men from the rear lines of the maniple would have had time to step into the gaps in the front line to replace the dead and wounded.

The stop and start model is supported by the extended time that some battles lasted. Livy has more than a few battles lasting several hours. The late military writer Vegetius claims battles often lasted two or three hours. For instance, in 49 at Ilerda in Spain, Caesar and Afranius and Petreius (Pompey's commanders in Spain) manoeuvred to gain an advantage over the other side. Both armies rushed to seize a hill which dominated the position and with it Caesar could cut the Pompeians off from their supplies. Caesar led three legions out of camp and drew them up for battle. He then ordered the front line of one of the legions to rush and seize the hill. At this Afranius sent forward units to contest the control of the hill. The battlefield was narrow, only wide enough for three cohorts of perhaps 1,200 men in total. Both sides rotated units in and out of battle for five hours until a charge decided the matter in Caesar's favour. Caesar's account focuses on the use of *pila* and missile weapons, although hand-to-hand fighting must have taken place. Caesar also supplies evidence of what the rear lines in a manipular conflict were for. He tells us that he and his opponents constantly rotated in new units, cohorts in the mid-first century.[56] In the manipular army or cohort army these would have been the units of the second line. Livy has a mechanical alteration of lines with the *hastati* withdrawing through the gaps between the maniples of the *principes* to the rear of the whole formation behind the *triarii* and their place being taken by the *principes*. It is far more likely that what happened was a piecemeal replacement of weakened maniples of the first line by those of the second until the whole line consisted of fresh troops.

The second and third lines could also be used to first hold and then extend the front line. At Zama, the maniples of the *hastati* had been thrown into confusion by the fierce attacks of the doomed Carthaginian first and second lines which, when they had fallen apart, were pursued off the field by the *hastati*. The line of the *principes* remained stationary while the wounded and dead were removed, and then, when the *hastati* had returned they reformed. Scipio brought up the *principes* and the *triarii* on the wings of the *hastati* and then advanced. It is important not to use too mechanical a model for the Roman formation which was, if anything, very flexible.

As the fights broke out along the line, more aggressive men pushed and shouldered their way into the opposing line, driving wedges into it. As long as both sides maintained their cohesion, casualties must have remained relatively light. The soldiers, given their equipment and the crowding as well as the dust of battle, must have had limited vision. As one side forced its way into the line of the other, the soldiers of the weakened line began to lose confidence. As the enemy pushed deeper into their formation, fear finally overcame the will to resist and the losing side's cohesion disintegrated. Not only had they lost the battle, but at this point they suffered the majority of their casualties from the pursuit, especially from light-armed infantry and cavalry. The loss of confidence was crucial in all of these battles as it has always been in war. Overwhelming numbers, weapon superiority, and attacks on the infantry's flanks or rear could all bring about the same result. In Roman warfare the infantry was the 'queen of the battlefield'; once it prevailed or was beaten, the outcome of the battle had been decided.

The Aftermath of Battle

The true cost in human lives and property damage can never be known. Battlefield casualties are often the best figures available, but they are subject to inaccuracy and bias. For instance, it is extremely rare for the casualties of allied or auxiliary forces to be given by Livy or other writers. Livy supplies figures for allied causalities only four times in eighty battles. In any war, there are skirmishes and smaller encounters where there is loss of life, but the sources give no figures for them. In the case of the Romans, available figures can be used in conjunction with census figures to give a general overview of the loss of life, but the accuracy of census figures is also subject of dispute. No source gives us any idea of the mortality figures for non-combatants. In his account of the slaughter of most of the inhabitants of New Carthage after Scipio Africanus took the town, Polybius gives no indication of the number of civilian dead.[57] At best, we can give an impressionistic portrait of the cost in human lives and suffering, but it is mostly limited to the battlefield.

In the massed, close order fighting of the ancient battlefield, the fighting left a distinctive pattern of dead and dying. The greatest number of casualties would have been at the point where the two sides first met. As the first men were killed or disabled, others would step in to take their place, leading to an increasing density of the dead and wounded. The decisive moment in the battle would come when one side's morale broke and its line lost cohesion. As the soldiers turned to flee, they would leave themselves defenceless and they would have been hindered in the flight by the men behind them, who in turn would run the risk of being trampled by those in the front line in their desperation to escape. This marked the point at which the greatest slaughter took place. As one moved away from this point, the density of casualties would diminish, although the way it decreased would vary according to the circumstances of each battle. For example, at Cannae where the mass of Roman infantry was surrounded, it is likely the highest number of casualties were concentrated towards the middle of the Roman infantry mass as it contracted as the enemy pressed in. In the crucial battle with the Goths in AD 378 at Adrianople (modern Edirne in Turkey), Ammianus Marcellinus describes a similar situation:

> *The foot-soldiers thus stood unprotected, and their companies were so crowded together that hardly anyone could pull out his sword or draw back his arm.*[58]

At the battle of the Metaurus (fought in 208 during the war against Hannibal), at Cynoscephalae and at Cannae, the attacks mounted against the rear of the enemy formations resulted in additional concentrations of dead and wounded.[59] The pursuit by the cavalry and light-armed infantry meant that bodies would be scattered about the countryside.

The wounded who were helped off the battlefield had varied chances of surviving their injuries. Those with flesh wounds, simple fractures and concussions had a reasonable chance of survival as long as they avoided infection. Those who had deep penetration wounds, which if they pierced the stomach or intestines often led to infection, and given the state of contemporary medicine, had little chance of survival. Unsurprisingly, among the Romans the wounded and killed included a high percentage of centurions. The Romans were later to develop the most advanced military medical practices of pre-modern times, but during the Republic, medicine in general and military medicine in particular, was quite primitive. The Romans did, however, take their wounded with them after battle, although it is questionable whether this practice raised or lowered death rates.[60] The same fate awaited those with severe concussions, which resulted in internal haemorrhaging. Those who were too severely wounded to move usually had little chance of survival; the wounded who remained on the field were often killed by the enemy. Livy gives a gruesome but probably accurate picture of the battlefield after Cannae:

> *The following day at dawn the [Carthaginians] set about collecting the spoils and surveying the carnage that even they found appalling. So many thousands of Roman corpses lay everywhere on the field [of battle] as chance had found them during the battle or flight. Some rose up from the middle of the bloody mass, tortured by their wounds which the cold of the morning had drawn tight, and were killed by the enemy. The enemy found some prone but still alive with their thighs and knees lacerated who bared their throats and necks demanding that their streaming blood should be drained. Others were found with their heads buried in ditches which they appeared to have dug and covering their faces with dirt, had suffocated themselves.*[61]

The sources as mentioned earlier do give casualty figures for the major battles, but the figures they give often differ from one another. It has been suggested that the figures are of little value. The sources seem to assume that units were at paper strength and ignore losses due to disease. It is true that many of the fatal diseases that later pre-modern armies were exposed to such as such as bubonic plague, cholera and syphilis were absent. The sources universally praise the discipline and order of the Roman army. Nonetheless, since in pre-modern armies, disease was a far greater killer than the actual fighting, it seems impossible to imagine that the legions were as disease free as they appear in the sources. One would suspect a deliberate silence.[62] This seems also to be true of desertion, which hardly ever appears as a factor in the sources, but surely must have been significant. This would especially have been true of the Spanish theatre of war in the last two centuries of the Republic.

Did the Romans ever possess accurate casualty figures? The answer seems to be that that the census partly supplied such figures. Every four years the census lists were revised. It played a vital role in assessing military obligations and political rights. Since it was used as the basis of the annual levy, it must have been crucial to assess as accurately as possible the losses from each battle and campaign for replacement purposes as well as for supplemental and annual levies. It must have helped that Roman soldiers camped in small units that would have made the absence of individuals obvious; in addition, the small size maniple would have made losses obvious.

It is not until the Second Punic War that we can establish an order of magnitude for Roman losses. From 218 to 215, approximately 50,000 citizens died. This was about one-sixth of the adult male population and 5 per cent of the total citizen body. These were the years that saw Hannibal's greatest victories, so losses were abnormally high. From 214 to 202 when the war ended, perhaps, an additional 75,000 Romans died. So that the total figure for deaths during the war was about 120,000. The total death rate for those eligible to serve was 18 per cent, which represented approximately 5 per cent of the total population. These casualty rates would not be matched again in Europe until the First World War. Roman allies, since they provided troops at least equal in number to the Romans, probably had even higher rates. These figures do not take into account service in the fleet, which probably involved about 60,000 men. The figures for naval casualties are not as reliable as they are for the legions. This scale of loss would have been unsustainable for any other Mediterranean power. It was the vast number of men that Rome had available including its allies that made its victory possible.

There is less evidence for the numbers of enemy casualties. They do occur in the sources, for instance, in the major battles against the Hellenistic monarchies. This is less true for campaigns in the western Mediterranean or north of the Alps. However, they are mentioned and it is not unlikely that at least a rough count was made, although again the reliability of such figures is in question. Commanders did send dispatches to the Senate after major operations. It may be that they contained numbers of both enemy and Roman losses. In addition, the number of enemy losses was a prerequisite for the award of certain military honours for the commander and this might have encouraged the counting of enemy losses, at least on occasions where the Romans emerged as victors. None of the arguments are conclusive, but they lend support to the possibility that the figures we have are at least indicative of the magnitude of the losses suffered. Nonetheless, writers could and did manipulate such figures for their own purposes, often to minimize Roman losses and maximize those of their enemies. Certainly, the disparities in the casualty figures for the major battles with the Hellenistic monarchies are striking. The fact that the differences are not as extreme in facing other types of armies does lend some credence to them. In Greek hoplite battles of the classical period where we have figures, the winning side suffered 5 per cent casualties while losers lost 14 per cent: almost three times as many.[63]

After the Second Punic War, military service continued to make significant manpower demands. In an average year during this period, nine legions saw service down to 168. This would mean about 50,000 citizens and 73,000 allies were in service in any one year. A study of battles between 200 and 168 shows losses in Roman victories to have been about 4.3 per cent of those engaged and 18 per cent in defeats. The figures for defeats are higher than they normally were because of several battles with exceptionally heavy losses. A comparison of battles fought in the Hellenistic east as against those fought in the west have average losses of 12.5 per cent in the west, while in the east casualties were about 2 per cent. It appears that western battles exacted a higher total of deaths.[64] The figures yield on the average a death rate of 0.5 per cent per year with about 2,300 citizens dying. The burden was a heavy one and in the long run created problems that were to appear at the end of the second century.

Despite quiet periods, there were years in the last century and a half of the Republic when major casualties were suffered. The largest losses came at a battle against the migrating German tribe of the Cimbri in October of 105, where between and 60,000 and 80,000 were killed along with 40,000 camp followers; however, there is some dispute about these figures.[65] The Social War with the Italian allies must also have taken a large toll, as well as the civil wars of the 80s. In addition, campaigning continued in Spain and the eastern Mediterranean. It was not until the 50s, when Caesar was active in Gaul, and more dramatically in the civil war that broke out between Caesar and Pompey in January of 49 and lasted until 45, that large-scale casualties were again incurred. Finally, in the last phase of the civil war in which Octavian and Marcus Antonius fought first Brutus and Cassius and then each other, another substantial number of Romans were killed or wounded. The end of the civil wars ended the haemorrhaging. In the following Imperial period, casualties were for the most part low, with a few exceptions such as Varus' defeat by the Germans in AD 9 in which three entire legions were lost.

Elephants at War

For over a century and a half, from Alexander's death in 323 to the middle of the second century, elephants appeared on western battlefields. Both the Indian and African varieties were used. The sources regularly state that African elephants were smaller than their Indian counterparts, and that African elephants were afraid to face their Indian cousins. The reason for this is that the Ptolemaic kingdom, the chief source for African elephants, used the forest elephant, the smaller of the two African species (the other is the bush elephant, which is smaller than the Indian).

While the Ptolemies monopolized the supply of African elephants, the Seleucids monopolized the supply of Indian ones. The number of elephants present at various major battles declined markedly in the course of the third century. Elephants are difficult to breed in captivity and overhunting was a factor in the extinction of the African elephants. The numbers of Indian elephants also declined sharply, due mostly to the loss of control in large areas like Bactria from which the Seleucids had obtained their supply.[66]

The animals presented substantial logistical problems. An African elephant could consume as much as 136–160kg of forage per day plus 72–180 litres of water. Further, the animals had problems with the European climate, which made it difficult to maintain large numbers of elephants in Italy or elsewhere in Europe.[67]

In Hellenistic warfare, elephants were used in three basic ways: as a screen against cavalry, to attack infantry and in siege operations to break into towns or fortifications. In major battles they were deployed at the front of the battle line often in conjunction with light infantry where they could screen and protect the infantry as they deployed and to prevent cavalry attacks, since untrained horses could not stand their smell. After 300, many of the larger elephants carried towers with two to four men who were armed with missile weapons. The elephants were armoured and on occasion even the tips of their trunks were protected.

The Romans first encountered them in the war with Pyrrhus at the battle of Heraclea in 280. His army was accompanied by twenty elephants, the first ever seen in Italy. The battle hung in the balance until Pyrrhus unleashed his war elephants against the Roman cavalry, which turned and fled, throwing the Roman line into confusion. That manoeuvre decided the battle. The next year at Asculum, worried by the impact of the elephants at Heraclea, the Romans devised what they thought was a solution to the problem. Polybius describes their tactics:

> Outside the battle line they stationed the light-armed troops and three hundred wagons, which they had readied for fighting the elephants. These wagons had upright beams on which were mounted movable traverse poles that could be swung round as quickly as thought in any direction. On the ends of the poles there were either tridents or sword-like spikes or scythes, all of iron; or they had cranes that hurled down heavy grappling-irons. Many of the poles had fire-bearing hooks, wrapped in tow and heavily daubed with pitch, projecting in front of the wagons. Men standing on the wagons were to set fire to them as soon as they came near the elephants and then use them to shower blows on the trunks and faces of the animals. In addition, standing on the four-wheeled wagons, were many light-armed troops.[68] The device failed. Although the wagons initially checked the advance of the elephants, light-armed troops in the elephants' castles as well as on the ground drove the wagons off. The failure of this manoeuvre opened the Roman line once again to an elephant charge which rolled up the line and decided the battle.[69]

During the First Punic War the Romans again encountered elephants in battle. Like other Hellenistic powers, Carthage maintained an elephant corps. Carthage's elephants were of the African forest species. Their size limited their load to only their riders, but they like their Indian cousins could inflict substantial damage. They first appeared in action during the

Roman attack on Agrigentum in Sicily in 262.[70] During the course of the successful siege, one large-scale action was fought in which elephants were in the battle line. They seemed to have accomplished little and were captured by the victorious Romans after the battle.[71]

They were far more effective in 255. In 256, the Romans had invaded Carthaginian home territory in the hope of bringing the war to a close. Following a victory over the Carthaginians, the Romans withdrew one consul and left behind the second, Atilius Regulus, with a consular army of two legions and allies. He advanced towards Carthage and established a base at Tunis across the bay. He then offered the Carthaginians unacceptable terms to end the conflict. Under the leadership of a Spartan mercenary commander, Xanthippus, the Carthaginian army recovered from its defeat and was ready to face the Romans. When the two armies met, the Romans formed up in their usual three lines; Xanthippus deployed his army in phalanx formation with his cavalry on the wings. In front of the phalanx he posted 100 elephants. The elephants charged the Roman centre, trampling men and creating havoc while the Punic cavalry outflanked and then surrounded the Romans. It was a crushing defeat in which the elephants had played a significant part. It was also the last significant encounter of the two sides on land. The war was decided at sea.[72]

In the Second Punic War elephants played a relatively minor role. Hannibal had begun his invasion of Italy with thirty-seven elephants, leaving twenty-one behind in Spain for his brother Hasdrubal.[73] The only time they were used with some success was at the Trebia soon after Hannibal entered Italy. He placed them in front of his infantry line on both wings close to the cavalry. The elephants were launched in an attack on the Roman centre and then transferred to an attack on the Gallic troops fighting with the Romans, where they were successful.[74] After Hannibal crossed the Apennines in the winter of 218/217, only one elephant survived. He did receive additional elephants, probably in 215, but they had little impact and played no role of any significance during the rest of the Italian war.

In Spain elephants appear at the decisive battle of Ilipa, fought in 206.[75] Hasdrubal Gisgo, the Carthaginian commander, had thirty-two elephants at this battle.[76] He deployed with the elephants stationed in two groups, most likely consisting of sixteen elephants each in front of each wing. Polybius claims that as a result of Scipio's outflanking manoeuvre the attack of elephants, assailed by the missiles of the cavalry and *velites* and harassed on every side and suffering heavily did as much damage to their own side as to the enemy.[77] This type of behaviour was a constant problem with elephants, which often did as much or more damage to their own troops as to those of the enemy.

The last large-scale encounter involving elephants was the battle of Zama.[78] Hannibal had at least eighty elephants as he prepared to fight Scipio. Although the battle was decided by the Roman infantry in conjunction with Roman and Numidian cavalry, the elephants did play a role in the battle. At Zama they were posted in front of the army. Scipio deployed his three lines so that the maniples of each line were behind those of the line in front of them. By doing so he created lanes that he filled with javelin men. The lanes were to serve as channels down which the elephants were to be driven and then bombarded with missiles as they ran down the lanes. The tactic was highly successful. Except for the casualties caused by the elephants when they attacked the *velites* in the lanes, the arrangement worked as Scipio had hoped, and after passing through the lanes, the surviving elephants ran off the field.

Despite these failures, the Romans were sufficiently impressed by the battlefield performance of the elephants that as part of the peace treaty of 201 that ended the war, they required the Carthaginians to surrender their elephants.[79]

At Cynoscephalae, in the war with Philip V, Roman elephants played an important role.[80] Flamininius had posted his elephants on his right wing.[81] Seeing his left in danger from the Macedonian phalanx, he launched an attack with his right on Philip's centre and left which had not yet deployed from column into line to try to relieve the pressure on his left. The lack of cohesion opened the Macedonians to a devastating attack by the Roman elephants, which destroyed the right wing of Philip's army.[82] The disintegration of the king's centre and left allowed maniples to be moved to the Roman left and that decided the battle. Elephants were used once again at the battle of Pydna against Philip's son Perseus. At Pydna, the Romans had twenty-two elephants. These elephants played a significant role on the Roman right, which assaulted the Macedonian left and in conjunction with the Roman cavalry drove off the Macedonian cavalry which were panicked by the elephants. In doing so, they exposed the left of the phalanx, opening it to attacks on its rear and flanks.

The Romans had faced elephants in the battle with Antiochus III at Magnesia.[83] Despite the efforts made by the king after his wars with the Ptolemies, Antiochus was able to muster only fifty-four elephants for the battle.[84] The Romans had deployed sixteen elephants of the smaller African variety, which they had presumably obtained from Carthage at the end of the Second Punic War and from the Numidians. These were no match for the Indian animals in Antiochus' army. Between each of the ten units of the phalanx forming the king's centre, two elephants were positioned. On the left sixteen elephants were deployed and the same number on the right wing. In the course of the battle, the Romans seemed to have had little trouble dealing with the elephants given their experience with them in the war with Carthage. During the pursuit of the king's beaten army, the elephants caused havoc by trampling their own men. The Roman elephants seemed to have been of no importance in the battle.

The Romans also employed elephants in their drawn out wars against the Celtiberians in Spain. In 153, the consul Fulvius Nobilior campaigned against them in Nearer Spain. His operations were marked by a number of defeats. Initially, he was ambushed and defeated by the tribe of the Arevaci. But the Spanish leader was attacked during a disorderly pursuit of Nobilior's men and killed along with 6,000 of his men. The Arevaci immediately elected replacements for the dead general and awaited the Romans. Nobilior moved up to Numantia and deployed before the city. He had with him ten elephants that the king of Numidia, Massinissa, had sent him. He placed them behind the army where they were not visible. The Celtiberian cavalry, never having encountered elephants before, turned and fled. However, he brought the elephants close to the city wall, and that was a serious mistake. One of the elephants, hit on the head by a stone, became enraged. His anger affected the other animals who began to run amok killing friend and foe. At this the enemy sallied out and defeated Nobilior, who lost 3 elephants and 4,000 men.[85]

Elephants would be employed on other occasions in Spain and in small numbers in Gaul and Britain. The last large-scale use came, appropriately, in North Africa at the battle of Thapsus in 46 between Caesar and his opponents in the civil war. The Republicans were led by Metellus Scipio; he possessed substantial forces which included 10 legions and 15,000 cavalry. He was allied with the Numidian king Juba who had brought 4 legions of Numidian infantry, light-armed infantry, cavalry and 120 elephants. Caesar's army was far weaker with 6 understrength legions, some light-armed troops and about 2,000 cavalry. After a first indecisive battle, the two armies came into contact near Thapsus, a port city, on 6 April. We are ill informed on the order of battle for both armies; we know little about the Republican order of battle, except that Scipio had unsurprisingly posted his elephants on his wings, presumably sixty on each wing.[86] Likewise, we have only partial information on Caesar's deployments. When both sides had formed up, Caesar's men launched a spontaneous attack. On Caesar's right, his slingers drove off Scipio's Numidian cavalry who panicked and fled, while the elephants turned to flee with them and began trampling troops in their path.[87] They headed for the fortification Scipio had constructed. The entire army now dissolved in flight.

After Thapsus, although elephants were used occasionally, they were never deployed in large numbers again. Although occasionally successful, they were more often a hindrance and only rarely made a decisive contribution. It was with inexperienced cavalry and infantry that they were the most effective. Once infantry had learned to deal with them, they presented more of a danger to their own forces than to the enemy. Given the problems they had with the European climate and the tremendous costs associated with them, it became clear that their contribution to victory was outweighed by the problems they created. At Rome, elephants were relegated to appearances as symbols of power in parades and at other functions.

CHAPTER NINE

A NEWER MODEL ARMY

The last century and half of the Republic witnessed a series of profound changes in the Roman army. They included a transformation in the structure and organization of the army, tactical changes, and an important modification of the relationship between Rome's army and Roman society. By the end of this period, the Roman army was no longer a militia of part-time soldiers: it had become a professional army.

The most important tactical change was the replacement of the maniple by a new tactical unit, the cohort. The sources provide no explicit evidence for the timing of the reform, the reasons for it or who was responsible for the change. The name in Latin signifies an enclosed space and was also applied to a defined company or group of individuals. It had long been used for units of the Italian allies, which numbered between 400 and 600 men. The allied cohort, commanded by a Roman officer the *praefectus cohortis* (cohort commander), was deployed on various duties including as a camp watch, and as a detached unit for foraging or various other duties.[1] At Pydna in 168, it was a skirmish between Perseus' Thracian troops and an outpost consisting of two cohorts of the Paeligni and the Marruncini and a unit of allied cavalry that started the battle.[2] It is likely though that in the battle line the allies fought in maniples to match the Roman units. Such a development is paralleled by their assimilation of Roman equipment.

Livy refers to legionary cohorts as early as 446 and they appear sporadically in his account of Rome's early wars. None of these early references can be accepted as genuine.[3] The first reliable mention of a Roman cohort occurs in Polybius' account of the battle of Ilipa in 206. At Ilipa, Scipio extended his wings in a successful attempt to outflank the army of the Carthaginian general Hasdrubal Gisgo:

> [Scipio] *taking the three leading* turmae *of cavalry from his right wing and placing in front of them the usual number of* velites *and three maniples – the Romans call this a cohort – from his right wing, while Marcius and Junius took the same units from the left, advanced straight at the enemy, wheeling his men to the left while Marcius and Junius wheeled theirs to the right. The units immediately following them wheeled in turn.*[4]

Polybius here defines a cohort as a unit of three maniples and their accompanying light-armed troops. The maniples presumably were drawn from the three lines of the legion that stood one behind the other. His use of the term indicates that the cohort was not a new unit, but had existed for some time. There is a reference to a Roman cohort and cavalry in Livy's account of the aftermath of the defeat and death of Scipio Africanus' father and uncle in 210.[5] The reference in this case is probably to be trusted. It is plausible that the name of the unit was derived from that of the allied units. It would have been natural to use the same name for Roman units of the same type. Like the allied units, they could be employed on various detached duties as necessary. Polybius again mentions the use of cohorts at another battle later in the year fought at the Ebro River, which was Scipio's final battle in Spain.[6] His opponent was Andobales, the chief of the Spanish tribe of the Ilergetes who lived north of the Ebro. Polybius writes that Scipio sent four cohorts to engage the Spanish army, which was deployed in the plain in conjunction with cavalry. The Spaniards were routed.

Livy mentions cohorts a number of times in his account of Roman campaigns in Spain during the second century. On occasion he will mention maniples in the same passage. Significantly, cohorts most frequently occur in his account of Rome's wars in the west, while maniples dominate his account of battles in the east. For instance, they are mentioned in his account of the battle against Antiochus III at Magnesia in 190.[7]

There are two significant source problems that create difficulties in understanding the development of the cohort. As in military matters in general, the literary sources are imprecise in their terminology. This is particularly the case in translating Latin terms into Greek. The second is anachronism. Polybius is the only extant historian who had direct acquaintance with the manipular army. Livy and other sources wrote after the maniple had disappeared as a tactical unit.

Given these limitations in our evidence, it appears that the cohort emerged during Roman operations in Spain.[8] In Spain, campaigns were often conducted against widely dispersed tribes that waged irregular warfare. Such warfare required operational groups that were smaller than the legions, capable of quick movement and able to protect themselves. This was a role that cohorts could fulfill. They also served as a partial solution to supply problems in a land with large unproductive or barren areas.

Individual maniples were too small to operate independently. The cohort was in effect a miniature legion composed of the three maniples that normally fought together and supported each other in large-scale battles. This was a decided advantage as the soldiers who composed the maniple had already trained together, and often had fought together. The unit was large enough to defend itself, fight independently and could easily be reintegrated into a legion when necessary. In the Spanish campaigns cohorts fulfilled many different functions. They are mentioned as city garrisons, as reserves or were dispatched on independent operations.

The mention of cohorts in the fifth century is anachronistic, obviously so, since it is likely that the phalanx was still the main Roman battle formation. Once the manipular legion replaced the phalanx, it is likely that units of three maniples were used in an ad-hoc manner for independent operations. That the Romans saw it as a suitable unit for such purposes is proved by the use of cohort-sized formations for the Italian allies. For operations that did not need the full legion, it would have made no sense to detach individual maniples as they were too small. The use of groups of cohorts as combat teams is mentioned by Caesar.[9] The slower introduction of the cohorts in the east was probably the result of several factors. Among them was the much greater wealth and urbanization of the East which allowed larger armies to support themselves with far less difficulty than in the West and the much greater importance of the set-piece battle in the east where entire campaigns could rest on the outcome of a single contest. There was no need to frequently dispatch troops on extended operations.

The key development was the replacement of the maniple by the cohort in the battle line. The last clear references in our sources to the use of the maniple in the battle line is to its employment by the consul Caecilius Metellus in the war against Jugurtha at the end of the second century. For instance, at a battle near the River Muthul (a tributary of the Bagradas River) in 109, Sallust writes that when the consul recognized that he was heading into an ambush he reinforced the maniples on the right side of his line with slingers and archers positioned between them.[10] Sallust also mentions the use by Metellus of cohorts in battle. Sallust claims the consul sent four cohorts against the Numidian infantry, which helped to bring about a Roman victory. A similar use of both cohorts and maniples is mentioned in 106 when Gaius Marius, Metellus' successor, was marching into winter quarters. In expectation of a possible attack, Marius had his men march in a hollow square; he positioned lightly equipped maniples to the front and rear of the square. He also sent four cohorts ahead along with cavalry to secure his camp.[11] These passages seem to indicate that the Jugurthine War was a transition point, when the cohort first co-existed with and then replaced the maniple as the main tactical unit.

It is for this reason that many scholars accept that it was Marius who introduced the cohort as the standard tactical unit in battle. However, no ancient source makes any reference to Marius' role in such a change. The only reforms directly attributed to Marius by the ancient sources are first the introduction of the eagle as a legionary standard, and a modification of the *pilum* to make it more difficult for an enemy to return it by substituting a wooden rivet for one of the two iron rivets. The weakened rivet would cause the spearhead to bend or break off more easily.[12] In addition, he took steps to increase the mobility of the army. He did away with camp followers who had accompanied Roman armies and shortened the legion's wagon train by having soldiers carry more of their own equipment. The soldiers took to calling themselves *muli Mariani* or 'Marius' mules'.[13] It has been suggested that it was during campaigns against the German tribes of the Cimbri and Teutones in 102 and 101 that he adopted the cohort as the main tactical unit because it could better cope with the irregular formations that these tribes used.[14] But the Romans had successfully fought the Celts and the Ligurians of northwestern Italy for some time with the existing manipular system.[15]

An important factor in the transition to the cohort was a change in legionary equipment in the 120s. The *triarii* who formed the rear line of the phalanx had kept the thrusting spear as their main offensive armament. In the 120s they adopted the same equipment as the first two lines. This development may in part have been due to the fact that the legionaries no longer bought their own equipment; it was now supplied by the state. Once the equipment was standardized it made little sense to reform the units on the battlefield into maniples.

The transition to the cohort as the main tactical formation in the battle line offered distinct advantages. The transmission of orders was simplified. Rather than having to pass orders to thirty units, they now need be transmitted to only ten. It also enabled troops to be moved around the battlefield more quickly to respond to threats to the rear and flanks of the line. The cohort organization also made the integration of the Italian allies easier as they were already formed in these units.

The majority of information on the structure and use of the cohort dates from after the end of the Republic. However, there is no reason to think that major changes had taken place between the army of the Republic and that of the early Empire. It was not until the end of the first century AD that changes were introduced in the composition of the leading cohort of the legion.

Each legion now consisted of ten cohorts. As with the maniples, the size of the cohort varied depending on legionary strength. For instance, at Pharsalus Caesar's cohorts on average were only 272 men strong as Caesar had been unable to replace casualties, while at the same battle Pompey's had an average strength of 409. In the Imperial period the standard strength of a cohort was 480 men. Within the cohort, the basic unit was the *contubernium,* a group of eight men who shared both living quarters and meals. It was probably to members of this group that the legionary developed his strongest sense of loyalty.[16] Maniples and centuries continued to be used as subdivisions. The persistence of these units can be seen as the result of at least two factors. The first is the innate conservatism of military forces in general and of the Roman army in particular. As an example, the terminology for distinguishing centurions was based on the three-line system of the manipular legion. It continued into the Empire when that system had long disappeared. The second was due to the size of the cohort which was simply too large to be a basic unit of administration. However, the cohort did influence the form of the Roman camp, which begins to show changes in the later second century caused by the cohort.[17]

Strangely, there is no evidence for a commander of a citizen cohort. Allied cohorts were commanded by Roman prefects. It is likely that the senior centurion within the cohort would have exercised overall command. He would have been the prior centurion of the *triarii*. The lack of such evidence is probably the result of the fact that the cohort did not have administrative functions that might have drawn the attention of the sources. The actions of military tribunes offer a parallel. It is only on rare occasions that we hear anything about their actions on the battlefield, even though we know they must have commanded in combat.

There is another aspect of the citizen cohort which is striking and further points to a late introduction of the cohort as a standard unit. It is most clearly visible in the Imperial period when the cohort had long been the standard tactical unit both for Roman and non-Roman troops. Religion was intimately bound up with service in the Roman army.[18] The army itself had a religious aspect, which is particularly clear in the Imperial period, when a major part of army religious life was centred on the cult of the legionary standards. The standards were kept in a special shrine and were paraded on various religious occasions. These standards included the legionary eagle as well as the standards of each century. There are a couple of references to the standard of the cohort in the early Empire, but its existence is contested.[19] There was in the same period an amply attested cult of the genius of the century, but there seems to have been no religious rite associated with the cohort. It seems to have been a unit of functional, but of no emotional significance.[20]

As in the case of the maniple, the question of how the unit was deployed is difficult to answer in absence of explicit information. One possibility is that it was usually deployed six men deep like the maniple. There is some support for this figure in the Imperial period in the contemporary account of the Jewish rebellion of AD 66–70 by the Jewish historian Josephus. He gives the order of march of the army commanded by the future emperor Vespasian into Galilee. He notes that the army marched in six columns. If this was the depth of the cohort, it would have made the transition of column into line a relatively easy manoeuvre. This would have meant that, given an average strength of about 480 men, the width of the cohort would again have been about 80 men. At 1.8 metres per man, that would have yielded a cohort with a width of about 152 metres. The frontage of eighty men would be about the strength of a century and so it is possible that the centuries fought one behind the other. This would also have allowed greater scope to the centurions to control their men. It is impossible to achieve certainty in this matter; depth and frontage varied according to circumstances. Julius Frontinus, a late first century writer with military experience, mentions that at Pharsalus, Pompey's cohorts were ten men deep. The depth may have been the result of an attempt by Pompey to strengthen his line as had been tried by the generals at Cannae. In that battle and at Pharsalus the troops were relatively new, untrained and facing veterans.[21]

In large-scale battles the cohorts were used in various formations that gave them a further advantage over the maniples, which had to maintain a three-line division. The most common deployment was in three lines, parallel to the three lines of the manipular system. As in the manipular system, it was the first two lines that were expected to bear the brunt of the fighting, while the third acted as a reserve. Occasionally, the sources mention a two-line formation. Lucius Afranius, facing Caesar at Ilerda in 49, deployed his first two lines consisting of cohorts drawn from five legions and a third line of auxiliary troops as a reserve.[22] In Africa in 46, Caesar deployed all of his cohorts in a single line. This was done to extend the line as far as possible since he was being attacked by light-armed infantry and cavalry, and wanted to protect his flanks as much as possible. He then had them face right or left in sequence, and attack in two directions. In this way, he broke the troops that encircled his legions.[23] What is striking is the way the system of deploying cohorts for the most part reproduced the system used for the manipular lines. Military conservatism must have played a part. It was certainly easier for Roman generals to continue using a familiar tactical disposition, but it is also true that the prior system had worked well. The cohort system in major battles, despite the similarities it had in common with the manipular legion, exhibited much greater flexibility.

It is likely that the cohorts maintained gaps, as the manipular lines had done, to allow the easy movement of the cohorts and the feeding in of reserve units when necessary. Were those gaps maintained as the cohorts closed with the enemy line? As with the maniples, it is likely that they did not close up. If they had formed a solid line, it would have been impossible for the centurions in charge of each of the cohorts to have kept control of their men. Both Caesar and Tacitus in the early Imperial period mention cohorts opening up to admit fugitives. If the line had formed one solid mass, this would have been impossible.[24]

In his description of the levy of the mid-second century, Polybius states that the light-armed soldiers were drawn from the youngest and poorest soldiers.[25] Roman citizens serving as light-armed troops had always been drawn from the poorer citizens, but not from the very poorest (the *capite censi*,) who normally had no obligation to fight. It is possible that they performed other sorts of military services.[26] We hear of a group called the *velati* or *accensi* who served as attendants for senior officers and did odd jobs.[27] Those who were slightly better off served as light-armed troops; these included javelin men, slingers and stone-throwers. The Romans seem to have had no native expertise as archers and in the later Republic they hired non-Roman troops, especially from Crete. The service of the poor as light-armed troops was partly a consequence of the fact that until the end of the second century Roman soldiers had to provide their own equipment; it simply would have been too expensive for the poor to afford the full kit necessary for legionary service.

Never a decisive arm in major battles, the light-armed infantry had other important functions on the battlefield. Occasionally, they did make a contribution to final victory as they did at Ilipa in 206, and again during the war against Philip in 199.[28] However, their normal functions were limited to screening the deployment of the legions, engaging the enemy's own light-armed troops and in pursuit after a defeated enemy had turned to flight. They often operated in conjunction with the cavalry and so were found on the wings of the legions.[29] They also served as camp guards. But in general, they were of marginal effectiveness.

It seems, although the terminology is a problem, that the early light-armed forces were known as *rorarii*. The appearance of the name *velites* is linked by Livy to an incident in the war against Hannibal. Livy claims that the *velites* dated from 211 at the siege of Capua and were a response to the superiority of Campanian cavalry. Young men were selected from the legions to ride into battle on the backs of the cavalry's horses and to dismount when they came into contact with the enemy cavalry. They would bombard them with missiles and so weaken their adversaries that the Roman cavalry could then deliver the final blow.[30] This cannot be correct. Light-armed troops armed in various ways had existed in Rome's military from the beginning. Such troops would not have been taken from the legions, but, as we know from Polybius, were levied as light-armed infantrymen. Riding into battle together with a cavalry trooper on the same mount is not mentioned again. Other armies did combine cavalry and light-armed infantry in battle: Caesar describes German infantry and cavalry operating together in this manner.[31]

The disappearance of these troops has been ascribed to Marius, although, as in the case with some of the other contemporary reforms credited to Marius, there is no explicit evidence to support this. All that can be said is that the last secure reference to *velites* occurs under Metellus, Marius' predecessor as commander in the war against Jugurtha.[32] The one reference we have involving Marius and the *velites* is a technical reform: the replacement of the round shield (*parma*) used by the *velites* with a rectangular shield similar to that of the legionaries. Presumably, it was a lighter version of the legionary shield, which itself would have been unsuitable for light-armed troops. This development fits with a general standardization of Roman equipment in this period.[33]

There is some evidence for the continuation of the *velites*. In 86, in the war against the Pontic king Mithridates Eupator, Roman *velites* are mentioned by Frontinus.[34] However, Frontinus can be unreliable and his notice has no supporting evidence. Certainly, by Caesar's time, Roman light-armed troops had disappeared from the battlefield.

It seems more likely, as in the tactical change marked by the introduction of the cohort, that it was a gradual change that was not the product of a single act or event. It was most likely the combination of several factors that led to the disappearance of the *velites*. Some link their disappearance to the introduction of the cohort in the battle line, but there is nothing to intrinsically connect the two reforms. Caesar in Gaul, and later in Africa, would clearly have benefitted from a substantial light-armed force.[35] The first factor that led to their disappearance was the repeated lowering of the census rating necessary for service as a legionary. Service as a legionary was probably more prestigious and perhaps better rewarded than as a light-armed soldier. As the minimum necessary for service in the heavy infantry fell, this would have contracted the pool of manpower available.[36] Added to that was the fact that the state now provided the necessary equipment which was purchased by a pay deduction, which further reduced the financial barrier to legionary service. By the end of the second century, Rome controlled a substantial territory consisting of provinces and areas which, while not directly administered, were under Roman control. This produced a vastly expanded pool from which light-armed troops could be drawn. Many of them had specialist skills that the *velites* had not possessed. Added to that was that this empire generated wealth not available earlier. In 167 the Roman war tax, the *tributum,* was abolished after wealth poured in to the treasury in the wake of Roman successes in the east. It is likely that – as was the case in other developments in this period – it was a slow dwindling of available recruits that finally led to the end of *velites*. This would explain the reference in Frontinus to *velites* fighting as late as 86. It might still have been possible, at that time, to find Romans who could be levied as *velites* when necessary.

Their final disappearance was made possible by the ability to call upon non-Romans to make up the deficit. Rome had long called upon non-Romans to fight in her armies; this was standard practice in Western Europe until the rise of national armies during and after the French Revolution. Initially, this was done on the basis of mutual alliances, which continued even when Rome had emerged by 260 as the dominant power in peninsular Italy. From the Second Punic War she had begun using non-Italian troops, especially Numidian cavalry and Spanish cavalry and infantry. As Rome's power expanded, she could draw such troops from her provinces and co-operative foreign states as well as from allies. Aetolian cavalry played a crucial role in Flamininius' victory over Philip V at Cynoscephalae in 197.[37] The need for such non-Italian troops became more pressing after the Social War of 90–88, which resulted in almost all of Italy being granted Roman citizenship.

The availability of these non-Italian troops probably accelerated the disappearance of the *velites*. They could offer specialist skills in archery or the use of the sling that could not be matched by Italian light-armed infantry.

Their extensive use in the armies of the civil war period probably played some role in the ability of all sides to raise what were huge armies. At the end of the civil wars after the defeat of Antony at Actium, and during the mopping up operations that followed, the victor Augustus had a combined force of sixty legions.

Foreign troops were employed extensively by all sides. There was an enormous number in Pompey's army especially, as he had no access to recruiting grounds in Italy. After the establishment of the Empire in the last decades BC, light-armed troops were drawn exclusively from non-Romans and became integral parts of the Imperial army.

The end of the second century and the beginning of the first seems to have been perhaps the most innovative period since the Servian reforms. It was marked by development of a new main battle unit for the heavy infantry – the cohort – the introduction of new march protocols and the end of the *velites*. There was also an alteration of the social composition of the army and signs of a transformation in the type of army that had so far proved so successful for Rome.[38] In addition to these developments, there was a further major change: the disappearance of Roman and Italian cavalry. We have evidence for both Roman and Italian cavalry in action in Spain in 139.[39] There is solid evidence for the presence of Italian allied cavalry in the war against Jugurtha, and uncertain evidence for the presence of Roman cavalry in 102 in fighting against the Germanic Cimbri.[40] Further attempts have been made to argue that Roman and citizen cavalry were in action in the 90s, but have not proved convincing. As with the cohort, we can only affirm with certainty that Roman and Italian cavalry had disappeared by the time of Caesar, to be replaced by cavalry drawn from subject peoples, allies and mercenaries.

Given the social and economic gulf that separated the wealthy men who staffed the Roman and Italian cavalry, and the poor who filled the ranks of the light-armed infantry, it is not likely that the same factors were operating in both developments. Cavalry service had changed its character during the second century; cavalrymen (*equites*) with a public horse still served and they were granted their mount by the state in expectation of service in the field. By this period, they were mostly senators' sons. Many would have been interested in a military career as a prerequisite for a political career. In theory, there was a ten-year military service requirement that had to be fulfilled before political office could be held. However, the majority of *equites* (cavalrymen) qualified solely on the basis of wealth. Within the larger group of *equites,* there was a much smaller one of extremely wealthy individuals who functioned as *publicani*. These were men who undertook government contracts for the supplying of the army or the collection of taxes in certain provinces and for a variety of other services. They were intimately tied to the senatorial order by economic and kinship ties. Many of these men would have been too old or simply physically unfit for military service. Despite what must have been substantial numbers unfit for war, as early as 225, Polybius claims that 17,000 to 18,000 men were available for active service.[41] The numbers of Roman citizens increased dramatically after citizenship was granted to practically all of Italy south of the Apennines in 88 after the Social War. Yet despite the vast pool of men available for cavalry service, Roman cavalry and Italian allied cavalry had disappeared.

The disappearance of this cavalry was made possible by the development of other sources of supply. With the Second Punic War, Rome began to use non-Italian cavalry on a large scale, starting with the cavalry of her Numidian ally Massinissa, whose men proved vital to the victory at Zama.[42] As Rome campaigned overseas in Spain and elsewhere, it became standard practice to recruit cavalry locally or to call upon allies for help. This was done despite numerous instances of disloyalty and desertion. It has been claimed that the use of foreign cavalry was the result of the poor performance of Roman cavalry in the Second Punic War. Recently an argument has been made that Roman cavalry was in fact effective.[43] Whatever the merits of the argument, there is definite evidence for Roman and allied cavalry serving for another century. So whatever the level of effectiveness, that was not the reason for its disappearance. It has also been suggested that it was the Social War that marked the disappearance of the citizen cavalry, because it created a need for citizen infantry and that a definite decision was taken to recruit potential cavalrymen into the legions.[44] This does not seem a convincing hypothesis. If the needs of the war absorbed cavalrymen into the infantry, why did the cavalry not return at the war's conclusion? The war did away with Italian cavalry, but the question of the disappearance of Roman cavalry still remains open.

As in the case in the *velites,* the factors that led to the end of the cavalry seem to have been not military, but social, and additionally in the case of the cavalry, political as well. By the beginning of the last century BC, the importance of military service for equestrians seeking political office declined in importance, although for those who sought the highest offices – such as the consulship – it still retained significance. The necessary period of service was shortened. It was no longer the ten years that it had been in the mid-second century. Two or three years were now sufficient. This service was now performed as a military tribune or as a legate, or as part of the commander's circle of young men and friends who commonly accompanied men taking up offices whether civilian or military. For instance, as a young man Julius Caesar first saw service with Marcus Thermus in the province of Asia in 81 at the age of 19, and then served in Cilicia. In neither case did he hold formal office.[45] Even more striking is the case of the famous orator Marcus Tullius Cicero. His only military service was under Pompeius Strabo, Pompey's father, during the Social War in 90–89, and under Cornelius Sulla in 88. In both cases the service lasted only for short periods. Despite almost no military experience, he was consul in 63 and commanded an army in the province of Cilicia in 51–50.

Service in the cavalry was no longer a prerequisite, nor an attractive option for young men on the make. The question is why this happened. The growing professionalism that gradually changed what had been a militia into a professional army may have been of some importance. Roman aristocrats shunned anything that smacked of a profession, especially one that entailed subordination to another. Service as a military tribune, which at least conferred the power of command, or informal duties in the suite of a commander, were far more attractive options. The availability of foreign cavalry made other choices possible. In fact, their use may by itself have made such service unattractive, as aristocrats would no longer be as visible to their fellow citizens, who could be called upon for vote at election time. In addition, serving in foreign theatres out of sight of the voters must have been an unappealing prospect. It might also make it more difficult to maintain a political position at Rome. Cicero's letters to his friend and informant Caelius at Rome, after he was forced by a change in the law on provincial governorships to serve in Cilicia, betray his longing for Rome and his unease about losing touch with the political life of the capital.

The disappearance of the cavalry was such that by Caesar's time it had ceased to exist. A revealing incident occurred during Caesar's first year of campaigning in Gaul in 58. The king of the Germanic tribe of Suebi, Ariovistus, had crossed the Rhine and had launched a series of attacks on Gallic tribes in eastern Gaul. These tribes appealed to Caesar for help, giving him the opportunity to end Ariovistus' expansion and at the same time to appear as the defender of these tribes.

Before the final clash, Ariovistus sent to Caesar asking for a meeting. A large open area, almost equidistant between the two camps, was selected. Ariovistus requested that each party be accompanied only by cavalry, an arm in which the Germans excelled. Caesar agreed to this. However, he had only Gallic cavalry with him, whom he did not fully trust. To solve the problem, he mounted his trusted Tenth Legion on horses taken from his Gallic cavalry. Throughout his time in Gaul, we hear only of Gallic or German cavalry serving with Caesar.[46] The only exception to this was the large number of Roman cavalry who served in the course of the civil war. This was an exceptional period which was also marked by the last large-scale levying of legions in Italy.

Despite all of these factors, this development remains something of a mystery. At a time when the burden of military service on the voters was increasing, it is hard to understand why they tolerated a decline in the participation of their elite, which had always made its own military service the most important component in its claims for support. The development is best seen as part of a longer term trend in Italy to the avoidance of military service by all elements in the eligible population. This trend culminated by the end of the first century AD with non-Italians forming a substantial majority of Rome's military forces.

During the conquest of Italy, Rome had required both its defeated enemies and its allies to supply troops to her armies and sustain them in the field. These troops served alongside the legions and the Roman cavalry. With her advance into southern Italy and the conquest of the Greek states there, Rome adopted a new approach to using her former enemies. The military traditions of these states were too different to have them serve as heavy infantry in the same manner as her other allies. However, they did have a strong tradition – which Rome lacked – in naval warfare, which the Romans made use of. They were required to supply ships and to help staff Rome's navy. They served in the First Punic War (264–241), which was primarily a naval war where the decisive battles were fought at sea, and allied contingents continued to provide rowers and especially personnel who could handle the technical aspects of warfare at sea.

It was the Second Punic War that marked the first introduction of a substantial number of non-Italian troops into Rome's military forces. The Romans recruited fighters from the Celtiberians of north–central Spain in their fight do drive the Carthaginians out of the peninsula.[47] These troops seem to have been mercenaries, and in 211, they were lured away by Carthaginian gold. Their desertion led to two catastrophic Roman defeats that almost drove them out of Spain.[48]

There are few references to the use of mercenaries in Roman forces, unlike the large number of references to such troops in the armies of the Hellenistic monarchies. The Romans viewed fighting as the right and duty of a citizen. They seem to have felt that there was something demeaning in employing mercenaries, although in certain circumstances they did use them. They turned to mercenary fighters for specialist skills that were not readily available among their citizens. Among the mercenaries they employed were Cretan archers, and slingers from the Balearic Islands and Rhodes. From the Third Macedonian War (171–168), these troops seem to have become a regular part of Roman forces along with the excellent Numidian light horse.[49]

The Second Punic War also saw the first large-scale use of non-Italian troops by the Romans in addition to mercenaries. The most significant instance occurred during Scipio Africanus' African campaign of 204–201. He had previously used allied Spanish troops in Spain, most notably at Ilipa in 206. In his dispositions for the battle, it is noticeable that he placed his Spanish troops in the centre of his line, while he sought a decision on his wings with his legions.[50] Clearly, Scipio did not fully trust them or their effectiveness. In Africa, Scipio established a close personal relationship with the Numidian prince Massinissa, who was hoping to establish a kingdom over all the Numidian tribes with Roman help. The relationship was beneficial to both in the end: Massinissa supplied Scipio with the excellent

Numidian light cavalry that played an important role during his campaign, and especially at the final battle of the war at Zama in 202; and the Roman defeat of Carthage allowed Massinissa to establish his kingdom.

The use of these foreign forces became a regular feature of Roman campaigns for the rest of the Republic and later. The varying levels of political and social development in the eastern and western Mediterranean led to significant variations in the sources of recruitment and the type of service of these troops. In the west, troops usually came from tribal groups and served in tribal units. In the east, the majority of troops were supplied by city-states and allied kings. Probably, the best known example are the forces supplied by the Aetolian League in central Greece. They bore the brunt of the fighting with Philip V during the First Macedonian War (215–205) and were instrumental in the Roman victories at Cynoscephalae and Pydna in the Second and Third Macedonian Wars. The Kingdom of Pergamum played a central role in the defeat of Antiochus III at Magnesia in 190. At sea, the island of Rhodes – an important naval power – also played a noteworthy role in Rome's various victories.

Despite the increasing use of foreign forces, the heavy infantry remained a Roman and Italian monopoly. The foreign troops served as cavalry or light infantry. As mentioned earlier, they had their uses, but the 'queen of the battlefield' remained the heavy infantry. The monopoly, in part, may have been psychological; it signified that it was Rome and her Italian allies who were the authors of victory. There was also the practical reason that it was command of citizens that gave the aristocracy the most important qualification for political office. In addition, the Romans and their Italian allies had developed a tactical system and a mode of fighting that had no parallels outside of Italy; to use foreign troops as heavy infantry would have required extensive training and arming of them on a large scale. All of these factors were compelling reasons to maintain the Italian and Roman monopoly in heavy infantry.

By the end of the Social War, the Romans had come to depend upon provincials or allied states for all of their cavalry, light-armed infantry and specialist troops. Caesar, during his campaigns in Gaul, relied on Gallic or German cavalry. The last century of the Republic saw an increased use of such troops. During the war against Jugurtha at the end of the second century, sizeable numbers of auxiliary cavalry and infantry were employed. In the course of the opening campaign of the civil war with Pompey and his allies, Caesar mentions that one of his opponents, Marcus Petreius, had 80 cohorts of infantry (perhaps 40,000 men) and 5,000 cavalry drawn from the Spanish provinces. Caesar himself remarks that he had 3,000 cavalry and 5,000 auxiliary infantry that had remained with him from his time as governor in Gaul.[51] At Pharsalus, Pompey fielded 7,000 cavalry and auxiliary infantry from all over the eastern Mediterranean. The use of auxiliary troops was so routine by the end of the first century that Caesar had a bodyguard of Spanish cohorts and the future emperor Augustus used another unit of Spanish troops in the same capacity.[52]

Despite the constant employment of auxiliary forces, the sources offer little information about their conditions of service or what happened to them after their service ended. We have, with rare exceptions, little information on how these troops were equipped and fought except for the specialist forces. Caesar's account of the techniques used by German cavalry is a rare exception.[53] There are also occasional references to particular weapons, such as the effective Spanish sword which the Romans adopted, but little other material. Their role in most battles goes unmentioned, except for some of the major encounters of the Second Punic War, during the following century at specific battles and in Caesar's account of his war with the Gauls. The sources fail to note not only the part they played in the action, but also omit their casualty figures. It is only on three occasions in the second century that we have separate figures for auxiliary casualties.[54] We have no information on how they were organized, but soldiers in both infantry and cavalry in the Imperial period were organized in units of between 500 and 1,000 men and these unit sizes may have had their origin in the late Republican period.

Command over these units, as was the case with all troops in the army, was vested in the senior Roman commander. However, at a lower level they were led by legates, military tribunes and sometimes by centurions. For instance, the auxiliary troops that fought Caesar in Spain at the opening of the civil war were commanded by two subordinate legates of Pompey, Lucius Afranius and Marcus Petreius, who from 55 had governed the two Spanish provinces *in absentia*. Officers called prefects are also recorded for some units. It is likely that the title was carried over from the prefects of the allies who commanded the Italian units. These officers often led a force comprised of a group of units, sometimes of combined arms. The names of only two such prefects are known from after the Social War. This is likely to be the result of the inadequacy of our sources. Allied troops were often led by native nobles including various kings, chiefs or nobles.

Parallel to the system for citizen troops, a series of rewards were created to act as an incentive for these soldiers. Auxiliaries could be awarded many of the same decorations as citizens. Medals and other decorations could be given for acts of exceptional courage as they were to Roman troops. Substantial material rewards were also possible. These included grants of land, which could be significant. Citizenship was also used as an incentive. The most famous instance of such an award was in 88 in the aftermath of the Social War. An inscription, found at the town of Ascoli Piceno in eastern Italy, commemorates the grant of citizenship by Gnaeus Pompeius Strabo, the father of Pompey, to a Spanish cavalry unit, the *turma Salluitana*, for its service during the war.[55] The extensive use of auxiliaries had by the 50s led to an occasional blurring of the line between auxiliary and citizen.

Caesar recruited his Fifth Legion, the Alaudae or Larks, from Gallic militia in 52.[56] The most prestigious and important awards were given to native commanders and leaders.[57]

The use of non-Italian troops had become a regular and important feature of Roman armies by the last century BC. Their use was finally regularized by Augustus. Half of the Imperial army consisted of auxiliary troops organized in cavalry and infantry formations under the command of equestrian officers. They were of three types: an infantry cohort of 500 or 1,000 soldiers; a cavalry unit, the *ala* or wing of 500 or 1,000 cavalry; and a part-mounted unit, the *cohors equitata* or 'mounted cohort', which was comprised of approximately 1,000 infantry and 240 cavalry. By the mid-first century AD, service in the *auxilia* had become an important pathway to citizenship; it was granted along with an honourable discharge at the end of the soldier's service.

During the second century, service in Rome's armies began to change. Rome's success in her wars had led to the creation of a series of provinces, first across the Mediterranean and then over the Alps in Gaul, in Asia Minor, Syria and in North Africa. The provinces originated as military districts and their governors had *imperium*. The earliest provinces, which were assigned to two praetors, were Sicily and Sardinia with Corsica created in 227. The first provinces that entailed substantial military commitments were the two Spains, Nearer and Farther, established in 197.[58] The Spains were a constant problem. The fighting went on until the reign of Augustus and the conditions of service were far from attractive. It was often hard, savage fighting, with little prospect of booty. Service there generated the most opposition. Between approximately 200 and 90, two or four legions saw service in Spain each year.[59] The expansion of empire led to legions being stationed in other provinces.

The development of garrisons in these provinces led to a change in the nature of military service. During the conquest of Italy, military service obeyed a seasonal rhythm, campaigning in the late spring and summer, and then a return to civilian life, most frequently to farming for the rest of the year. The Punic Wars altered this pattern. In the First Punic War legionary service in Sicily and for a short time in North Africa was relatively brief and close to home. The war against Hannibal saw prolonged service outside of Italy in Spain and for a shorter time in North Africa. It was after these wars that expansion in the east and west permanently altered the conditions of service.

With legions stationed overseas, the small farmers who formed the backbone of the army were faced with the prospect of an extended separation, far from their homes and families. How long that separation was is unclear. There is some evidence indicating that the average length of service was six years in the mid-second century, when Rome had an average of 75,000 men in service every year. This was not the men's full commitment. They were often allowed to return to Italy after four to six years, but that did not complete their military service. The theoretical obligation remained at sixteen years. Most of the evidence comes from Spain, which as mentioned above, was an especially difficult posting. It is significant that during the Second Punic War, there was a large-scale mutiny by men who had been in service there for over a decade.[60]

The response to this heavy burden of military service varied with the individual and the conditions of that service. As always, Spain generated the most dislike. In 151, reports of high casualty rates and constant fighting led to attempts to evade the draft. In 145, popular opposition to the draft was so strong that only new men were taken for service, while an exemption was granted to those who had just finished their service in the third war with Carthage or in Macedonia and Greece.[61] However, there were campaigns, such as the one against Perseus or the last war against Carthage, where the prospect of rich booty attracted many volunteers and there was no resistance to the levy.

The late third and second century were marked by declines in the minimum census rating necessary for service in the legions. As mentioned earlier, those who fell below the minimum rating, the *capite censi,* were still liable to some form of service, usually in the fleet, although in times of crisis they also served in the legions.[62] The figures for the Servian army specify property worth either 11,000 or 12,500 asses as the necessary minimum for legionary service. The *as* was the basic bronze coin of the early Republic. Its value was tied to its weight in metal; originally it equalled 329 grams or a Roman pound. The asses used in the figures for the Servian army are sextantal asses of two Roman ounces or about 41 grams. There is evidence in Livy that the sextantal *as* was still being used in 214. Polybius gives a substantially lower figure of 4,000 asses. It has been suggested that the change to the Polybian minimum occurred in 214 or 212/211. Scholars have pointed to the introduction of the *velites* as marking the change, but that seems to have been largely a name change. The increased number of legions necessary seems a more likely explanation for the change. 212 was the year when the maximum number of legions were fielded in the Second Punic War, and we know that the war created financial pressures. In 215, the war tax was doubled and still could not cover the war's necessary costs.[63] 214 seems a strong possibility; it would have allowed time for a modification of the census which would have made possible the raising of twenty-five legions in 212. In Cicero's dialogue on the Republic, which has a dramatic date of 129, it appears that the census rating had declined further to 1,500 asses.[64] The second reduction must have happened between about 170 and 129. The continued campaigning in the course of the second century and the growth of overseas garrisons must have made a permanent reduction in the census requirement an attractive option. There is no explicit statement in any ancient source that there were reductions in the minimum census figure, but it is clear that they happened.

The need for more manpower played a part in the lowering of the requirement, but it is also likely that it reflected a change in economic conditions. The early Roman economy, as most ancient economies, was agrarian. It included both the great estates of a landowning aristocracy that was partially identical with a political oligarchy, and a large mass of self-sufficient peasant farmers with small plots that were marked by low productivity. These small farmers were dependent on supplementing their income by the use of the public land that Rome had confiscated from its opponents during its conquest of Italy. The small farmers produced enough for their own immediate needs and for taxes.

The war against Hannibal, both the fighting and the long occupation of southern and parts of central Italy, led to extensive devastation. The worst effects were felt outside of Latium, but even in Latium there were repercussions. The consuls of 206 were instructed by the Senate to reset-tle peasants who had been uprooted by the war.[65] Livy states that many farmers had been killed, slaves were hard to find, and that cattle had been destroyed. Some of the inhabitants of the Latin colonies in the north had fled to the cities and it seems clear that cities were a refuge everywhere that war affected people's lives. The scale of the disruption can be gauged from a program of colonization in northern and southern Italy between 194 and 177 that resettled about 100,000 men, women and children on plots of such small size that they point to the poverty from which the settlers came. These allotments were presumably supplemented with common land. The state of areas ravaged by the war must have adversely affected the mili-tary manpower available for the legions or allied forces since many would have now fallen below the census minimum.

Other developments also worked towards the same end. Of these, the most important was the length and scope of the military effort during the second and first centuries. The scope of the Roman war effort in the years 200–168 and 80–50 was staggering. The median army of the last two centu-ries totalled 13 per cent of all male citizens. To obtain an army of this size, if we take seven years of service as the norm, the drafting of approximately 50 per cent of the adult Roman male population was necessary. The figure is striking.[66] There is continued controversy about the reliability of ancient census figures that are crucial to these estimations. Despite such difficul-ties, it is clear that the number of citizens serving was extremely high.

As mentioned earlier, much service was now overseas separating men from their families and friends. The length of service increased this isola-tion. Complaints of men serving far from home for extended periods of time rarely occur in the sources. However, there are occasional examples. In 199, the consul Publius Villius Tappulus was given the command of the war against Macedonia. The troops that Tappulus took over, were part of the army defeated at Cannae and who had then served with Scipio in Africa from 204 to the end of the Second Punic War. By the time Tappulus assumed command they had been in service for at least the supposed maximum of sixteen years. They had suffered disgrace because of their supposed cowardice at Cannae, and this may be what led to their prolonged service. The 2,000 men involved had been posted to Macedonia, listed as volunteers. They claimed they had been forcibly re-enrolled, and pleaded to return home. They said that they had been absent from Italy for years and had grown old in service, worn out by their efforts and weakened by their wounds. Despite their unusual situation, their complaints must have been typical of those who had to endure long service abroad. Such service not only affected men's bodies, but also inflicted the psychological pain of separation from home and family.[67]

Untypical in the length and in the success of his career was Spurius Ligustinus, who had been born on a small Sabine peasant holding just before the outbreak of the Hannibalic War. The source for the speech that Livy attributes to him is unknown.[68] It occurs in the context of a dispute over the levy of 171 for the war in Macedonia. Spurius and some other men who had previously held the post of leading centurion in a legion felt that they had been unfairly assigned a lower rank. In his defence against such treatment, Spurius recounted his service record, which, by this time, had reached a total of twenty-two years. Probably, few achieved Spurius' level of accomplishment or duration of service, but he illustrates the extreme of what was possible. The context of the speech indicates that the burden of service fell heavily on the rural population, and on those at the bottom of the census classes. Spurius' speech notes that he first saw service in 200 in the war against Philip V and served until that war ended in 196. He then volunteered for and served in Spain in 195, and between 191 and 188 fought against Antiochus III. His second period of service in Spain came in the late 180s and early 170s. He had fought in every major campaign since 200, and had risen to the position of *primus pilus,* the most senior centurion in a legion. His career highlights the growing frequency of overseas warfare, although there was still fighting in northwestern Italy in this period. It also makes clear that by the early second century it was possible for an individual to pursue what amounted to a professional military career, given the frequency of Rome's wars and the need for extended military service overseas. By 140, there were Roman military forces in Spain, Macedonia and Greece and in North Africa.

The separation of the soldiers from Italy and frequent warfare were bound to have effects on the peasant farms these men came from. It deprived them of a major source of labour, when there was little margin between subsistence and economic disaster for small farmers. Given the small size of their plots, most peasants needed to find additional sources of income. Public land offered one way and tenancy another, as well as casual labour on the farms of the rich. Even if the head of the family was not drafted as seems to have been the case, his sons living under the same roof were, and this diminished the pool of available labour.

The severing of the peasant from his land was intensified by another factor, the economic wealth that these wars produced. Much of the wealth found its way into the pockets of the upper class as the distribution of booty was at the discretion the general.[69] In addition, provincial governors siphoned off wealth from their provinces. For the most part, the nobility and the wealthy in general looked to land-holding as the primary area for investment. It offered both status and security. This was, in part, the product of the absence of alternate forms of investment that carried the same benefits.[70] Peasant farms in trouble offered tempting targets for investment. This would have put greater pressure on peasant land-holdings, especially as the peasants divided up their farms among their heirs. In conjunction with this trend there was a growth in villas that depended on slave labour. It is likely that the increase in large estates came at the expense of small holders who were unable to maintain themselves. The importation of slaves meant a decline in tenant farming and the need for free seasonal employment on the farms of the wealthy. It also meant that that access to public land became more and more limited. By the late 130s, there was an attempt to impose acreage limits on the use of public land in an effort to increase the number of those eligible for the legions.[71] Despite these laws, the villa continued to flourish and there was a large increase in their numbers from the 80s onward.

The second century was the period when a large number of slaves were imported into Italy and Sicily. It was marked by a series of major slave revolts in Sicily for 138 to 132 and then again from 104 to 101. There were also smaller-scale revolts in Italy during the same period. It has been estimated that between the beginning of the Second Punic War in 218 and the mid-second century, approximately 500,000 slaves were imported into Italy.[72]

A further problem for peasant farmers was the gradual loss of the largest market in Italy: the city of Rome. From the beginning of the second century, Rome began drawing, in the form of taxation, on the grain production of Sardinia and Sicily to supplement Italian grain. These tithes helped feed the city of Rome as well as Roman armies. From 123, the grain supply for the city of Rome was for most of the period subsidized by the state. Granted that subsistence farmers could produce little beyond what was necessary for their own needs, it is likely that imports, although not a crucial factor, played some part in making it more difficult for a small farmer to make a living.[73] Another large market – the army – was increasingly out of reach as more of the legions were stationed overseas. These developments created transport problems which often forced the peasant to sell to local aristocrats who had the money and connections to successfully move large amounts of agricultural produce.

Also in the course of the mid-second century, there seems to have been an increase in the population of the countryside. If we accept the general accuracy of the census figures and assume they represent adult males, there was an increase of 75,000. In 163 the censors registered 337,000; by 124 the figure stood at 395,000. It is likely that much of this resulted from a combination of population growth and the influx of small farmers into surrounding citizen communities, which allowed men from the country-side to be more easily counted. It has been convincingly suggested that certain census figures in the mid to late second century show a downward trend in population. This was the result of the increasing impoverishment of the rural peasantry, not a true decline in population.[74] As always, the poor tend not to be counted. This must have led to increasing pressure on those qualified for service in the legions and must have forced many off their land. All of these developments led to increasing impoverishment of the class that formed the backbone of the legions and is reflected in the decline of the minimum census requirement in this period.

Signs of strain were apparent, especially in the Spanish theatre. It is significant that, when Scipio Aemilianus was elected consul for the second time in 134 and assigned to conduct operations against the Celtiberian city of Numantia in east central Spain, the Senate refused him both men and money with the claim that Italy had been stripped of men. By using his own resources and those of his friends, he was able to secure sufficient funds, as well as to gather a force of 4,000 men by calling on cities and kings who were personally connected to him as well as enroll volunteers. There is no doubt that the Senate's behaviour was partly the result of polit-ical struggles. Even if the excuse about lack of manpower is a gross exag-geration, there is good reason to see it as reflecting a real concern. For the excuse to work it had to be plausible. Already by 133, one Roman politi-cian, Tiberius Gracchus, had decided that a manpower crisis loomed and decided to do something about it.[75]

In 111 war broke out between Rome and the ruler of Numidia, Jugurtha, who in the course of dispossessing his relatives emerged as sole ruler. The year before, he sacked the kingdom's capital of Cirta, killing a number of Italian merchants in the process. The Senate was forced to declare war. The next two years saw two ineffectual Roman commanders. Finally, in 109 Caecilius Metellus, one of the consuls, was assigned the command. He was an extremely effective general, who forced Jugurtha to conduct a guerilla war which would only end with his capture. Marius was serving on his staff as a legate and had been effective in his role.[76] He came from Arpinum, a town in Latium not far from Rome. Despite having held office, he had not been accepted by the inner circle of the elite. Asking permis-sion to return to Rome to stand for one of the consulships of 107, Marius' request was denied by Metellus. Marius returned to Rome anyway and, although a man without consular ancestors, was elected. The popular assembly voted to have Marius replace Metellus in Numidia. This illustrates a tendency in appointments to command – which would intensify in the first century – for the popular assembly rather than the Senate to appoint generals and extend the terms of generals and governors.

Marius quickly gathered supplies and money, and began a levy to supplement the troops in Africa. He also solicited volunteers, as Scipio had done a quarter of a century earlier. Among the volunteers he enrolled were men whose property fell below the census minimum. The Senate opposed Marius' actions, but did nothing to hinder them. This used to be thought of as a significant departure from prior Roman practice. It was not. Marius, perhaps in response to the continuing pressure of poverty on the rural population, simply brought the repeated lowering of the census rating to its logical conclusion.[77] Those with little property had been recruited before, but only in emergencies.[78] The sources exaggerated the effect of this levy, which was only a supplementary draft for the legions already in service. They were right in perceiving that the enrollment of men whose present and future security depended on military service was the beginning of a growing distance between the Roman state and its army.

Marius' action was not the end of the traditional levy based on the census classes; it continued to function. The need for large numbers of troops, especially during Rome's civil wars, kept the traditional draft going. For instance, during the Social War 150,000 men were mobilized. This figure was dwarfed by the 420,000 drafted into service between 49 and 31, when the civil wars finally came to a close.[79]

The abolition of the minimum census requirement simply did away with a formal process that no longer corresponded to a social or economic reality. The difficult conditions in the countryside had forced many families off the land, although the majority of the army was still recruited from rural areas. Life in the urban areas brought its own problems. The most pressing was the problem of debt, which reflected the hardship that city life brought and which paralleled the economic problems in the countryside. The situation was intensified by the civil wars which produced untold hardship. For instance, after his victory over his opponents in the first of Rome's civil wars, Sulla demobilized his army of about 120,000 men in 82 and set about providing his veterans with land near Rome to stabilize and support his regime. He provided them with ten colonies, and settled about 80,000 on plots of expropriated land. It was not only senators and wealthy equestrians who lost their land, but thousands of peasants as well.[80] The need to do something about debt and land hunger was a major political theme of in the politics of the 60s.[81]

Military service offered an escape for those who found their livelihood either threatened or gone. The conditions of service were not attractive.

Pay was low and the soldier faced stoppages for food, clothing and equipment. There were also the dangers of combat and the threat of disease, although there are few references in the sources to Roman armies struck by epidemics. Discipline was harsh and the commander was entitled under certain circumstances to inflict the death penalty, not only on individuals but on whole units, if he chose.

Despite these disadvantages, military life had substantial attractions to men living on the margins. It provided regular meals and lodging; it also offered companionship and an opportunity for male bonding. Each legionary belonged to a smaller unit, the *contubernium* of eight men. He took his meals with his fellow members, shared fatigue duties with them, slept next to them and probably served in the battle line with them. Such intimate contact was bound to generate a sense of group loyalty and of belonging.[82] There was also the feeling of being part of a group larger than oneself. It was no accident that part of Marius' reforms included the introduction of a new symbol for the legion – the eagle – in place of an earlier multiplicity of standards.[83] Each maniple had two standards, one for each century and the century standards were retained after the transition to the cohort as the main battle unit.

The emotive power of those standards and the strong affective tie between soldiers and their units are illustrated several times in Caesar's *Gallic Wars*. During the invasion of Britain in 55, the bearer of the eagle of the Tenth legion, when he saw that his comrades were reluctant to advance to the shore from their boats, leapt over the side bearing his eagle towards the shore. The loss of the legion's eagle would have brought immense dishonour and so the men followed.[84] Combat also offered a theatre in which to display a man's courage or his *virtus*.[85]

Finally, the pay may have been small, but it was regular, there was the prospect of booty and during the first century, when colonies began to be established outside of Italy, of land for settlement and farming. The clearest evidence of the importance of booty is the contrast in the second and first century between service in Spain and service in the Greek east. The former promised hard fighting and little prospect of booty and so excited resistance to the levy. The latter presented the possibility of substantial financial gain because of the abundant plunder available. When war was declared on Macedonia in 171, there was a rush of volunteers.[86] The same thing happened in 149 when war was declared on Carthage, which it was thought would be over quickly and produce immense booty.[87] The same was true of Rome's first century wars. Pompey's campaigns in the east from 66–63 produced immense amounts of booty, as Caesar's later did in Gaul.[88] It was standard practice to turn the soldiers loose when a city fell to plunder and slaughter. There were also cash rewards distributed by generals at the end of a successful campaign. The army offered the prospect of economic mobility when there were few other avenues open to poor men.

Service lasted at least eight years, and often for periods of eight to ten years in the first century. An extreme example is provided by a group of soldiers variously called after their commanders, the Valerians or Fimbrians. They were formed from parts of two existing legions, and then sent east with their commander Valerius Flaccus to fight Mithridates, king of Pontus in northern Asia Minor in 86. Flaccus' greed led to a mutiny in which he was killed. He was replaced by his legate Flavius Fimbria. With interruptions due to discharges and even a mutiny, these men served in the East for over twenty years, far longer than the traditional maximum of sixteen years, if that was still in effect. What is striking is they retained their identity as a unit through a series of commanders and discharges. In all but name, they were professionals and they illustrate the effect of civil war and prolonged service as factors that fostered the trend towards a fully professional army. Some of Caesar's legions, like his favoured Tenth, saw service for extended periods. The Tenth was already in Gaul when Caesar arrived as governor in 58. It served with Caesar throughout his campaigns in Gaul, and then it fought for him in the civil war that followed, including at the battle of Pharsalus. In 47, its legionaries were among the troops that mutinied because of what they felt was a failure to keep a pledge to discharge them and to pay a promised bonus. Caesar managed to quiet them and they returned to service.[89] They were still with him during the last battle of the civil war at Munda in Spain in 45.

It is no coincidence that in the second half of the first century we begin to have an epigraphic record produced by common soldiers, primarily consisting of grave inscriptions and dedications. Caesar's men and those who followed identified themselves as soldiers and as veterans in their grave inscriptions and in the records of their gifts. Their personal identity was bound up with their military service. Unlike Spurius Ligustinus, for whom soldiering was simply an aspect of a citizen's obligations to the community, by the 40s being a soldier was to lay claim to a particular occupational and personal status.[90]

The same trend toward professionalization can be seen among the officers of the legion. There had always been a rigid class distinction between the centurion and the military tribune, or cavalry prefect, and those of higher rank, but the development of the professional army changed this as well. After Marius and then Sulla, we begin to see soldiers rising to the centurionate and then subsequently becoming officers or holding higher posts. There was Lucius Petronius,[91] who became an equestrian while serving under Marius or Lucius Fufidius, a centurion of Sulla, who became governor of one of the Spanish provinces.[92] The wealth provided by the civil wars led to increased social mobility among all ranks, especially under Sulla and Caesar. The development of a professionalized military is also signalled by the rise in the first century of the term *homo militaris* or 'military man'. That is no longer a citizen under arms, but a man whose profession was army service.[93]

During this period the relations of the army to its commander changed. This was due, in part, to the increasing use of the extraordinary command. This command can be defined as extraordinary in terms either of the powers conferred, or the length of tenure, or both. The Romans had used this expedient earlier. The Scipio brothers had held a seven-year command in Spain from 218 till their deaths in 211, and Scipio Africanus, who replaced them, held Spain from 210–206. But the extraordinary commands of the Late Republic were longer on the average. Pompey and Caesar provide the most famous and striking examples, but they are not alone. Caesar's command in Gaul lasted nine years from 58–50. Pompey commanded in Spain from 77–71. He was then appointed to command against the pirates. The three-year command extended to the whole Mediterranean basin. He next commanded in the east from 66–63 and then was awarded a five-year term as governor of the Spains, which he could and did exercise through legates in 55.[94] The command was renewed in 52, and was prolonged for another five years.[95] The length of these commands and the responsibility for a growing empire meant that the important commands were now conferred on proconsuls; consuls only infrequently served outside of Italy. Until the first century, commands had normally been assigned by the Senate, with a few exceptions. Important commands were now usually granted by the popular assembly. The real significance of this development lay in the nature of the new army and the troops that constituted it.

The length of these commands could and did, at times, lead to a closer association between the men and their commander. Often, they were serving far from Italy and their living conditions were dependent on their commander. Perhaps the most striking example was the loyalty of Caesar's troops to their general. Even after Caesar's assassination, many of his men revered his memory and were proud to be identified as Caesar's men. Augustus, adopted as Caesar's heir, did all he could to strengthen his identification with the dead dictator. It would be an exaggeration to say he owed everything to his position as Caesar's heir, but his political rise would have been impossible without that connection.[96]

Lucius Licinius Lucullus, one of the consuls of 74, received a command in Cilicia at the end of his consulship. When Mithridates of Pontus launched his attack on the new Roman province of Bithynia, Lucullus forced him out of the province and back into Pontus. Gradually, Lucullus was assigned control of the provinces in Asia Minor and overall direction of the war against Mithridates, which dragged on. In 68, the Romans lost the battle of Zela to Mithridates. Lucullus rushed to bring aid to his battered forces, but upset over the defeat and the harsh discipline he imposed on them, his men mutinied and refused to march further. This plus the machinations of his political enemies meant the end of Lucullus' command.[97]

Prolonged commands offered the possibility that close mutual ties might develop between the legionaries and their general, but there was no certainty that either would benefit, as is clear from the case of Lucullus. As in most pre-modern armies, semi-professional or professional soldiers basically had a contractual relationship. Violation of it by either party was fatal to the contract.

The semi-professional army of the late Republic was no longer as anchored in the state as the militia that preceded it had been. The Senate provided no mechanisms to reward or to regularize an army that was no longer a militia and was composed of men with no prospects after they had completed their military service. The soldiers needed the help of a powerful Roman noble if there was to be any possibility of reward for their service. It was that man's political abilities and strength that would give them what they wanted.

The commander, if successful, could give his troops immediate rewards in the form of booty and promotion and denying those rewards could lead to trouble, as it did for Lucullus. The problem remained, what would happen to them after their service was over. The answer to that problem, in a predominantly agricultural economy, was a grant of land. Grants of land had been made in the form of individual allotments or as part of colonial foundations within Italy and overseas in the late third and the first half of the second century. Already by the end of the Third Samnite War in 290, demobilized Roman soldiers were given land in Samnium.[98] At the termination of his successful campaign to expel the Carthaginians from Spain in 206, Scipio had founded the Roman colony of Italica as well as Latin colonies such as Cordoba. There had also been extensive assignments of land to individuals and the foundation of colonies in Cisalpine Gaul, which ceased by 170.

By the 130s, a reflection of the continued pressure on the peasantry can be seen in the tribunate of Tiberius Gracchus, in which the distribution of public land became an issue and continued to be so after his death.[99] During the civil war period, starting in the late 80s and again in the last phase of the civil war beginning in 49, land was confiscated from private individuals and distributed to veterans. Such distributions were not always successful. Many of Sulla's recipients of confiscated land had little or no experience or tolerance for farming and during the 70s many abandoned their farms and returned to service.[100]

For many legionaries, land grants would have been the most significant reward for their service. Soldiers could never be sure they would receive their grants. There were interests opposed to them. The lower classes of the city of Rome offered formidable opposition because of the threat it posed to their own economic interests. The plebs had little interest in military service, but were jealous of any special consideration given to others. The theme of the tension between countryside and city runs like a thread through the history of the last century of the Republic. The plebs were especially opposed to concessions to Rome's Italian allies which implied that they might have to share the profits of empire. Even the Social War, which resulted in a grant of citizenship to all of the allies south of the Po, had little effect on their attitude. At times, when public land was at issue, many members of the elite joined in opposition. They feared that the distribution of public land would impact their property.

It was only generals who had the support of a strong political faction and could mobilize the votes of their soldiers – such as Marius, Sulla, Pompey and Caesar – who were able to secure such grants. Even Pompey had severe difficulties when he returned to Rome with his men from his eastern campaigns. It was only with the assistance of Caesar as consul in 59, and Crassus that land legislation could be literally forced through. The prospect of rewards after service, gifts of money (donatives), promotions and access to booty were at the discretion of the general. He could use them to foster a sense of loyalty to himself. The Republic had lost control of its army, it had become a 'name without substance or form'.[101]

It was the votes of Pompey's veterans that secured the passage of a land bill to grant them allotments put forward by Caesar in 59. Such actions created a bond that persisted after service. In 81, at the end of the first civil war, Sulla settled his men in a series of ten colonies surrounding Rome to provide protection for him and his political programme. He especially concentrated them in those areas where his enemies had drawn their strength.[102]

Nevertheless, as mentioned earlier, the relationship was not automatic. For example, in 107 Marius was able to take over the command in the war against Jugurtha because the previous commander, Caecilius Metellus, although successful had alienated his men by his harshness and disdain. Even Caesar, who forged perhaps the closest relationship with his men of any commander, faced mutiny in 47. Veterans awaiting discharge in Italy rebelled because of unfulfilled promises and marched on Rome. Caesar spoke to the mutineers, using a subtle mixture of threats and promises, especially pointing out the rich booty they would earn them if they campaigned with him in North Africa. He was able to finally regain control. The sources claim that it only took his addressing them as citizens instead of fellow soldiers, implying dismissal from service, to bring them to heel.[103]

Some of the major land distributions affected tens of thousands of soldiers. Sulla, with twenty-three legions to demobilize, settled something like 80,000 to 100,000 veterans on land confiscated from his opponents. The last decades of the Republic, starting with Marius at the beginning of the first century, were marked by the large-scale overseas colonization. Marius' men were settled on the North African coast, in southern France and in Spain. Perhaps as many as 100,000 men were settled in these colonies.

The last large-scale land distributions in Italy came during the final phases of the civil war. Caesar started settling his veterans after Pharsalus and land distributions continued until his assassination in 44. Approximately 20,000 were settled in Italy. However, Caesar also settled veterans and civilians in the provinces. He established colonies in Africa, Spain, Illyricum, Macedonia and in the East. In all, he seems to have settled about 100,000 including families.

Augustus and his allies Antony and Lepidus began a land distribution programme after their victory over Brutus and Cassius at Philippi in 42. They had to find land for 45,000 veterans in Italy when there was little available land left. They solved their problem by selecting eighteen cities and dispossessing many of their inhabitants and by adding land from adjacent cities when they needed to. Unlike Caesar, they founded only one colony outside of Italy, in Macedonia at the site of their victory.

In 36, after a victory over Sextus Pompeius, Augustus began another round of colonization under pressure from his soldiers. He distributed substantial cash bonuses and demobilized somewhere between 20,000 and 40,000 legionaries. An additional distribution marked Augustus' victory over Antony at Actium in 31. This seems to have been the largest of his land distributions. In his autobiography he claims to have settled 120,000, although it is not entirely clear who was included in this total.

The end of the civil wars did not end his settlement programme. Between 26–15, additional veterans were established in colonies in Africa, Gaul, Spain and the East. Augustus claims that approximately 500,000 citizens took their military oath to him. He goes on to state that of these, he settled on the land or gave cash distributions to 300,000 of them.[104] After his victory at Actium he had a force of sixty legions. It was a force that the empire could not support. He demobilized thirty-two legions and kept twenty-eight in service down to AD 9. In AD 9, three were lost fighting the Germans at the Teutoburg Wood. They were never replaced; the army remained at twenty-five legions for the rest of his reign and also under his successor Tiberius.

After 14, land distributions ceased being the regular reward for the legionary's successful completion of his service. The establishment of a fully professional army in AD 13 led to the substitution of a cash bonus at the end of service in place of land distributions.

CHAPTER TEN

THE LATE REPUBLICAN ARMY

The Army in Combat

The expansion of the Roman Empire in the course of the second and first centuries led to conflict in extremely varied settings, ranging from the cold and snow of Gaul to the deserts of Syria. The century also witnessed bloody civil wars in the late 80s, and then from 49 until the final end of civil conflict in 31. For the first time, Roman armies encountered each other in battle.

The ability to operate in such different environments was the result of a superb logistical system. It was probably the best organized and effective military supply system until modern times.[1] The semi-professionalization of the army also contributed to Roman success. The value of men with long experience was clear. At Mutina in 43, in a battle between Antony and Octavian and his allies, Appian recounts the fighting of veteran units against each other and its effect on raw recruits:

> Urged on by their mutual dislike and ambition, they attacked each other, thinking it was their own affair and not their generals'. As veterans, they raised no battle-cry, since they could not hope to terrify each other, they fought in silence, both as victors or losers. Since neither flanking nor charging was possible amid marshes and ditches, they met together in close order, and as neither side could force back the other, they were forced together with their swords, as if they were wrestlers. No blow missed its mark. There were wounds and slaughter, but no cries, only groans; and when one fell he was instantly carried away and another replaced him. Neither admonition nor encouragement were needed. Experience made each one his own general. When exhausted they separated to catch their breath, like athletes, and then attacked each other again. The new recruits who had come up were struck with amazement, seeing a fight carried out with such precision and in such deep silence.[2]

The increasingly professional character of these men must have facilitated the training of new recruits and the imposition of army discipline on new soldiers. On the battlefield they stiffened the ranks of less experienced men. The absence of veterans in the ranks at Cannae was a major weakness of the legions facing Hannibal.[3] Professionalism also meant that legions now enjoyed a continuity that must have contributed to their sense of community. The expansion of empire also made a difference. Troops had earlier spent time overseas for prolonged periods in Spain and elsewhere; but after the completion of a campaign the legions were normally disbanded and replaced with new recruits. During the final fifty years of the first century, legions began to have a semi-permanent existence. Many of the Caesarean legions remained in being, and along with the legions recruited during the last phase of the civil war, were retained as permanent units in the Imperial army.

Alongside the personnel changes, a new method of training was introduced, probably by Marius at the end of the second and beginning of the first century. It was based on the drills that his consular colleague in 105, Rutilius Rufus, had introduced doubtless in preparation for the German invasions of Italy that followed. The impetus was probably a series of Roman defeats at the hands of the Germans in the preceding ten years. These losses persuaded Marius to follow Rufus' methods. It was primarily a weapons training programme based on that of the gladiatorial schools. It appears that prior to the reform there had been no systematic programme of weapons training.[4]

Another development that separates the army of the last century from earlier Roman armies is the substantial use of field fortifications. In prosecuting sieges, the Romans had developed exceptional skills in the construction of circumvallations and contravallations, perhaps best illustrated by Caesar's siege fortifications in the Gallic War at the siege of Alesia in 52.[5] In addition, the practice of constructing a fortified marching camp at the end of each day's march enhanced Roman skills. In 86, in the first phase of his war with Mithridates, Sulla met Mithridates' general Archelaus at Chaeronea in central Greece. Sulla countered Archelaus' overwhelming numerical superiority by the construction of field trenches and towers to protect his flanks.[6] Probably, the most extensive use of field fortifications was by Caesar during the civil war. At Dyrrachium in 48, he was able to place the much larger army of Pompey under siege using fortifications, even if he was not in the end successful. At Uzita, during the war in Africa in 46, both Caesar and his Republican opponent Scipio used a series of field fortifications to try to gain tactical advantage.[7]

There was also an increase in the tactical employment of combined arms, especially of both heavy and light cavalry. Nevertheless, the heavy infantry still remained the most important Roman arm. The lack of heavy infantry mobility when facing a mobile enemy strong in cavalry – such as the Parthians – could end in disaster, as it did for Crassus at Carrhae in 53 BC.[8] Caesar, as always an imaginative commander, dealt with attacks by cavalry and by light-armed troops by selecting and training legionaries from the front ranks of the line, presumably the youngest, to operate with less equipment to counter these more mobile enemies [9]

The greatest change of all was the central role the army assumed in politics. Earlier Roman history had been marked by occasional mutiny as a means to bring about political and social change. However, these actions were directed to specific ends, rather than being an attempt to dominate the state. The army of the Late Republic remained a potent force in Roman politics for a century. It was only with the victory of Augustus in the last civil war, that the emperor removed the army from politics by professionalizing it and relocating on the imperial frontiers. Even though this proved a long-lasting solution, it did not permanently exclude the army as a political factor. In AD 68–69 and then again in AD 193–197, it temporarily played a crucial role in politics; by the middle of the third century it had become the dominant political force in a beleaguered empire.

The Battle with the Nervii

After his initial victories over the Helvetii and Ariovistus (the chief of the Germanic Suebi) in 58, during his first year as governor in Gaul, Caesar set off to carry out his official duties in Cisalpine Gaul. Provincial governors often had a heavy burden of judicial work that consumed most of the late autumn and winter months. While attending to business, he heard that the tribes of northeastern Gaul, the Belgae, were organizing an attack on his army. Central Gaul had been pacified in 58 and the Belgae must have feared – as it turned out with reason – that their turn would come next. The stationing of legions on their borders intensified their fear.

With his customary speed, Caesar raised two legions without the Senate's authorization. They were sent north commanded by a legate as soon as the campaigning season opened. Caesar, as soon as there was fodder for his accompanying cavalry, headed north over the Alps. He entered the territory of the Belgae and found allies and supplies only among the Remi, who lived near the modern city of Chalons-en-Champagne. As he advanced into Belgic territory, Caesar encountered a combined Belgic army on the banks of the Aisne River. After failing to cut off Caesar's supplies or to bring him to battle the tribes – themselves short of food – disbanded their army and returned to their homes with the intention of fighting him separately.

Caesar defeated them individually. By late summer he was east of the Somme on the borders of the Nervi, whose capital was at ancient Bagacum or Bavacum (modern Bavay near Valentines). After a three-day march through their territory, Caesar reached within 14km of the Scheldt River.[10] There he discovered that the Nervii were encamped on the opposite bank of the river with their allies the Atrebates and Viromandui.

He found out that the Gauls were observing the Roman order of march and that they had decided to launch an attack while the Romans were in marching formation. The normal marching order was that each legion had its baggage to its rear, so that the legions were separated from each other by their equipment. In addition, the men normally carried heavy packs which would hinder their movements in a fight. Some Gauls suggested to the Nervii that they should attack the first legion to appear once it was entering the Roman camp, before the others came up, and plundered its baggage. They said that once this happened the other legions would put up no resistance and flee.

The camp was located on a hill that sloped down to the Scheldt. Caesar, aware that the enemy was near, had changed his order of march. The legions, lightly equipped, marched together with their baggage to the rear. Cavalry and light-armed troops were sent across the river to screen the camp's construction. The two new legions that Caesar had raised were some way back and had not yet reached the camp. The Nervii had decided to launch their attack when the baggage train came into view; as soon as they saw the baggage, the Nervii launched a swift and strong assault across the river. The speed of the attack created serious difficulties. Caesar makes it clear that it was the legions' prior experience in battle that enabled them to meet the attack, as he had hardly any time to issue orders.

Caesar came up to encourage his men and to issue such orders as he could. The Roman battle order was haphazard as there had been no time to form up. The combat was chaotic with fighting breaking out at various points along the line and the men facing in all directions. It was difficult to get any overall sense of the battle, as thick hedges obscured the view and made it difficult to issue general orders or direct support to where it was needed. On the Roman left, the Atrebates were winded by their dash across the river and by fighting the Ninth and Caesar's favourite Tenth Legion; the legions were advancing downhill against them, and the Atrebates were driven back across the river. The two legions then attacked across the river and defeated the Gauls opposite them. The Eleventh and Eighth Legions in the centre also defeated the enemy facing them. They moved to continue the fight on the riverbank. The Seventh and Twelfth Legions formed the right wing and were covering the Roman camp, but the forward movement of the rest of the line exposed the front and left side of the camp.

The Nervii, noticing the situation, took advantage of it. They formed a compact column and marched on the exposed portions of the camp. Part of the column attempted to encircle the legions on their exposed left flank while the rest made for the camp. They swept aside the Roman cavalry and light-armed troops who had fled to the camp for safety and then, as the Nervii continued to advance, resumed their flight.

Caesar noticed that the Twelfth Legion on his right was so densely packed together that they could not use their weapons effectively. The situation was quickly worsening with men stationed at the legion's rear leaving the battle line to avoid the enemy's missiles. Caesar snatched a shield and made his way to the front of the line. He ordered the troops there to open up their formation so that they could use their weapons effectively. His presence and his orders partially restored the situation and checked the Nervii's progress.

The Seventh Legion, which was close to the Twelfth, was also hard pressed. He ordered the legions to gradually close up and for their rear ranks to face about so that they could fight off the attacks on their rear. This restored the situation. The newly raised legions with the baggage train, learning of the plight of their fellow soldiers, rushed to aid their comrades. Caesars' legate Labienus also moved to assist. The enemy was now exposed on his flanks and rear. The Nervii resisted courageously, but it was a hopeless situation. The Roman victory was complete.[11]

The battle was essentially a soldier's battle. It was the experience of the troops and their skill that turned what could have been a disaster into a victory. Much of the responsibility for the near disaster must rest with Caesar. Granted, the topography presented scouting difficulties; nonetheless, Caesar was aware of the enemy's position. His changed marching order is evidence of that. If he had drawn up a battle line facing the river and the enemy, while detailing perhaps a third of his men to camp construction, he could have met the attack much more easily. Aemilius Paullus had successfully constructed his camp at Pydna in the face of the Macedonians in just this way.[12] It was Caesar's impetuosity and haste that created the real danger. It was a trait that he displayed on many occasions, especially during his invasion of North Africa in the civil war. The professionalism of his troops – centurions and officers in this case – more than compensated for his errors.

The Parthians and Carrhae

The coalition of three men – Pompey, Caesar and Marcus Crassus – known as the First Triumvirate, had no legal standing but had been formed in 60 or early 59 to allow each man to achieve his immediate political goals. Caesar had obtained a five-year provincial command in Gaul and Illyricum. Pompey had the arrangements he had made in the east after his successful war against Mithridates ratified, as well as land grants for his veterans. Crassus had obtained debt relief for the men who collected the taxes in Asia and thereby solidified his ties to them.

Although the coalition weathered some difficult moments, it held together and the three renewed their pact in 56. Pompey and Crassus were elected as consuls for 55 and Caesar's governorship in Gaul was extended for another five years. Pompey received a command in Spain for a five-year period which he could hold *in absentia* and Crassus was allotted the province of Syria for five years. Crassus felt this command was vital to his political future. Pompey and Caesar had won immense wealth and glory as a result of their military successes. Crassus was probably richer than either of his two political partners, but he lacked the military prestige they had won. His only large-scale independent military command had been in the slave uprising of 73–71 led by Spartacus. Crassus triumphed, but it was an inglorious slave war and Pompey had stolen some of the credit for his victory. Syria was an attractive command. It was rich and Pompey's easy victories there seemed to promise a painless path to military glory.

The Parthian kingdom would be his major adversary. In the late 50s, the kingdom had been passing through a period of instability as rival claimants fought for the throne. The Romans saw this as an invitation to intervene and Crassus' predecessor as governor had almost done so.

Unfortunately, there is little information about the Parthians, who are mostly known from Greek and Roman literary sources and archaeological evidence. They entered the northern part of Parthia, which lay southeast of the Caspian, in the mid-third century and established themselves in this formerly Seleucid territory. Their kingdom was centred on the Iranian plateau with their capital at Ctesiphon on the right bank of the Tigris River. The relation of the king to his nobles, who retained a high degree of autonomy, is hard to understand. He seems to have exercised a general control of the kingdom with a highly organized central bureaucracy. Certainly, from the first century BC until its fall in the mid-third century AD, it was the only powerful organized state on the borders of the Roman Empire. The Romans recognized its power and treated the Parthians as equals, despite constant border wars, especially over the fate of Armenia.

The army was controlled by the king. There must have been a small standing army, probably consisting of mercenaries who served as palace guards and garrisoned the main cities and strongpoints. However, for large-scale conflict the king depended on his nobles who mobilized their tenants, slaves and followers. In what manner these groups were coordinated when mobilized is unknown, although on campaign there was usually a noble in overall command as was the case at Carrhae. At times, these nobles could be a threat to the king and disciplining them must not have been easy.

Unlike the Roman army, where the heavy infantry dominated the battlefield, Parthian infantry was its weakest component. Parthian strength was in cavalry. With their control of the northern Iranian plateau they possessed one of the great horse breeding areas of the ancient world. Their cavalry was of several types. There was a heavy cavalry unit, the cataphracts or *clibanarii,* who were protected head to foot with mail and carried a heavy thrusting spear as their main offensive weapon and a sword as secondary armament. Their horses were also armoured. They could not successfully charge heavy infantry in formation, but they were effective once the formation was broken up, and against enemy cavalry. The other main cavalry arm was the horse archers, famed for the over-the-back Parthian bow shot. The cataphracts could keep enemy infantry penned in, while the archers bombarded a formation with missiles until it disintegrated.

During the winter of 54/53, Crassus returned to Syria from Rome. The sources, which are heavily biased against him, claim that he spent that winter in dissipation. It is more likely that he was assembling the necessary funds and supplies for the coming campaigning season of 53. The one serious omission in his preparations appears to have in the training of legions to operate as an effective and cohesive whole. A welcome addition was the arrival of his son, the younger Marcus Licinius Crassus, with 1,000 Gallic cavalry; he had been serving as a legate of Caesar's in Gaul and the cavalry was likely a gift from Caesar.

The king of Armenia, Artavasdes, approached Crassus with an offer of 6,000 cavalry and the promise of additional troops in the future. But the offer came with unacceptable conditions and Crassus refused it, although the additional cavalry strength would have been welcome.

In the spring of 53, Crassus crossed the Euphrates, which marked the unstable border between Roman and Parthian territory. He commanded seven understrength legions, totalling perhaps 28,000 men, along with 4,000 light infantry and 4,000 cavalry. He directed his march to the valley of the Balikh River, a tributary of the Euphrates. As he marched towards the river valley, he was met by local allies who joined his army. He followed an old caravan route which provided the needed supplies, and in early June, he finally reached the Balikh.

The Parthian king, in response to the invasion, divided his army into two parts. One he sent towards Armenia to distract Artavasdes; the other under the command of Surena, the king's chief general and greatest nobleman, was dispatched to face Crassus.[13] It was a much smaller army than Crassus', perhaps 10,000 cataphracts and horse archers and other mounted men.[14] Since the army was primarily cavalry, this lower figure is understandable. Infantry in armies in the Mediterranean theatre normally outnumbered cavalry by a ratio of ten to one. A key innovation by the Parthian general was a pack train of 1,000 camels which carried a reserve supply of arrows. This compensated for a weakness of the horse archer, the limited supply of ammunition he carried. Interestingly, this innovation was never, as far as we know, repeated. Why this was so is hard to explain. A possible reason lay in the nature of the Parthian army; since it consisted of the levies by the great nobles, it had little institutional memory and so innovations were not likely to be passed on.

Crassus was moving east along the river when the two armies met. Both armies faced difficulties in dealing with each other. The Roman heavy infantry, the heart of Crassus' army, was well protected by its defensive equipment. If it could maintain its battle order, the Parthians could not defeat it (and later on, they consistently failed to do so). Parthian attacks were most successful against isolated detachments or lines of communication. Such attacks could create problems, but rarely could they be decisive.

The problem for the Romans in fighting the Parthians was their mobility. If they could take away their mobility or fix them to a particular spot they could defeat them. It was also possible, if they had sufficiently effective missile forces, to nullify the key Parthian advantage.[15]

The most detailed account we have of the battle at Carrhae is Plutarch's *Crassus*. There are some problems of detail, such as the formation Crassus adopted at the beginning of the battle, but the general development of the action is clear as well as the reasons for Crassus' defeat.

Crassus' first hint of the approach of the Parthian army was a report from his cavalry scouts that the enemy was close. Plutarch's account is strongly biased against him. It claims that the news rattled the general and that he first spread out his line with cavalry on the wings, as was their usual position in the battle line. The purpose of this formation was, according to Plutarch, to keep the force from being surrounded. Caesar adopted the same arrangement while campaigning in North Africa seven years later.[16] It may be that Crassus then realized that the terrain was too open for such a manoeuvre to succeed, as he then deployed his men in a hollow square which was a standard Roman defensive marching formation. He posted a *turma* of cavalry with each cohort.

It is at this point that Plutarch's description of the Roman formation becomes difficult to understand. He claims that Crassus was in command of the centre, while his son commanded one wing and Gaius Cassius – the later assassin of Caesar – commanded the other. A square obviously has no wings. One further problem is the role of the cavalry, who would later ride out to confront their Parthian opposites. What was the purpose of posting them with each cohort? This would have robbed them of their ability to stage a massed attack and would also have broken the square's cohesion. Cavalry would normally be deployed outside the square where they had room to manoeuvre and to scout. There is no clear answer to these difficulties.

Crassus advanced to the Balikh. The men wanted to camp next to the river since they were worn out by thirst and heat, but Crassus, spurred on by his son, decided to attack. The Romans advanced at a slow, steady pace until they came in sight of the enemy. At first glance, the Parthians did not appear formidable. Surena had screened his army with an advance guard and the men had been instructed to cover their armour to make their appearance less frightening. The Parthian commander was also aiming at a psychological impact on the enemy. When the Romans came into sight, he ordered the war drums to be beaten, and as the drums reached a crescendo the soldiers stripped off their cloaks and revealed their armour gleaming in the blazing sunlight. The noise and the sudden gleam of the armour must have had a powerful effect.

Hoping to take advantage of this display, the Parthians decided on an initial charge by their cataphracts, but seeing the close formation of the heavy infantry, thought better of it. This was their first full-scale battle against the Romans and they were not used to their opponents' tactics.

The Parthians surrounded the Roman infantry square and hemmed it in, restricting its room to manoeuvre. In response, Crassus sent his light infantry forward, probably to bombard the Parthians surrounding the square and drive them off. The tactic failed; the enemy's horse archers met the Roman light-armed troops with such a barrage of arrows that they were driven back to the protection of their own heavy infantry. Their flight disorganized the square, which had to open to admit them. The waves of arrows also affected the heavy infantry. They now saw that their defensive equipment was not proof against the rain of arrows, which were shot with such force that they penetrated armour. The Parthian horsemen used the Asiatic composite bow, which was made from a variety of different materials, principally horn and wood laminated together. These bows were small enough to be easily used on horseback, but required strength and lengthy training to be effective. They were effective against individuals at about 60 metres and against formations such as the Roman square at about 150 metres.[17] They were also capable of penetrating about 2.5mm of metal.

The Parthians then spread out their lines and began to bombard the square with their arrows. The heavy infantry was in an impossible situation: if they kept their ranks, they were helpless against the enemy archers; but if they set out in pursuit, they could not catch them. In doing so, they made their square more vulnerable and exhausted themselves in the desert heat to no advantage.

At this point, Crassus sent orders to his son to move forward to try to close with the enemy. His son took a force of 1,300 horse – of whom 1,000 were Gallic cavalry – 500 archers and 8 cohorts, probably numbering about 3,000–4,000 men. The Parthians turned their horses and retreated. Most likely it was an attempt to lure Crassus' force away so that it would be isolated from the other Roman units. On its own it could be surrounded and attacked.

Once the Parthians had lured Crassus and his men sufficiently far from the safety of the rest of the Roman army, the Parthians turned and began to attack. They stationed their cataphracts opposite the Roman formation to contain it while their archers rode around it and launched a constant wave of arrows at it. The dust thrown up by the Parthian horses and the rain of arrows forced the Roman soldiers into an ever tighter mass that was a helpless prey for the archers. Crassus launched an attack to rescue the isolated formation with his Gallic horse, but the attack failed. The survivors retreated to a small hillock which afforded them no relief. Finally, Roman resistance totally collapsed. According to Plutarch, only 500 survived to be taken prisoner. The Parthians beheaded Crassus' son and turned their attention to the main Roman force.

Crassus drew his men up on a slight rise, hoping it would impede the enemy cavalry, and waited for the return of his son. He received a request for help from his son, but was afraid to endanger his main force by sending support. While he was torn between fear for his army and fear for his son's life, the main Parthian force rode up and the second phase of the battle began. The Parthians had affixed his son's head on a spear and displayed it. Crassus was no longer in any doubt about his son's fate.

The enemy's attack mimicked the tactics they had used against the younger Crassus. The horse archers rode around the formation showering it with arrows, while the cataphracts used their long spears to force the Romans into an ever denser mass. Sporadic charges were mounted against the cataphracts, but they ended in failure. Finally, as night approached, the Parthians broke off their attack. They informed Crassus that they granted him a respite until morning. He could renew the struggle on the following day or agree to journey to the Parthian king Arsaces to negotiate.

The Romans passed the night in utter despair. They were in a flat plain with no cover and with no obvious way to escape the Parthians. They were also worried about what to do with their wounded. Plutarch paints a picture of Crassus sunk in misery, unable to take any action. He claims that his quaestor Cassius and his legate Octavius, ignoring Crassus, started the army moving. It was a difficult and erratic advance, particularly troubled by the needs of the wounded. An advanced cavalry unit made it to Carrhae, delivered a message that there had been a great battle with the Parthians and then quickly fled farther, finally arriving at Zeugma on the Euphrates. The commander of the garrison of Carrhae, upset by the news, set out to meet Crassus and finding him, brought him back to the city.

At dawn, the Parthians attacked the Roman camp, slaughtering 4,000 men who had been left in camp. In addition, a unit of four cohorts which had become lost during the night was surrounded and destroyed. The Parthians let twenty of these men survive and sent them on ahead to Carrhae. Plutarch claims it was a reward for their courage; it is more likely that they were to serve as a warning of the fate awaiting the city.

The next day, Surena arrived with his army at Carrhae. He was unsure of Crassus' fate. To see if he was in the city, he sent a message that he wanted to parlay. Crassus appeared on the city wall and so ended any doubt about his whereabouts. Surena proposed a truce and offered Crassus a safe conduct to meet the king, if Crassus would agree to make an alliance and leave Mesopotamia. Crassus agreed and asked for a place and time to meet with Surena.

The Parthians attacked the city: this persuaded the Romans that their only safety lay in flight. Misled by a guide who favoured the Parthians, some of Romans abandoned this guide and made their way to safety; a number did survive and many deserted their commander. Surena and his men caught up with Crassus and his party. Crassus was killed and beheaded. The survivors in his party surrendered to the Parthians. Plutarch states that 20,000 Romans died. The sources offer no figures for Parthian casualties.

Perhaps the most important effect of the battle was not in the East, but in the West. The two surviving members of the triumvirate, Caesar and Pompey, would now face each other without any balancing force. Their struggle for supremacy would lead to almost twenty years of continuous warfare.

Pharsalus

Caesar's rapid conquest of Italy in January 49 ended the first phase of civil war. In response, Pompey hastily evacuated Italy, leaving from the port of Brundisium to rally support in the east. Caesar did not immediately pursue him, but turned west to conquer Spain. He did not want to leave the only sizeable Pompeian army at his back when he turned to cross the Adriatic in pursuit of Pompey. Lucius Afranius and Marcus Petreius, the Pompeian legates in Spain, had together a sizeable force of 5 legions and 80 auxiliary cohorts as well as 5,000 cavalry drawn from their province. Caesar defeated the Pompeians within forty days by manoeuvre and without a major battle.

After leaving Italy, Pompey had encamped at the seaport of Dyrrachium (Durres in modern Albania) in Epirus on the other side of the Adriatic. It gave him access to the sea and stood at the beginning of the great east–west route of the Via Egnatia which ran through Macedonia to the harbour and ports which were the starting points for the passage to Asia. The forty days that Caesar spent in Spain were enough time for Pompey to assemble a force of nine legions, including the five he had brought from Italy and others levied in the east. He also had a force of 7,000 cavalry, as well as numerous light-armed troops, including archers and slingers. His campaigns in the east had won him the support of numerous eastern kings, some of whom owed their thrones to him. He was also awaiting the arrival of his ally Metellus Scipio with two legions from the latter's province of Syria. Pompey's fleet dominated the Mediterranean and was stationed in the Adriatic to prevent Caesar crossing to Dyrrachium and gaining access to the Via Egnatia.

Caesar decided to fight in the Balkans rather than wait for Pompey to attack Italy. In this way he could spare Italy the devastation that war brings and strike before Pompey could assemble an even larger army. However, he was in difficulties. He had twelve understrength legions and cavalry at Brundisium, but no way to transport them across the Adriatic. Furthermore, he had no fleet to contest the Pompeian domination of the sea. Despite these seemingly insurmountable difficulties, he was able to find enough ships to bring over 7 legions totalling 15,000 infantry and 500 cavalry. Because it was winter, when no one would expect a crossing, he was able to elude detection by the enemy's fleet. But he had to leave four legions with Marc Antony at Brundisium to follow when circumstances permitted. On his arrival, he had to further weaken his army. He sent five cohorts to Aetolia in central Greece in an attempt to alleviate his food supply problems, and also sent an additional two legions to Macedonia to try to prevent the junction of Pompey's and Scipio's armies. In the spring, Antony finally was able to bring the remaining four legions across.

Caesar, because of his supply problems and rightly convinced that his men were the more effective soldiers, was anxious to bring Pompey to battle. Trying to repeat his success in Spain Caesar attempted to outmanoeuvre Pompey. He was unsuccessful and decided to try to confine Pompey to the port of Dyrrachium despite the fact than his adversary enjoyed superior numbers. He began the construction of large-scale siege works; Pompey built counterworks. In the end Caesar's attempt failed: Pompey had access to the sea for supplies and a fleet that could keep that access open. Caesar claims that he constructed the fortifications to restrict the enemy's foraging since he had an overwhelming preponderance in cavalry. It is not hard to think that the siege works were in fact meant as psychological warfare, as a means to force Pompey to fight by damaging his troops morale.

In the end the siege created more difficulties for Caesar than for Pompey. Caesar was beset by severe supply difficulties. Those difficulties multiplied when the Pompeians launched a strong assault on the southern part of Caesar's fortifications that resulted in severe losses among Caesar's troops.

These setbacks, in combination with a severe grain shortage, finally compelled Caesar to move in hopes of obtaining supplies and drawing Pompey after him. He set off southeast to one of the more fertile areas of Thessaly where he could obtain the needed supplies and link up with Domitius and his two legions. This would offer him the opportunity to prevent the junction of his enemy's forces. In addition, the move to confront Scipio should draw Pompey away from the coast and Caesar might finally, by restricting Pompey's supplies, bring about the battle he desired.

The manoeuvre worked. Pompey pursued Caesar into Thessaly. The area was friendly to Caesar and offered an abundant supply of grain. He successfully joined his army to Domitius' two legions. But Scipio had now united his legions with those of Pompey. Now that his forces had linked up, Caesar decided to bring Pompey to battle. Pompey was encamped on a hill near Pharsalus or near a site known as Old Pharsalus where a previous Roman army had camped in 169 during the Third Macedonian War. The site of Old Pharsalus is not securely located, but it is generally agreed that modern Farsala is the site of ancient Pharsalus. The site of the plain where the battle was fought is also uncertain. The only definite feature is the Enipeus River (Enipeas), a tributary of the Peneus (Pineios) River flowing to the north of Pharsalus. The sources seem to indicate that the battle was fought to the north of the river and that Pompey was encamped on one of the hills on its northern bank.

Caesar tried to tempt Pompey to commit his forces. He initially drew up his men for battle near his camp and then on successive days moved his battle line closer and closer to Pompey's camp. Pompey's response was draw up his troops on the lower slopes of the hill on which he was camped. Caesar wisely refrained from attacking such a formidable position. His men would have had to run uphill and so lose much of the impetus of their attack. Pompey had once again checkmated Caesar. As at Dyrrachium, Caesar was forced to move because of a lack of supplies and in the hope that Pompey might pursue him and perhaps expose himself to battle.

Surprisingly, Pompey accepted battle just as Caesar was ready to march. Caesar fails to explain this change of plan. However, unlike Caesar, Pompey did not have full control over his own campaign. The aristocrats such as Scipio who were with his army were his equals, and their combined pressure could easily have led to the change of plan. Plutarch's account of the battle suggests that this was a crucial factor.[18]

Pompey deployed his troops so that his right flank was protected by the Enipeus, facing east with the sun at his back. His infantry cohorts were deployed in the typical three-line formation. In all he had eleven legions and additional auxiliary cohorts. In total Caesar says that he had 45,000 soldiers, plus 2,000 veterans who had previously fought with him.[19] In addition, there were numerous eastern contingents.[20] The cohorts were deployed to a greater than normal depth of ten men, a sign of his lack of trust in his army's capabilities. Three of his legions were raw recruits, while another two had served with Caesar in Gaul. Another legion, the Cilician, had formed the garrison of that province and had recently fought with the Parthians and so was in a weakened state. Given the superior fighting skills of Caesar's infantry, this was the best course open to him. The order he gave to his infantry to hold their ground and await Caesar's attack was another sign of his lack of confidence. He intended to win on his left flank where he had massed his overwhelmingly superior cavalry along with archers and slingers. He planned to have it drive off the cavalry on Caesar's right wing and then sweep around that flank to take Caesar's army in the rear. Given all of his problems with his infantry, it made good tactical sense for Pompey to try to strike the decisive blow with his cavalry. Pompey himself commanded the left of his line, with Scipio in command of his two Syrian legions in the centre. Cornelius Lentulus, the consul of the year before, may have been on the right wing where Afranius was also stationed.[21]

Caesar had far fewer troops. He claims that he had 22,000 men in 80 cohorts, the equivalent of 8 legions. This works out to 275 men per cohort, which is little more than half the usual paper strength for a cohort. He sent two cohorts to guard his camp, which further weakened his line. He also deployed his infantry in the standard three-line formation. He had only 1,000 cavalry, most of which he placed on his left wing. Anticipating Pompey's plan, which must have been evident from the massed cavalry on Pompey's left, he took one cohort from each of the legions and formed them into a fourth line and placed them opposite the Pompeian cavalry. He had instructed these men to retain their *pila* and to use them as thrusting spears against the cavalry.

Once the cavalry had been deployed and each commander had given the usual speech of encouragement to his troops, the battle began. Pompey's infantry initially held their ground as planned. Their instructions were that they should receive the enemy infantry where they stood, break the force of its charge and then launch their own attack. This would force the Caesareans to run twice the normal distance and wear them out, while Pompey's men would be fresh. It would also limit the impact of the enemy *pila* as they would be receiving them standing still. These are the reasons that Caesar alleges. It seems likely that given the inexperience and different units he had in his army, that he thought standing in place would allow them to maintain their ranks and not run the risk of falling into disorder.

The Caesareans charged, holding their *pila* level; as they approached, they saw that the enemy was stationary. It was at this point that their training and experience made a significant difference. Noticing that the Pompeians were not moving, they halted and rested. They then resumed their charge, throwing their javelins and drawing their swords as they closed with the enemy. The Pompeians, in response, threw their own javelins and drew their swords.

Simultaneously, the Pompeian cavalry on the left charged forward along with the archers and slingers. The small number of cavalry on Caesar's right wing were driven back. The Pompeian cavalry, now attacking Caesar's flank, began to surround the rear of Caesar's line. Caesar now gave the order to his fourth line to attack the cavalry using their *pila* as thrusting spears.[22] The Pompeian cavalry gave way and fled. The slingers and archers now without cavalry protection were pursued and killed. These same cohorts now surrounded the left wing of the Pompeian infantry who had held their position.

At the same time Caesar ordered his third line, which had not so far been involved in the battle, to advance. The combination of these fresh troops and the attack in the rear by the fourth line was too much for the Pompeian infantry who now turned and joined the cavalry in flight. Caesar rightly claims that it was to his fourth line that he owed his victory.

Caesar now moved to attack the Pompeian camp. After a fierce battle, he took it. When it seemed as if the camp was about to fall Pompey fled, later meeting his death in Egypt. After the camp was taken, Caesar moved on to the final act. A number of Pompeians had taken refuge on a nearby hill; seeing Caesar's attempt to cut them off, they fled, but were intercepted and forced to surrender.

So ended the greatest battle of this phase of the civil war. Caesar claims that he suffered 200 dead while the Pompeians lost 15,000 killed and 24,000 captured. The prolonged pursuit and the slaughter of the light-armed troops must have substantially added to his opponent's casualties, as well as the disparity in training and experience between the two armies. So his figures should be accepted. Pharsalus was to be followed by a series of conflicts in North Africa and then once more in Spain. Although sometimes in trouble because of his haste, the famous Caesarean *celeritas*, Caesar was above all an excellent tactician, who could meet the challenges presented by different enemies in a variety of circumstances.[23]

The Carrot and the Stick

In his account of the Roman army, Polybius discusses the Roman system of military rewards, which he regards as an admirable mechanism to persuade the Roman soldier to face and surmount the dangers of battle. He sees it, along with a parallel system of punishments, as key elements in Rome's success.[24] The system he describes was elaborate and detailed; it makes a striking comparison with the system of rewards developed in Greek city-states which, although they had a limited number of honours for military prowess, focused their rewards system on athletic success.

The Carrot: Rewards

As in most areas of Roman political and social life, rewards were assigned not only on the basis of courage or success, but also on a scale based on an individual's social status. The system combined tangible and intangible awards, with the latter conferring the highest prestige. The same dichotomy is found in Greek athletic prizes. In a highly military society such as Rome's, these rewards would bring social prestige, and material rewards could and did follow. For the upper class, it could help in the quest for office; lower down the social scale it could result in a promotion to the rank of centurion or other positions which brought an increased share of booty and higher pay. In the late Republic, a centurion's pay was fifteen times that of a common legionary. Even when promotion was not awarded, there was a chance for gifts of money and increased rations.

Initially, most rewards seem to been granted on the basis of what had been done regardless of social rank or position. The first awards appear in sources in the mid-fifth century. However, by the last third of the second century, the system described by Polybius was in place. It was further elaborated in the first century and in many respects continued into the imperial period. It has been suggested, probably rightly, that this development may have been tied to the evolution of a professional army. Such organizations tend to be more conscious of rank and structure.

The most common class of awards was also the least important. The most comprehensive evidence for these awards is found in the Imperial period, especially on tombstones. A full-size spear, first referred to in Polybius, was conferred on a soldier who killed an enemy in a single combat which the soldier could have avoided.[25] Torques, or decorated metal collars which seem to have had a Celtic origin, were given for various reasons. There is no indication of any specific act or rank that was a necessary condition to receive an award. Metal disks called *phalerae* were given to cavalry troopers and *phiale* to the infantry. The *phalerae* were given as decoration for the trooper's horse. What *phiale* were is uncertain; they may have been the same award with some indication that the recipient was an infantryman. The first clear evidence for the *phiale* dates to the early first century at the same time as the torque. These classes of decorations appear to have been limited to soldiers of the rank of centurion or below. This type of award also includes the *vexillum,* a miniature reproduction of a battle standard. The evidence for it mostly postdates the Republic. It indicates that there were a variety of forms and a lack of standardization.[26]

Although under the Empire these awards were only given to Roman citizens, there are occasional examples in the Republican period of these awards being given to non-citizens. The most important purpose of such awards was to express gratitude to foreign rulers for their participation in Rome's wars. Citizenship was also awarded for service by non-citizens; Spanish cavalry serving in the Social War received it, as did a whole legion of Caesar's – the Fifth – during his years in Gaul. During the Empire the incorporation of a large body of non-citizens into the army seems to have ended the practice of individual grants of citizenship. From the mid-first century AD, citizenship was regularly awarded to auxiliary soldiers at the completion of their service. The rewards given were practical. By the early third century, the practice of granting citizenship ceased. It may be that the extension of citizenship in AD 212 to almost all inhabitants of the empire made the practice redundant.

The major symbolic awards were crowns. For the most part, they were woven from the leaves of various trees or plants. The siege crown, made of grass, was bestowed by the besieged on the commander who lifted a siege. It was the second most prestigious award next to the triumphal crown.[27] The sources only mention six occasions when this was conferred. Next to it in prestige was the civic crown, made of oak leaves and bestowed for saving a fellow citizen's life. There were also crowns awarded for the first man to scale the enemy's battlements in a siege and a parallel crown for the first man over the wall of an enemy's camp. These, along with a crown awarded for extraordinary naval service, were made of gold.

There were even more prestigious awards than the crowns. One was the *spolia opima* ('the highest spoils'), which in historical times was limited to a Roman commander who personally defeated and killed an enemy commander in battle and then took his weapons and equipment. There is some slight evidence that at an earlier period a soldier other than the commander could win the *spolia opima*.[28] The award was given rarely; only three occasions are attested. The first was the mythical victory of Romulus over Acro, king of the king of the city of Caenina who had made war on Romulus because of the rape of the Sabine women.[29] Romulus carried off the dead king's armour and weapons, suspended on an oak frame. This practice has parallels elsewhere in the ancient Mediterranean. He carried the spoils back to Rome where he built a small temple dedicated to Jupiter Feretrius in which he dedicated the spoils. The second award was to Cornelius Cossus. He won it either in 437 or 428. Part of the problem with the dating is the attempt by the first emperor, Augustus, to question the status of Cossus for reasons of personal prestige. He is said to have killed Lars Tolumnius, the king of Veii, in battle. Most scholars accept this event as historical. The final example is that of Marcus Claudius Marcellus, consul in 222, who killed the Gallic king Viridomar at a battle near Clastidium. This award is definitely historical.

The reasons for the origin of the ritual of the *spolia opima* are obscure. The Greeks erected trophies consisting of a wooden cross from which were hung the weapons of the defeated enemy. There is no evidence for such a custom at Rome. It may have been borrowed from the Greeks. It has been suggested that the origin of the ceremony was as an expiation of blood guilt. However, it seems more like an affirmation of personal prowess. Its rarity is partially to be explained by the fact that, unlike many cultures, the Romans did not accept single combat as a way of deciding battles.[30]

The most prestigious and important of all military awards was the triumph. It has been suggested that it is also a ritual of purification. It seems more likely that it is a celebration of the elements that led to victory, the commander, his army and the community as personified in its chief god *Jupiter Optimus Maximus* ('Jupiter the Best and Greatest').

Its origins are obscure, but many Greek and Etruscan elements that went into the development of the ceremony have been identified. Etruscan borrowings are the most important; this is hardly surprising, as Roman dress and insignia of office, including the ring given to Roman cavalry to symbolize their status, have Etruscan precedents. For instance, the costume worn by the triumphing general has similarities to the dress of Etruscan kings. Despite these borrowings, the rite does not seem to have been of Etruscan origin, but rather to have had a Latin source. There is support for this view in the fact that the rite could be and sometimes was celebrated on the Alban Mount, which was sacred to Jupiter Latiaris, the common god of the Latins, and a site sacred to a number of Latin communities. The palm-embroidered toga and sceptre of the triumphing commander are derived from the attributes of the god.

If the Senate agreed to a triumph, it voted the necessary funds. The Centuriate Assembly then had to vote to grant *imperium* to the general for the day of his triumph, since a commander's *imperium* lapsed once he crossed the *pomerium* (the religious boundary of the city) and its absence would invalidate his claim to hold a triumph. Some sources claim that there were specific rules for such a grant, probably the most famous being the requirement that 5,000 of the enemy had been killed in a single battle.[31] But it seems more likely that the grant was not bound by rules, but was at the discretion of the Senate and people.[32] The vote could be subject to political infighting and generals were refused permission and funds. If that happened, an alternative was open to them; those who were refused could celebrate a triumph on the Alban Hill. There was also the possibility of being voted a lesser triumph called an ovation (*ovatio*), which was a far less spectacular affair. The general walked on foot instead of riding in a four-horse chariot. He wore the *toga praetexta,* a toga with a purple border, instead of the triumphal toga and he was crowned with myrtle not laurel. Basically, the elements that linked the general to Jupiter were absent.

The ceremony began with an assembly of the army and its general in the Campus Martius, an area especially associated with warfare. The army hailed its victorious leader and the commander responded in kind, handing out prizes and rewards to individual soldiers. Then began a triumphal march that went from the southern end of the Campus Martius through the *Porta Triumphalis* ('Gate of Triumph'), and the made its way through the vegetable and cattle markets to the Circus Maximus.[33] It then wound around the Palatine Hill and through the Forum and then up the Capitoline Hill to the temple of Jupiter. The circuit was traditional and probably went back to the origins of the celebration.

The triumphal parade itself consisted of three distinct parts: first, the booty and prisoners; then the triumphing commander; and finally, the portion of the army that had been assembled for the parade. Given the size of Roman armies, it is doubtful if the whole army ever participated.

The *triumphator* (triumphing general) was positioned at the centre of the parade between the booty he had won and the army that he had commanded. He rode in a four-horse chariot, dressed in a tunic decorated with gold thread decorations, wearing over it a purple toga similarly adorned. He carried a laurel branch in one hand and an ivory sceptre topped with an eagle in the other. The laurel was sacred to Mars, the god of war, and the eagle was the sacred bird of Jupiter. His face was painted red and on his head he wore a laurel crown that was also worn by the other participants. A late source claims that a slave stood behind the general in the chariot, holding a gold crown over his head and repeating, 'Look behind you, remember you are mortal.'[34] The *triumphator's* younger children rode beside him in the chariot, while his older boys accompanied him on horseback. Scipio Aemilianus, who was about 17, rode beside his father Aemilius Paullus during the latter's triumph over Perseus.[35] The ceremony not only reflected glory on the commander, but also on his family.

The parade ended at the temple of Jupiter, where white oxen were sacrificed as a thanks-offering to the gods for the granting of victory. The scale and brilliance of the triumphs varied greatly. Perhaps the most lavish of them all was Pompey's in 61. It was granted for his victories over the pirates who had infested the Mediterranean, including in their depredations descents on the coast of Italy, and Mithridates of Pontus who had waged two hard-fought wars against Rome. Mary Beard sums up the spectacle:

> It was a ceremony that put on show at the heart of the metropolis the wonders of the East and the profits of empire: from cartloads of bullion and colossal golden statues to precious specimens of exotic plants and other curious bric-à-brac of conquest. Not to mention the eye-catching captives dressed up in their national costumes, the placards proclaiming the conqueror's achievements (ships captured, cities founded, kings defeated ...), paintings recreating crucial moments of the campaigns, and a bizarre portrait head of Pompey himself, made (so it was said) entirely of pearls.[36]

Usually the celebration lasted a single day, but occasionally it extended over several days. In August 29, Augustus celebrated a three-day triumph over Egypt. During the Empire, the triumph was monopolized by the Imperial family, although the generals who actually fought in the wars were awarded triumphal ornaments which consisted of a wreath of bay leaves (a symbol of purification), a vest decorated with a golden palm symbolizing victory, and a gold-embroidered purple cloak.

The Stick: Punishment

The most common judgement on Roman military punishment in the sources is that it was harsh, but effective. In his account of the Roman army, Polybius comments on the harshness of Roman military discipline. In his discussion of the night watch in marching camps, he claims that:

> It is because the Romans punish so harshly and implacably that their night guards carry out their duties without fault.

His general opinion of punishment reflects the same point of view:

> They have chosen the most effective practices to inspire terror and dismay and to repair the harm done.[37]

The sources claim that such punishments in combination with a system of rewards, were crucial to Rome's military success. The sources offer anecdotes that confirm this general impression. The most striking is the story of the consul Manlius Torquatus and his son during the war with the Latins in the mid-fourth century.[38] The son was challenged, while on patrol, by an enemy commander and killed him in single combat. He brought his spoils back to his father, the commanding general, and was executed for having disobeyed the order not to engage the enemy.[39] The historicity of this event is uncertain, but there are definitely attested incidents of harsh discipline. Scipio Africanus crucified Roman and beheaded Latin deserters at Carthage.[40] The proconsul Fabius Maximus Servilianus, campaigning in Spain in 141, had the hands of a group of deserters cut off as an object lesson to the rest of his troops.[41]

These examples could be multiplied; nevertheless, they should be viewed with caution. They have an exemplary purpose and focus on the exceptional. The number of mutinies recorded in the sources should be a warning not to take the severity portrayed in the sources as normal or frequent. Discounting the numerous mutinies connected with the struggle between plebeians and patricians, all later periods of Republican history include mutinies of various types. In 206, a major mutiny broke out in Spain among the soldiers of Scipio Africanus. In this case, the grievance at issue was the lateness of the men's pay and what the soldiers felt was an inadequate distribution of booty. When their officers refused to join the rank and file in revolt, they were driven from the camp. Scipio finally restored order among the 8,000 troops, but did execute 35 ringleaders.[42] In 47, Caesar had issued marching orders to his Gallic legions, who were stationed in Campania, to prepare for a crossing to Africa to fight the Pompeians. Instead, his troops marched on Rome to demand back pay, discharges, and promised bonuses. The sources stress the force of Caesar's personality. He assembled the mutineers and merely by addressing them as fellow citizens – instead of as fellow soldiers – ended the mutiny.[43] The truth is less flattering to Caesar. Caesar faced a situation in which he had to attack the Pompeians in Africa with all the forces at his disposal; despite this, as a result of the mutiny, he was forced to discharge four of the legions with pay and awards of land, and the other five accompanied Caesar to Africa and were later discharged with substantially higher pay. No soldier was punished in 47. The next year, when Caesar was in a far stronger position, five of the ringleaders were executed.[44] Both the harsh punishments and the apparent clemency of these anecdotes support the view that there was no written code of military justice, but rather a set of customary rules. Much depended on the character of the general in whom the power to punish was vested. This is supported by a situation that is often noted in the sources. The portrayal of an effective general is often highlighted by his arrival at his post to find a situation of lax discipline. For instance, after two years of unsuccessful fighting with Jugurtha, Metellus, now in command, arrived to find Roman forces:

> *Dispirited and unwarlike, incapable of encountering either danger or fatigue; more ready with the tongue than with the sword; accustomed to plunder our allies, while it was the prey of the enemy; unchecked by discipline, and void of all regard to its character.*[45]

Sallust praises his restoration of the traditional discipline, which allowed the army to face the enemy with confidence. The theme of the restoration of discipline as the mark of an excellent commander continued with the army of the emperors. This seems to have been especially true of legions stationed in the East.[46]

The ultimate responsibility for discipline in an army rested on the commanding general. It was inherent in the *imperium* that gave him the power to command. If a consul or praetor, it was simply an extension of the power that allowed him to perform his magisterial duties. If the commander was a promagistrate, it was based on a special grant of *imperium* that accompanied the prolongation of his responsibilities after his year in office. The power of the commander to punish had its foundation in magisterial power. The soldiers as citizens had voted for war and elected the magistrates who led them. The fact that the soldiers still regarded themselves as citizens, even in the army, is clear from an incident during the Second Punic War. After both Scipios had been killed in 211, the remnants of their army retreated north to the Ebro River. They then elected a Roman knight, Lucius Marcius, as their general, conferring *imperium* as the centuriate assembly would have in Rome.[47] The basic difference between normal actions of a magistrate and a general was the extent of the general's power. Until the second century, the right of a commander to inflict punishments appears to have been unlimited. In civilian life, the same magistrate was limited by laws that allowed appeal to the popular assembly in the case of serious crimes. In addition, a further significant difference from civilian justice was the ability of the general to inflict collective punishments on units. This was never allowed in civilian penalties. It is important to note that officers were subject to the same penalties as legionaries and this may have helped persuade legionaries to acquiesce in harsh punishments for themselves.

The military tribunes administered justice among the rank and file, including the imposition of fines, and the infliction of beatings, as well as death sentences. They tried those accused of wrongdoing and decided on appropriate punishments, if they were found guilty. In the case of allied or auxiliary troops serving with the army, the role of the tribune was taken over by the prefects of the allies. The punishment of officers was vested in the commanding general. Those below the rank of tribunes, the centurions and their junior officers exercised disciplinary authority, but did not administer justice. They seem to have carried out the punishments ordered by the tribunes. Unlike the case in a modern army, imprisonment was not a punishment. Prisons existed, but they seem to have been used for detention before a penalty was exacted.

Although there were standard punishments, the rules allowed for flexibility. There were mitigating factors such as length of service, prior conduct and personal character. These factors, in conjunction with the type of offence, affected the severity and type of punishment inflicted.

Penalties can be divided into two general categories depending on whether the offence was committed by an individual or a group. Individual offences included disobedience, cowardice or desertion, theft in camp, falling asleep on guard duty or losing the password while on guard. Collective offences normally included cowardice of a unit and its refusal to obey orders. In these cases, the Romans imposed punishment on the whole unit, including those who were not guilty. For instance, because of their behaviour at Cannae, the surviving legionaries were given barley instead of wheat for a period of seven years and suffered from other disabilities as well.[48] Perhaps the most famous of Roman collective penalties is that of decimation: if a unit retreated in battle without permission, a tribune selected by lot one-tenth of the unit and these men were beaten to death by their fellow soldiers.[49] In 71, Marcus Crassus decimated 500 soldiers who had fled from a battle with the slave army of Spartacus.[50] Such punishments seem to have been designed to create a situation in which the members of the unit policed each others' behaviour.

This system of punishments appears to have endured, but underwent modification after the end of the Republic. The development of a professional army was the most important agent of change. Demotion was now a much more effective punishment as well as loss of pay or of a retirement bonus. Collective punishments like decimation generally disappeared. Too much time and effort had been invested in training and equipping the soldiers to allow the investment to be lost, except in extreme circumstances. What did not change was the centrality of the concept of discipline as the key to Roman success. Writing at the end of the fourth century, Vegetius' opening section of his handbook on military affairs focuses on discipline as one of the keys in Roman success:

> *By no other means, do we see that the Roman people conquered the world than through training in arms, the discipline of the camp and constant practice of the arts of war.*[51]

Another Carrot: Booty

War in the ancient world was as much an economic as a political and social activity. For instance, in Celtic society aristocratic status and power depended on an aristocrat's ability to maintain a large entourage of followers. Some of these were as large as 10,000 men.[52] Crucial to that ability was the raid that rewarded the noble's followers and provided wealth for social display which could be used to attract additional clients. It was one method to quickly amass wealth in a world of low productivity.

The Romans not only carried off plunder, but also confiscated land. In Italy, defeated enemies normally had to forfeit a third of their land. It was a substantial economic blow in a world that depended on agriculture for the production of most of its wealth. The land was either made into public land, assigned to citizens in individual allotments or used for colonies. The practice was later extended to areas outside of Italy. Moveable wealth in the form of precious metal, slaves or other property could be kept in its original form and allotted to officers or troops. Normally, it was sold at auction to the camp followers who trailed along with the army and the proceeds distributed. This was especially necessary when there were large numbers of slaves, such as the 150,000 brought back to Italy by Aemilius Paullus after his victory over Perseus.[53]

The booty of a successful campaign was divided into two parts, the *praeda* ('booty in general') which was what the soldiers had looted and which belonged to them, and *manubiae,* which was the state's portion. In theory, it was public property, but in practice it often became part of the commander's personal property.[54] All of the booty could be assigned to the state's portion, but this was rarely the case. A part of the commander's portion was generally distributed to the troops and a further amount usually deposited in the state treasury. If a commander did not want to alienate his troops who were both fellow citizens and voters, the distribution to the troops was a necessity. In 167, Aemilius Paullus gave his troops smaller sums than they had expected and almost lost his right to triumph as a result.[55] Despite these distributions, the commander often benefitted handsomely.

Although booty was a major source of wealth for commanders, it is only from the second century that we hear of generals launching campaigns for financial gain. Warfare served other functions as well. Roman commanders normally brought along friends, especially young men, who accompanied them to gain experience in military affairs and administration. The custom created social and political bonds with the commander or governor. They were often employed on the recommendation of the commander's peers and could serve to create obligations that might prove to be politically or personally useful. It was on Cicero's recommendation that Caesar found a position for a young jurist Gaius Trebatius, who later followed Caesar in the civil war and tried to convince Cicero to do so as well.[56]

Buildings and other monuments were constructed out of the proceeds of a successful campaign to memorialize the victor's success and his family. In 146, after the end of the fourth and final Macedonian War, the victor Caecilius Metellus built two temples from the proceeds of the booty: one to Juno and another to Jupiter in the Campus Martius. Marcus Fulvius

Nobilior, proconsul in Greece in 187, built a temple of Hercules and the Muses after his victory over the Aetolians.[57] In 196, Lucius Sertinius, who had been proconsul the year before, set up the earliest known triumphal arch to commemorate his successes in Spain.[58]

Its presence in a triumph was an advertisement of the commander's success and enhanced his prestige. Livy in his description of the triumph of Papirius Cursor as consul in 293 mentions the crowd's assessment of the wealth displayed and their comparison of it with the display of wealth in other triumphs.[59]

Booty was a major incentive for soldiers. It explains the contrast between the ease with which troops were levied for the wars in the East and the resistance to the draft for service in Spain.[60] Although they had no legal right to booty soldiers had a reasonable expectation that they would receive a portion of it, in addition to what they had plundered on their own. The desire for booty could be so strong that it overcame military discipline and endangered the safety of the troops. In 52, during the Gallic rebellion against Roman domination, Caesar warned his legates not to allow their men to disperse in search of plunder.[61] The orders were disobeyed and the men suffered as a consequence. In the great battle fought at Telamon in Etruria in 225, the Romans were intimated by the size and appearance of the enemy, but when they saw the gold ornaments that the Gauls wore, their enthusiasm for battle soared.[62]

By the 170s and except for a short time from 130–115, land distributions in Italy ceased and when land became available it was increasingly directed to relieving the problems of citizenry as a whole. Although by the end of the second century, soldiers had begun to be given land overseas, the place of land grants was taken by the distribution of cash bonuses, which the Romans called donatives.[63] In the course of the second century, the amount distributed to the troops gradually increased. The distribution was normally double the soldier's annual pay. It was even more important for centurions and other lower grade officers whose normal pay was a multiple of the legionaries'.[64]

Of course there were additional motives for fighting beyond the financial ones, including patriotism and the attractions – especially for young men – of danger and adventure. In addition, even for the ordinary soldier there was the possibility of increased social prestige. Polybius points this out in his description of the benefits in civilian life of winning a crown:

> *For the recipients of such awards, apart from becoming famous in the army and in civilian life, are specifically marked out in religious processions when they have returned. No one is allowed to wear decorations except those on whom these honours for bravery have been conferred by the consul. In their houses, they hang up the spoils they have won in the most prominent places, considering them a sign and evidence of their courage.[65]*

Polybius describes a procedure for gathering booty that the Romans employed after the capture of a city, in this case New Carthage in 209:

> The following is a description of the Roman procedure for dealing with booty employed after the capture of cities. When this happens, sometimes a contingent of soldiers from each maniple, and at other times a number of maniples, in accordance with the size of the city are detailed for this task; at any rate, they never assign more than half of the army to this duty. The rest of the force remains under arms and keeps watch sometimes outside, sometimes inside the city as dictated by the danger involved. The force is, for the most part, divided into two Roman legions and two allied units. On rare occasions, they assemble a force of four legions. All of the men assigned to this mission carry back to each legion the plunder allotted to it. After the sale of the spoils, the military tribunes give an equal share to all, not only to those on guard duties, but also to the men guarding the tents, to the sick and to those absent on some special assignment. No one steals any of the booty, but they keep the oath that all swear when they first assembled and were about to march out to war.[66]

Polybius' picture is obviously idealized. In practice, the procedure was far more variable and the soldiers less principled. In particularly difficult sieges, where the loss of life would have been greater than in open battle, commanders could and did let their troops into a conquered city to plunder and kill until they were satisfied. Scipio did this after the sack of New Carthage in 209. In general, the armies of the Republic were far more unrestrained and savage in their violence than their Hellenistic contemporaries. Livy mentions that the wars in the East against Philip V and Antiochus III had made soldiers rich. This could only have happened if soldiers kept booty for themselves. If the donatives mentioned earlier are any indication of the scale of booty they would have received from their commander, then the way to riches was to keep as much as one could for oneself.

Booty also served as an incentive for the Italian allies. The allied cities could use it to recoup some of the costs of supplying their troops, and it was an incentive for the allied soldiers in the same way as it was for the Romans. Moveable booty was more important to them as they could not join in the land distributions given to Roman citizens. The allies had no legal claim to the booty, but the Romans were well aware of its value in helping to hold the alliance together. The sources are not clear on the amount of booty that the allies received, but the little evidence that we have points to the soldiers receiving about the same amounts as their Roman comrades.

The Army of the Empire[67]

The assassination of Caesar, in March 44, served as the prelude to the final round of civil war which was only concluded by the victory of his adopted son and heir Augustus (C. Iulius Caesar Octavianus) at Actium in western

Greece in early September 31. Antony and Cleopatra fled to Egypt, pursued there by the victor and were to both perish in the following year. The military power that had been fragmented after Caesar's death was now united in the hands of one man.

The civil war had witnessed the mobilization of manpower on a scale without precedent. It has been estimated that approximately 250,000 Italians served in the armies of the period. A force of this size was neither desirable nor financially sustainable, and Augustus discharged perhaps 80,000 from service by 29. As he had after his victory over Sextus Pompeius at Naulochus, Augustus attempted to disrupt existing property relations as little as possible, and the need to find sufficient funds to buy land caused delay. His veterans wanted land and the mutiny of troops sent back to Italy in 30 is evidence of their impatience. Finally, the conquest of Egypt and the enormous booty it generated allowed the demobilization to proceed. Veterans were settled in both Italy and provinces in various phases over an extended period of time. In total the sources claim that twenty-eight colonies were founded, probably mostly between 30–14. Increasingly the colonies were overseas; they were established in Pisidia in Asia Minor, Spain, Sicily and Gaul. The sixty legions in service at Actium were reduced to twenty-six legions with two more added in 25 when Galatia became a province. Twenty-eight legions remained the standard number until the catastrophic loss of three legions in AD 9, which were not replaced.

These demobilizations allowed Augustus to undertake a radical reform of Rome's army. Despite the growing number of men who chose to make an army career, the majority of soldiers during the civil war period had been raised through the traditional levy and sought a return to civilian life as soon as they possibly could. It is of some significance that in the demobilization of troops after the victory over Brutus and Cassius at Philippi in October 42, of the 44,000 men offered discharge only 8,000 chose to remain in service. These demobilizations formed a background to a radical reform, the creation of a long-service professional army to replace the traditional system.

This change was not carried out abruptly, but was the culmination of a process that had its roots in Caesar's army and in the formations of the civil war period. Caesar's legions had seen long service in Gaul and during 49–44 most had been disbanded as was normally done in the Republic after their term of service had expired. However, long service and a network of personal ties and economic interest bound his veterans together so that in the months after his death, Octavian and Antony were able to reconstitute many of the Caesarean legions from these veterans and many of these legions continued in existence for the next 200 years.

The transition to a fully professional army was carried out in a relatively short time. Though direct evidence for Augustus' reasons for instituting this change is lacking, a number of plausible reasons can be suggested. First, Augustus' power rested on his control of Rome's armies. In the late Republic, it had been the ability of competing aristocrats to mobilize military force against each other and the senate that had destroyed the state. The retention of soldiers in service for most of their working lives would allow the emperor to construct close and lasting ties of patronage which would allow the emperor to monopolize military patronage. These ties consisted of a nexus of material and emotional links between the emperor and his soldiers. In his account of his own achievements, Augustus specifies at length the vast sums he spent to buy land for and to pay bonuses to discharged soldiers. In AD 6, he was instrumental in setting up and funding a new military treasury that provided discharge bonuses. It furnished a powerful incentive for the troops to remain in service and to maintain their loyalty to the ruling dynasty. These monetary ties were further enhanced by the distribution of money bonuses and gifts during service. Further, though the level of army pay was hardly generous, for the majority of recruits who came from a background of rural poverty, military service at least offered a steady wage, food and medical attention when needed, with the prospect of a substantial bonus at the end of service which would enable them to buy farmland. Soldiers also enjoyed special privileges in making wills and in property transactions.

An additional factor in developing bonds between the emperor and his troops was the monopolization of military glory by the emperor. From 38, Augustus officially bore the title of the victorious general, *imperator,* as part of his name. Numerous public monuments constructed at Rome and in the cities of the empire celebrated his military victories. The acclamation and the triumph became imperial monopolies in the course of Augustus' reign. The last triumph celebrated by an individual outside of the Imperial family was that of Cornelius Balbus for his victory over the tribe of the Garamantes in North Africa in 19. The soldiers' oath, that during the Republic had been given to his commander at the commencement of service, was now sworn only to the emperor and renewed annually on 3 January each year. Imperial images appeared along with the standards in legionary shrines, and legions and other units received titles and emblems with Imperial titles. For instance, the legion stationed in the province of Africa was the III Augusta. In AD 69, legions in upper Germany showed their displeasure with a new emperor by stoning his images.[68] Such ties could only be created with a standing military force.

The other advantage that a standing army offered the emperor was the opportunity to remove the army from politics. It had been the link between the political struggles of the elite and interests of Rome's citizen soldiers that had led to the destruction of the Republic. The institution of a standing army whose benefits were guaranteed by the emperor was crucial in breaking the link to political infighting. It severed the ties of self-interest which had bound politicians and the armies of the Republic. A further factor of importance was the stationing of the army away from the political centre on the borders of the empire, which made it less susceptible to manipulation by politicians at Rome.

Augustus devised a system that would guarantee that he retained direct control over these forces through a seemingly Republican device. In 23, the Senate granted him the province of Spain, Gaul and Syria for ten years with a proconsular *imperium* greater than other governors, and which allowed him to interfere in other provinces as he saw fit. He ruled his provinces through a series of deputies, the *legati Augusti propraetore,* who were directly responsible to him. This command contained the majority of the empire's armed forces. For most of his reign, the emperor retained direct control over all military forces, except for the single legion under the senatorial governor of Africa.

The professionalization of the legions was also extended to Rome's auxiliary forces. A large number of auxiliary units, both tribal and supplied by various client kings, had fought in the civil war. A level of professionalization was already evident during the civil war with named units recorded as serving overseas for extended periods. Although, many of these units were disbanded at the end of fighting, the Gallic and Spanish cavalry were retained and are mentioned under Augustus as serving in various parts of the empire. Little is known about their conditions of service, but their numbers were substantial. For instance, seventy infantry cohorts and fourteen mounted regiments are on record during the Pannonian rebellion of AD 6–9. The figure of 150,000 auxiliaries attested in the first years of Augustus' successor is evidence for a substantial development of permanent long-term auxiliary units. The use of auxiliaries as garrison troops in the new province of Judaea in AD 6 is a further indication for the permanence of these units.

The necessity of a standing army for the disguised military monarchy that Augustus created is clear, but less obvious is the combination of factors that governed the size of the army. Various scholars have argued that the standing army of approximately 300,000 legionaries and auxiliaries that Augustus created was far too small for its task of further conquests and protecting the existing borders of the empire. Yet in the following 200 years, although the army was occasionally defeated, there were no major external threats; the most serious conflicts were civil wars. It is important to realize that the Augustan army was far larger than the armies of the Republic except during the civil wars; in the mid-first century, the Republic fielded an average of twelve to fourteen legions a year and at the outbreak of the civil war in 49 the total available was twenty-one. So despite the vastly increased size of the empire resulting from the wars under Augustus, his army represented a substantial increase in available military forces, if one includes auxiliary forces roughly equal in numbers to the legions. Finances were the major constraint on the size of the armed forces. The army was by far the most significant state expense, consuming more than 50 per cent of its total income. However, cost alone could not have been the decisive factor. Later emperors were able to increase the number of legions, though there is no evidence that their incomes were substantially higher than Augustus'. Only a minority of the troops ever saw combat, and probably many never engaged in large-scale warfare after the first years of Augustus. This is reflected in the absence of the mobilization of additional troops for the campaigns on the Rhine and Danube during the reign. The only exception seems to have been the great Pannonian revolt of AD 6–9 which severely taxed Imperial financial and manpower resources.[69] This seems to suggest that Imperial defence was not the most important aspect in Augustus' determination of army size. One factor seems to have been of greater importance: a force of this size, loyal to the emperor, was beyond the capacity of any possible internal military challenge to his supremacy and so there was no need to increase the financial burden. The system worked with occasional exceptions for two and a half centuries until changed conditions on Rome's borders overwhelmed the old army. Even in such a situation, the state was powerful and flexible enough to create a new and very different army that allowed a refashioned empire to survive for another millennium.[70]

NOTES

Introduction

1. The readiness of the Romans to acknowledge borrowing of both tactics and weapons from their enemies is evident in a collection of anecdotes written in Greek. The anecdote (*Ineditum Vaticanum* 3) is presented as a dialogue between a Roman named Kaeso, probably a member of the powerful Fabian clan, and an unknown Carthaginian on the eve of the First Punic War. The historical accuracy of the material is questionable, but the anecdote makes clear the readiness of the Romans to learn from their opponents. Kaeso says, 'Our nature is such that (I will only mention examples that are beyond dispute, so that you can report it to your city) we engage our enemies on their own terms and we have as far as foreign methods go, surpassed those who have had long experience in them.'

2. For the Roman alliance system see p.138.

3. For a discussion see A. M. Eckstein, *Rome enters the Greek East: From Anarchy to Hierarchy in the Hellenistic Mediterranean, 230–170 BC,* Blackwell (Malden, MA, 2008) p.8.

4. M. M. Austin, 'Hellenistic Kings, War and the Economy', *Classical Quarterly* 38 (1986) pp.457–460.

5. Not necessarily in acquiring territory, but rather in extending its influence and its ability to compel other states to follow its dictates.

6. *Res Gestae* 13.

7. There is a possibility that there were more years of peace than Augustus admits. S. Oakley, 'The Roman Conquest of Italy', in J. Rich and G. Shipley (eds.) *War and Society in the Roman World,* Routledge (London and New York, 2002) pp.14–16 has shown that there were several periods of peace but that after 440 an almost yearly pattern of warfare developed.

8. Caesar, *The Gallic War* 5.41.

9. On Sallust's political views see D. C. Earl, *The Political Thought of Sallust,* Cambridge University Press (Cambridge, 1961). For the war against Jugurtha see the short account in H. H. Scullard, *From the Gracchi to Nero,* Routledge (Abingdon, 2011) pp.39–47.

10. Sallust, *The War against Jugurtha* 41.

11. R. I. Frank, 'The Dangers of Peace', *Prudentia* 8 (1976) pp.1–7 and C. A. Barton, 'The Price of Peace in Ancient Rome', in K. A. Raaflaub, (ed.) *War and Peace in the Ancient World,* Blackwell Publishing (Malden, MA, 2007) pp.245–255.

12. The ten years were served either in the cavalry or as a military tribune attached in a legion. For a concise account of the military tribunate see Michael M. Sage, *The Republican Roman Army: A Sourcebook,* Routledge

(New York and London, 2008) pp.104–106. For a detailed discussion, J. Suolahti, *The Junior Officers of the Roman Army in the Republican Period, Suomalainen Tiedeakatemia,* (Helsinki, 1955) pp.35–57.

13. H. Beck, A. Dupla, M. Jehne, and F.P. Pina (eds.) *Consuls and Res Publica: Holding High Office in the Roman Republic,* Cambridge University Press (Cambridge, 2011) pp.1–16.

14. Appian, *The Spanish Wars* 49.

15. N. Rosenstein, *Imperatores Victi (Military Defeat and Aristocratic Competition in the Middle and Late Republic,* University of California Press (Berkeley, 1990) has argued that military defeat was no impediment to holding future office. This counterintuitive argument has been successfully challenged by J. Rich, 'Roman attitudes to defeat in battle under the Republic', in Simon, F. M, Polo, Francisco Pina and Rodriguez, J. R. (eds.) *Vae Victis! Perdedores En El Mundo Antiguo,* Collecció Instrumenta, 14. Barcelona: Universidad de Barcelona, (2012) pp.83–111.

16. For Caesar's departure for his governorship, see Suetonius, *Caesar* 18.1.

17. Suetonius, Caesar 24.1 and M. M. Sage, *Roman Conquests: Gaul,* Pen & Sword Military (Barnsley, 2011) p.64.

18. For the authority of the general over booty see I. Shatzman, 'The Roman General's Authority over Booty', *Historia* 21 (1972) pp.177–205. The most striking example of the display of booty in a triumph was Pompey's triumph of 61. For discussion of it and its significance see M. Beard, *The Roman Triumph,* Belknap Press of Harvard University (Cambridge, MA and London, 2007) pp.7–41.

19. They are first attested in 212 and then subject to a charge of fraud in connection with the delivery of supplies to the Roman armies in Spain in 210 see Livy, *History of Rome* 24.18.1–3, 10–11 and 25.3.10.

20. These small scale merchants along with prostitutes are mentioned in connection with the armies of the late Republic. There is no reason to doubt that they were present from the earliest period that Roman armies began to operate at some distance from the city. Since they were generally unarmed they were especially vulnerable to attack. See Caesar, *The African War* 75.

21. Plutarch, *Pompey* 14.4.

22. Livy, 42.32.6.

23. W. V. Harris, *War and Imperialism in Republican Rome 327–70 B.C.,* Clarendon Press (Oxford, 1984) p.44.

24. For instance, see M. Torelli, 'The Topography and Archaeology of Republican Rome', in N. Rosenstein and R. Morstein-Marx (eds.) *A Companion to the Roman Republic,* Blackwell Publishing (Malden, MA, 2006) pp.87–98.

25. N. Rosenstein, *Rome at War,* University of North Carolina Press (Chapel Hill and London, 2004) p.21.

Chapter 1: The Sources

1. On Livy see T.J. Luce, *Livy. The Composition of his History,* (Princeton, 1977), G. B., Miles, *Livy. Reconstructing Early Rome,* (Ithaca and London 1995) and G. Forsythe, *Livy and Early Rome: A Study in Historical Method and Judgement,* Historia Einzelschriften 132 (Stuttgart, 1999).

2. E. Gabba, *Dionysius and the History of Archaic Rome*, Sather Classical Lectures 56, University of California Press (Berkeley and Los Angeles, 1991). F. Walbank, *Polybius, Rome and the Hellenistic World*, Cambridge University Press (Cambridge, 2002).

3. E. Rawson, 'The Literary Sources for the Pre-Marian Army', *Papers of the British School at Rome* 39 (1971) p.27.

4. See K. Sacks, *Diodorus Siculus and the First Century*, Princeton University Press (Princeton, 1990).

5. On the Roman annalists see G. Forsythe, *A Critical History of Early Rome*, University of California Press. (Berkeley and Los Angeles, 2005) pp.60–64.

6. On Timaeus see F. W. Walbank, *Polybius, Rome and the Hellenistic World*, pp.165–177.

7. See F. W. Walbank, *Polybius, Rome and the Hellenistic World* (Cambridge, 2002).

8. D. Magnino and K-L, Elvers. 'Appianus', in H. Cancik and H. Brill's New Pauly Antiquity volumes edited by H. Cancik and H. Schneider, Brill Online 2016.

9. See M. Griffin (ed.), *A Companion to Julius Caesar*, Wiley-Blackwell (Chichester, 2009).

10. M. M. Sage, *Roman Conquests: Gaul*, Pen & Sword Military (Barnsley, 2011) p.27.

11. *Letters to his Friends* 5.12.10.

12. For Sallust see R. Syme, *Sallust*, Sather Classical Lectures, University of California Press (Berkeley, 1964).

13. E. Rawson, *Intellectual life in the late Roman Republic*, Johns Hopkins University Press (Baltimore, 1985).

14. See H. I. Flowers, *Roman Republics*, Princeton University Press (Princeton, 2010).

15. See B. Campbell, 'Teach Yourself to be a General', *Journal of Roman Studies* 77 (1987) 13–29.

16. Vegetius' *On Military Matters* dates from the end of the fourth century and the authorship and date of the manual ascribed to the Emperor Maurice's are uncertain. It may have been written anywhere from the sixth to the ninth centuries.

17. A. Degrassi, *Fasti Anni et Elogia Inscriptiones Italiae*, vol. 13.2) (Rome 1963).

18. On the Fasti, see R. M. Ogilvie and A. Drummond, 'The Sources for Early Roman History', in F. W. Walbank, et al., *The Cambridge Ancient History, Vol. VII, 2*, Cambridge University Press (Cambridge, 1989) pp.11–15.

19. T. J. Cornell and K. Lomas (eds.) *Urban Society in Roman Italy*, University College Press (London, 1995) p.125 and S. P. A. Oakley, *A Commentary on Livy Books VI-X* vol. I, Clarendon Press (Oxford, 1997) p.346.

20. M.J. Dobson, *The Army of the Roman Republic: Polybius and the Camps at Numantia Spain*, Oxbow Books (2007).

Chapter 2: The Army of the Kings

1. T. J. Cornell, *The Beginnings of Rome*, Routledge (London, 1995) pp. 259–260.

2. M. Torelli, 'Archaic Rome between Latium and Etruria,' in F. W. Walbank et al., *The Cambridge Ancient History* vol. 7.2, Cambridge University Press (Cambridge, 1989) p.36.

3. Vesta was the goddess of the hearth and home and played an important role in family life. The Regia was probably part of a royal residence. After the expulsion of the kings it served as the residence of the *rex sacrorum* ('king of sacrifices') and then the *pontifex maximus* who was the chief priest of the Roman state religion.

4. G. Forsythe, *A Critical History of Early Rome,* University of California Press (Berkeley and Los Angeles, 2005) pp.86–91.

5. See C. J. Smith, *Early Rome and Latium: Economy and Society (1000–500 BC),* Oxford University Press (Oxford, 1996) pp.86–100.

6. For early Greek practice see H. Wees, *Greek Warfare Myth and Realities,* Duckworth (London, 2004) p.58.

7. The *tribuni* survived in a cult, participating in the Salian festival celebrated on 19 March, which had military overtones. See R. M. Ogilvie, *A Commentary on Livy Books 1–5,* Clarendon Press (Oxford, 1965; reprinted with addenda, 1970) p.83.

8. T. J. Cornell, op. cit. p.294.

9. See J. Keegan,*The Face of Battle,* Viking Press (New York, 1976) pp.221–222.

10. Livy, *History of Rome 1.37,* Dionysius of Halicarnassus, *Roman Antiquities* 3.51.

11. Dionysius, *Roman Antiquities* 3.65.6. Tarquinius Priscus made his nephew Arruns commander of the Etruscan auxiliaries in a battle against the Sabines.

12. Livy, *History of Rome* 1.54.4.

13. For a thorough discussion of the *gens,* see C. J. Smith, *The Roman Clan,* Cambridge University Press (Cambridge, 2006).

14. For a good short summary of the background to the problem see T. J. Cornell, op. cit. pp.295–298; for a lucid summary of the evidence see P. Erdkamp, 'Army and Society', in N. Rosenstein and R. Morstein-Marx (eds.) *A Companion to the Roman Republic,* Blackwell Publishing (Malden, MA and Oxford, 2006) p.280.

15. For the inscription and interpretation see H. S. Versnel, 'Historical Implications', in *Lapis Satricanus,* C.M. Stibbe, G. Colonna, C. De Simone, and H.S. Versnel (eds.) *Scripta Minora* 5 (The Hague, 1980), pp.97–150.

16. For a typical view of the deleterious effects of wealth see Sallust, *Cataline* 10–12 with J. Ramsey, *Sallust's Bellum Catalinae,* Oxford University Press (Oxford, 2007) p. 84, and Livy, *History of Rome,* Preface 11–12.

17. For a survey of chariot finds see P. F. Stary, *Zur eisenzeitlichen Bewaffnung und Kampfesweise in Mittelitalien ca. 9. bis 6. Jh. v. Chr.,* P. Von Zabern (Mainz, 1981) pp.42–45.

18. T. J. Cornell, op.cit. pp.163–165.

19. The usual dates are 925–500. For a short summary see G. Forsythe, op. cit. pp.25–56.

20. Oakley, S. 'The Roman Conquest of Italy,' in J. Rich and G. Shipley (eds.) *War and Society in the Roman World,* Routledge, (London and New York, 1993) pp.13–14.

21. Livy, *History of Rome* 3.7.1. At 6.12.2-6 expresses amazement that the Aequi and Volsci could be constantly defeated and slaughtered, yet return again in full strength the next year. Livy presents three possible explanations, but misses the true one, which is that the large-scale battles of the sources were in reality raids.

22. T. J. Cornell, op. cit. pp.173–178.
23. The accounts are found at Livy, *History of Rome* 1.42.5-43.10, Dionysius *Roman Antiquities* 4.16-18 and Cicero *On the Republic* 2.47-9.
24. Although the sources for the organization of the classes are mostly in agreement, they are not identical. The weapons of some of the classes differ in Livy and Dionysius. I have used Livy's account for the fourth class. The fifth class is simply the light-armed troops assigned to the legion. The fourth class, although this is less certain, appears also to belong to that category and so the heavy infantry consisted only of the first 3 classes for a total of 120 centuries.
25. It was not until 289 that Rome created special officials concerned with coinage and in 269 the first mint was opened at Rome. But the dates for coining of various denominations are controversial. See W. Scheidel, I. Morris, and R. Saller (eds.) *The Cambridge Economic History of the Greco-Roman World,* Cambridge University Press (Cambridge, 2007) pp.502–503.
26. *Histories* 6.39.12.
27. It is also used to signify a fleet. The basic meaning appears to be a military unit either naval or land-based.
28. N. Rosenstein, 'Phalanges in Rome?' in Garrett, G., Fagan G. C. and Trundle, M. *New Perspectives on Ancient Warfare,* Brill (Leiden and Boston, 2010) pp.289–302 has challenged the view that there was ever a hoplite reform at Rome. I do not think his argument is convincing. He argues that the majority of equipment finds are clearly ceremonial or luxury goods and more closely related to ritual than warfare. That the finds are often of expensive and not very effective equipment is by itself not compelling. There are finds of equipment in Etruria predating the introduction of hoplite equipment that are clearly ceremonial such as a set of shields from Veii, Rome's close neighbour. But similar, if less luxurious equipment was used in warfare. Grave goods are often used for display or as religious tokens, but they often consist of goods used in life and their existence cannot be used to show they had no function in warfare. Rosenstein advances two other equally unconvincing arguments. First, that the Greek phalanx was not totally formed until the fifth century, has already been dealt with, see p.24 above. The second, that there was no event which could produce such a change in this period, is unprovable. There were according to the historical tradition several large-scale battles including Lake Regillus at the beginning of the following century, which might have provided the impetus. More importantly, borrowing of equipment or other cultural traits does not need a specific occasion or event. Proximity will often be effective, but it may be that sixth century Rome was simply keeping up with its peers.
29. H. van Wees, 'The Development of the Hoplite Phalanx: Iconography and Reality in the Seventh Century', in H. Van Wees (ed.) *War and Violence in Ancient Greece,* Duckworth and University Press of Wales (London, 2000) pp.155–156.
30. There is some ancient evidence that the Romans borrowed the hoplite system from Etruria, Diodorus Siculus, *Library of History* 23.2.1-2 and *Ineditum Vaticanum* III. These sources are late and are influenced by a Roman motif of borrowing a method of fighting from an enemy and then defeating him with

it. It is far more likely that Rome as well as the remainder of Latium, where other evidence for hoplites has been found, were simply part of the same economic and cultural area.

31. There are suggestions in the sources that the army had been doubled to 6,000 men before Servius Tullius. The doubling of the army is ascribed to several kings including Servius' immediate predecessor Tarquinius Priscus, but the uncertainty of the sources would make it more likely that it was Servius' redefinition of citizenship and the growing population that led to the increase in the number of the soldiers. For this view see T. J. Cornell, op. cit. p.183.

32. T. J. Cornell, op. cit. pp.208–14.

Chapter 3: A Time of Troubles

1. Livy, *History of Rome* 3.44-48.
2. G. Forsythe, *A Critical History of Early Rome* p.149.
3. Livy, *History of Rome* 2.9-14.
4. Tacitus, *Histories* 3.72.
5. Dionysius, *Roman Antiquities* 5.36.1-3.
6. The first year of the Republic is traditionally dated to 509, but other dates appear in the sources. Of the first consuls only Marcus Horatius is authentic. For the powers of the king see p.10. The consuls adopted many elements of the king's insignia, but emphasized their collegiality by sharing the axes that represented the power to inflict capital punishment.
7. Collegiality and limited tenure were common to almost all Roman offices.
8. Recently an argument has been made that magistrates did not possess *imperium* within the *pomerium,* or sacred boundary of the city. They relied on the powers inherent in their office and only used *imperium* in the field. This was certainly true of less senior magistrates who did not possess *imperium*. For this argument see F. K., Drogula, 'Imperium, Potestas, and the Pomerium in the Roman Republic', *Historia* 56 (2007) pp.419–452.
9. This is the well-known thesis of P. Fraccaro, *Opuscula, III, Scritti di Topografia e di Epigrafia.* Vol. I, La Revista Athenaeum (Pavia, 1957) pp.287–292. The major objection to this thesis has been the argument that only the first class of forty centuries constituted the phalanx. But this view is based on a mistaken notion of the development of the Greek phalanx.
10. A tribune in command of a detachment, Livy *History of Rome* 35.5.1; general duties, *Digest of Justinian* 49.16.12.2; crucial role on the battlefield, Polybius, *Histories* 18.26 a tribune plays a decisive role in the battle of Cynoscephalae in 197.
11. T. J. Cornell, *The Beginnings of Rome* p.227 for dictators in other Latin cities.
12. G. Forsythe, *A Critical History of Early Rome* p.150.
13. M Sage, *The Republican Roman Army* p.102
14. C. J. Smith, *The Roman Clan,* Cambridge University Press (Cambridge, 2006) p.260.
15. A. Drummond, 'Rome in the Fifth Century I: The Social and Economic Framework', *Cambridge Ancient History* vol. VII pt. 2 (Cambridge and New York, 1989) pp.130–131.

16. A. Drummond, 'Rome in the Fifth Century: The Social and Economic Framework' in F. W. Walbank, A. E. Astin, M. W. Frederickson (eds.) *The Cambridge Ancient History* vol. 7.2, Cambridge University Press (Cambridge, 1989) pp.130–131.

17. The most sensible discussions are T. J. Cornell, *The Beginnings of Rome* pp.281–283, and J.-C. Richard, 'Les origines de la plèbe romaine', *Bulletin d'école française de Rome* 232 (1978) pp.496–498.

18. W. Broadhead, 'Colonization, Land Distribution, and Veteran Settlement', in P. Erdkamp (ed.) *A Companion to the Roman Army,* Blackwell Publishing (Oxford and Malden, MA, 2007) pp.148–149.

19. T. J. Cornell, *The Beginnings of Rome* pp.192–194.

20. Zonaras, *Epitome* 7.19. A twelfth century AD chronicler who depended heavily on Dio.

21. Livy, *History of Rome* 4.6.5-8.

22. G. Forsythe, *A Critical History of Early Rome* p.236, accepts the military origin of the tribunate, citing the creation of the quaestorship and censorship in the 440s as evidence for a major military reform. This is not convincing. We have no evidence for any reform in this period. What would it have been? Further, when the consulship was revived there was a reversion to two commanders with a potential subordinate commander in the new office of praetor which halved the number of commanders available.

23. *Roman Antiquities* 6.10.2.

24. For the battles see Dionysius, *Roman Antiquities* 6.5.4-12.6 and Livy, *History of Rome* 2.19-20.

25. For the text see Dionysius, *Roman Antiquities* 6.95.2.

26. Festus p.276.

27. Festus p.276, under praetor.

28. Livy, *History of Rome* 2.41, and Dionysius, *Roman Antiquities* 4.49.

29. E. T. Salmon, *The Making of Roman Italy,* Thames and Hudson (London, 1982) pp.7–8.

30. 9.13.7. See F. Braudel, *The Mediterranean and the Mediterranean World in the Age of Philip II,* vol I, Harper and Row (New York, 1972) p.66, and S. Oakley, 'The Roman Conquest of Italy' in J. Rich and G. Shipley (eds.) *War and Society in the Roman World,* Routledge (London and New York, 1993) p.13.

31. A. Eckstein, *Mediterranean Anarchy, Interstate War, and the Rise of Rome,* University of California Press (Berkeley and Los Angeles, 2005) pp.139–140.

32. 6.12.2-6.

33. J. W. Rich, 'Warfare and the Army in Early Rome', in Erdkamp, P. (ed.), *A Companion to the Roman Army,* Blackwell (Oxford and Malden, MA, 2007) p.13.

34. Livy, *History of Rome* 1.17-20. Numa is portrayed as the peaceful opposite to the warlike Romulus. He is said to have been the founder of many of the religious institutions of the city. Ancus Marcius the fourth king is said to have been of Sabine background as well.

35. Dionysius, *Roman Antiquities* 2.37.

36. Livy, *History of Rome* 3.15, and Dionysius, *Roman Antiquities* 10.14-16.

37. Livy, *Periochae* 11 and on Dentatus M. Jehne, 'The Rise of the Consular as A Social Type in the Third and Second Centuries BC' in H. Beck, A. Duplà, M.

Jehne and F. P. Polo (eds.), *Consuls and the Res Publica,* Cambridge University Press (Cambridge, 2011) p.219.

38. On the triumph see pp.263–265.
39. Livy, 3.26-29 and Dionysius RA 10.23-25.
40. Livy 3.26.7 sums up the exemplary nature of dictator and provides an insight into Roman aristocracy values: 'What followed merits the attention of those who disdain all human qualities except for wealth, and think there is no room for great honours or worth except amidst a profusion of it.'
    H. W. Litchfield, 'National Exempla Virtutis in Roman Literature', *Harvard Studies* 25 (1914) pp.1–71, especially pp.1–7 and D. C. Urban, 'The Use of Exempla from Cicero to Pliny the Younger' (2011). Publicly Accessible Penn Dissertations, Paper 591, http://repository.upenn.edu/edissertations/591.
41. For Sallust see p.ix.
42. Livy 4.26.4-7.
43. Diodorus Siculus, writing in the middle of the first century, has an anecdote about the battle that centres on the relationship of the dictator and his son. The son leaped out from the battle line that his father had established and was then executed by his father for disobedience. Diodorus and Livy express disbelief about the dictator's execution of his own son. There is a later and more widespread version of the same story told of one of the consuls of 340, Titus Manlius Torquatus. It seems likely that both stem from independent family traditions. This passage has been used as evidence for the use of the hoplite army whose success depended on keeping position in battle. However, such an interpretation is hardly compelling. At base these are examples of appropriate behaviour between fathers and sons; at the core of each is the moral imperative to place duty to one's own country above family obligations. Support for this view is visible in the fact that both commanders are successful in serious battles that have momentous consequences for the community. There is nothing to link the Tubertus episode with the use of a hoplite formation. Any mass formation requires some form of order and the Romans presumably used ordered formations before they adopted the phalanx as they did after they discarded it.
44. Livy 2.39 and Dionysius, RA 8.14-36, see *Cambridge Ancient History* VII.2 (1989) p.288.
45. T. J., Cornell, 'Coriolanus: Myth, History and Performance', in Braund, D. and Gill, C. (eds.) *Myth, History and Performance,* University of Exeter Press (Exeter, 2003) pp.73–97.
46. Livy 4.38
47. R. M. Ogilvie, *A Commentary on Livy, Books 1–5* (Oxford, 1965) p.282 argues that the battle is family legend though it is not clear what family he means. He admits the reality of the redeeming figure of Sextus Tampanius, who in Livy's account gallantly tries to retrieve the Roman defeat but fails. See T. J. Cornell, op. cit. p.291.
48. T. J. Cornell, *The Beginnings of Rome,* p.308.
49. Livy 2.2-3, Diodorus Siculus 14.117.1-3 and Plutarch, Camillus 33.1-35.1.
50. J. Black, *European Warfare 1494–1660,* Routledge (London and New York, 2002) pp.7–13.

51. *On the Agrarian law*, 2.73.
52. G. Bradley, 'The Nature of Roman Strategy in Mid-Republican Colonization and Road Building', in T. D. Stek and J. Pelgrom (eds.), *Roman Republican Colonization: New Perspectives from Archaeology and Ancient History,* Papers of the Royal Netherlands Institute 62 (2014) p.61.
53. *History of Rome* 4.11.3.
54. It has been suggested that the gap was the result of deteriorating relations between Rome and its Latin allies, see S. Oakley, *The Roman Conquest of Italy,* p.19.
55. M. Pallotino, *Histoire de la première Italie,* Fré (Strasbourg, 1993) pp.63–64.
56. M. Torelli, 'Greek Artisans in Etruria: A Problem Concerning the Relationship Between Two Cultures', *Archaeological News* 5 (1976) pp.136–138. For recent archaeological progress in research on urbanization in Etruria see S. Steingraber, 'The Process of the Urbanization of Etruscan Settlements from the Late Villanovan to the Late Archaic Period (End of the Eighth to the Beginning of the Fifth Century B.C.): Presentation of a Project and Preliminary Results', *Etruscan Studies* 8 (2001) pp.7–33.
57. On the Cremera see pp.14–15.
58. G. Forsythe, *A Critical History of Early Rome* for the sources for the second war.
59. T. J. Cornell, *The Beginnings of Rome,* p.313.
60. Ironically, terracotta statuettes from Veii of Aeneas (the Romans' ancestor) carrying Anchises from the burning ruins of Troy, were formerly dated to the sixth or fifth century, but are now seen as possibly belong to the fourth or third century.
61. 4.58.
62. 5.19.1.
63. M. Beard, *The Roman Triumph,* Belknap Press (Cambridge, MA and London, 2007) passim.
64. Livy 6.9.4.
65. 5.21.1-4.
66. On the rite see R. M. Ogilvie, *Commentary on Livy Books 1 to 5,* Clarendon Press (Oxford, 1965) pp.672–673.
67. See S. H. Rutledge, 'The Roman Destruction of Sacred Sites,' *Historia* 56 (2007) pp.180 and 191 n.50.
68. Livy 5.22.1. See G. Forsythe, *A Critical History of Early Rome* p.250.
69. W. V, Harris, 'Roman Warfare in the Economic and Social Context of the 4th Century BC', in W. Eder (ed.), *Staat und Staatlichkeit in der frühen römischen Republik,* F. Steiner (Stuttgart, 1990) pp.498–499.
70. K. Bradley, *Slavery and Society at Rome* (Cambridge, 1994).
71. H. H. Scullard, *Festivals and Ceremonies of the Roman Republic,* Thames & Hudson (London, 1981) pp.92–95 and 193–194.
72. M. M. Sage, *Warfare in Ancient Greece: A Sourcebook,* Routledge (New York and London, 1996) Introduction pp.xx-xxi.
73. Livy, *History of Rome* 4.59 and Diodorus Siculus, *Library of History* 14.16.5.
74. Livy, *History of Rome* 4.59-60. The pay in unworked, irregular lumps of bronze, which the Romans called *aes rude,* was conveyed to the treasury in carriages according to Livy. The ingots were not coins in the strict sense as their value was determined by their weight. They seem to have been in use

by the mid-fifth century. See M. Pobjoy, 'Epigraphy and Numismatics', in N. Rosenstein and R. Morstein-Marx (eds.) *A Companion to the Roman Republic,* Blackwell (Malden, MA and Oxford 2006) p.64. The Latin word for military pay is *stipendium*.

75. For a further discussion, see pp.51–52.
76. Tacitus, *Annals* 11.24.
77. *Geography* 4.4.2-5.
78. Ibid.
79. 5.30.2
80. D. Rankin, *The Celts and the Classical World,* Routledge (London and New York, 1987) p.209.
81. *Histories* 2.30.8.
82. Caesar, *The Gallic War* 5.19.
83. 5.37. See J. Rich, 'Roman attitudes to defeat in battle under the Republic', in F. M. Simón, F. Pina Polo and J. R. Rodríguez (eds.) *Vae Victis! Perdedores en el Mundo Antiguo,* Instrumenta (Barcelona, 2012) p.97–98.
84. It was also supposedly the date of the defeat at the Cremera (see p.14).
85. A. M. Eckstein, *Mediterranean Anarchy, Interstate War, and the Rise of Rome,* University of California Press (Berkeley and Los Angeles, 2006) p.133.
86. V. Rosenberger, 'The Gallic Disaster', *Classical World* 96 (2003) pp.367–368.

Chapter 4: Recovery and Expansion

1. Livy, *History of Rome* 5.32, R. M. Ogilvie, *A Commentary on Livy* pp.698–699.
2. Livy, *History of Rome* 5.33.1 'Thus was sent into exile the citizen, if anything is certain in human affairs, who would have prevented the capture of the city.'
3. Plutarch, *Camillus* 23.6 and Livy, *History of Rome* 5.43-45.
4. The Greek geographer Strabo, a contemporary of the Emperor Augustus, had a very different version in which it was the people of the Etruscan city of Caere who won this victory when the Gauls were returning north with the ransom, and then returned it to the Romans (*Geography* 5.2.3).
5. This account accepts the arguments of T. J. Cornell, *The Beginnings of Rome* p.318–319 and G. Forsythe, *A Critical History of Early Rome* p.257. Both of these scholars accept the main lines of Livy's account of these years.
6. See P. J. E. Davis, 'The Archaeology of Mid-Republican Rome: The Emergence of a Mediterranean Capital', in J. D. Evans (ed.) *A Companion to the Archaeology of the Roman Republic,* Blackwell, (Oxford and Malden, MA 2013) pp.422–423.
7. See p.43 above and S. P. Oakley, *A Commentary of Livy Books VI–X,* Clarendon Press (Oxford, 1997–98) p.350.
8. See p.33.
9. See pp.60–61.
10. See the convincing arguments of T. J. Cornell, *The Beginnings of Rome* pp.337–8.
11. Livy 7.6.8.
12. C. J. Smith, *The Roman Clan* p.182.
13. Although among the largest Latin cities, they were diminutive in comparison to Rome.
14. Livy, *History of Rome* 7.9-11.

15. On single combat see, S. P. Oakley, 'Single Combat in the Roman Republic', *Classical Quarterly* 35 (1985) pp.392–410 and T. Wiedemann, 'Single Combat and Being Roman', *Ancient Society* 27 (1996) 91–103.
16. Diodorus Siculus, *Library of History* 5.29.
17. *Histories* 6.54.3-4.
18. On the development of the concept of manliness, see M. McDonnell, *Roman Manliness,* Cambridge University Press (Cambridge, 2006).
19. Plutarch, *Marcellus* 7-8.
20. J. W. Rich, 'Augustus and the Spolia Opima', *Chiron* 26 (1976) pp.85–127.
21. Justin, *Epitome* 20.5.4-6. See M. M. Sage, *Warfare in Ancient Greece* pp.198–199.
22. T. J. Cornell, *The Beginnings of Rome* p.324 suggests that this renewal of the treaty between Rome and the Latins was more favourable to Rome than the Cassian treaty had been. In fact, Rome's growing aggressiveness may have compelled the Latins to obtain whatever terms they could. It is not mentioned in the sources but it is possible that these Latins saw the Gauls as potential allies.
23. Polybius, *Histories* 2.18.9.
24. Livy, *History of Rome* 7.15.10.
25. See L. Bonfante, *Etruscan Life and Afterlife: A Handbook of Etruscan Studies,* Wayne State University Press (Detroit, 1986) p.262. Recent archaeological excavations at Tarquinia have yielded evidence for human sacrifice.
26. Pliny, *Natural History* 30.3.12.
27. W. V. Harris, *Rome in Etruria and Umbria,* Oxford University Press (Oxford, 1971) pp.41–48.
28. Livy 8.4.
29. M. McDonnell, *Roman Manliness* p.200 for references and some interesting observations.
30. See last note.
31. For example, Livy, *History of Rome* 10.19.11.
32. Livy, *History of Rome* 7.30.
33. Livy, *History of Rome* 8.11.16.
34. See p.60.
35. T. J. Cornell, *The Beginnings of Rome* p.349.
36. Livy, *History of Rome* 8.17.12.
37. The Romans practised partible inheritance, which distributed the deceased's property to his sons in equal portions. Given birth and death rates it was not unlikely that peasant holdings would after a few generations become too small to carry the requisite census for legionary service. See P. Erdkamp, 'Soldiers, Roman Citizens, and Latin Colonists in Mid-Republican Italy', *Ancient Society* 41 (2011) p.111.
38. J. R. Patterson, 'Rome and Italy', in N. Rosenstein, and R. Morstein-Marx (eds.) *A Companion to the Roman Republic,* Blackwell, (Oxford and Malden, MA, 2006) p.607.
39. R. Laurence, 'Roads and Bridges', in J. D. Evans (ed.) *A Companion to the Archaeology of the Roman Republic,* Wiley-Blackwell (Malden, MA and Oxford, 2013) p.299.
40. The text is at Polybius, *Histories* 3.24. For a discussion see D. Hoyos, *The Carthaginians,* Routledge (London and New York, 2010) p.179.

41. Polybius, *Histories* 3.25.

42. Livy, *History of Rome* 7.10.

43. Oscan was spoken by the peoples of the southern Apennines, the Samnites, Lucanians and Bruttians as well as most of Campania.

44. T. J. Cornell, 'The Conquest of Italy', in *The Cambridge Ancient History* vol. VII, pt. 2 (Cambridge, 1989) p.359.

45. *Geography* 5.3.5.

46. The Opici seem to have been the pre-Oscan population of Campania.

47. P. Connelly, *Greece and Rome at War*, Greenhill Books (London and Mechanicsburg, PA, 1996) pp.107–112.

48. One of the northeastern gates of the city.

49. T. J. Cornell, 'Deconstructing the Samnite Wars: An Essay in Historiography', in H. Jones (ed.), *Samnium. Settlement and Cultural Change*. The Proceedings of the Third E. Togo Salmon conference on Roman studies. Providence, Rhode Island: Center for Old World Archaeology and Art, Brown University. *Archaeologia Transatlantica* 22 (2004) pp.115–131 has recently challenged the idea of separate Samnite wars with the claim that ancients had no such schema. Livy does seem to have seen them as a single conflict that encompassed all of the fighting between Rome and the Samnites. The passage in Livy *History of Rome* 7.29 that it is claimed supports this thesis is less certain support than it seems, since the Samnite conflict is being placed in the same class as the fight against Pyrrhus which was a definite conflict with a limited duration. The point here is that Livy is simply naming what he calls the larger conflicts that Rome had previously fought with no specification of their nature or numbers. As Cornell admits there are hints in other writers that the idea of some sort of division existed for ancient writers.

50. See Florus, *Epitome* 1.16.

51. Livy, *History of Rome* 7.30-31. The speech itself is a composition by Livy since there is no reason to suppose a record of the original speech existed. It was normal for ancient historians to recast even actual speeches in their own style and, in cases where no record survived to have their speakers say what the historians thought was appropriate to the occasion. 343 is far too early for there to have been any record of such a speech. As has been pointed out the speech is reminiscent of a speech in Thucydides the Greek historian of the Peloponnesian War; Thucydides probably served as at least a partial model. On this point see G. Forsythe, *A Critical History of Early Rome* pp.285–286.

52. E. T. Salmon, *Roman Colonization under the Republic*, Cornell University Press (Ithaca, 1970) pp.55–56.

53. Dio, *History of Rome* 60.6.1.

54. Dionysius of Halicarnassus, *Roman Antiquities* 15.6.

55. Livy, *History of Rome* 8.22.

56. Livy, *History of Rome* 8.25.

57. Livy, *History of Rome* 8.23.10-12: 'Since the time for elections was drawing near, and it was not in the public's interest to summon home Publilius, who was threatening the enemy's walls and was expecting to capture their city any day, the Senate persuaded the tribunes that they should bring before the assembly a proposal that when Q. Publilius Philo finished his magistracy, he should conduct operations as proconsul until the defeat of the Greeks.'

58. Livy, *History of Rome* 8.25.
59. Livy, *History of Rome* 8.27.
60. *History of Rome* 8.40.
61. Caesar, *The Gallic War* 1.7.4 records that the Gallic Helvetii had defeated and killed the consul Lucius Cassius Longinus and made his army pass under the yoke in 107.
62. N. Horsfall, 'The Caudine Forks: Topography and Illusion', *Papers of the British School at Rome* 50 (1982) pp.45–52.
63. T. J. Cornell, *The Cambridge Ancient History* vol. VII, pt.2 p.370.
64. Roman writers tried to lessen the shame of the defeat by claiming it was the result of trickery.
65. Livy, *History of Rome* 9.7 and Diodorus Siculus 18.44. The uncertainty about who commands in Livy is worrying. It may point to a fictitious encounter especially with the Samnites.
66. Livy *History of Rome* 9.20.
67. Livy, *Periochae* 9.14.
68. Livy, *History of Rome* 9.20.
69. Livy, *History of Rome* 9.20.
70. Livy, *History of Rome* 9.23 and Diodorus Siculus, *Library of History* 19.73.
71. E. T. Salmon, *Roman Colonization under the Republic* p.58-59.
72. See above p.65.
73. Livy, *History of Rome* 9.44.
74. Livy, *History of Rome* 9.45.
75. Livy, *History of Rome* 9.32 and Diodorus Siculus, *Library of History* 20.35. For the suggestion that it was the central Etruscan cities see T. J. Cornell, *The Beginnings of Rome* p.355. The best discussion of this conflict is W. V. Harris, *Rome in Etruria and Umbria,* Oxford University Press (Oxford, 1971) pp.49–60.
76. Livy, *History of Rome* 9.32. and Diodorus, *Library of History* 20.35.
77. Livy, *History of Rome* 8.25 and 9.20.
78. Livy, *History of Rome* 8.25. A rumour that the Tarentines were going to offer Naples help against the Romans.
79. Livy, *History of Rome* 10.2. Diodorus has a different version of Cleonymus' campaign. He claims that acting in Tarentum's employ, he brought the Lucanians into an alliance with his employers then persuaded the Lucanians to join in attack against Metapontum that led to their surrender. Given later Roman interest in Thurii, Livy's version seems more likely.
80. G. Forsythe, *Critical History of Early Rome* p.327. Livy several times is reduced to reporting alternate accounts of events with no way to decide between them.
81. A. Degrassi, *Inscriptiones Latinae Liberae Rei Publicae,* La Nuova Italia (Florence, 1957) n.309. It is generally thought to date from the early second century. It replaced an earlier inscription.
82. Livy, *History of Rome* 10.4. He received a triumph for his victory.
83. *History* 2.18.1-4.
84. Livy, *History of Rome* 10.12. But other sources give variant details of the campaigns of both consuls of 298.
85. Livy, *History of Rome* 10.15.
86. Livy, *History of Rome* 10.18.
87. Livy, *History of Rome* 10.21.

88. As has been pointed out by P. Sommella, *Antichi campi di battaglia in Italia,* Quaderni Inst. Topograf. University, Roma 3 (Rome, 1967) p.35, various sources offer different lists of those who fought the Romans in the battle. He opts as most scholars rightly do for Livy's combatants. Some of the sources give fantastic figures for the dead of the allied army which would support an immense force. Such exaggeration is not uncommon in ancient writers, but there is no reason to suspect that it was appreciably larger than the Roman force.

89. Livy 10.30. Livy rightly remarks that the absence of the Etruscans and Umbrians was crucial to the Roman victory.

90. Livy 10.27 The citation of legion numbers is striking and would seem to enhance the authenticity of Livy's description.

91. See p.55–6 above.

92. This *devotio* is usually accepted as authentic, see p.63–4 above.

93. Livy, *History of Rome* 10.37.

94. W. V. Harris, *Rome in Etruria and Umbria* p.78.

95. *History of Rome* 10.38.

96. Livy, *History of Rome* 10.38.

97. Livy, *History of Rome* 22.38.

98. Dionysius of Halicarnassus, *Roman Antiquities* 10.18.2.

99. Livy, *Periochae* 11.

100. Velleius Paterculus, *History* 1.14.6-7. See G. Forsythe, *Critical History of Early Rome,* p.335.

101. The transition to the manipular legion will be discussed below.

102. Livy, *History of Rome* 9.30.

103. E. T. Salmon, *Roman Colonization under the Republic* pp.70–81.

104. See p.74 above.

105. For these events see Polybius, *Histories* 2.19.7-13.

106. Polybius, *Histories* 2.20.1-6. There are chronological and other difficulties with the events of 284–282. For an attempt to solve them see G. W. Morgan, 'The Defeat of L Metellus Denter at Arretium', *Classical Quarterly* 22 (1972) pp.309–325.

107. See p.76 above.

108. Dionysius of Halicarnassus, *Roman Antiquities* 19.13 and 16.

109. A. M. Eckstein, *Mediterranean Anarchy: Interstate War and the Rise of Rome,* University of California Press (Berkeley, New York and London, 2006) p.155.

110. A. M. Eckstein, *Mediterranean Anarchy: Interstate War and the Rise of Rome* p.153.

111. See p.75.

112. A famous episode, see Dionysius, *Roman Antiquities* 19.5.1-6.1.

113. H. H. Scullard, *The Elephant in the Greek and Roman World,* Thames and Hudson, (London, 1974) and M. B. Charles and P. Rhodan, '"Magister Elephantorvm": A Reappraisal of Hannibal's Use of Elephants', *Classical World* 100 (2007) pp.363–389.

114. Plutarch, *Life of Pyrrhus* 13.1.

115. Plutarch, *Life of Pyrrhus* 17.4

116. Polybius, *Histories* 9.5 and Livy, *History of Rome* 26.7-11.

117. Also known as Ausculum. Coins minted by the city can be used to justify either name.
118. Polybius, *Histories* 18.28.10.
119. Dionysius, *Roman Antiquities* 20.1.8 provides figures for the forces on both sides, Pyrrhus had 70,000 infantry, while Romans had a force of approximately the same size, of whom 20,000 were Romans. The Romans had 8,000 horse and Pyrrhus slightly more cavalry and 19 elephants. The figures for the cavalry and elephants are acceptable, infantry figures are not. The number 10,000 seems to be based on the assumption of a 4 legion army with a complement of 5,000 men each, which is high, but not impossible; 50,000 allies seems incredible. When we do have figures for Roman armies normally the allies number about the same as the Roman troops or somewhat more but not two and a half times as much. Also there is no hint in Dionysius' account that there was any sizeable disparity between the size of the two forces, so 40,000 on both side is the more acceptable figure.
120. Wheeling or formations opening and riding through each other was the normal practice in antiquity and in later periods, see M. M. Sage, *The Republican Roman Army: A Sourcebook*, Routledge (New York and London, 2008) p.93.
121. See P. R. Franke, 'Pyrrhus' in *The Cambridge Ancient History* vol. VII, pt.2 p.476. Franke's account is the best introduction to Pyrrhus in Italy and Sicily.
122. There is no continuous source for these years. The disparate evidence is collected by T. R. S. Broughton, *The Magistrates of the Roman Republic*, vol. I, American Philological Society (New York, 1951) pp.194–195.
123. P. Lévêque, 'Pyrrhos,' *Bulletin des École Français d'Athènes et de Rome,* fascicule 185 (Paris, 1957) p.525 points out that there is an uncertainty in the sources about whether Beneventum was a defeat for Pyrrhus. Given Pyrrhus' reaction, a defeat – although perhaps not a decisive one – seems the likeliest outcome.
124. Malventum most likely meant 'ill wind' and Beneventum 'good wind'; the terms could also refer to a bad or good arrival. The first set of meanings seems more likely.

Chapter 5: A New Model Army I

1. *Histories* 6.19-42.
2. Ovid, *Fasti* 3.115-117.
3. Polybius, *Histories* 24.1 and Livy, *History of Rome* 8.8 offer a divergent account of the organization of the army. While Polybius has ten maniples per lines for a total of thirty, Livy's legion has fifteen per line for a total of forty-five, and ninety centuries to Polybius' total of sixty centuries. Polybius is certainly right. In no other source is the legion assigned more than sixty centuries. There are also problems in the legion's third line. In Polybius it simply consists of the *triarii,* while Livy has a number of other troops, some of whose titles are real but who most likely are light-armed. Livy's date for the army he is describing 340, is far too early the transition to a full manipular army.
4. E. Rawson, 'The Literary Sources for the Pre-Marian Army', *Papers of the British School at Rome* 39 (1971) p.25.

5. Livy, *History of Rome* 9.32.

6. Livy, *History of Rome* 8.8. 12.

7. *Jewish War* 3.124.

8. Polybius, *Histories* 3. 113.1.

9. 19.2.

10. *Histories* 18.28.1-32.5.

11. For the battle see pp.186–189.

12. Polybius, *Histories* 15.9.7.

13. Polybius, *Histories* 15.14.3.

14. A. M. Eckstein, *Mediterranean Anarchy, Interstate War, and the Rise of Rome* (Berkeley and Los Angeles, 2006) p. 219.

15. For a full treatment see M. McDonnell, *Roman Manliness,* Cambridge University Press (Cambridge and New York, 2006).

16. M. McDonnell, *Roman Manliness* p.2.

17. Plautus, *Amphitruo* 648-653. For the quote and a discussion of it see J. E. Lendon, 'War and Society', in *The Cambridge History of Greek and Roman Warfare* vol. I, Cambridge University Press (Cambridge, 2007) pp.509–516.

18. D. Braund. 'After Alexander: the Emergence of the Hellenistic World 323–281', in A. Erskine, *A Companion to the Hellenistic World,* Blackwell (Malden, MA and Oxford, 2005) p.29.

19. M. M. Austin, 'Hellenistic Kings, War and the Economy', *Classical Quarterly* 36 (1986) pp.457–459.

20. N. Sekunda, *Hellenistic Infantry Reform in the 160s,* Lódz: Oficyna Naukowa (2001). See the important review of the book by P. Beston, *Classical Review* 52 (2002) pp.388–389

21. See p.40 above. It is true that Livy and Dionysius assign the *scutum* to classes II-IV of the Servian army but this is probably not accurate.

22. H. van Wees, 'The Development of the Hoplite Phalanx: Iconography and Reality in the Seventh Century', in H. van Wees, ed., *War and Violence in Ancient Greece* (London, 2000) p.127, admits that the hoplite shield was less suitable for use outside the phalanx, but makes the claim that the wearing of a cuirass would compensate for that. Even if one accepts this, the issue of the cost of such equipment would still remain an issue.

23. R. Ling, *Roman Painting,* Cambridge University Press (Cambridge, 1991) p.10.

24. P. Connolly, *Greece and Rome at War,* Greenhill Books (Westport, CT, 2006) p.131. On the *scutum,* M. Feugère, *Les armes des Romains,* Éditions France (Paris, 1993) p.93. There is also evidence for the spread of the shield to the Hellenistic east Mediterranean. See P. Sabin, H. van Wees and M. Whitby (eds.) *The Cambridge History of Greek and Roman Warfare* vol. I, Cambridge University Press (Cambridge, 2007) p.339ff.

25. Livy, *History of Rome* 9.41.17-19. See also Plutarch, *Marius* 20.1: 'But Marius, sending his officers to all parts of the line, exhorted the soldiers to stand firmly in their lines, and when the enemy had got within reach to hurl their javelins, then take to their swords and crowd the barbarians back with their shields…'

26. M. T. Burns, 'The Homogenisation of Military Equipment Under the Roman Republic', in *Romanization,* Digressus Supplement 1 (2003) p.70.

27. M. T. Burns, 'The Homogenisation of Military Equipment Under the Roman Republic', p.74.

28. P. Connolly, *Greece and Rome at War* p.124 and M. C. Bishop and J. C. N. Coulston, *Roman Military Equipment*, Oxbow Books (Oxford, UK, 2006) pp.65–66. See also P. Connolly, 'The Roman Fighting Technique deduced from Armour and Weaponry', in V. A. Maxfield, and M. J. Dobson (eds.), *Roman Frontier Studies* 1989 (Exeter, 1991) pp.358–360.

29. *Histories* 2.23.

30. Livy, *History of Rome* 9.40 and Polybius, *Histories* 2.22. Unfortunately, no Roman examples of the greave have survived.

31. M. Feugère, *The Arms of the Romans,* p.92.

32. Polybius, *Histories* 1.40.12. The term *pilum* does occur in a speech by a Roman general, before a battle in 295. But the rhetorical context is suspicious.

33. Plutarch, *Marius* 25.1.

34. 29.33.

35. Caesar, *The Gallic War* 1.25.

36. Caesar, *The Civil War* 3.93.5-6.

37. 8.8.

38. A. L. Goldman, 'Weapons and the Army', in J. D. Evans (ed.), *A Companion to the Archaeology of the Roman Republic,* Wiley-Blackwell (Malden, MA and Oxford, UK, 2013) p.133.

39. M. C. Bishop and J. N. C. Coulston, *Roman Military Equipment,* p.56.

40. A. L. Goldman, 'Weapons and the Army' p.133.

41. *History of Rome* 24.48.

42. Polybius, *Histories* 10.20.17. We are much better informed about military training in the Imperial period. The best account is Vegetius, *Epitome of Military Science* 1.11-12.

43. Valerius Maximus, *Memorable Sayings and Deeds* 2.3.2.

44. P. Krentz, 'The Nature of Hoplite Battle', *Classical Antiquity* 4 (1985) p. 54.

45. Polybius, *Histories* 2.33.7. This was against the Gauls in 233. The same technique is mentioned in the battle of Cynoscephalae in 198 against the Macedonians, Polybius, *Histories* 18.8.4.

46. Dionysius of Halicarnassus, *Roman Antiquities* 14.10.17 and Vegetius, *Epitome of Military Science* 1.12.

47. Caesar, *The Civil War* 3.89.

48. See p.149.

49. *Histories* 6.21.9.

50. Livy, *History of Rome* 26.4.

51. *Histories* 6.22.

52. Cicero, *The Brutus* 271.

53. Livy *History of Rome* 31.35.5-6.

54. J. E. Lendon, *Soldiers and Ghosts,* Yale University Press, (New Haven and London, 2005) p.179.

55. Polybius, *Histories* 6.19.1.

56. Livy, *History of Rome* 5.7.5. Livy dates the reform to 403.

57. *Histories* 6.25.

58. See the useful discussion of the question by J. B. McCall, *The Cavalry of the Roman Republic,* Routledge (London and New York, 2002) pp.29–33.

59. Josephus, *The Jewish War* 3.96 and Arrian, *Tactics* 4.7-9.
60. *Indian Wars of Mexico, Canada and the United States 1812–1900,* Routledge (London and New York, 2006) p.56.
61. R. E. Gaebel, *Cavalry Operations in the Ancient Greek World,* University of Oklahoma Press (Norman, OK, 2002) p.11.
62. See in general, P. Sidnell, *Warhorse: Cavalry in Ancient Warfare,* Hambledom Continuum (London and New York, 2006).
63. Dionysius of Halicarnassus, *Roman Antiquities* 20.1.1-2.
64. F. Jacoby, *Die Fragmente der Griechischen Historiker* 839 F1. It is quoted in Diodorus Siculus, *Library of History* 23.2.1 and Athenaeus, *Deipnosophistae* 6.273.
65. *Ineditum Vaticanum* 3, for its text see M. M. Sage, *The Republican Roman Army: A Sourcebook,* Routledge (London and New York, 2008) pp.17–18.
66. Sallust, *Cataline* 51.37-8.
67. D. Briquel, 'La tradition sur l'emprunt d'armes samnites par Rome', in A.-M. Adams and S. Rouveret, *Guerre et sociétés en Italie aux Ve et IVe siècles avant J-C,* Presses de l'Ecole Normale Supérieure (Paris, 1986) p.79.
68. J.B. McCall, *The Cavalry of the Roman Republic,* p.31.
69. See p.54.
70. *History of Rome* 8.8.1.
71. See p.63.
72. It is likely he copied the description of another annalist who was equally ignorant of the manipular formation. See E. Rawson, 'The Literary Sources for the Pre-Marian Army' p.29.
73. Varro, *On the Latin Language* 5.89 is an example.
74. See pp. 49–50 and p.59.
75. 40.4.
76. E. Rawson, 'The Literary Sources for the Pre-Marian Army' pp.24–25 has argued that the reference probably comes from a historical source.
77. E. Rawson, 'The Literary Sources for the Pre-Marian Army' p.24 note 41. For references to cavalry of this type fighting in major battles see M. M. Markle III, 'Use of the Sarissa by Philip and Alexander of Macedon,' *American Journal of Archaeology* 82 (1978) p.492.
78. 21.6.
79. For example Alexander's Illyrian campaign of 335. For it, see Arrian, *Anabasis* 1.2.
80. Livy, *History of Rome* 7.5.9.
81. Livy, *History of Rome* 9.30.3.
82. Orosius, *Against the Pagans* 4.1.3.
83. For a fuller discussion of the levy see pp.119–122.
84. *History of Rome* 7.38. See E. Gabba, 'Instituzione militari e colonizzazione in Roma medio-repubblicana (IV-III sec. AC.)', *Rivista di filologia e di istruzione classica* 103 (1975) pp.147–154.
85. *History of Rome* 7.41-42.
86. See pp.107–108.
87. *Histories* 1.33.9.
88. *Histories* 1.40.10.

89. Livy, *History of Rome* 22.57.12.
90. Livy, *History of Rome* 24.16.7.
91. Livy, *History of Rome* 10.21.3.
92. Cassius Hemina, *Fragment* 21.
93. 151 Livy, *Periochae* 48 and 55, Appian, *The Spanish Wars* 49; 138 Cicero, *Brutus* 85.
94. Valerius Maximus, *Sayings and Deeds of Famous Men* 6.3.4. On the penalties see C. Nicolet, *The World of the Citizen in Republican Rome,* University of California Press (Berkeley, 1980) pp.99–102.
95. Livy, *History of Rome* 24.56.9-13.
96. C. Nicolet, *The World of the Citizen in Republican Rome,* p.100.
97. For a table of census figures between 265 BC and AD 14, see L. De Ligt, 'Roman Manpower and Recruitment during the Middle Republic', in P. Erdkamp (ed.) *A Companion to the Roman Army,* Blackwell (Malden, MA and Oxford, 2007) p.118.
98. The standard work on Roman manpower is P. A. Brunt, *Italian Manpower (225 BC–AD 14),* Oxford University Press (Oxford, 1971). For second century figures and their significance see L. De Ligt, 'Roman Manpower Resources and the Proletarianization of the Roman Army in the Second Century BC', in O. Hekster, G de Kleijn and D. Slootjes (eds.) *Crises and the Roman Empire,* Brill (Leiden and Boston, 2007) pp.167–182.
99. E. Gabba, 'Instituzione militari e colonizzazione', in *Roma medio-repubblicana* p.152.
100. See pp.51–52.
101. On the *tumultus* see p.57 above.
102. P. A Brunt, *Italian Manpower* p.625.
103. E. Rawson, 'The Literary Sources for the Pre-Marian Army' p.14.
104. P. A Brunt, *Italian Manpower* p.628.
105. This account follows Polybius, *Histories* 8.19.5-21.
106. Junior tribunes had five years' prior service, while senior tribunes had ten.
107. See p.118.
108. Appian, *The Spanish Wars* 49.
109. Livy, *History of Rome* 29.13.8.
110. On the formula see D. W. Baronowski, 'The Formula Togatorum', *Historia* 33 (1984) pp.248–252 and P. Erdkamp, 'Soldiers, Roman Citizens, and Latin Colonists in Mid-Republican Italy', *Ancient Society* 41 (2011) pp.119–123 and 133–135.
111. N. Rosenstein, *Rome at War: Farms, Families, and Death in the Middle Republic* (Chapel Hill and London, 2004) pp.20–29.
112. See pp.272–273.
113. See pp.14–15.
114. Livy, *Periochae* 56 and Appian, *Spanish Wars* 84.
115. Livy, *History of Rome* 43.14.2-6.
116. *Histories* 6.21-23.
117. *History of Rome* 10.38.
118. *Roman Antiquities* 10.18.2.
119. *History of Rome* 22.38.1-5.
120. *Histories* 6.33.1-2.

121. *Attic Nights* 16.4.2.
122. On the development of the oath in the Late Republic see A. Keaveney, *The Army in the Roman Revolution,* Routledge (London and New York, 2007) pp.71–76. On the oath of 32 see *The Achievements of the Divine Augustus* 25.2.
123. Tacitus, *Histories* 1.55.

Chapter 6: A New Model Army II

1. See pp.70–71.
2. D. W. Baronowski, 'Roman Military Forces in 225 BC (Polybius 2.23-4)', *Historia* 42 (1993) pp.196–197.
3. For the early use of legates see pp.125–126.
4. *History of Rome* 22.49.15.
5. *History of Rome* 44.182–4.
6. Plutarch, *Caesar* 1.18-2.7 and Suetonius, *Julius Caesar* 4.
7. Appian, *The Mithridatic War* 93 and Velleius Paterculus, *History of Rome* 2.31.
8. Appian, *Civil War* 2.18, Plutarch, *Pompeius* 53.1 and Dio, *History of Rome* 39.39.1-4.
9. Cicero, *Letters to his Friends* 15.6. This is a letter to Cato attempting to justify the award of a triumph for his victory.
10. *Histories* 6.24.
11. *Histories* 6.24.2.
12. Varro, *On the Latin Language* 5.91.
13. On this problem see G. A. Ward, *Centurions: The Practice of Roman Officership,* dissertation, the University of North Carolina at Chapel Hill (2012) p.68–73.
14. *The Gallic War* 6.40.8.
15. *The Gallic War* 2.25.
16. *The Gallic War* 6.40.7.
17. *The Civil War* 3.53.
18. *Histories* 6.39.12.
19. D. Rathbone, 'Warfare and the State', in P. Sabin, H. Van Wees and M. Whitby, *The Cambridge History of Greek and Roman Warfare Vol. II Rome from the Late Republic to the Late Empire,* Cambridge University Press (Cambridge and New York, 2006) p.161.
20. For military awards see pp.261–265.
21. G. A. Ward, *Centurions* p.73.
22. *Histories* 6.24.9.
23. *The Gallic War* 2.25.
24. *The Gallic War* 3.5.
25. *The Gallic War* 6.38.
26. *The Gallic War* 5.44-45.
27. G. Webster, *The Roman Imperial Army of the First and Second Centuries,* University of Oklahoma Press (Norman, OK, 1998) plate 1 for an example of a tombstone, and M. C. Bishop and J. C. N. Coulston, *Roman Military Equipment* p.10.
28. Tacitus, *Annals* 1.23.3.
29. Livy, *Periochae* 57 and Sallust, *The War against Jugurtha* 45.
30. S. E. Phang, *Roman Military Service: Ideologies of Discipline in the Late Republic and Early Principate,* Cambridge University Press (Cambridge, 2008) p.129.

31. *The Gallic War* 2.17.
32. The phrase is ascribed either to Frederick the Great or Napoleon. It is recorded in English from the early twentieth century, see E. Knowles, *The Oxford Dictionary of Phrase and Fable*, Oxford University Press (Oxford, 2006).
33. See M. van Creveld, *Supplying War*, Cambridge University Press (Cambridge, 1977).
34. For the environment in which these campaigns took place see M. Cary, *The Geographic Background of Greek and Roman History*, Oxford University Press (Oxford, 1949) and the groundbreaking study of F. Braudel, *The Mediterranean and the Mediterranean World in the Age of Philip II* vol. 1 Harper & Row (New York, 1972).
35. Two important general studies on supplying the Roman army are J. P. Roth, *The Logistics of the Roman Army at War (264 BC – AD 235)*, Brill (Leiden, 1999) and P. Erdkamp, *Hunger and the Sword: Warfare and Food Supply in Roman Republican Wars (264–30 BC)*, Dutch Monographs on Ancient History and Archaeology (Book 20), Brill (Leiden, 1998).
36. Livy, *History of Rome* 38.37.9.
37. Polybius, *Histories* 6.39.13-15.
38. Plutarch, *Marius* 7.3.
39. M. Van Creveld, *Supplying War* p.6.
40. Frontinus, *Stratagems* 4.1.6.
41. *Histories* 6.39.12.
42. P. Erdkamp, 'War and State Formation in the Roman Republic', in P. Erdkamp (ed.) *A Companion to the Roman Army*, Blackwell (Malden, MA and Oxford, 2007) p.102.
43. *The Gallic War* 7.3.
44. Frontinus, *Stratagems* 4.1.7. For a discussion of the reform see B. Rankov, 'Military Forces' in P. Sabin, H. Van Wees and M. Whitby (eds.) *The Cambridge History of Greek and Roman Warfare Vol. II Rome from the Late Republic to the Late Empire*, Cambridge University Press (Cambridge and New York, 2006) p.31.
45. J. P. Roth, *The Logistics of the Roman Army at War* p.75.
46. Aristophanes, *The Peace* line 1183 implies three days' rations.
47. J. P. Roth, *The Logistics of the Roman Army at War* p. 77.
48. J. P. Roth, *The Logistics of the Roman Army at War* p.81.
49. Despite Cato the Elder's claim that they could in Gellius, *Attic Nights* 6.3.7.
50. See p.129 above.
51. *Histories* 3.89.8.
52. Livy, *History of Rome* 22.37. On the relationship between Rome and Hiero II, see P. J. Burton, *Friendship and Empire*, Cambridge University Press (Cambridge, 2011) p.165–169.
53. Livy, *History of Rome* 36.4.
54. J. P. Roth, *The Logistics of the Roman Army at War* p.158.
55. Livy, *History of Rome* 25.20.1-2.
56. Livy, *History of Rome* 42.48.
57. Livy, *History of Rome* 42.47.
58. See G. Rickman, *The Corn Supply of Ancient Rome*, Clarendon Press (Oxford, 1980).

59. C. Nicolet, *The World of the Citizen in Republican Rome* p.112.
60. *History of Rome* 2.15.2.
61. L. de Ligt, 'Roman Manpower and Recruitment During the Middle Republic' p.117
62. M. Sage, *The Republican Roman Army* p.125.
63. T. P. Wiseman, *New Men in the Roman Senate 139 BC – AD 14*, Oxford University Press (Oxford, 1971) Chapter 3.
64. An early case of admitting a foreign aristocrat into the Roman elite is Attus Clausus, a Sabine aristocrat, see p.12.
65. (Anonymous), *De Viris Illustribus* 36.1, Florus, *Epitome of Roman History* 1.2.1 and Valerius Maximus, *Memorable Doings and Sayings* 9.1.
66. Baronowski, D. W., 'The "Formula Togatorum"', *Historia* 33 (1984) p.250. For further discussion, see P. A. Brunt, *Italian Manpower 225 BC – AD14*, Oxford University Press (Oxford, 1971) p.545–549.
67. *Roman Antiquities* 20.4.1.
68. See pp.219–225.
69. Dionysius, *Roman Antiquities* 20.1.5. P. Erdkamp, 'Polybius and Livy on the Allies in the Roman Army', in L. De Blois et al. (eds.) *The Impact of the Roman Army (200 BC – AD 476)* in Impact of Empire 6 (Leiden and Boston, 2007) p.48 thinks the reference is a fantasy, but parallel information about Pyrrhus' deployment in the same battle makes it likely that it is factual.
70. See Polybius, *Histories* 18.28.10.
71. Sallust, *The War against Jugurtha* 95.1 and 105.2.
72. *Histories* 6.26.7.
73. Polybius, *Histories* 6.26.5.
74. Livy, *History of Rome* 8.8.
75. *History of Rome* 29.15.
76. This is clear from a decree of the senate in 186 addressed to the allies that forbade the practice of the cult of Bacchus, see Livy, *History of Rome* 39.8-19.

Chapter 7: The Army on Campaign I

1. Fragment 99 B-W.
2. For Greek concepts of the laws of war see A. Lanni, 'The Laws of War in Ancient Greece', *Law and History Review* 26 (2008) pp.469–489.
3. *On Duties* 1.34-35.
4. For the procedure see Livy, *History of Rome* 1.32.
5. T. Wiedemann, 'The Fetiales: A Reconsideration', *Classical Quarterly New Series* 36 (1986) pp.478–490.
6. For a full discussion of these procedures see J. W. Rich, 'Declaring War in the Roman Republic in the Period of Transmarine Expansion', *Collections Latomus* 149 (1976) pp.13–18.
7. H. H. Scullard, *Festivals and Ceremonies of the Roman Republic,* Thames and Hudson, (Bungay, 1981) pp.85–86.
8. H. Le Bonnec, 'Aspects religieux de la guerre à Rome', in J. P. Brisson (ed.) *Problèmes de la guerre à Rome,* Mouton (Paris-La Haye, 1969) p.102.

9. H. H. Scullard, op. cit. pp.95–96.
10. On lustration before battle Dio, *History of Rome* 47.38; and in the course of a campaign, Appian, *Spanish Wars* 19.
11. *The Civil War* 5.96.
12. Livy, *History of Rome* 21.63, Cicero, *On Divination* 1.77.
13. Suetonius, *Tiberius* 2.2 among many others. The earliest source for the incident is Polybius, *Histories* 1.52-53 who attributes the defeat to incompetence on the part of the consul.
14. Cicero *On Divination* 2.76. See J. W. Rich, 'Augustus and the Spolia Opima', *Chiron* 26 (1996) pp.101–105.
15. J. W. Rich, 'Roman Rituals of War' in B. Campbell and L. A. Tritle (eds.) *The Oxford Handbook of Warfare in the Classical World,* Oxford University Press (Oxford and New York, 2013) pp.550–551.
16. See p.145.
17. *Histories* 6.40.
18. Josephus, *The Jewish War* 3.6.2.
19. Onasander, *The General* 6.6.
20. Plutarch, *Crassus* 23.3-4.
21. Caesar, *The Gallic War* 2.19.
22. *The Gallic War* 6.6.
23. Sallust, *The War against Jugurtha* 46.6.
24. *On the Military Institutions of the Romans* 1.9.
25. *Histories* 3.68.3.
26. For the Caudine Forks see p.72–3 above. On Trasimene, J. F. Lazenby, *Hannibal's War,* University of Oklahoma Press (Norman, OK, 1998) p.65.
27. N. J. E. Austin and N. B. Rankov, *Exploratio: Military and Political Intelligence in the Roman World from the Second Punic War to the Battle of Adrianople,* Routledge (London and New York, 1995) p.10.
28. Caesar, *The Gallic War* 1.21.
29. *Gallic War* 2.19 and M. M. Sage, *Roman Conquests: Gaul* pp.54-55.
30. F. Russell, 'Finding the Enemy: Military Intelligence', in *The Oxford Handbook of Warfare in the Classical World,* Oxford University Press (Oxford, 2013) p.475.
31. See p.125.
32. *Gallic War* 4.22.
33. N. J. E. Austin and N. B. Rankov, *Exploratio* pp.102–107.
34. Sallust, *The War against Jugurtha* 44.
35. Vegetius, 1.21-25.
36. P. Southern, *The Roman Army: A Social and Institutional History,* ABC-Clio Inc. (Santa Barbara, 2006) p.29.
37. F. J. Wiseman, *Roman Spain,* Bell (London, 1956) p.139.
38. L. J. F. Keppie, *The Making of the Roman Army: From Republic to Empire,* B. T. Batsford (London, 1984) p.22.
39. *The Gallic War* 3.17-19.
40. B. Dobson, 'No Holiday Camp: The Roman Republican Army Camp as a Fine-Tuned Instrument of War', in J. D. Evans (ed.) *A Companion to the Archaeology of the Roman Republic,* Wiley-Blackwell (Malden, MA and Oxford, 2013) pp.217–222.

41. *The Gallic War* 2.19.
42. For a good account of the layout of a camp see, L. Keppie, *The Making of the Roman Army: From Republic to Empire* pp.21-22.
43. *The Gallic War* 5.49-51.
44. *Histories* 6.42.1-5.
45. H. van Wees, *Greek Warfare: Myth and Reality*, Bristol Classical Press (King's Lynn, 2004) p.107.
46. Diodorus Siculus, *Library of History* 11.21.1-3.
47. Arrian, *Anabasis* 3.9.1.
48. S. E. Phang, *Roman Military Service: The Ideologies of Discipline in the Late Republic and Early Principate*, Cambridge University Press (Cambridge, 2008) pp.67–68.
49. Appian, *The Wars in Spain* 86.
50. Sallust, *The War against Jugurtha* 44.
51. Sallust, *The War against Jugurtha* 45.
52. *Histories* 6.33.
53. See below p.268.
54. *Roman Antiquities* 6.45.2.
55. For a good discussion of the cult in the Imperial period see O. Stoll, 'The Religions of the Armies' in P. A. Erdkamp (ed.) *Companion to the Roman Army*, Blackwell (Oxford and Malden, MA, 2007) pp.457ff.
56. Seneca, *Letters* 95.
57. *Histories* 1.1.5.
58. For a general account of the period see A. Erskine (ed.) *A Companion to the Hellenistic World*, Blackwell (Malden, MA and Oxford, 2005).
59. M. M. Austin, 'Hellenistic Kings, War and the Economy', *Classical Quarterly* 38 (1986) pp.450–466.
60. For the thesis of a major change see, N. Sekunda, *Hellenistic Infantry Reform in the 160s BC*, Oficyna Naukowa MS. (Lodz, 2001) and the judicious review by P. Beston in *Classical Review New Series* 52 (2002) pp.388–389.
61. *Histories* 18.28.1-32.5.
62. Plutarch, *Paullus* 19.1-2.
63. P. R. Franke, *The Cambridge Ancient History* vol. 7.2 (Cambridge, 1989) p.433.
64. P. R. Franke, op. cit. p.432.
65. On Gallic military equipment and tactics see pp.54–55.
66. On the *Gaesati* see pp.54–55.
67. Polybius, *Histories* 2.24.2. For the enumeration of manpower in this chapter, see p.173.
68. The praetor's name is unknown.
69. A cult of human sacrifice and of the severed head is an important feature of Celtic religion, see D. Rankin, *The Celts and the Classical World*, Routledge (London and New York, 1987) p.11.
70. *Histories* 2.27.5-7.
71. See p.163.
72. *Histories* 2.30.7.
73. For Gallic equipment, see p.163.
74. Polybius, *Histories* 2.31.1. The figure of 40,000 is repeated in the other sources.
75. For a general treatment of Carthage see D. Hoyos, *The Carthaginians*, Routledge (London and New York, 2010).

76. D. Hoyos, *Carthage* p.50.

77. For their equipment, see pp.55–56.

78. D. Hoyos, *The Truceless War: Carthage's Fight for Survival, 241 to 237 BC,* Brill (Leiden and Boston, MA, 2007).

79. See P. Hart, *The Great War: A Combat History of the First World War,* Oxford University Press (Oxford, 2013) p.78.

80. A. M. Eckstein, *Mediterranean Anarchy, Interstate War, and the Rise of Rome,* University of California Press (Berkeley and Los Angeles, 2006) pp.1–34.

81. Plutarch, *Pyrrhus* 21.3-4.

82. See W. Ameling, 'The Rise of Carthage to 264' in D. Hoyos (ed.) *A Companion to the Punic Wars,* Blackwell (Malden, MA and Oxford, 2011) p.56.

83. Polybius, *Histories* 1.7.6.

84. For the development of the Roman navy see later in this chapter.

85. On the Barcids see D. Hoyos, *Hannibal's Dynasty: Power and Politics in the Western Mediterranean, 247–183 BC,* Routledge (London and New York, 2003).

86. Hoyos, *A Companion to the Punic Wars* p.71.

87. For this interpretation see. A. M. Eckstein, 'Polybius, the Gallic Crisis, and the Ebro Treaty', *Classical Philology* 107 (2012) pp.219–220.

88. There has been much controversy about the chronology of whatever arrangement there was. Some have argued for a formal alliance that predated the signing of the Ebro treaty, although there is no evidence for any exception for Saguntum in that treaty. For this view see A. K. Goldsworthy, *The Fall of Carthage: The Punic Wars 264–146 BC* (London, 2000) p.149. The more common view is a good faith agreement between the two. But the mystery remains as to why such an agreement was ever entered into. It may be that the Romans purposely did establish some sort of relation to give them a reason to intervene in Spain, if they felt the need to do so.

89. P. J. Burton, *Friendship and Empire: Roman Diplomacy and Imperialism in the Middle Republic (353–146 BC),* Cambridge University Press (Cambridge and New York, 2011) p.22.

90. J. F. Lazenby, *Hannibal's' War,* University of Oklahoma Press (Norman, OK, 1998) p.26.

91. On various figures for casualties, see A. K. Goldsworthy, *The Fall of Carthage: The Punic Wars 265–1 46 BC,* p.189.

92. Livy, *History of Rome* 22.36 See also pp.122–4.

93. Livy, *History of Rome* 22.38.

94. *Histories* 3.107.1.

95. Ironically, a second battle of Cannae was fought in AD 1018 between the Byzantines and the Lombards.

96. J. Briscoe, 'The Second Punic War', in A. E. Astin et al. (eds.) *Cambridge Ancient History, Vol. VI.2: Rome and the Mediterranean to 133 B.C.,* (Cambridge, 1989) pp.51–52.

97. Polybius, *Histories* 3.110.10.

98. *Histories* 3.113.

99. G. Daly, *Cannae: The Experience of Battle in the Second Punic War,* Routledge (London and New York, 2002) p.29.

100. Ibid.

101. *Histories* 3.117.4-5

102. *History of Rome* 22.49. His figure for the surviving cavalry is also different.
103. *Histories* 3.117. See the discussion of G. Daly, *Cannae*, pp.198–199.
104. *History of Rome* 2.49.
105. Livy, *History of Rome* 28.12.

Chapter 8: The Army on Campaign II

1. Appian, *The Illyrian War* 7.17-8.22. For a reconstruction of the events leading to the First Illyrian War see R. M. Errington, 'Rome and Greece to 205 BC', in A. Astin et al. (eds.) *The Cambridge Ancient History Vol. VIII: Rome and the Mediterranean to 133 B.C.*, Cambridge University Press (Cambridge, 1989) pp.85–88.
2. For the Roman settlement see A. M. Eckstein, *Rome enters the Greek East: From Anarchy to Hierarchy in the Hellenistic Mediterranean, 230–170 BC*, Oxford University Press (Oxford, 2008) p.42ff.
3. On Philip's ambitions and its relation to Rome see A. M. Eckstein, *Rome* pp.78–91. For a text of the treaty see Polybius, *Histories* 7.9.
4. Polybius, *Histories* 15.20.
5. *Histories* 16.27.1.
6. Livy, *History of Rome* 31.6-7.
7. The most important source is Polybius, *Histories* 18.21-26.12.
8. Demetrias in Thessaly was one of the three Macedonian 'Fetters of Greece', along with Chalcis on the island of Euboea and the Acrocorinth at the Isthmus. These fortresses were located at choke points crucial in controlling Greece.
9. Peltasts carried a characteristic crescent-shaped wicker shield and normally employed javelins as their main offensive weapon, although they occasionally used heavy thrusting spears.
10. See p.150.
11. See p.197.
12. The comparison of the manipular legion and the phalanx is at *Histories* 18.28.2-32.5. See also p.160 above.
13. Polybius, *Histories* 5.79.4 and 31.3.5.
14. P. Sidnell, *Warhorse: Cavalry in Ancient Warfare,* Hambledon Continuum (London and New York, 2006) p.143.
15. There are two surviving accounts of the battle, Livy's at 37.37-44 and Appian, *The Syrian Wars* 31-35. Preference is usually given to Livy's account, but there are problems with both of them. For an excellent modern account, see B. Bar-Kochva, *The Seleucid Army: Organization and Tactics in the Great Campaigns,* Cambridge Classical Studies 28, Cambridge University Press (New York and London, 1976) pp.163–172.
16. *History of Rome* 37.44.
17. *The Syrian Wars* 37.
18. For other measures taken by Perseus see P. S. Derow, 'Rome, the Fall of Macedon and the Sack of Corinth, in A. E. Astin et al. (eds.) *The Cambridge Ancient History VIII* pp.300–301.
19. Plutarch, *Paullus* 15.
20. Livy, *History of Rome* 44.37 and Plutarch, *Paullus* 17.
21. *Histories* 29.16.

22. See p.192.
23. The Paeonians had once been an independent people living in the Axius (Vardar) river valley and the surrounding areas and along the Strymon River. They now formed part of Macedonia.
24. *Paullus* 19.
25. Plutarch, *Paullus* 20.1-2.
26. *History of Rome* 44.41.
27. *Paullus* 21.6 and *History of Rome* 44.42.
28. Plutarch, *Paullus* 19.4-10 and Livy 44.43.
29. *History of Rome* 5.19 and 21. See also pp.49–50.
30. Polybius, *Histories* 10.10.1-15.10 offers the best account of the siege.
31. *On Siegecraft* 10.2.-26.
32. D. Campbell, *Besieged: Siege Warfare in the Ancient World,* Osprey Publishing (Oxford and New York, 2006) p.9.
33. For Carthaginian siege technology see Diodorus Siculus' account of the sieges of Himera in north central Sicily in 409 (13.59).
34. See J. P. Roth, *The Logistics of the Roman Army at War (264 B.C. – A.D. 235),* Brill (Leiden and Boston, 1999) p.288 and Polybius, *Histories* 1.17.
35. *The Civil War* 3.47. Barley has only about half the nutritional value of wheat.
36. N. Rosenstein, *Rome at War: Farms, Families and Death in the Middle Republic,* University of North Carolina Press (Chapel Hill and London, 2004) p.130.
37. Caesar, *The Gallic War* 2.32.
38. Livy, *History of Rome* 28.3.
39. *Histories* 10.15.4-8.
40. *The Face of Battle,* Viking Press (New York, 1976).
41. For instance, for an attempt to reconstruct hoplite battle see V. D. Hanson, *The Western Way of War,* University of California Press (Berkeley, CA and London, 2009). For attempts at reconstructing Roman battle conditions see P. Sabin, 'The Roman Face of Battle', *Journal of Roman Studies* 90 (2000) pp.1–17 and G. Daly, *The Experience of Battle in the Second Punic War,* Routledge (London and New York, 2002).
42. Page 315ff.
43. See pp.97–98.
44. See p.221.
45. P. Sabin, 'The Roman Face of Battle', p.4.
46. Tacitus, *Histories* 3.15.
47. For Polybius' assessment of the characteristics of a good commander, see *Histories* 2.36.3.
48. Plutarch, *Pompey* 59.2.
49. Caesar, *The Civil Wars* 1.63-1.86.
50. *The Gallic War* 2.25.
51. A. D. Lee, 'Morale and the Roman Experience of Battle', in A. B. Lloyd (ed.) *Battle in Antiquity,* Duckworth in association with the Classical Press of Wales (London, 1996) p.200.
52. See p.168.
53. See the convincing discussion of M. Taylor, 'Roman Infantry Tactics in the Mid-Republic: A Reassessment', *Historia* 63 (2014) p.302.

54. For a collection of the evidence see A. Zhmodikov, 'Roman Republican Heavy Infantrymen in Battle', *Historia* 49 (2000) pp.67–76.

55. S. Koon, 'Phalanx and Legion: the "Face" of Punic War Battle', in D. Hoyos (ed.) *A Companion to the Punic Wars,* Wiley-Blackwell (Malden, MA and Oxford, 2011) p.89.

56. See pp.257–261.

57. See p.106.

58. 31..13.2 quoted in G. Daly, *Cannae: The Experience of Battle in The Second Punic War,* p.194 and Livy, *History of Rome* 28.14-15.

59. For Cannae and Cynoscephalae see pp.177 and 188 above. For the battle of the Metaurus see Polybius, *Histories* 11.1.2-3.6 and Livy, *History of Rome* 27.48.

60. J. P. Roth, 'War', in *The Cambridge History of Greek and Roman Warfare* vol. I, p.395.

61. *History of Rome* 22.51.5-8.

62. For a different view see N. Rosenstein, *Rome at War,* University of North Carolina Press (Chapel Hill and London, 2004) p.24.

63. P. Krentz, 'Casualties in Hoplite Battles', *Greek Roman and Byzantine Studies* 26 (1985) p.18.

64. The table from which these data are drawn was constructed by N. Rosenstein, *Rome at War,* p.110.

65. See P. A. Brunt, *Italian Manpower: 225 BC to AD 14,* Oxford University Press (Oxford, 1971) p.85.

66. Bactria is the ancient name for a region that included parts of modern Afghanistan and Tajikistan.

67. On elephants in general, see H. H. Scullard, *The Elephant in the Greek and Roman World,* Thames & Hudson (London, 1974), M. B. Charles and P. Rhodan, '"Magister Elephantorvm": A Reappraisal of Hannibal's Use of Elephants', *Classical World* 1000 (2007) pp.363–389.

68. Dionysius of Halicarnassus, *Roman Antiquities* 20.6-7.

69. Plutarch, *Pyrrhus* 21.7.

70. See p.168.

71. Polybius, *Histories* 1.19.11.

72. See p.167-9 above.

73. Polybius, *Histories* 3.33.16 and 42.11.

74. M. B. Charles and P. Rhodan, '"Magister Elephantorvm"', pp.372–376.

75. See pp.178–181.

76. This Hasdrubal is to be distinguished from Hasdrubal Barca, the brother of Hannibal, who was killed at the Metaurus the year before. For the elephants see Polybius, *Histories* 11.20.2.

77. Polybius, *Histories* 11.20 and Livy, *History of Rome* 28.14-15

78. See p.111.

79. Polybius, *Histories* 11.18.4 and Livy, *History of Rome* 30.43.

80. See p.188.

81. Livy, *History of Rome* 33.8.

82. Polybius, *Histories* 18.25.7. and Livy, *History of Rome* 33.9.

83. See pp.192–193.

84. Livy, *History of Rome* 37. 39.

85. Appian, *The Spanish Wars* 46.
86. Caesar, *The Spanish War* 81.
87. Caesar, *The Spanish War* 83.

Chapter 9: A Newer Model Army

1. Polybius, *Histories* 6.35.5.
2. For Pydna see p.197 above.
3. 3.69.7. None of these references to cohorts can be considered historical. They are the result of the anachronistic picture of the early army found in Livy and other sources.
4. *Histories* 11.23.1-2. The usual number of *velites* in this case was probably 120 men, as 40 were normally assigned to each maniple.
5. Livy, *History of Rome* 25.39.
6. *Histories* 11.33.1.
7. See pp.191–4 above; Appian, *The Syrian Wars* 31 also mentions maniples.
8. The classic account of the development of the cohort as a tactical unit is M. J. V. Bell, 'Tactical Reform in the Roman Republican Army,' *Historia* 14 (1965) pp.40–422.
9. For instance, *The Civil War* 1.70.
10. Sallust, *The War against Jugurtha* 49.3-6.
11. Sallust, *The War against Jugurtha* 100.2.
12. For the eagle see Pliny, *Natural History* 10.16; for the *pilum,* see Plutarch, *Marius* 25.1-2.
13. For the reforms see Plutarch, *Marius* 13.1 and Frontinus, *Stratagems* 4.1.7. For the problems see B. Rankov, 'Military Forces', pp.31–32.
14. For instance, H. M. D. Parker, *The Roman Legions,* W. Heffer & Sons (Cambridge and New York, 1971) p.29.
15. L. Keppie, *The Making of the Roman Army: From Republic to Empire,* Barnes & Noble Books (Totowa, NJ, 1984) p.63.
16. P. Southern, *The Roman Army: A Social and Institutional History,* ABC-Clio Inc. (Santa Barbara, CA, 2006) pp.99–100.
17. B. Dobson, 'No Holiday Camp', in J. D. Evans (ed.) *A Companion to Archaeology of the Roman Republic,* Wiley-Blackwell (Malden, MA and Oxford, 2013) pp.224–225.
18. For the army and the major religious ceremonies see p.51.
19. Tacitus, *Histories* 1.44.2 and *Annals* 1.18.3.
20. J. E. Lendon, *Soldiers & Ghosts,* p.231.
21. Frontinus, *Stratagems* 2.32.2. For maniple depth see the data collected by M. J. Taylor, 'Roman Infantry Tactics in the Mid-Republic: A Reassessment', *Historia* 63 (2014) pp.12–13.
22. Caesar, *The Civil War* 1,83.
23. Caesar, *The African War* 1.17.
24. Caesar, *The Gallic War* 2.25.
25. *Histories* 6.21.3.
26. The *capite censi* could be subject to the levy in emergencies. The only certain recorded instance was in 280.

27. The identity and functions of the *accensi* and *velati* in the army are a problem as the sources provide inadequate information. For a short account of what is known see Michael M. Sage, 'Velites', in B. Campbell and L. Tritle (eds.) *Encyclopedia of Ancient History,* vol. 10, Wiley-Blackwell (Malden, MA and Oxford, 2012).

28. Ilipa, Polybius, *Histories* 11.22.8-10 and the fight between the consul P. Sulpicius Galba and Philip in Illyria see Livy, *History of Rome* 31.35.5-6.

29. Vegetius, *On Military Matters* 1.20.

30. *History of Rome* 26.4.3-10.

31. *The Gallic War* 1.48.

32. Sallust, *The War against Jugurtha* 46.7 and 49.6.

33. Festus, *On the Meaning of Words* 26M.

34. *Stratagems* 2.3.17.

35. For an attempt to link the introduction of the cohort and the end of the velites see N. Rankov, 'Military Forces', pp.32–3.

36. For the decline in the census rating and its effects, see p.234 below.

37. See p.187.

38. For these changes see p.230ff.

39. Dio Cassius, *History of Rome,* Fragment 78.

40. For citizen cavalry Valerius Maximus, *Memorable Deeds and Sayings* 5.8.4, and for allied cavalry see Sallust, *The War against Jugurtha* 95.

41. Polybius, *Histories* 24.14.

42. See p.207.

43. J. B. McCall, *The Cavalry of the Roman Republic* pp.101–108.

44. J. B. McCall, *The Cavalry of the Roman Republic* p.102.

45. Suetonius, *Julius Caesar* 3.

46. Caesar, *The Gallic War* 1.42.

47. For the Celtiberians see B. Cunliffe, *The Ancient Celts,* Penguin Books (Harmondsworth, 1999) pp.133–144. The hiring of mercenaries, Livy, *History of Rome* 24.29.

48. For the deaths of the Scipios see Polybius, *Histories* 10.6.2 and 7.1, Livy *History of Rome* 25.32-36 and 26.2.5 and Appian, *The Spanish Wars* 16.

49. For the question of mercenary service in the Roman army see J. R. W. Prag, 'Troops and commanders: *auxilia externa* under the Roman Republic Troops and Commanders', pp.107–108.

50. For instance at the battle of Ilipa see p.180.

51. *The Civil War* 1.39.

52. On these developments see D. B. Saddington, *The Development of the Roman Auxiliary Forces from Caesar to Vespasian (49 BC – AD 79),* University of Zimbabwe (Harare, 1982) p.26.

53. *The Gallic War* 1.48.

54. P. Erdkamp, 'Polybius and Livy on the Allies in the Roman Army', in L. De Blois and E. Lo Cascio (eds.) *The Impact of the Roman Army (200 BC – AD 476),* Brill (Leiden and Boston, 2007) p.61.

55. *Inscriptiones Latinae Selectae* 8888.

56. Suetonius, *Julius Caesar* 24.2.

57. J. R. W. Prag, 'Troops and Commanders: *auxilia externa* under the Roman Republic', p.111.

58. Nearer Spain comprised the area of the present day provinces of Catalonia and Valencia, while Further Spain included the Guadalquivir valley and extended to Portugal, Extremadura and Galicia.

59. P. A. Brunt, *Italian Manpower*, pp.661–665.

60. N. Rosenstein, *Rome at War*, pp.189–190.

61. On this resistance, see A. E. Astin, *Scipio Aemilianus*, Oxford University Press (Oxford, 1967) pp.167–172.

62. See p.307 n.26.

63. Livy, *History of Rome* 23.31.1

64. *De Re Publica* 2.40. The hypothesis was first put forward by E. Gabba, 'The Origins of the Professional Army at Rome: The Problem of the Proletarii and Marius' Reform', in E. Gabba, *Republican Rome, the Army and the Allies*, University of California Press (Berkeley and Los Angeles, 1976) pp.6–7. See the remarks of L. De Ligt, 'The Proletarianization of the Roman Army', in L. de Blois et al. (eds.) *The Impact of the Roman Army (200 BC–AD 476)*, Brill (Leiden and Boston, 2007) pp.17–18.

65. Livy, *History of Rome* 28.11.

66. These are the calculations of K. Hopkins, *Conquerors and Slaves, Sociological Studies in Roman History* vol. 1, Cambridge University Press (Cambridge, 1978) p.35.

67. Livy, *History of Rome* 32.3.1-6.

68. *History of Rome* 42.34.1-11

69. N. Rosenstein, *Rome at War* p.9, argues that there is no evidence for an increase in the wealth of the elite in this period. He also points to the constraints of political competition among the elite. But this is anecdotal evidence and it seems extremely unlikely that the elite as a whole would not benefit from the rich booty that the eastern wars produced.

70. Cicero, *On Duties* 1.151 writes that 'of all those ways in which wealth can be acquired nothing is better, sweeter, more fruitful or more worthy of a free man than agriculture.'

71. Such a limit was part of the legislation of Tiberius Gracchus in 133, see Plutarch, *Tiberius Gracchus* 8.

72. On the effects of the importation of slaves on other economic developments to 133, see J. P. Morel, 'Early Rome and Italy', in W. Scheidel, I Morris and R. Saller (eds.) *The Cambridge Economic History of the Greco-Roman World*, Cambridge University Press (Cambridge and New York, 2007) pp.506–509.

73. On Rome's grain supply see G. Rickman, *The Corn Supply of Ancient Rome*, Oxford University Press (Oxford, 1980).

74. L. De Ligt, 'Roman Manpower Resources and the Proletarianization of the Roman Army in the Second Century BC', in *The Impact of the Roman Army (200 BC – AD 476)*, pp.4–10.

75. On Gracchus there is a good short account in H. H. Scullard, *From the Gracchi to Nero*, Routledge (New York and London, 2010) pp.20–26.

76. On Marius see T. F. Carney, *A Biography of C. Marius*, Argonaut (Chicago, 1970).

77. Sallust, *The War against Jugurtha* 86.2, Aulus Gellius, *Attic Nights* 16.10.14.

78. See p.116 above.

79. On this see C. Nicolet, *The World of the Citizen in Republican Rome*, p.130.

80. Appian, *The Civil Wars* 1.100 and 104. See also A. Keaveney, *Sulla: The Last Republican,* (London and New York, 2005) pp.152–155.
81. T. P. Wiseman, 'The Senate and the *Populares* 69–60 BC', in J. Crook, A. Lintott and E. Rawson (eds.) *Cambridge Ancient History IX,* Cambridge University Press (Cambridge and New York, 1991) pp.346–351.
82. But see the reservations of J. F. Lendon, 'The Roman Army Now', *The Classical Journal* 99 (2004) pp.444–446.
83. Pliny the Elder, *Natural History* 10.16.
84. 4.25.
85. See pp.97–98.
86. Livy, *History of Rome* 42.32.6.
87. Appian, *The African Wars* 75.
88. M. Beard, *The Roman Triumph* pp.7–35; and R. A. Billows, *Julius Caesar: The Colossus of Rome,* Routledge (London and New York, 2009) p.161.
89. Suetonius, *Julius Caesar* 70.
90. L. Keppie, 'Military Service in the Late Republic: The Evidence of Inscriptions', in M. Feugère (ed.) *L'équipement militaire et l'armement de la république (IVe–Ier s. avant J.-C.), Proceedings of the Tenth International Roman Military Equipment Conference,* Montpellier, 1996, Journal of Roman Military Equipment Studies 8 (1997) pp.3–11.
91. E. Bispham, *From Asculum to Actium,* Oxford University Press (Oxford and New York, 2007) p.361.
92. Orosius, *The History against the Pagans* 5.21.
93. Sallust, *Cataline* 45.2 and 59.6; Cicero, *Against Piso* 54.
94. Appian, *The Civil Wars* 2.18 and Dio Cassius, *History of Rome* 39.3. 6.
95. Plutarch, *Pompey* 55.7 and Appian, *The Civil Wars* 2.24.
96. R. Syme, *The Roman Revolution,* Oxford at the Clarendon Press (Oxford, 1939) pp.116–118.
97. See E. S. Gruen, *The Last Generation of the Roman Republic,* University of California Press (Berkeley and Los Angeles, 1974) p.261.
98. Valerius Maximus, *Memorable Deeds and Sayings* 4.3.5.
99. D. Stockton, *The Gracchi,* Clarendon Press (Oxford and New York, 1979).
100. A. Keaveney, *Sulla, The Last Republican,* p.182.
101. Suetonius, *Caesar* 77.
102. P. A. Brunt, *Italian Manpower,* p.300.
103. Suetonius, *Julius Caesar* 69.
104. Augustus, *The Achievements of the Divine Augustus* 3.3.

Chapter 10: The Late Republican Army

1. P. Erdkamp, *Hunger and Sword: Warfare and Food Supply in Roman Republican Wars 264–30 BC,* and J. P. Roth, *The Logistics of the Roman Army at War, 264 BC – AD 235.*
2. Appian, *Civil Wars* 3.68.281.
3. Polybius, *Histories* 3.109.
4. The best guide to this training, although mostly concerned with the training of the army of the Empire is Vegetius, *On Military Matters* 1.8-20.
5. Caesar, *The Gallic War* 7.72-73.

6. Plutarch, *Sulla* 18.1 and 21.1; Frontinus, *Stratagems* 2.3.17
7. Caesar, *The African War* 49.
8. See p.254ff.
9. Caesar, *The African War* 70.
10. The identity of this river is a problem. For a suggestion that it was the Scheldt and not the Sambre, see M. M. Sage, *Roman Conquests* p.53.
11. Caesar, *The Gallic War* 2.16-27.
12. See above p.191
13. The recurrence of the name in later Parthian history may indicate that this was a title and not a personal name.
14. Plutarch, *Crassus* 21.6. The figures are uncertain.
15. On eastern and more particularly Parthian tactics see E. L. Wheeler, 'The Army and the Limes in the East', in P. Erdkamp (ed.) *A Companion to the Roman Army,* pp.258–262.
16. Caesar, *The War in Africa* 17.
17. P. Hunt, 'Military Forces', in P. Sabin, H. Van Wees and M. Whitby (eds.) *The Cambridge History of Greek and Roman Warfare* vol. I, p.122 and S. Anglim et al. (eds.) *Fighting Techniques of the Ancient World 3000 BC – 500 AD,* pp.82-83.
18. Plutarch, *Caesar* 41 and Appian, *The Civil Wars* 2.67.
19. Caesar, *The Civil War* 3.88. Caesar's account at 3.94-97 is our best source.
20. For a list see Appian, *The Civil Wars* 2.71.
21. Appian, *The Civil Wars* 2.76. Caesar, *The Civil War* 3.88 mentions only Afranius, but does not say he commanded the wing.
22. Appian, *The Civil Wars* 2.78.
23. See the appreciation of Caesar as a tactician by N. Rosenstein, 'General and Imperialist', in M. Griffin (ed.) *A Companion to Julius Caesar,* pp.94–94.
24. *Histories* 6.39.1-11.
25. *Histories* 6.39.3-4. There is some controversy over whether the Romans awarded a spear without a spear point. It seems likely that it did have a point.
26. On these awards see V. Maxfield, *The Military Decorations of the Roman Army,* University of California Press (Berkeley and Los Angeles, 1981) pp.67–101.
27. See p.262.
28. J. W. Rich, 'Augustus and the Spolia Opima', *Chiron* 26 (1976) pp.86–91.
29. Livy, *History of Rome* 1.10.
30. S. P. Oakley, 'Single Combat in the Roman Republic', *Classical Quarterly* 35 (1985) p.398.
31. Valerius Maximus, *Memorable Deeds and Sayings* 2.8.
32. M. Beard, *The Roman Triumph* pp.191–192.
33. The location of the gate is uncertain.
34. Tertullian, *Apology* 33.4.
35. Polybius, *Histories* 31.29.
36. M. Beard, *The Roman Triumph* p.7.
37. For these comments see *Histories* 6.37.6 and 38.4.
38. See above p.266
39. Livy, *History of Rome* 8.6-8.
40. Valerius Maximus, *Memorable Deeds and Sayings* 2.7.12.
41. Valerius Maximus, *Memorable Deeds and Sayings* 2.7.11; Frontinus, *Stratagems* 4.1.42

42. For an analysis of the mutiny see S. G. Chrissanthos, 'Scipio and the Mutiny at Sucro, 206 B.C.', *Historia* 46 (1997) pp.172–184.

43. Suetonius, *Julius Caesar* 70 and Plutarch, *Caesar* 51.

44. For this reconstruction of the mutiny, see S. G. Chrissanthos, 'Caesar and the Mutiny of 47 B.C.', *Journal of Roman Studies* 91 (2001) pp.63–75.

45. Sallust, *The War against Jugurtha* 44.

46. One noted case during the Empire is that of Gnaeus Domitius Corbulo, who on his arrival in AD 58 to take up the command against the Parthians under Nero used harsh methods to restore army discipline (Tacitus, *Annals* 13.35-36). He had done the same on taking up the post as governor of Lower Germany in 47 (*Annals* 11.18).

47. Livy, *History of Rome* 25.37.

48. The affected unit was also forced to camp outside fortifications which involved greater exposure to enemy attack, Polybius, *Histories* 6.38.3.

49. On this subject see S. Phang, *Roman Military Service: Ideologies of Discipline in the late Republic and the Early Principate* p.123–129.

50. Plutarch, *Crassus* 10.2 and Appian, *The Civil Wars* 1.118.

51. *On Military Matters* 1.1.

52. Caesar, *The Gallic War* 1.4.

53. Polybius, *Histories* 30.15.

54. The prevailing view was that of L. Shatzman, 'The Roman General's Authority over Booty', pp.177–205. He argued that the *manubiae* were the general's private property. It has now been convincingly refuted by J. B. Churchill, '*Ex qua quod vellent facerent:* Roman Magistrates' Authority over *Praeda* and *Manubiae*', *Transactions of the American Philological Association* 129 (1999) pp.85–116.

55. Livy, *History of Rome* 45.35-36.

56. Cicero, *Letters to his Friends* 7.8 and 17.

57. Pliny, *Natural History* 35.66.

58. Livy, *History of Rome* 33.27.4.

59. *History of Rome* 10.46.5.

60. See p.121.

61. Caesar, *The Gallic War* 7.45.

62. On Telamon see p.161–4 above.

63. There were also distributions during the civil wars of the first century, see p.257 above.

64. *Histories* 6.39.12.

65. *Histories* 6.39.9-10.

66. *Histories* 10.16.1-17.

67. For a general overview of the Imperial army see B. Campbell, *Warfare and Society in Imperial Rome, 31 B.C. – A.D. 280,* Routledge (New York 2002) and Y. Le Bohec, *The Imperial Roman Army,* B. T. Batsford (Frome, 1994).

68. The emperor was Galba, Tacitus, *Histories* 1.55.

69. E. S. Gruen, 'The Expansion of the Empire under Augustus', in Bowman A. K., Champlin E. and Lintott A. (eds.) *The Cambridge Ancient History Vol. X The Augustan Empire, 43 B.C – A.D. 69,* Cambridge University Press (Cambridge, 1996) pp.176–178.

70. The exceptions were the civil wars of 69–70 and 193–197.

SELECT BIBLIOGRAPHY

General and Introduction

Adcock, F.E. (1940) *The Roman Art of War under the Republic,* Harvard University Press: Cambridge, MA.

Astin, A. E. et al. (eds.) (1989) *The Cambridge Ancient History Vol. VIII: Rome and the Mediterranean to 133 B.C.,* Cambridge University Press: Cambridge.

Bowman A. K., Champlin E. and Lintott A. (eds.) (1996) *The Cambridge Ancient History Vol. X: The Augustan Empire, 43 B.C–A.D. 69,* Cambridge University Press: Cambridge.

Broughton, T. R. S. (1951 and 1952) *The Magistrates of the Roman Republic,* Vols. I and II, American Philological Society: New York.

Campbell, B. and Tritle, L. A. (2013) *The Oxford Handbook of Warfare in the Classical World,* Oxford University Press: Oxford and New York.

Cary M. (1949) *The Geographic Background of Greek and Roman History,* Oxford University Press: Oxford.

Connolly, P. (1998) *Greece and Rome at War,* Greenhill Books: London and Mechanicsburg, PA.

Dobson, B. (2008) *The Army of the Roman Republic,* Oxbow Books: Oxford.

Eilers, C. (2009) *Diplomats and Diplomacy in the Roman World,* Brill: Leiden and New York.

Erdkamp, P. (2006) 'Army and Society', in N. Rosenstein and R. Morstein-Marx (eds.) *A Companion to the Roman Republic,* Wiley: Malden, MA and Oxford, pp.278–296.

Evans, D. (ed.) (2013) *A Companion to the Archaeology of the Roman Republic,* Wiley-Blackwell: Malden, MA and Oxford.

Fagan, G. G. and Trundle, M. F. (eds.) (2010) *New Perspectives on Ancient Warfare,* Brill: Leiden and Boston.

Gabba, E. (1976) *Republican Rome, the Army and the Allies,* University of California Press: Berkeley and Los Angeles.

Garlan, Y. (1975) *War in the Ancient World: A Social History,* trans. J. Lloyd, Chatto and Windus: London.

Gilliver, C.M. (2001) *The Roman Art of War,* Stroud: Charleston, SC.

Goldsworthy, A. K. (2000) *Roman Warfare,* Cassell: London.

Goldsworthy, A. K. (2003) *The Complete Roman Army,* Thames & Hudson: London.

Keppie, L. (1984) *The Making of the Roman Army: From Republic to Empire,* Barnes & Noble Books: Totowa, NJ.

Lendon, J. E. (2005) *Soldiers and Ghosts: A History of Battle in Antiquity,* Yale University Press: New Haven and London.

M. McDonnell (2006) *Roman Manliness,* Cambridge University Press: Cambridge and New York.

Nicolet, C. (1980) *The World of the Citizen in Republican Rome,* University of California Press: Berkeley.

Potter, D. (2004) 'The Roman Army and Navy', in H. I. Flower (ed.) *The Cambridge Companion to the Roman Republic,* Cambridge University Press: Cambridge, pp.66–68.

Raaflaub, K. (ed.) (2007) *War and Peace in the Ancient World,* Blackwell: Malden, MA and Oxford.

Rich, J. and Shipley, G. (eds.) (1993) *War and Society in the Roman World,* Routledge: London and New York.

Rosenstein, N. (2003) 'Republican Rome', in K. Raaflaub, and N. Rosenstein (eds.) *War and Society in the Ancient and Medieval World,* Center for Hellenic Studies: Cambridge, MA, pp.226–244.

Sabin, P., Van Wees H. and Whitby M (eds.) (2006) *The Cambridge History of Greek and Roman Warfare Vol. II, Rome from the Late Republic to the Late Empire,* Cambridge University Press: Cambridge and New York.

Sabin, P., Van Wees, H. and Whitby, M. (eds.) (2007), *The Cambridge History of Greek and Roman Warfare Vol. I: Greece, the Hellenistic world and the Rise of Rome and Vol. II Rome from the Late Republic to the Late Empire,* Cambridge University Press: Cambridge.

Sage, M. M. (2008) *The Republican Roman Army: A Sourcebook,* Routledge: New York and Oxford.

Sage, M. M. (2013) 'The Rise of Rome', in B. Campbell and L. A. Tritle (eds.) *The Oxford Handbook of Warfare in the Classical World,* Oxford University Press: Oxford and New York, pp.216–235.

Walbank, F. W., Astin, A. E. and Drummond, A. (eds.) (1989) *The Cambridge Ancient History Vol. VII, pt. 2,* Cambridge University Press: Cambridge.

Warry, J. (1995) *Warfare in the Classical World,* University of Oklahoma Press: Norman, OK.

Chapter I: The Sources

Bispham, E. (2007) 'Literary Sources', in N. Rosenstein, and R. A. Morstein-Marx, R, *A Companion to the Roman Republic,* Blackwell: Malden, MA and Oxford, pp. 29–50.

Cornell, T. J. (1995) *The Beginnings of Rome: Italy and Rome from the Bronze Age to the Punic War (c. 1000 BC–264 BC),* Routledge: New York and London.

Cornell, T. J (2003) 'Coriolanus: Myth, History and Performance', in D. Braund and C. Gill (eds.) *Myth, History and Performance,* University of Exeter Press: Exeter, pp. 73–97.

Cornell, T.J. (2005) 'The Value of the Literary Tradition concerning Archaic Rome', in K. A. Raaflaub (ed.) *Social Struggles in Archaic Rome: New Perspectives on the Conflict of the Orders,* Blackwell: Malden, MA.

Earl, D. C. (1961) *The Political Thought of Sallust,* Cambridge University Press: Cambridge.

Forsythe, G. (1999) 'Livy and Early Rome: A Study in Historical Method and Judgement', *Historia Einzelschriften* 132: Stuttgart.

Gabba, E. (1991) *Dionysius and the History of Archaic Rome,* Sather Classical Lectures 56, University of California Press: Berkeley, CA.

Horsfall, N.M. (1987) 'Myth and Mythography at Rome', in J.N. Bremmer and N.M. Horsfall (eds.) *Roman Myth and Mythography,* University of London, Institute of Classical Studies Bulletin Supplement 52, pp.1–11.

Litchfield, H. W. (1914) 'National Exempla Virtutis in Roman Literature', *Harvard Studies in Classical Philology* 25, pp.1–71.

Luce, T.J. (1977) *Livy. The Composition of his History,* Princeton University Press: Princeton.

Miles, G. (1995) *Livy: Reconstructing Early Rome,* Cornell University Press: Ithaca and London.

Oakley, S. P. A. (1997) *A Commentary on Livy Books VI–X Vol. I,* Clarendon Press: Oxford.

Rawson, E., (1971) 'The Literary Sources for the Pre-Marian Army', *Papers of the British School at Rome* 39, pp.13–31.

Sacks, K (1990) *Diodorus Siculus and the First Century,* Princeton University Press: Princeton.

Wiseman, T.P. (1987) 'The Credibility of the Roman Annalists', in T. P. Wiseman, *Roman Studies: Literary and Historical,* F. Cairns: Liverpool, pp. 293–296.

Chapter II: The Army of the Kings

Barker, G. and Rasmussen, T. (1998) *The Etruscans,* Blackwell: Oxford.

Bonfante, L. (1986) *Etruscan Life and Afterlife: A Handbook of Etruscan Studies,* Wayne State University Press: Detroit.

Cornell, T. J. (1995) *The Beginnings of Rome: Italy and Rome from the Bronze Age to the Punic War (c. 1000 BC–264 BC),* Routledge: New York and London, pp.173–194.

Crawford, M. H. (1974) *Roman Republican Coinage,* Cambridge University Press: Cambridge.

Crawford, M. H. (1985) *Coinage and Money under the Roman Republic,* University of California Press: Berkeley and Los Angeles.

Forsythe, G. (2005) *A Critical History of Early Rome,* University of California Press: Berkeley and Los Angeles, pp.111–114.

Forsythe, G. (2007) 'The Army and the Centuriate Organization in Early Rome', in Erdkamp, P. (ed.) *A Companion to the Roman Army,* pp.24–41.

Holloway, R. Ross (1994) *The Archaeology of Early Rome and Latium,* Routledge: London and New York.

Krentz, P. (1985) 'The Nature of Hoplite Battle', *Classical Antiquity* 4, pp.50–61.

Last, H. (1945) 'The Servian Reforms', *Journal of Roman Studies* 35, pp.30–48.

Morel, J. P. (2007) 'Early Rome and Italy', in W. Scheidel, I. Morris and R. Saller (eds.) *The Cambridge Economic History of the Greco-Roman World,* Cambridge University Press: Cambridge and New York, pp.487–510.

Nilsson, M. P. (1929) 'The Introduction of Hoplite Tactics at Rome', *Journal of Roman Studies* 19, pp.1–11.

Ogilvie, R. M. (1976) *Early Rome and the Etruscans,* Fontana/Collins: London.

Pallottino, M. (1991) *A History of Earliest Italy,* trans. M. Rye and K. Soper, University of Michigan Press: Ann Arbor, MI.

Rich, J. (2007) 'Warfare and the Army in Early Rome', in Erdkamp, P. (ed.) *A Companion to the Roman Army*, pp.7–23.

Ridley, R. T. (1975) 'The Enigma of Servius Tullius', *Klio* 57, pp.147–177.

Rosenstein, N. (2010) 'Phalanges in Rome?', in G. Garrett, G. C. Fagan and M. Trundle (eds.) *New Perspectives on Ancient Warfare*, Brill: Leiden and Boston pp.289–302.

Smith, C. J. (1996) *Early Rome and Latium: Economy and Society c.1000–500 BC*, Oxford University Press: Oxford.

Smith, C. J. (2006) *The Roman Clan*, Cambridge University Press: Cambridge.

Snodgrass, A. M. (1965) 'The Hoplite Reform and History', *Journal of Hellenic Studies* 85, pp.110–122.

Sumner, G. V. (1970) 'The Legion and the Centurionate Organization', *Journal of Roman Studies* 60, pp.67–78.

Thomsen, R. (1980) *King Servius Tullius: A Historical Synthesis*, Copenhagen.

Torelli, M. (1989) 'Archaic Rome between Latium and Etruria', *The Cambridge Ancient History*, Vol. 7.2, pp.30–51.

Versnel, H. S. (1980) 'Historical Implications', in G. Colonna, C. De Simone, and H. S. Versnel (eds.) *Lapis Satricanus*, Scripta Minora 5, Nederlands Historisch Instituut te Rome: The Hague.

Watson, G. R. (1958) 'The Pay of the Roman Army: The Republic', *Historia* 7, pp.113–120.

Wees, Van H. (2000) 'The Development of the Hoplite Phalanx: Iconography and Reality in the Seventh Century', in H. Van Wees (ed.), *War and Violence in Ancient Greece*, Duckworth and University Press of Wales: London, pp.125–166.

Chapter III: A Time of Troubles

Adcock, F. E. (1957) 'Consular Tribunes and their Successors', *Journal of Roman Studies* 47, pp.9–14.

Boddington, A. (1959) 'The Original Nature of the Consular Tribunate', *Historia* 8, pp.356–364.

Brunt, P.A. (1971) *Social Conflicts in the Roman Republic*, Chatto & Windus: London.

Cornell, T.J. (1989) 'Rome and Latium to 390 BC', in A. E. Astin, F. W. Walbank, M. W. Frederiksen, and R.M. Ogilvie *The Cambridge Ancient History*, vol. VII, pt. 2, pp.243–308.

Cornell, T. J. (2004) 'Deconstructing the Samnite Wars: An Essay in Historiography', in H. Jones (ed.) *Samnium. Settlement and Cultural Change.* The Proceedings of the Third E. Togo Salmon Conference on Roman Studies. Providence, Rhode Island: Center for Old World Archaeology and Art, Brown University. *Archaeologia Transatlantica*. 22, pp.115–131.

Cunliffe, B. (1999) *The Ancient Celts*, Penguin Books: Harmondsworth.

Drummond, A. (1989) 'Rome in the Fifth Century I: The Citizen Community', in A. E. Astin, F. W. Walbank, M. W. Frederiksen, and R.M. Ogilvie *The Cambridge Ancient History*, vol. VII, pt. 2, pp.172–242.

Raaflaub, K. (ed.) (1986) *Social Struggles in Ancient Rome: New Perspectives on the Conflict of the Orders*, University of California Press: Berkeley, pp. 356–364.

Rankin, D. (1987) *The Celts and the Classical World*, Routledge: London and New York.

Rosenberger, V. (2003) 'The Gallic Disaster', *Classical World* 96, pp.365–373.
Staveley, E.S. (1953) 'The Significance of the Consular Tribunate', *Journal of Roman Studies* 43, pp.30–36.

Chapter IV: Recovery and Expansion

Erdkamp, P. (2011) 'Soldiers, Roman Citizens, and Latin Colonists in Mid-Republican Italy', *Ancient Society* 41, pp.109–146.
Franke, P. R. (1989) 'Pyrrhus', in F. W. Walbank, A. E. Astin and A. Drummond (eds.) *The Cambridge Ancient History,* vol. VII, pt.2, pp.456–485.
Harris, W. V. (1971) *Rome in Etruria and Umbria,* Oxford University Press: Oxford.
Harris, W. V. (1990) 'Roman Warfare in the Economic and Social Context of the 4th Century BC', in W. Eder (ed.) *Staat und Staatlichkeit in der frühen römischen Republik,* F. Steiner: Stuttgart, pp.494-510.
Keaveney, A. (1987) *Rome and the Unification of Italy,* Bristol Phoenix Press: London.
Oakley, S. P. (1993) 'The Roman Conquest of Italy', in J. Rich and G. Shipley (eds.) *War and Society in the Roman World,* pp. 9–37.
Rich, J. W. (2008) 'Treaties, allies and the Roman conquest of Italy', in P. de Souza and J. France (eds.) *War and Peace in Ancient and Medieval History,* Cambridge University Press: Cambridge, pp.51–75.
Salmon, E. T. (1967) *Samnium and the Samnites,* Cambridge University Press: Cambridge.
Salmon, E. T. (1970) *Roman Colonization under the Republic,* Cornell University Press: Ithaca.
Salmon, E. T. (1971) *The Making of Roman Italy,* Thames & Hudson: London.

Chapter V: A New Model Army I

Bishop, M. C. and Coulston, J. C. N. (2006) *Roman Military Equipment,* Oxbow Books: Oxford.
Brunt, P. A. (1987) *Italian Manpower 225 BC – AD 14,* Oxford University Press: Oxford.
Burns, M. T. (2003) 'The Homogenisation of Military Equipment under the Roman Republic: Romanization?', *Digressus, The Internet Journal of the Classical World* Supplement 1, http://www.digressus.org/, pp.60–85.
Campbell, D (2013) 'Arms and Armor', in B. Campbell and L. A. Tritle (eds.) *The Oxford Handbook of Warfare in the Classical World,* Oxford University Press: Oxford and New York, pp.419–437.
Connolly, P. (1985) 'The Roman Saddle', in M. Dawson (ed.) *Roman Military Equipment: The Accoutrements of War,* BAR International Series 336, pp.7–27.
Connolly, P. (1989) 'The Roman Fighting Technique Deduced from Armour and Weaponry', in V. A. Maxfield and M. J. Dobson *Roman Frontier Studies,* pp. 358–363.
De Ligt, L. (2007) 'Roman Manpower and Recruitment during the Middle Republic', in P. Erdkamp (ed.) *A Companion to the Roman Army,* pp.114–131.
Feugère, M. (2002) *Weapons of the Romans,* trans. D.G. Smith, Tempus: Charleston, SC.

Gaebel, R. E. (2002) *Cavalry Operations in the Ancient Greek World,* University of Oklahoma Press: Norman, OK.

Goldman, A. (2013) 'Weapons and the Army', in J. D. Evans (ed.) *A Companion to the Archaeology of the Roman Republic,* Blackwell: Malden MA and Oxford, pp.123–140.

Harris, W.V. (1990) 'Roman Warfare in the Economic and Social Context of the 4th Century BC', in W. Eder (ed.) *Staat und Staatlichkeit in der führen römischen Republik,* pp. 494–510.

Hyland, A. H. (1990) *Equus: The Horse in the Roman World,* Batsford: London.

McCall, J. B. (2002) *The Cavalry of the Roman Republic,* Routledge: London and New York.

Millar, F. (1984) 'The Political Character of the Classical Roman Republic, 200–I50 B.C.,' *Journal of Roman Studies* 74, pp.1–19.

Moore, R (2013) 'Generalship: Leadership and Command', in B. Campbell and L. A. Tritle (eds.) *The Oxford Handbook of Warfare in the Classical World, Vol. II,* Oxford University Press: Oxford and New York, pp.457–473.

Sage, Michael M. (2013) 'Velites' in R. S. Bagnall (ed.) *Encyclopedia of Ancient History,* Vol. 10, Wiley-Blackwell: Malden, MA and Oxford.

Chapter VI: A New Model Army II

Baronowski, D. W. (1993) 'Roman Military Forces in 225 BC (Polybius 2.23-4)', *Historia* 42, pp.181–202.

Duplà, A., M. Jehne and F. P. Polo (eds.) (2011) *Consuls and the Res Publica,* Cambridge University Press: Cambridge.

Engles, D. (2013) 'Logistics: The Sinews of War', in B. Campbell and L. A. Tritle (eds.) *The Oxford Handbook of Warfare in the Classical World,,* pp.351–368.

Erdkamp, P. (1998) *Hunger and the Sword: Warfare and Food Supply in Roman Republican Wars (264–30 BC),* Giesen: Amsterdam.

Erdkamp, P. (2007), 'Polybius and Livy on the Allies in the Roman Army', in L. De Blois et al. (eds.) *The Impact of the Roman Army (200 BC–AD 476),* Brill: Leiden and Boston, pp.47–74.

Gabba, E. (1976) *Republican Rome, the Army and the Allies,* trans. P.J. Cuff, University of California Press: Berkeley.

Harris, W. V. (1984) 'The Italians and the Empire', in W. V. Harris (ed.) *The Imperialism of Mid-Republican Rome,* Papers and Monographs of the American Academy in Rome 29, pp.89–109.

Höleskamp, K.-J. (1993) 'Conquest, Competition and Consensus: Roman Expansion in Italy and the Rise of the *Nobilitas*', *Historia* 42, pp. 12–39.

Jashemski, W. F. (1950) *The Origins and History of the Proconsular Imperium to 27 BC,* University of Chicago Press: Chicago.

McDonald, A.H. (1944) 'Rome and the Italian Confederation (200–186 BC)', *Journal of Roman Studies* 34, pp.11–33.

Rich, J W. (2008) 'Treaties, allies and the Roman conquest of Italy', in de Souza, P. and France, J. (eds.) *War and Peace in Ancient and Medieval History,* Cambridge University Press: Cambridge, pp.51–75.

Rosenstein, N. (1990) *Imperatores Victi: Military Defeat and Aristocratic Competition in the Middle and Late Republic,* University of California Press: Berkeley.

Rosenstein, N. (1993) 'Competition and Crisis in Mid-Republican Rome', *Phoenix* 47, pp.313–338.

Rosenstein, N. (2007) 'Military Command, Political Power, and the Republican Elite', in P. Erdkamp (ed.) *Companion to the Roman Army*, Blackwell: Malden MA and Oxford, pp.132–147.

Rosenstein, N. (2007) 'Aristocratic Values', in Rosenstein, N. and Morstein-Marx, R. A. (eds.) *Companion to the Roman Republic*, pp.365–383.

Rosenstein, N. (2011) 'War, Wealth and Consuls', in B. Beck, A. Dupla, M. Jehne, and F. Pina Polo (eds.) *Pina Consuls and Res Publica: Holding High Office in the Roman Republic*, Cambridge University Press: Cambridge, pp. 133–157.

Roth, J. P. (1999) *The Logistics of the Roman Army at War (264 BC–AD 235)*, Brill: Leiden and Boston.

Ward, G. A. (2012) *Centurions: The Practice of Roman Officership*, Dissertation, University of North Carolina: Chapel Hill.

Chapter VII: The Army on Campaign I

Ameling, W. (2011) 'The Rise of Carthage to 264', in D. Hoyos (ed.) *A Companion to the Punic Wars*, Wiley-Blackwell: Malden MA and Oxford, pp.39–57.

Austin, J. E. and Rankov, N. B. (1995) *Exploratio: Military and Political Intelligence in the Roman World from the Second Punic War to the Battle of Adrianople*, Routledge: London and New York.

Briscoe, J. (1989) 'The Second Punic War', in A. E. Astin et al. (eds.) *Cambridge Ancient History, Vol. VII.2: Rome and the Mediterranean to 133 B.C.*, pp.44–80.

Connolly, P. (1998) *Greece and Rome at War*, Greenhill Books: London and Mechanicsburg, PA pp.135–140.

Daly, G. (2002) *Cannae: The Experience of Battle in the Second Punic War*, Routledge: London and New York.

Dobson, B. (2013) 'No Holiday Camp: The Roman Republican Army Camp as a Fine-Tuned Instrument of War', in J. D. Evans (ed.) *A Companion to the Archaeology of the Roman Republic*, pp.214–234.

Goldsworthy, A. K. (2000) *The Fall of Carthage: The Punic Wars 264-146 BC*, Cassell: London.

Goldsworthy, A. K. (2001) *Cannae: Hannibal's Greatest Victory*, Cassell's Fields of Battle, Cassell: London.

Hoyos, D. (2010) *The Carthaginians*, Routledge: Abingdon.

Hoyos, D. (2011) *A Companion to the Punic Wars*, Wiley-Blackwell: Malden, MA and Oxford.

Lazenby, J. F. (1998) *Hannibal's War*, University of Oklahoma Press: Norman, OK.

Rich, J, (2013) 'Roman Rituals of War', in B. Campbell and L. A. Tritle (eds.) *The Oxford Handbook of Warfare in the Classical World*, pp.542–568.

Rich, J. W. (1976) 'Declaring War in the Roman Republic in the Period of Transmarine Expansion', *Collections Latomus* 149 (1976).

Richardson, J. S. (1996) *The Romans in Spain*, Blackwell: Cambridge MA.

Russell, F (2013) 'Finding the Enemy: Military Intelligence', in B. Campbell and L. A. Tritle (eds.) *The Oxford Handbook of Warfare in the Classical World*, Oxford University Press: Oxford, pp.474–492.

Scullard, H. H. (1981) *Festivals and Ceremonies of the Roman Republic*, Thames & Hudson: London.

Shipley, G (2000) *The Greek World after Alexander, 323-30 BC,* Routledge: London and New York.

Stoll, O. (2007) 'The Religions of the Armies', in P. A. Erdkamp (ed.) *A Companion to the Roman Army,* pp.451–476.

Walbank, F. W. (1957) *A Historical Commentary on Polybius, Vol I,* Clarendon Press: Oxford, pp.709–714.

Whitby, M. (2006) 'Reconstructing Ancient Warfare', in Sabin, P., van Wees, H. and Whitby, M. (eds) *Cambridge History of Greek and Roman Warfare Vol. I,* Cambridge University Press: Cambridge, pp.54–81.

Wiedemann, T. (1986) 'The Fetiales: A Reconsideration', *Classical Quarterly* 36, pp.478–490.

Chapter VIII: The Army on Campaign II

Austin, M. M. (1986) 'Hellenistic Kings, War and the Economy', *Classical Quarterly* 36, pp.450–466.

Bar-Kochva, B. (1976) *The Seleucid Army: Organization and Tactics in the Great Campaigns,* Cambridge Classical Studies 28, Cambridge University Press: New York and London.

Braund, D. (2005) 'After Alexander: The Emergence of the Hellenistic World 323-281', in Erskine, A. (ed.) *A Companion to the Hellenistic World,* Blackwell: Malden, MA and Oxford, pp.19–34.

Campbell, D. (2006) *Besieged: Siege Warfare in the Ancient World,* Osprey Publishing: Oxford, UK and New York.

Charles, M. B. and Rhodan, P. (2007) 'Magister *Elephantorvm:* A Reappraisal of Hannibal's Use of Elephants', *Classical World* 100, pp.363–389.

Daly, G. (2002) *Cannae: The Experience of Battle in the Second Punic War,* Routledge: London and New York.

Derow, P. S. (1989) 'Rome, the Fall of Macedon and the Sack of Corinth', in A. E. Astin et al. (eds.) *The Cambridge Ancient History, Vol VIII,* Cambridge University Press: Cambridge, pp.290–323.

Eckstein, A. M. (2006) *Mediterranean Anarchy, Interstate War, and the Rise of Rome,* University of California Press: Berkeley and Los Angeles.

Eckstein, A. M. (2008) *Rome Enters the Greek East,* Blackwell: Malden, MA and Oxford.

Errington, R. M. (1989) 'Rome and Greece to 205 BC', in A. E. Astin et al. (eds.) *The Cambridge Ancient History Vol. VIII,* pp.81–106.

Hanson, V. D. (2009) *The Western Way of War,* University of California Press: Berkeley and London.

Keegan, J. (1976) *The Face of Battle,* Viking Press: New York.

Kern, P.B. (1999) *Ancient Siege Warfare,* University of Indiana Press: Bloomington, IN.

Lee, A. D. (1996) 'Morale and the Roman Experience of Battle', in A. B. Lloyd (ed.) *Battle in Antiquity,* Duckworth in association with the Classical Press of Wales: London, pp.199–217.

Paul, G.M. (1982) 'Urbs Capta: Sketch of an Ancient Literary Motif,' *Phoenix* 36, pp.144–155.

Rance, P (2007) 'Battle', in P. Sabin, H. Van Wees and Whitby, M. (eds.) *The Cambridge History of Greek and Roman Warfare Vol. II,* pp.342–378.

Sabin, P. (2000) 'The Roman Face of Battle', *Journal of Roman Studies* 90, pp.1–17.

Scullard, H. H. (1974) *The Elephant in the Greek and Roman World*, Thames & Hudson: London.

Walbank, F. W. (1967) *Philip V of Macedon,* Cambridge University Press: Cambridge.

Zhmodikov, A. (2000) 'Roman Republican Heavy Infantrymen in Battle', *Historia* 49, pp.67–78.

Ziolkowski, A. (1993) '*Urbs direpta* or How the Romans sacked Cities', in J. Rich and G. Shipley (eds.) *War and Society in the Roman World,* Routledge: London and New York, pp.69–91.

Chapter IX: A Newer Model Army

Adams, C. (2007) 'War and Society', in P. Sabin, H. Van Wees, and M. Whitby, *The Cambridge History of Greek and Roman Warfare Vol. II,* Cambridge University Press: Cambridge, pp.198–232.

Astin, A. E. (1967) *Scipio Aemilianus,* Oxford University Press: Oxford.

Bell, M.J.V. (1965) 'Tactical Reform in the Roman Republican Army', *Historia* 14, pp.404–422.

Blois de, L. (2007) 'Army and General in the Late Roman Republic', in P. A. Erdkamp (ed.) *A Companion to the Roman Army,* Blackwell: Malden, MA and Oxford, pp.164–179.

Brunt, P.A. (1962) 'The Army and the Land in the Roman Revolution', *Journal of Roman Studies* 52, pp.69–86.

Brunt, P.A. (1987) *Italian Manpower 225 BC – AD 14,* 2nd ed., Oxford University Press: Oxford.

Cagniart, P. (2007) 'The Late Republican Army (146-30 BC)', in P. A. Erdkamp (ed.) *A Companion to the Roman Army,* Blackwell: Malden, MA and Oxford, pp.80–95.

Carney, T. F. (1970) *A Biography of C. Marius,* Argonaut: Chicago.

Cheeseman, G. L. (1914) *The Auxilia of the Roman Imperial Army,* Oxford Clarendon Press: Oxford.

De Blois, L. (1987) *The Roman Army and Politics in the First Century B.C.,* J. C. Gieber: Amsterdam.

De Ligt, L. (2007) 'Roman Manpower and Recruitment during the Middle Republic', in P. Erdkamp (ed.) *A Companion to the Roman Army,* Blackwell: Malden, MA and Oxford, pp.114–131.

De Ligt, L. (2007) 'Roman Manpower Resources and the Proletarianization of the Roman Army in the Second Century BC', in 'The Impact of the Roman Army (200 BC–AD 476)', in L. De Blois et al. (eds.) *Impact of Empire 6,* Brill: Leiden and New York, pp.3–20.

Erdkamp, P. (2006) 'The Transformation of the Roman Army in the Second Century B.C.', in T. Ñaco del Hoyo et al. (eds.) *War and Territory in the Roman World: Guerra y territorio en el mundo romano,* British Archaeological Reports 1530, pp.41–51.

Evans, R. J. (1994) *Gaius Marius: A Political Biography,* Praetoria: University of South Africa.

Gabba, E. (1976) 'The Origins of the Professional Army at Rome: The Problem of the Proletarii and Marius' Reform', in E. Gabba, *Republican Rome, the Army and the Allies,* University of California Press: Berkeley, pp.1–12.

Goldsworthy, A. K. (1996) *The Roman Army at War (100 BC – AD 200),* Clarendon Press: Oxford.

Keaveney, A. (2007) *The Army in the Roman Revolution,* Routledge: London and New York.

Kertész, I. (1976) 'The Roman Cohort Tactics: Problems of Development', *Oikumene* 1, pp.89–97.

Parker, H. M. D. (1971) *The Roman Legions,* W. Heffer & Sons: Cambridge, UK and New York.

Prag, J. R. W. (2010) 'Troops and Commanders: *auxilia externa* under the Roman Republic', in Bonanno, D., Marino, R and Motta, D, (eds.) *Truppe e commandamti nel mondo antico,* Università degli Studi di Palermo, pp.101–113.

Rich, J. W. (1983) 'The Supposed Roman Manpower Shortage of the later Second Century BC', *Historia* 32, pp.287–331.

Rosenstein N. (2004) *Rome at War: Farms, Families and Death in the Middle Republic,* University of North Carolina Press: Chapel Hill and London.

Saddington, D. B. (1982) *The Development of the Roman Auxiliary Forces from Caesar to Vespasian (49 BC – AD 79),* University of Zimbabwe: Harare.

Smith, R E. (1958) *Service in the Post-Marian Army,* Manchester University Press: Manchester.

Taylor, M. (2014) 'Roman Infantry Tactics in the Mid-Republic: A Reassessment', *Historia* 63, pp.301–322.

Chapter X: The Late Republican Army

Beard, M. (2007) *The Roman Triumph,* The Belknap Press: Cambridge, MA and London.

Campbell, B. (2002) *Warfare and Society in Imperial Rome, 31 B. C. – A.D. 280,* Routledge: London and New York.

Curtis, V. S. and Stewart, S. (2007) *The Age of the Parthians,* I. B. Tauris: New York and London.

Flower, H. I. (2000) 'The Tradition of the Spolia Opima: M. Claudius Marcellus and Augustus', *Classical Antiquity* 19, pp.34–64.

Gelzer, M. (1968) *Caesar Politician and Statesman,* trans. P. Needham, Harvard University Press: Cambridge, MA.

Goldsworthy, A. (2006) *Caesar: The Life of a Colossus,* Yale University Press: New Haven and London.

Gwatkin, W. E. Jr. (1956), 'Some Reflections on the Battle of Pharsalus', *Transactions of the American Philological Association* 87, pp.109–124.

Le Bohec, Y. (1994) *The Imperial Roman Army,* B. T. Batsford: Frome.

Marshall, B. A. (1976) *Crassus: A Political Biography,* A. M. Hakkert: Amsterdam.

Maxfield, V. (1981) *The Military Decorations of the Roman Army,* University of California Press: Berkeley and Los Angeles.

Pelling, C. B. R. (1973) 'Pharsalus', *Historia* 22, pp. 249–259.

Phang, S. E. (2008) *Roman Military Service Ideologies of Discipline in the Late Republic and Early Principate,* Cambridge University Press: Cambridge and New York.

Rice Holmes, T. (1971) *Caesar's Conquest of Gaul,* AMS Press: New York.

Rich, J. W. (1976) 'Augustus and the Spolia Opima', *Chiron* 26, pp.85–127.

Sage, M. M. (2011) *Roman Conquests: Gaul,* Pen & Sword Military: Barnsley.

Ward, A, M. (1978) *Marcus Crassus and the Late Roman Republic,* University of Missouri: Columbia, MO and London.

Watson, G. R. (1969) *The Roman Soldier,* Thames & Hudson: London.

Index

Achaea, 3, 192

Achaean League, 3, 158, 186

Acilius Glabrio, 191

Acquarossa, 29

Acro, 263

Actium, 137, 227, 245, 271–2

Ad Maecium, 43

Adrianople, 210

Adriatic, 56, 75, 79, 91, 129, 137, 162, 183, 189, 195, 257

Aegean, 48, 104, 158, 185, 191

Aemilius Barbula, proconsul, 85

Aemilius Paullus, commander, 96, 99, 109–10, 151, 160, 197, 251, 269

Aequi, 20, 33, 38, 40–5, 59–60, 66, 75–6, 115

Aeson river, 198

Aetolian League, 158, 184–5, 189, 191, 231

Aetolians, 184, 186–7, 189–91, 270

Africa, 4–5, 150, 164, 174, 177–8, 214, 224, 226, 230, 236, 239, 245, 248, 266, 273–4

Ager Gallicus, 161

Agincourt, battle of, 204

Agnania, 38

agreement, 3, 27, 37, 73–4, 76, 89, 116, 130, 169

Agrigentum, 168, 200–202

Aisne River, 249

Alalia, 167

Alaudae, 233

Alba, 12

Alba Longa, 11

Alban Hills, 11, 43, 45, 264

Alban Mount, 11, 263

Albania, 83, 129, 201, 257

Alesia, 200, 248

Alexander, vii, 2, 44, 82–4, 96, 155, 158–60, 192, 213

Algidus, 41–3

Allia, battle, 15, 56, 59

alliance, vii, 37–8, 43, 47, 61–4, 66, 68–9, 71, 74–5, 80–2, 91, 137–8, 161, 173, 178, 184–6, 194, 226, 256, 271

allies, 29, 33, 43–5, 49, 52, 60, 63–5, 67–8, 71, 73, 75–7, 79–80, 85–9, 91, 113, 115, 121, 126, 134, 136–42, 148–9, 151, 154, 162, 165, 168–9, 171–3, 178–9, 183–4, 186, 189–91, 193–7, 202, 212–13, 215, 219, 221–2, 226–8, 230–2, 244–5, 247, 249, 253, 257, 267, 271

Alps, 150, 161–2, 164, 171, 212, 233, 249

Ambracia, 87, 137

Ammianus Marcellinus, 204, 210

Anagnini, 74

ancient world, 54, 61, 204, 252, 268

Andobales, chief, 220

Anio, 38, 41, 61

Antiochus, king, xi, 136, 140, 159, 161, 185, 189–94, 196, 216, 220, 231, 236, 271

Antium, 15, 42

Apennines, 31, 38–9, 42, 47, 50, 56, 60, 66–8, 91, 132, 161–2, 172, 215, 228

Appia, 65, 73, 90

Appian, 3, 86, 147, 193, 247

Appius Claudius Caecus, senator, 86

Appius Herdonius, 41

Apulia, 56, 70–3, 76, 81, 86, 89, 91, 173

Aquilonia, 78

Arausio, x, 126, 157

Archelaus, general, 248

archers, 19, 85, 103, 150, 221, 224, 230, 252–3, 255–7, 259–60

Archytas, 82

Ardea, 45–6, 59, 73

Arevaci, 217

Argos, 90

Aricia, 30, 45

Arienzo, 72

Ariovistus, 229, 249

Armenia, 252–3

Arminium, 91, 137, 161–2

armour, 12, 16, 18–19, 24–5, 54, 78, 84, 159–60, 192, 214, 252, 254–5, 263

arms, viii, 11, 16, 19, 24, 31, 62, 84, 98, 103, 106, 112, 135, 148, 158, 210, 225, 229, 232, 242, 248, 252, 268, 271

Arpaia, 72

Arpi, 88

Arpinum, 238

Arretium, 74, 76, 78, 80, 172
arrows, 90, 129, 253, 255–6
Arruns, 30
Arsaces, king, 256
Artavasdes, king, 253
Ascoli Piceno, 232
Asculum, 86, 111, 113, 115, 140, 159, 214
Asia, 1, 48, 53, 83–4, 115, 140, 157–8, 166,
    184–5, 189–92, 194, 202, 228, 233, 241–2,
    251, 255, 257, 272
Athens, vii, 51, 158, 185
Atilius Regulus, consul, 78, 162, 215
Atrax, 186
Atrebates, 249–50
attack, x, 29, 43, 45, 50, 57, 59, 62, 68–70, 73–5,
    77, 82, 84–5, 87–8, 90, 95–8, 103, 109–10,
    129–31, 135, 145, 147–51, 153–4, 160–1,
    163–4, 167–8, 170–1, 176–80, 183, 186,
    188, 192–3, 195, 197–9, 201–203, 205, 207,
    209–10, 214–17, 221, 224, 229, 242, 247–51,
    253–7, 259–60, 266
Attalids, 158
Attus Clausus, Sabine chief, 12
Atuatucae, 203
Aufidus River, 86, 174–5, 177, 204
Augustus, Emperor, vii–viii, xii–1, 7, 53, 99,
    105, 122, 124, 227, 232–3, 242, 245, 249, 263,
    265, 271–5
Aulus Gellius, author, 124
Aulus Hostilius Mancinus, consul, 195
Aulus Postumius Tubertus, dictator, 42
Aurunci, 69
Aventine Hill, 147
axes, 17–19

Baecula, 179
Baetis River, 179
Bagacum, 249
Bagradas River, 164, 221
Balearic Islands, 103, 230
Balikh River, 253–4
Balkans, 137, 183, 189–90, 194, 257
battlefield, 13, 19, 61, 63, 78, 83–4, 86, 90, 96–7,
    106–107, 131, 140, 148, 173–5, 177, 189, 196,
    204–206, 208–11, 213, 216, 222–3, 225, 231,
    247, 252
battles, vii, 5–7, 11–16, 18, 20, 23, 30–1, 37,
    40–3, 53–7, 61, 63, 67–8, 72–9, 81, 83–5,
    87–8, 90–1, 93–7, 99–103, 105–108, 111,
    113–17, 123, 128–30, 134, 137, 140–2, 147–
    51, 153–4, 159–63, 167–9, 171–81, 185–91,
    193, 196–98, 201, 204–17, 219–22, 224–6,

230–2, 240–2, 247, 249–51, 254, 256–64, 268,
    270–1
Bavacum, 249
Bay of Naples, 68, 70
Bedriacum, 206
Belgae, 149, 151, 249
Beneventum, 72, 91, 115
Bithynia, 242
bodies, 10–12, 18, 20, 26, 32, 54, 64, 84, 87, 89,
    98, 107, 138, 146, 151, 159–60, 208, 210, 212,
    232, 236, 262
Boii, 56, 81, 161, 163–4
Bologna, 19
borders, 40, 45–6, 69, 73, 75, 79, 136, 145, 158,
    162, 183, 186, 189, 194, 249, 252–3, 264,
    274–5
Bovianum, 74
bows, 55, 192, 255
Britain, 55, 151–2, 162, 217, 240
bronze, viii, 17–20, 23, 39, 51, 54, 67, 100, 112,
    114, 197, 207, 234
Brundisium, 257–8
Bruttians, 81, 85, 87, 89, 91
Brutus, 213, 245, 272
burials, 16–17, 19, 24–5
butts, 24, 39, 95, 104, 106, 109, 208

Caecilius Metellus, consul 239, 150–1, 156, 221,
    238–9, 244, 269
Caenina, 263
Caere, 47–9, 62, 64, 80, 167
Caesar, vii–viii, x, 1, 4–5, 14, 54–6, 102–103,
    107, 112, 114, 126–7, 129–31, 135, 145,
    149–51, 153–5, 200–208, 213, 217, 221–22,
    224–9, 231–3, 240–2, 244–5, 248–51, 253–4,
    257–62, 266, 269–72
Calabria, 81
Calatia, 74
Cales, 69, 73
Callinicus, 195
Camarina, 200
Camerinum, 74
Camillus, leader, 49–50, 57, 59–60, 114
camp, viii, 7, 30–1, 56, 78, 88, 101, 105, 124,
    126, 129–31, 133–4, 140, 148, 150, 152–7,
    162, 172, 175, 177, 179–81, 187–8, 192–3,
    196–8, 200–202, 205, 208, 213, 219, 221–2,
    225, 229, 248, 250–1, 254, 256, 259–60, 262,
    265–6, 268–9
campaigns, xi, 4, 13, 27, 30, 35–6, 38, 41–3,
    49, 51–2, 54, 59–60, 69, 71–5, 78–9, 83, 85,
    89–90, 105, 116, 118–19, 121–3, 126, 128–9,

132–3, 136–9, 142, 146–8, 150–3, 159, 162, 164, 169, 171–3, 175, 178–9, 185–6, 189, 191, 195, 205, 211–13, 220–1, 229–31, 233–4, 236, 240–1, 243–4, 248–9, 252–4, 257, 259, 265–6, 269, 275

Campania, 15, 24, 47–8, 63–5, 68–70, 72–4, 89, 116, 140, 167–8, 225, 266

Campi Arusini, 90

Campus Martius, 119, 146, 264, 269

Cannae, x, 85–6, 95, 111, 117, 123, 126, 157, 172–5, 177–8, 184, 193, 204–205, 210–11, 223, 236, 247, 268

Canosa, 56

Cape Bon, 164

Capena, 49

Capitoline, viii, 9, 12, 57, 59, 62, 119–20, 147, 264

Capua, 64–6, 68–9, 86, 116, 136, 225

Carrhae, 149, 248, 251–2, 254, 256

Carthage, ix, 2–3, 27–8, 48, 65–6, 83, 88–9, 97, 102–103, 106, 111–12, 117, 122, 125, 136, 147, 155, 157–8, 164–73, 175–81, 185, 190–1, 195, 199–203, 209–11, 214–16, 219, 230–1, 234, 240, 243, 266, 271

Casilinum, 136

Cassivelaunus, 55

casualties, 77, 85–6, 88, 90, 125, 142, 162, 172, 177–8, 189, 193, 196–9, 204, 209–13, 216, 222, 232, 234, 257, 261

Catadas, 164

catapult, 200–201

Caudine Forks, 72–3, 150

cavalry, ix, 10–13, 19–20, 22, 27, 31, 37, 44, 55, 61, 64, 77, 83–90, 103, 107–13, 115, 118–20, 128–9, 134–5, 137–8, 140–2, 146, 148–51, 153–7, 159–60, 162–3, 165–6, 172–80, 184, 186–8, 191–3, 195–7, 202, 204, 206–207, 209–10, 214–17, 219–21, 224–33, 241, 248–50, 252–60, 262–3, 274

Celtic, 52–7, 99–101, 103, 107, 159, 161–3, 165–6, 178, 222, 262, 268

Cenabum, 135

Cenomani, 56

census, 21–3, 30, 52, 106–107, 116, 118–19, 121, 137, 139, 143, 209–11, 226, 234–6, 238–9

centuries, vii, ix, xi–7, 9–27, 29, 31–5, 38–53, 55–6, 59–60, 62, 65–71, 76, 78, 80–4, 86, 88, 93–105, 107, 109–12, 114–20, 122, 124–28, 132–5, 137–8, 140–1, 146, 148–50, 152–3, 157–61, 164–5, 167, 169, 180, 183, 198–201, 204, 206–207, 209, 211, 213, 219–28, 230–44, 247–9, 252, 261–2, 266–70, 274–5

centurions, 12, 95, 105, 107, 127–32, 153, 156, 205, 207, 210, 222–4, 232, 236, 241, 251, 261–2, 267, 270

ceremonies, 51, 123, 146–7, 263–5

Chaeronea, 248

Chalons-en-Champagne, 249

chariots, 17, 55, 146, 162–3, 192–3, 264–5

chest protector, 17, 24, 39, 99–100, 117

children, 39, 56, 67, 98, 235

Cilicia, 127, 151, 228–9, 242, 259

Cimbri, 213, 222

Cimetra, 76

Ciminian forest, 74

Ciminian mountains, 74

Cincinnatus, consul, 41, 123

Cineas, advisor, 83, 86

Circus Maximus, 264

Cirta, 238

Cisalpine Gaul, 243, 249

citizens, viii, xi–xii, 10–11, 20–2, 26–7, 32–4, 41–2, 45–6, 50–3, 57, 60, 64–5, 75, 79–80, 84, 89, 98, 106, 108, 117–18, 120, 123–4, 137–9, 142, 161, 166, 173, 199, 212–13, 223–4, 226–33, 235, 238, 241–2, 244–5, 262, 266–7, 269–1, 273

civil wars, viii, xi, 3–5, 45, 67, 103, 124, 126, 129, 201, 206, 213, 217, 227, 229, 231–2, 239, 241, 243–5, 247–9, 251, 257, 261, 269, 271–2, 274

Claudius, emperor, 53, 69, 86, 147–8, 178, 263

Cleonymus, commander, 75

Cleopatra, 272

Clusium, 29, 162

coalition, 29–30, 43, 48, 55, 59, 61, 77–9, 81, 86, 157, 186, 251

coast, vii, 9, 14, 29, 38–9, 42, 48–9, 56, 63, 65, 68–9, 73, 79–81, 83, 88, 127, 136, 151, 153, 157, 162, 164–5, 169–70, 172, 178–9, 183, 190, 195, 200, 202, 244, 258, 265

cohorts, 121, 130, 139–40, 150, 207–209, 219–24, 226–7, 231–3, 240, 254–60, 274

colonies, 9, 19, 40, 44–8, 50, 59–60, 65–6, 69–70, 73–5, 78–80, 91, 142, 161, 164–5, 199, 235, 239–40, 243–5, 269, 272

colonists, 46–7, 60, 65, 73, 76, 161, 164, 199

combat, 7, 11, 16, 18, 44, 55, 61–2, 97–9, 101, 106, 115, 117, 128, 131, 149, 204, 207–208, 210, 221, 223, 240, 247, 250, 262–3, 266, 275

communities, ix, 9, 13, 21, 38–9, 41, 46, 54, 60, 64, 67, 73, 75, 80, 121, 138–43, 238, 241, 248, 263–4

conflict, viii, x, 9, 14, 20, 32, 36–7, 40–4, 48–9,

51, 53, 61, 63, 69, 74–6, 80–1, 89, 104, 107, 150, 157–8, 165, 167–8, 171, 184, 191–2, 195, 209, 215, 247, 252, 261, 274

conquest, vii–ix, 1, 7, 48, 52–3, 55, 79, 82–3, 89, 91, 137–8, 158, 184, 186, 230, 233, 235, 257, 265, 272, 274

consuls, ix–x, 4, 7, 14–15, 21, 30–7, 41, 45, 51–2, 60, 63, 69–74, 76–81, 86–90, 105–106, 116, 118–26, 134, 139–42, 146–7, 152, 161–2, 168, 172–3, 177–8, 183, 185, 188, 191, 195, 203, 205, 215, 217, 221, 228–9, 235, 238, 242, 244, 251, 259, 263, 266–7, 270

contubernium, 205, 222, 240

Cora, 44

Cordoba, 243

Coriolanus, Roman commander, 42–3

Cornelius Balbus, 273

Cornelius Cossus, 62, 263

Cornelius Dolabella, 81

Cornelius Lentulus, 259

Corsica, 48, 100, 165, 167, 169, 171, 233

Cremera, 14–15, 48–9

Cremera River, 48

Crete, 103, 224

crossbow, 200

cuirass, 23, 99–100, 108–109, 160

Cumae, 48, 66, 68

Curius Dentatus, commander, 41, 80, 90, 119

Cynoscephalae, 96, 160, 186–8, 192, 198, 210, 216, 226, 231

Cyrenaica, 164

daggers, 17, 19, 104–105

dead, 25, 88, 168, 198, 208–10, 217, 242, 261, 263

death, vii, 33, 77, 83, 88, 96, 146, 158–9, 168, 183, 198, 204, 211–13, 220, 240, 242–3, 260, 267–8, 272

Decius, 63, 77, 86, 140

defeat, viii, x–xi, 3, 14–15, 30, 38, 40–1, 43, 45, 48, 56–7, 59–64, 68, 72–81, 88–91, 94–5, 97, 109, 112, 117, 125, 137, 147, 151, 157, 160, 162, 165, 167–8, 172–3, 176, 178–9, 184–6, 189–90, 194–5, 197, 201, 206, 213, 215, 217, 220, 225, 227, 230–1, 236, 242, 248–50, 253–4, 257, 263, 265, 269, 274

Delos, 104

Delphi, 99, 109

Demetrias, 183–4, 187, 194

deployment, 24, 94–5, 97–8, 107, 111, 117, 140, 148, 175–6, 179, 181, 192, 206–207, 217, 224–5

Diodorus Siculus, author, 1–2, 51, 54–5, 75, 200

Dionysius, author, 1–2, 5–6, 14, 21, 37, 56, 62, 101, 113, 115, 123, 140, 157, 199–201

disease, 116, 203, 211, 240

Dium, 186, 195

Dora, 74

Drepana, 148

Dyrrachium, 129, 201–202, 248, 257–9

Ebro River, 169–70, 178, 220, 267

Egnatia, 257

Egypt, 4, 84, 91, 99, 159, 185, 190, 260, 265, 272

elephants, 83–90, 96–7, 103, 166, 172, 179–80, 187–8, 191–3, 197, 213–18

Elpeus River, 195–6

embassy, 80, 82, 145–6, 170, 183, 185, 195

emigration, 46, 66

empire, vii–viii, xii, 6, 45, 68, 70–1, 83, 122, 127, 129, 137–8, 146, 157, 164–5, 169, 191, 222–3, 226–7, 233, 242, 244–5, 248–9, 262, 265, 271, 273–5

Emporion, 169

enemy, vii–ix, xi, 4, 11, 14, 33, 43–4, 54–5, 60–4, 77, 79, 83, 87, 94–6, 98–103, 106–108, 110–12, 114, 126, 129, 134–5, 137, 145–6, 148–1, 153–4, 160–1, 163, 166–7, 172, 175–7, 180, 191, 198, 206–12, 215, 217–19, 221, 224–5, 230, 242, 244, 248, 250–2, 254–6, 258, 260–4, 266–7, 270

Enipeus River, 258–9

Epirus, 82–3, 85, 88, 183, 257

equipment, 5, 7, 15–20, 22–7, 39–40, 44, 48, 53–4, 62, 67, 84, 93, 96, 98–101, 104–10, 112–13, 115–17, 131, 135, 140, 142, 159, 163, 165, 188, 192, 201, 205–209, 219, 221–2, 225–6, 240, 248, 250, 253, 255, 263

Esquiline Hill, 17, 99

Etruria, 9, 11, 14, 17–21, 24–5, 27, 29–30, 33, 36, 39–41, 45–50, 56, 59, 62–3, 66, 74–81, 85–6, 91, 94, 100–101, 104, 112, 136, 138, 147, 162, 167, 172, 263, 270

Etruscan, 9, 12, 14, 16, 18–19, 24–5, 27, 29–30, 40, 47–50, 62–4, 74–7, 80, 98, 100, 104, 138, 167, 263

Euboea, 191

Eumenes, 194

Fabian clan, 14–15

Fabii, 2, 14–15, 20, 49, 74, 77, 99, 173

Fabius Gurges, consul, 79

Fabius Maximus, consul, 31, 74, 76–7, 80, 172, 266

Fabius Maximus Servilianus, proconsul, 266
Fabius Pictor, historian, 2, 15, 111, 117
Fabricius Luscinus, consul, 81
Falerii, 62–3, 76
Fidenae, 14, 49
Fifth Legion, 233
First Illyrian War, 183
First Macedonian War, 184, 189, 231
First Punic War, viii, 2–3, 5, 51, 102, 104, 111,
    117, 120, 136, 141, 147, 164–5, 167, 169, 171,
    200, 214, 230, 233
First Samnite War, 116
First Triumvirate, 251
First World War, 12, 166, 204, 212
Flavius Fimbria, 241
fleet, 48, 126–7, 137, 141, 147, 166, 168–9, 171,
    183, 190, 195, 202, 212, 234, 257–8
forces, 3, 13, 29–30, 33, 37, 44, 68–9, 72, 77,
    81–3, 88–9, 97, 102, 106, 109, 115–16, 121–2,
    126, 129, 135, 137–8, 140–2, 150, 153, 161,
    165, 168, 171, 174–6, 178–81, 183, 187, 192,
    195–6, 206, 209, 217–18, 222, 225, 230–2,
    235–6, 242, 254, 258–9, 266–7, 274–5
Fregellae, 69–70, 73
Fufius Cita, 135

Gades, 179
Gaesati, 54, 162–3
Gaius Cassius, 254
Gaius Domitius Ahenobarbus, legate, 99, 192,
    258
Gaius Flaminius, 147, 150, 161, 172
Gaius Marius, commander, 150, 206, 221
Gaius Sempronius Atratinus, commander, 43
Gaius Sulpicius Peticus, dictator, 62
Gaius Trebatius, jurist, 269
Galatia, 272
Galilee, 95, 223
Galli, 52
Gallic War, 4, 103, 130, 240, 248
Gallicus, 57, 161
Gaugamela, 155
Gauls, viii, x, 2, 4, 7, 43, 48, 52–7, 59, 61–2, 65,
    76–7, 79–81, 86, 91, 103, 114, 126, 129–31,
    142, 149–51, 153–5, 161–4, 169, 171–2, 174,
    213, 217, 226, 229, 231–3, 240–3, 245, 247,
    249–51, 253, 259, 262, 270, 272, 274
Gauls Viridomar, 61
Gaza, 190
Gellius Egnatius, commander, 77
Gelon, 155
generals, x, 82, 125, 147–8, 150, 166, 192,

223–4, 239–40, 244, 247, 264–5, 269
Genucian Law, 60, 116
Germans, 53, 129, 213, 229, 245, 248
Gerunium, 173–4
Glabrio, 191
Gnaeus Manlius Vulso, consul, 52
Gnaeus Naevius, 5
Gnaeus Octavius, 195
Gnaeus Pompeius Strabo, 127, 232
Gnaeus Servilius Geminus, 172
Goliath, 61
Greece, 4, 21, 23–5, 56, 87, 90, 101, 104, 115,
    132, 158–9, 166, 184–6, 190–1, 194, 198, 200,
    231, 234, 236, 248, 258, 270, 272
Gulf of Actium, 137
Gulf of Tarentum, 75, 81
Gulf of Tunis, 164

Hadria, 79
Hadrumentum, 164
Halicarnassus, 1
Hamilcar Barca, 169
Hannibal, x, 3, 43, 85–6, 97, 103, 111, 143, 150,
    157, 165–6, 169–9, 181, 183–6, 190, 200, 210,
    212, 215, 225, 233, 235–6, 247
Hasdrubal Gisgo, general, 169, 179–1, 215, 219
hasta velitaris, 93, 107, 116
hastati, 93–4, 97, 103, 116, 128, 141, 149, 156,
    209
helmets, 17–19, 22–3, 39, 54, 56, 67, 78, 99–100,
    107–109, 112, 114, 116
Helvetii, 103, 150, 249
Heraclea, 85–6, 91, 214
Hercules, 197, 270
Hernici, 38, 42–4, 59–60, 74–5
hoplites, 18, 21, 23–6, 31, 39–40, 44, 48, 84, 94,
    98, 100–102, 106, 112–13, 117, 135, 140, 159,
    192, 198, 208, 212
Horatius, 63
horses, 11, 13, 31, 37, 54, 70, 84–5, 103, 105,
    108, 110–11, 134, 137, 146–7, 156, 166, 173,
    175, 177, 186, 192, 202, 214, 225, 227, 229,
    252, 255, 262

Ilerda, 206, 208, 224
Ilipa, 178–9, 181, 207, 215, 219, 225, 230
Illyria, 136, 166, 183–4, 187
Illyricum, 245, 251
Ineditum Vaticanum, 111–13
infantry, 10–12, 21–7, 30–1, 37, 77, 83–4,
    87–90, 93–4, 101, 103, 105–11, 113, 119, 121,
    134–5, 137, 140, 142, 148–9, 151, 154, 156–7,

159–60, 162–3, 165–6, 172–80, 186–8, 191–3, 196–8, 204, 207, 209–10, 214–18, 221, 224–8, 230–3, 248, 252–3, 255, 257, 259–60, 262, 274

Insubres, 56, 161, 163

invasion, 9, 33, 39, 68–9, 74, 76, 88–9, 106, 117, 137, 143, 151, 161–2, 165, 168, 171, 178, 183, 186, 215, 240, 248, 251, 253

iron, 17, 19, 24, 39, 47, 54–5, 87, 100, 102, 104, 114, 146, 199, 207, 214, 221

Iron Age, 18–19, 46

Italy, xi, 1–2, 9–10, 17, 19, 21, 24, 29, 32–34, 38–39, 46–7, 50, 52, 54, 56, 61–2, 64–6, 68–70, 74–5, 77, 79, 81–3, 85–6, 89–1, 98–101, 104–105, 112, 118, 121–2, 126–7, 129, 132, 136–8, 141–3, 161–2, 164–5, 167, 169, 171–3, 178–9, 183–4, 194–5, 200, 214–15, 222, 226–38, 240, 242–5, 248, 257, 265, 269–70, 272

javelin, 1, 12, 19, 22, 24, 39, 55, 67, 93–4, 97, 101–103, 106–108, 112, 114, 116, 160, 165–6, 216, 224, 260

Judaea, 274

Jugurtha, 5, 151, 156, 221, 225, 227, 231, 238, 244, 267

Jugurthine War, 156, 221

Julius Frontinus, writer, 223, 225–6

Junius, 219

Kaeso, Roman envoy, 111–2

kardiophylax, 100, 112

Kasr el-Harit, 99

killed, x, 62, 67, 77–8, 80–81, 91, 131, 135, 163, 168, 172, 177–8, 183, 189, 193, 196, 205, 207, 210–11, 213, 217, 235, 241, 257, 260–4, 266–7

kings, vii–ix, 3, 10–14, 21, 27, 29–32, 36, 41, 44, 47, 49, 51, 53, 61, 83–91, 96, 98–9, 105, 109, 122, 126, 136, 147, 151, 158–60, 165, 167, 178, 183–7, 189–98, 201, 213, 216–17, 225, 229–32, 238, 241, 252–3, 256–7, 263, 265, 274

knives, 17, 19

Labici, 42, 45

Lacinian Promontory, 82

Lacus Regillus, 31, 37

Laevinus, 85

Lake Trasimene, 147, 150, 161, 172

Lake Vadimon in Etruria, 81

lances, 108–9, 146, 192

land, xi, 24, 32–4, 38, 44–6, 48–50, 59, 61, 64–5, 68–9, 78–81, 84, 89, 91, 117, 126–7, 129, 132, 137, 141, 152, 161, 169, 171, 174, 183, 187,

191, 202, 215, 220, 232, 235–40, 243–5, 251, 266, 269–73

Lanuvium, 43, 59

Larissa, 137, 195

Lars Porsenna, 29

Lars Tolumnius, 263

Latina, 65, 69, 86

Latium, 9, 15–17, 19–20, 25–8, 38–45, 47, 49, 62, 65, 68–9, 73, 75, 86, 91, 235, 238

Lautulae, 73

laws, 33–4, 36, 46, 60, 82, 116, 123, 145, 161, 169, 174, 229, 237, 267

leaders, 11, 13, 15, 20, 33, 36–8, 59–60, 77, 82, 94, 127, 131, 153, 163, 215, 217, 233, 264

leather, 17–18, 23, 67, 106, 108–109, 112

legates, viii, 79–80, 125–7, 130, 146, 149–51, 154, 191–2, 228, 232, 238, 241–2, 249, 251, 256–7, 270, 274

legionaries, xi, 23, 30, 65, 95, 99, 101, 103–104, 106–107, 116, 127, 130, 153–4, 157, 196–8, 205, 207–208, 219, 221–3, 225–6, 234, 240–41, 243, 245, 261, 267–8, 270, 273–4

legions, ix–xi, 22, 26, 30–1, 34–5, 45–6, 51, 77, 79, 85, 87–8, 94, 96, 99, 104, 106, 108, 113–15, 118–21, 125, 127–30, 133–5, 139–42, 148–50, 152–4, 156–7, 160, 162, 172–3, 176, 186, 192–3, 195–8, 207–208, 211–13, 215, 217, 219–22, 224–5, 227–30, 233–41, 244–5, 247–51, 253, 257–60, 262, 266–7, 271–5

Lepidus, 193, 245

levies, xi, 12, 31, 33, 35, 40, 44, 52, 79, 84, 89, 106, 116–22, 124, 128, 139, 165, 201, 211, 224, 229, 234, 236, 239–40, 253, 272

Liguria, 105, 173, 195, 197, 222

Liris, 38, 42, 68–9

Liris River, 42, 68–9

Livy, xi, 1–3, 5–7, 14, 20–1, 29, 31, 35, 37, 40, 43–5, 49–51, 56–7, 59, 61–3, 67–70, 72–9, 99, 101, 103–105, 107–108, 113–14, 116, 123–6, 132, 136, 140-42, 173–4, 177, 193, 196–8, 205, 208–209, 211, 219–20, 225, 234–6, 270–1

Locri, 81, 89

Longanus River, 168

losses, vii, ix, xi, 30, 37, 46, 48, 67, 76, 82–3, 85–6, 89–90, 117, 125, 129, 137, 163, 165–7, 171, 177–8, 180, 186, 191, 193, 197, 209–13, 237, 240, 248, 258, 268, 271–2

Lucania, 71, 73, 75–6, 81–2, 85, 87, 89–91

Luceres, 10

Luceria, 72–3

Lucilius, centurion, 131

Lucius Aemilius Pappus, consul, 162

Lucius Aemilius Paullus, consul, 126, 173, 195
Lucius Afranius, commander, 208, 224, 232,
   257, 259
Lucius Cornelius Scipio Barbatus, consul, 76
Lucius Fufidius, governor, 241
Lucius Licinius Lucullus, consul, x, 242–3
Lucius Marcius, Roman knight, 219, 267
Lucius Petronius, equestrian, 241
Lucius Quinctius Cincinnatus, dictator, 41
Lucius Scipio, consul, 191–2
Lucius Sertinius, proconsul, 270
Lucius Sextius, plebeian, 60
Lucius Vorenus, centurian, 131, 205

M. Furius Camillus, dictator, 49–50, 57, 59–60,
   114
Macedonia, 3, 5, 13, 83–5, 87–8, 90, 95–6, 99,
   108–109, 113, 115, 122, 126, 136–7, 151,
   158–60, 166, 183–90, 194–8, 216, 230–1,
   234–6, 240, 245, 251, 257–8, 269
magistrates, 6–7, 10, 15, 30–6, 48, 66, 71, 80,
   118, 126, 139, 142, 190, 267
Magnesia, 140–1, 191–2, 196, 198, 207, 216,
   220, 231
Malventum, 89–91
Mamertini, 89, 167–8
maniples, 93–7, 103, 106–107, 113, 117, 127–30,
   134, 139–40, 149, 156–7, 160, 163, 176–7,
   180, 188, 205, 207–209, 211, 216, 219–24,
   240, 271
Manius Curius Dentatus, consul, 41, 118
Marc Antony, commander, viii, 227, 245, 247,
   258, 272
Marcellus, 61–2
Marcus Antonius, 213
Marcus Cassius Scaeva, centurion, 129
Marcus Claudius Marcellus, consul, 263
Marcus Fannius, 99
Marcus Minucius Rufus, 173
Marcus Petreius, commander, 208, 231–2, 257
Marcus Terentius Varro, writer, 5, 93, 173–6
Marcus Thermus, 228
Marius, 1, 102, 114, 122, 133, 135, 150, 206,
   221, 225, 238–41, 244, 248
Marruncini, 219
Marseille, 48
Marsi, 75–6
Masinissa, 136, 217, 230–1
Massilia, 48, 169–70
Massinissa, prince, 228, 230
Mediolanum, 56
Mediterranean, vii, xii, 2–3, 11–12, 16, 24, 27,
   48, 51, 53–6, 62, 84, 90, 98, 111, 122, 127,
   132–3, 135, 157–9, 164–6, 183–4, 199, 201,
   205, 207, 212–13, 231, 233, 242, 253, 257,
   263, 265
Megalopolis, 3
Menapii, 149
mercenaries, 44, 54, 56, 62, 77, 84–90, 98, 102,
   104, 159, 162, 165–70, 178, 187, 192, 196,
   199, 227, 230, 252
Mesopotamia, 190, 256
Messana, 167–8
Messapia, 81–2, 85, 91
Messina, 167
Metapontum, 91
Metaurus, 210
Metellus Denter, commander, 80
Metellus Scipio, 217, 257
Meuse, 149
Mevania, 75
Milo, 83
mines, 47, 164, 169, 198
Minturnae, 63
Minucius Thermus, consul, 105, 173, 177
missiles, 17, 19–20, 24, 84, 87–8, 96–7, 101, 103,
   107–108, 149, 153, 155, 159, 163, 180, 193,
   200, 208, 214–16, 225, 250, 252, 254
Mithridates Eupator, king, 225, 242, 248, 251,
   265
monarchy, vii, 1, 10, 13–14, 27–9, 31–2, 60, 84,
   158–60, 165, 198, 212, 230, 274
Monti Lepini, 42, 44
Motya, 165, 200
Mount Algidus pass, 45
Mount Vesuvius, 63
Mt Olympus, 195
Mt. Soracte, 49
Munda, 241
Murlo, 29
Muthul River, 221
Mutina, 247
Mylae, 168

Naples, 47, 68–71, 75, 86
Narnia, 79
Naulochus, 272
Nepet, 45, 50, 59, 63
Nervii, 131, 149, 151, 153–4, 205–206, 249–51
New Carthage, 106, 169, 178, 199, 203, 210, 271
Nola, 70
Norba, 44
North Africa, vii, 106, 164–5, 168, 171, 217,
   233, 236, 244, 251, 254, 261

Numa Pompilius, viii, 41
Numantia, 7, 101, 131, 152, 156, 217, 238
Numidia, ix, 5, 105, 122, 136, 165–6, 176–8, 216–17, 221, 226, 228, 230, 238–9

oath, 15, 78–9, 122–4, 139, 145–6, 156–7, 173, 245, 271, 273
Octavian, 147, 213, 247, 272
Octavius Mamilius of Tusculum, 36
operations, 31, 51–2, 70, 73, 121–2, 127, 132, 136–7, 139, 171, 174, 179, 199, 201, 212, 214, 217, 220–21, 227, 238
Opici, 67
opposition, xi, 30, 43, 56, 59, 66, 77, 90, 97, 122, 157, 162–3, 165, 168, 181, 190, 195, 209, 217, 220, 231, 233–5, 239, 243–4, 255
Orgetorix, Helvetian noble, 14
Oso River, 161
Otranto, 183

P. Decius Mus, consul, 86
P. Rutilius Rufus, consul, 106, 248
P. Sulpicius Saverrio, consul, 86
Padua, 105
Paeligni, 75, 140, 197, 219
Paestum, 91
Palatine Hill, 9, 264
Palestine, 166, 185
Panormus, 102, 117, 165
Papirius Cursor, 270
Pappus, 162–3
parma, 107–109, 225
Parthia, 149, 151, 248, 251–7, 259
patricians, 10, 32, 35–6, 51, 60, 123, 266
Paullus, 96, 174–7, 195–7
peace, viii-x, 37, 60, 62–3, 69, 74, 76, 89, 166–7, 169, 184–5, 189, 195, 216
Pedum, 42
Peloponnese, 3, 51, 158, 186
Peloponnesian War, 51
peltasts, 187, 192, 196
Peneus River, 258
Pentri, 74
Pergamum, 84, 158, 184–5, 190, 192, 194, 231
Perseus, king, xi, 3, 99, 109, 122, 151, 160, 187, 194–8, 204, 216, 219, 234, 265, 269
Persia, vii, 48, 186, 190, 199
Perusia, 78
Petra, 195
phalanx, 5, 23–6, 37, 40, 61, 84–8, 93–8, 103–104, 106, 111–15, 159–60, 187–9, 192–3, 196–8, 215–16, 220–2

phalerae, 262
Pharsalus, 103, 106, 187, 206–207, 222–4, 231, 241, 245, 257–9, 261
Pherae, 187
Philip, xi, 84, 96, 160, 183–90, 192, 194, 200–201, 216, 225–6, 231, 236, 271
Philippi, 245, 272
Philo, 70–1
Phoenice, 183–4
Phoenicia, 48, 164–5, 167, 199
Phrygios, 192
Phthiotic Thebes, 158, 187
Picenum, 79
pikes, 84, 87, 96–7, 159
pila, 94, 102–103, 206–208, 260
pilani, 94
pilum, 1, 94, 101–103, 107, 115, 221
pilus, 128, 236
Pindus Mountains, 132, 195
Pisa, 137, 162
plebeians, 32–3, 35–6, 51, 59–60, 70, 119, 121, 123, 243–4, 266
Plutarch, 4–5, 57, 96, 114–15, 133, 196–8, 254–7, 259
Po valley, 24, 47–8, 56, 161, 164, 172, 244
Polybius, 3, 5, 23, 27, 55, 61, 76, 81, 93, 95–6, 100–10, 113, 116–17, 120, 122–4, 128, 130, 132–5, 137, 139–40, 145, 148–50, 152–3, 155–7, 159–63, 166, 168, 174–8, 180, 189, 196–7, 203–204, 210, 214–15, 219–20, 224–5, 228, 234, 261–2, 265, 270–1
Pompeius Strabo, 228
Pompey, xi, 103, 107, 127, 129, 147, 201–202, 206–208, 213, 222–3, 227–8, 231–2, 240, 242, 244, 248, 251–2, 257–61, 265–6
Pomptine Plain, 42–3, 45, 60
Pontus, 241–2
Porta Decumana, 154
Porta Praetoria, 154
Porta Principalis Dextra and Sinistra, 154
Porta Triumphalis, 264
ports, 15, 39, 70, 81, 100, 148, 164, 167, 169, 179, 202, 217, 257–8
Postumius Albinus, dictator, 37
Praeneste, 42–3, 61–2, 64
praetors, 71, 80, 125, 141, 162, 177, 195, 233, 267
primus pilus, 128, 236
prisoners, 77, 81, 86, 151, 162–3, 172, 177, 255, 264
Ptolemaic, 83–4, 91, 98, 158–9, 166, 185, 190, 213, 216

Ptolemy Ceraunus, 83
Publicus Decius Mus, consul, 63
Publilius Cornelius Scipio, consul, 172
Publius Cornelius Scipio, 178
Publius Licinius Crassus, consul, 195
Publius Sulpicius Galba, consul, 185
Publius Valerius, 15
Publius Villius Tappulus, consul, 235
Punic, 167, 169, 171, 174, 178, 215, 233
Punic Wars, 118, 233
Puteoli, 68, 70
Pydna, 96, 99, 160, 196, 198, 206, 216, 219, 231, 251
Pyrgi, 167
Pyrrhic War, 2, 115
Pyrrhus, 2, 66, 83–91, 111, 113, 115, 118, 140, 159, 167–8, 183, 214
Pythium, 195

Quinctius Cincinnatus, consul, 41
Quintana, 154
Quintus Cicero, viii, 4, 6, 21, 45, 127, 129, 131, 135, 145, 148, 151, 154, 205, 228–9, 234, 269
Quintus Ennius, 5
Quintus Fabius Maximus Rullianus, consul, 74, 76, 80, 172
Quintus Marcius Philippus, consul, 195
Quintus Publilius Philo, consul, 70
Quintus Statorius, Roman centurian, 105

Ramnenses, 10
ranks, vii, 70, 97, 111, 113, 126–7, 129–30, 135, 163, 177, 180, 204, 207, 227, 236, 241, 247, 255, 260–2, 266–7
Raphia, 159, 190
rations, 133–5, 139, 261
Ravenna, 161
rear, 26, 77, 79, 88, 94, 96, 113–14, 128, 134, 141, 148–50, 154, 159–60, 177, 188, 192, 195, 205, 207–10, 216, 221–2, 249–51, 259–60
rebellion, 76, 116, 189–90, 223, 270, 274
Regia, 147
Regulus, commander, 117, 162–3
reign, viii, xii, 3, 11–12, 27, 49, 84, 99, 233, 245, 273–5
Renieblas, 101, 152
reserves, 22, 44, 46, 77, 87, 94, 96, 117–18, 137, 160, 191, 206, 220, 224
Rhegium, 81–2, 89, 91, 139, 167–8
Rhodes, 103, 127, 158, 184–5, 194, 231
river, 9, 14, 49, 57, 68, 85, 132, 136, 151, 153, 164, 169, 172, 174–5, 177–8, 192, 249–51,

253–4, 258–9
Romulus, 7, 10–11, 49, 62, 263
Rusellae, 78
Rutulians, 46

Sabellians, 38, 66, 68
Sabines, 13, 38, 40–1, 43, 67, 79, 162
Sabinus, 153
Sacco River, 41
sacrifice, 39, 62–3, 67, 78, 109, 146–8, 197, 265
Saguntum, 170–1
Sambre River, 153
Samnite Wars, 11, 65, 74, 113
Samnites, 38, 43, 63–4, 66–81, 85, 87, 90–1, 101, 107, 112–13, 115–16, 118, 123, 125
Samnium, 70–4, 76, 78–9, 82, 86, 89, 243
Sardinia, 136–7, 162, 165, 169–71, 233, 237
Sardis, 192–3
sarissa, 84, 96, 115, 159–60, 197
Satricum, 15, 43, 59
Scheldt River, 149, 249–50
Scipio, 3, 97, 106, 156, 172, 178–81, 196, 203, 209, 215–17, 219–20, 230, 236, 239, 243, 258–59, 266–7, 271
fortification, 217
Scipio Aemilianus, consul, 3, 122, 131, 156, 174, 238, 265
Scipio Africanus, commander, 3, 97, 103, 106, 150, 166, 174, 191–2, 199, 203, 207, 210, 220, 230, 242, 266
Scipio brothers, 242
Scipio Corculum, 204
Scotussa, 187
scutum, 19, 26, 67, 98–100, 112, 142, 163, 198
scythes, 87, 214
Second Macedonian War, 108, 184
Second Punic War, x, 1–3, 23, 97, 104, 109, 117–19, 121, 125, 136–7, 139, 142, 165–7, 169, 185–6, 191, 193, 212, 215–16, 226, 228, 230, 232, 234, 236–7, 267
Second Samnite War, 69, 76, 82, 99, 150
Sempronius Sophus, 74
Sena Gallica, 79, 81, 161
Senate, 2, 4, 12, 14, 21, 30, 32–3, 36, 45–6, 51–3, 61, 68, 86, 91, 119, 121–2, 125–7, 137–9, 142, 146, 168, 172–4, 177, 183–5, 189, 194, 212, 227, 235, 238–9, 242–3, 249, 264, 273–4
Senones, 56, 62, 81, 161
Sentinum, 63, 77, 79–80, 86
Servia, 7, 23, 25–6, 30, 44, 59, 101, 107, 111–12, 115–16, 119, 227, 234
service, ix, xi–xii, 10, 22, 26–7, 33, 45–6, 51–2,

54, 56, 60–1, 65, 78, 84, 107–108, 116–18, 120–3, 125, 127, 134, 139–40, 142–3, 156, 174, 184, 205, 212, 223–9, 231–6, 238–45, 262, 268, 270, 272–4
Servius Tullius, king, 10, 13, 20–1, 27, 93
settlement, 9, 27, 29, 37, 39, 46–8, 56, 59, 64, 69, 138, 183, 189, 198, 235, 240, 245
Sextus Baculus, commander, 130, 205
Sextus Pompeius, 245, 272
shields, 17–20, 22–3, 26, 39–40, 54, 67, 84, 87, 95–6, 98–100, 103, 106–109, 112–14, 116, 130, 142, 146–7, 149, 159–60, 165, 192–3, 197, 206–208, 225, 250
ships, 66, 75, 80, 136, 141, 147, 183, 198, 257, 265
Sicily, 2, 83, 88–9, 125, 137, 147–8, 165, 167–72, 199–200, 215, 233, 237, 272
Sidicini, 63, 68–9, 140
siege, xi, 3, 49–51, 68, 70–1, 73–4, 82, 84, 86, 114, 117, 131, 135–6, 139, 154, 164, 168–70, 187, 198–203, 214–15, 225, 248, 258, 262, 271
Signia, 44
Silarus River, 68
Silver Shields, 192, 197
Sinuessa, 63
Siris River, 85
slaves, 21, 40–1, 50–1, 64, 117–18, 124, 134, 138, 156, 168, 172, 235, 237, 252, 264, 269
Social War, 127, 138, 213, 226, 228, 231–2, 239, 244, 262
soldiers, x–xi, 26, 40, 49, 78–80, 93–4, 98, 100–101, 103, 105–106, 112, 114, 116, 121, 123–4, 128–36, 139, 142, 150, 153, 156–7, 159, 188, 193, 204–11, 219–21, 224–6, 232–3, 236, 240–1, 243–5, 247, 251, 254–5, 258–9, 262–4, 266–73
Somme, 204, 249
Soria, 101
Sorrentine Peninsular, 68
Spain, viii, x–xi, 4, 7, 48, 101–102, 104–106, 118, 121–2, 127, 131, 142, 152, 157, 164–6, 169–72, 178–9, 181, 183, 195, 206, 208, 213, 215, 217, 220, 227–8, 230, 232–4, 236, 238, 240–5, 248, 251, 257–8, 261, 266, 270, 272, 274
Sparta, 51, 158
Spartacus, 252, 268
spears, 17, 19–20, 22–4, 39, 53, 55, 67, 72, 84, 93–6, 102–105, 108, 112, 114–15, 117, 146, 159–60, 188, 197–8, 206, 221–2, 252, 256, 260, 262
spikes, 87, 138, 214

Spurius Cassius, consul, 37, 129, 213, 245, 254, 256, 272
Spurius Ligustinus, primus pilus, 236, 241
Strabo, geographer, 53, 56, 67
Straits of Messina, 167
Straits of Otranto, 183
strength, 27, 50, 55, 68, 73, 77, 82, 85, 89, 96, 99, 102, 104, 106–107, 114, 119, 123, 151, 155, 160, 168, 194–5, 205, 211, 222–3, 242–4, 252–3, 255, 259
Suessa, 116
suffering, 79, 89, 210, 215
Sulla, xi, 239, 241, 243–4, 248
supplies, x, 4, 6, 19, 22, 27, 52, 64, 77, 83–4, 126, 132–7, 141–2, 147, 151, 154, 160, 162, 164, 168, 171, 173–5, 179, 196, 202, 208–209, 213, 228, 239, 249, 253, 258–9
Surena, 253–4, 256
surrender, 60–2, 68, 72–3, 75, 91, 150, 153, 158, 169–70, 188, 191, 195, 198, 203, 216, 257, 261
Sutrium, 45, 50, 59, 63, 74, 94
swords, 17–20, 22–4, 39, 53, 55, 87, 94–5, 97, 99, 101, 103–10, 112, 114–15, 131, 159–60, 163, 197–8, 207–208, 210, 214, 232, 247, 252, 260, 267
Sybaris, 47
Syphax, king, 105
Syracuse, 56, 62, 88–9, 136, 155, 165, 167–8, 199–200, 203
Syria, 149, 158, 166, 185, 190, 233, 247, 251–3, 257, 259, 274

Tacitus, 224
Tappulus, 235
Tarentines, 82, 85, 87
Tarentum, 39, 47, 70, 75, 81–3, 85–8, 90–1, 139, 167, 173
Tarquinius Priscus, king, 10–13, 21, 27, 29, 36, 47, 62
Tarquinius Superbus, king, 12, 29
Taurisci, 162–3
taxes, xi, 33, 52, 118, 125, 164–65, 198, 226–7, 234–5, 237, 251, 275
Telamon, 56, 101, 161–2, 169, 270
temple, viii, 12, 25, 32–3, 50, 61–2, 64, 263–5, 269–70
Tenth Legion, 229, 250
Terracina, 42–3, 73
territory, viii, xi, 26–7, 37–8, 40–5, 48–50, 59–60, 64, 67, 70–1, 73, 75–6, 78–9, 82, 89, 103, 117, 120, 126, 145–6, 149–50, 153–4, 158–9, 161, 164, 168, 184–6, 189–91, 193–4,

200, 202, 215, 226, 249, 252–3
Teutones, 222
Thapsus, 217
Thessaly, 99, 137, 186–7, 191, 195, 258
Third Macedonian War, 3, 137, 230–1, 258
Third Samnite War, 41, 75, 80, 123, 243
Thrace, 190
Thurii, 75, 81–2, 91
Tiber, vii, 9, 14, 27, 33, 38, 41, 47, 49–50, 56–7, 69, 74, 172, 238, 243, 245
Tiberius Gracchus, politician, 238, 243
Tibur, 27, 42–3, 61–2, 64
Ticinus River, 172
Tifernum, 74
Tigris River, 252
Timaeus, 2
Titienses, 10
Titurius Sabinus, Caesar's legate, 153
Titus Aebutius, 37
Titus Manlius Torquatus, nobleman, 61
Titus Pullo, centurion, 131, 205
Titus Quinctius Flamininus, commander, 147, 150, 161, 172, 186–8, 216, 226
Tivoli, 27
tomb, viii, 17, 33, 99–100
training, 6, 103, 105–106, 127, 156, 173–4, 176, 179–80, 186, 205, 231, 247–8, 253, 255, 260–1, 268
treaties, x, 27–8, 37–8, 44, 48, 60, 62, 64–6, 68, 73–6, 78–80, 82–3, 138, 141–2, 145–6, 152, 167–9, 184–5, 189, 216
Trebia, 172, 176, 193, 215
Trebia River, 43
Trebium, 42
Trerus Valley, 38
triarii, 93–5, 97, 104, 114–15, 128, 141, 149, 156, 160, 205, 209, 222–3
tribes, x, 10, 12, 21, 30, 38, 40, 50, 52, 55–6, 59–60, 62, 66, 73–5, 81, 101, 110, 116, 120, 149, 153, 157–8, 161, 164–5, 170, 189, 217, 220–2, 229–30, 249, 273
tributum, 52, 60, 226
Trifanum, 63
troops, x–xi, 7, 12, 20, 24, 26, 31, 40, 44, 52, 56, 63–6, 78, 81, 83–8, 90, 93–7, 102–103, 105–108, 112–14, 116–17, 120–2, 125, 131, 133–6, 139–40, 142, 147–50, 153–6, 159–60, 162–3, 165–6, 173–5, 178–81, 183, 187–9, 192–3, 195–7, 201–203, 205–209, 212, 214–15, 217, 219, 221–7, 230–3, 235, 239, 241–3, 248, 250–1, 253, 255, 257–61, 266–7, 269–5
Troy, 49

Truceless War, 166, 169
Tullus Hostilius, king, 11
Tunis, 164, 215
turmae, 13, 108, 140, 192, 219
Tusculum, 37, 41, 60
Twelfth Legions, 129, 250
Tyrrhenian Sea, 38, 47–8, 68, 79, 91, 137, 161

Umbria, 45, 67, 74–9, 99
units, 10, 12–13, 21, 23, 26, 35, 47, 55, 61, 77, 87, 91, 94–5, 108, 113, 116, 119, 121, 127–8, 130, 135, 139–41, 148, 150, 153–5, 159–60, 165–6, 174, 176–7, 180, 192, 197–8, 205–206, 208–209, 211, 216, 219–24, 231–3, 240–1, 247–8, 255–6, 260, 267–8, 271, 273–4
Utica, 164

Vaccei, x
Vadimon, 81
Valencia, 170
Valerius Flaccus, commander, 241
Valerius Laevinus, consul, 85
Veii, 14, 18, 40, 47–51, 57, 59, 62, 79, 108, 113–14, 198–9, 263
velites, 107–109, 114, 140, 180, 215–16, 219, 225–8, 234
Velitrae, 42, 44
Venelli, 153
Veneti, 153
Venusia, 79, 85, 177
Verrugo, 43
Veseris, 63, 77, 113–14, 142
Veseris River, 63
Vesuvius, 63
Vetelia, 42
veterans, 154, 174, 224, 239, 241, 243–5, 247, 251, 259, 272
victory, viii, x, 2, 37, 41–2, 44–5, 50, 52, 57, 59, 61–4, 67–9, 72, 74–7, 79, 81–2, 84–5, 88, 97–9, 109, 111, 116–17, 125, 127, 132, 138, 145, 148, 157–9, 163, 165–9, 171, 176–7, 186, 189–90, 192, 195, 197, 207, 212, 215, 218, 221, 225–6, 228, 231, 239, 245, 249, 251–2, 260, 263, 265, 269–73
Villanovans, 18, 46–7
Viridomar, king, 61, 263
Viridovix, 153
Viromandui, 249
virtus, 97–8, 205, 240
Volsci, 20, 33, 38, 40, 42–5, 49, 59–60, 64–6, 68, 115
Volsinii, 78, 138–9

Volterrae, 76
Volturnus River, 68, 79, 136

war, vii–xi, 1–7, 10–12, 14–17, 19–21, 23–5, 27,
   33, 35, 37–42, 44–5, 48–9, 51–6, 60–84, 86,
   88–90, 96–8, 100–101, 103–104, 108, 110,
   112–26, 128–30, 132, 135–6, 141–2, 145–7,
   151–2, 154–5, 157–71, 173–4, 178, 181,
   183–7, 189–91, 194–5, 198–201, 203–206,
   209–17, 219–21, 225–45, 247–9, 251–2, 254,
   256–8, 261–72, 274–5
warriors, 14, 16, 19–20, 23, 25, 39, 53–5, 72, 78,
   112, 205
warships, 80, 141, 151, 171

weapons, 1, 5–7, 16–17, 19–20, 22–4, 39, 51, 67,
   78, 84, 88, 93–4, 96–7, 101–109, 112, 114–16,
   123, 131, 140, 147, 153, 157, 159–60, 163,
   174, 177, 192, 205, 207–209, 214, 232, 248,
   250–2, 263
wounded, 88, 130, 133, 155, 172, 178, 193, 198,
   205, 208–11, 213, 256
wounds, 198, 200, 210–11, 236, 247, 264

Xanthippus, commander, 215

Zama, 97, 103, 111, 166, 181, 207, 209, 215–16,
   228, 231